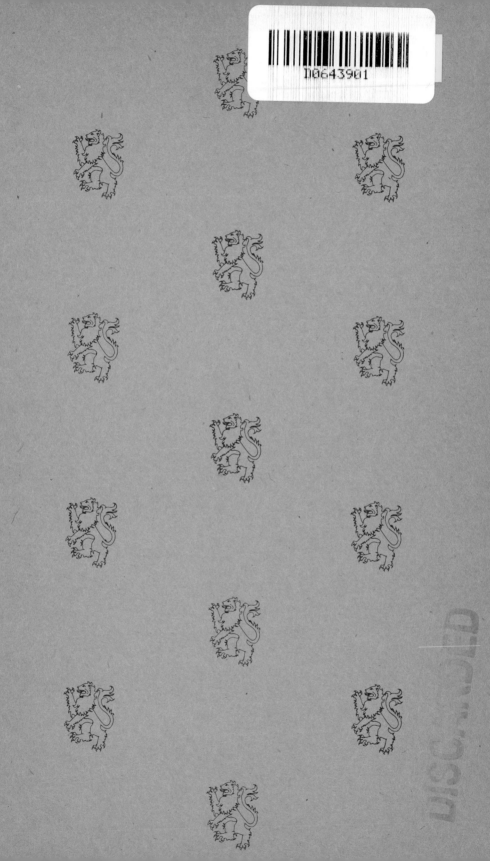

VOLUME ONE

Britain and the War for the Union

Britain
&the War
for the Union

Volume One

Brian Jenkins

McGill-Queen's
University Press

Montreal London
1974

This book has been published with
the help of a grant from the Social
Science Research Council of Canada
using funds provided by the Canada
Council.

International Standard Book
Number 0-7735-0184-3
Library of Congress Catalog
Number 74-77503
Legal Deposit 4th quarter 1974
Bibliothèque nationale du Québec

Design by Ronald Caplan
Printed in Canada by
The Bryant Press Limited

FOR

Charles Arthur Jenkins

1909–1970

CONTENTS

PREFACE

THIS IS THE FIRST OF A PAIR OF VOLUMES. The division may appear arbitrary to some readers but there are good reasons for it and these are indicated in the concluding chapter. The selection of a descriptive title presented a problem, for whatever the choice it was certain to echo that of one or more of the many books on the American Civil War that have preceded mine. In this case the magnificent studies of Allan Nevins spring to mind, but I chose to call the book *Britain and the War for the Union* not from a reckless desire to emulate or to invite comparison with the work of a master historian but because that does seem the most apt title. Of course, like other historical studies this one rests upon the work of many scholars. For a discussion of the wealth of secondary material I refer the reader to the Bibliographical Essay. It is by no means exhaustive, as cross-checking with the notes will demonstrate.

My thanks are due to those of my colleagues who have been generous with advice, to my wife who has been constant in her encouragement, and to my good friends William and Margaret MacVean who have done much more than friendship could demand. For their financial support of the research for this study I wish to thank the Canada Council and my own University, which together with the Social Science Research Council of Canada has also helped to defray publication costs.

In conclusion, I wish to thank His Grace the Duke of Norfolk, and His Grace's Archivist and Librarian, Francis W. Steer, for permission to quote from the Lyons Papers; the Editor of the London *Times* for permission to use the Printing House Square Papers, and H. C. Erwin for permission to quote from the Cobb Papers. Quotations from the Adams Papers are from the microfilm edition, by permission of the Massachusetts Historical Society. Those from the Palmerston and Shaftesbury Papers are by permission of the Trustees of the Broadlands Archives, while the Milne Papers have been quoted by permission of the Trustees of the National Maritime Museum. I wish to thank the British Museum, the Library of University College, London, the University of Nottingham Library, the Manuscript Division of the New York Public Library, the Library of Congress, the Houghton Library, Harvard University, the University of Rochester

Library, the University of North Carolina Library, Duke University Library, the University of Georgia Library, and the Alabama Department of Archives and History for permission to use the manuscripts in their possession.

BRIAN JENKINS
University of Saskatchewan
Saskatoon

ONE

The King was in his counting house

ON DECEMBER 20, 1860, South Carolina seceded from the Union and the South began to travel a road that proved both long and winding before it petered out in a Virginia hamlet on April 9, 1865. At first there was no hint of the despair and disaster that lay ahead. The Palmetto State was quickly joined by Mississippi, Florida, Alabama, Georgia, Louisiana, and Texas. The first few days of February 1861 saw delegates from these states gather in Montgomery, the sleepy but central Alabama capital, where they created the Confederate States of America and organized a provisional government. In unity lay domestic strength and the assurance of foreign fellowship, and the following month three commissioners were despatched to Europe to secure international recognition of the new Republic. Although these representatives were accredited to Great Britain, France, Russia, and Belgium, they concentrated their activities and the Confederate public fixed its attention on Britain.

From the outset of the secession crisis Southerners had counted upon British support. They did not expect sympathy, for of all the Abolition wolves none was more voracious than the British. They had eradicated slavery from their own territories in 1833 and then promptly turned to the task of promoting universal emancipation. The World Antislavery Conventions were held in London in 1840 and 1843 with Americans in attendance. British money had been sent to the United States and British abolitionists had toured there. In short, they had not scrupled to intervene directly in this most sensitive of domestic controversies. Not surprisingly, many Southerners had made what they could of these opportunities to damn abolition as an alien movement. It was the "English policy" and its supporters were financed by "English gold." To be English was itself sufficient occasionally to rouse Southern suspicions of abolitionist sym-

1

pathies, while to be opposed to slavery was tantamount to an admission of anglophilia. The conclusion was inescapable. On grounds of sentiment the British would sympathize with the North, which Southerners envisaged and portrayed as one vast lair of abolitionists.

Fortunately for their own peace of mind the advocates of secession knew that nations acted not from sympathy but self-interest, and economic self-interest at that. Like Thomas Gradgrind, disunionists willingly reduced everything to a "a mere question of figures, a case of simple arithmetic." In fact, they spent so much time talking and writing about the material benefits of secession, and the material interests that would compel Britain and France to recognize them that they earned William Howard Russell's description of "great materialists." In cotton, Southerners repeatedly reassured one another, they possessed a commodity not merely regal but omnipotent. As Senator Louis Wigfall of Texas put it during a debate in the upper chamber on December 12, "I say that cotton is King, and that he waves his scepter not only over these thirty-three States, but over the island of Great Britain and over continental Europe, and that there is no crowned head upon that island, or upon the continent that does not bend the knee in fealty and acknowledge allegiance to that monarch."[1] He was simply claiming, a colleague remarked irreverently, that cotton would "govern all creation."[2]

Wigfall was no master of the art of understatement yet he had merely recited the Southern creed. The 1850s had been happy and confident years for the cotton producers of the South. Only once during the decade had the price of the staple slipped below 10 cents a pound, and for much of the period it had been well above this comfortably profitable level. Their cotton was in demand and the need for it would compel the industrial and commercial North, which by 1860 was consuming about a fifth of the entire Southern crop, to accept peacefully the secession of the cotton-growing states. This same craving would leave the British, who took three times as much cotton as the North, no other choice than recognition of an independent South. And in the unlikely event that the North attempted to coerce the seceding states the greater necessity of Britain would force her to intervene on their behalf. The British simply could not afford to allow their vital textile industry to be disrupted by any inter-

2

ruption of the supply, because an estimated 5 millions of them were dependent upon it for their livelihood. Of course, even to admit that the North might seek to hold the South by force was an admission that the power of cotton was limited. Nevertheless, the omnipotence of the staple was stated and restated until it became an article of Confederate faith.

Yet there was one question which threatened to strike at the heart of the secessionist argument—would the British escape their indenture to the Cotton South by opening alternative areas of supply? This was the doubt voiced by those opposed to the frantic pace of secession, and they pointed to the activities of the Cotton Supply Association which had been founded in England for just this purpose. Its agents were busy throughout the world seeking new sources of the staple and nothing was more certain than that cotton culture would be stimulated elsewhere if American commerce was deranged by a prolonged domestic political crisis. But these warnings could not stem the onrushing tide of disunion which gained further power from the admitted British failure to increase significantly their supply from India, generally considered their likeliest alternative source of the fibre.

The failure of the opponents of the pell-mell pace of secession to shake the widespread confidence in the international might of Southern cotton did not entirely exhaust their opposition to the course of events. They also resorted to nationalist appeals and warnings against greater dependence upon Britain. Few followed the *Richmond Dispatch* in advocating a unifying war against England, but the *New Orleans Daily Picayune* published a letter from its London correspondent that cast a sinister light on the British response to the crisis in the United States. He reported that many English secretly, and some openly, rejoiced at "the possible wreck of the grand structure which our fathers wrested from their fathers' grasp." He also warned that Britain might seize advantage of the disruption of the Union to interfere in Mexico. "She would gladly see a rupture, which would make us weak and herself strong. We should forget the petty ills, which sometimes vex the Union, and turn our eyes to Mexico."[8] Similarly, Sam Houston of Texas and Governor Ellis Conway of Arkansas discerned in the American turmoil the left hand of Britain. Conway issued an address to the state's militia in which he expressed the conviction "that the settled and secret policy of the British Government is to disturb the domestic tranquillity

3

of the United States; that its object is to break up and destroy our Government, get rid of a powerful rival, extend the area of British dominions on this Continent, and become the chief and controlling Power in America."[4]

These public appeals to national and traditional distrust and dislike of Britain were frantically endorsed by John Floyd—a Southerner, and the secretary of war in the Buchanan administration, although he was soon to depart from it amidst rumours of malfeasance and treason. "The South can never count upon the friendship of England or upon her toleration of evils not her own," he wrote in a letter for publication. "Once within her power, she will fix upon us forever the badge of inferiority which we are now ready to destroy the Union to escape, and will foster our products so far, and so far only, as may be absolutely necessary to supply her wants." Above all, Floyd warned, England would insist upon making good her record on slavery. The *Richmond Enquirer* agreed, for any attempt by a British ministry to espouse the proslavery side, whatever the commercial profit or material welfare at stake, "would produce a vote of censure in the House of Commons, so immediate and decided as to throw the Ministry out of power before the lapse of twenty-four hours."[5]

All such cautions were ignored by a press lately reassured by a startling story in a Canadian newspaper. The *Toronto Leader*'s assertion on January 24 that the British government would recognize the independence of a Southern Confederacy as soon as it was formed was widely reported. It attracted so much attention because the *Leader* was generally regarded as the official organ of the Canadian government and thus one that it was all too easy to believe was privy to British intentions. The result was a spate of editorials not only asking but answering the question: "Will England Recognize a Confederacy?"

The urgent need for a new nation state, created from the seceded states, was clear. "We must meet Lincoln with a President of our own," wrote William Henry Trescot, the former assistant secretary of state in the Buchanan administration, "we want the military resources of the South concentrated at once and above all our foreign relations ought to be assured as quickly as possible. No attempt at foreign negotiations ought to be made by simple states." This was all-important, Trescot insisted in his correspondence with the influential Howell Cobb of Georgia. "The condition of weakness and confusion which will result

4

from four or five floating about is indescribable. Weld them together while they are hot."[6]

By the time then that the degates to the Southern Convention assembled in Montgomery, the necessity of a common policy had been recognized, indeed its outlines had been publicly drawn. Southerners saw in cotton the means either of inducing or of coercing the British into a helpful course. In fact on this point there was apparently even greater unity at the beginning of February than there had been earlier. Some of those who had discreetly and ineffectually challenged the diplomatic influence of cotton by suggesting that the British might obtain it from elsewhere now absolved themselves of the sin of doubt, while many newspapers published encouraging British statements acknowledging the crucial importance of American cotton. "Nobody but crazy-headed abolitionists ever supposed for a moment that England would not recognize the Southern Confederacy, should one be formed out of the slave states," a forgetful *Richmond Whig* declared on February 8. For the South would be her chief customer, whereas the North was Britain's industrial rival. More important, Britain was heavily dependent on the Gulf states for cotton. Therefore, she and the Confederacy would be bound by a communion of interests.

Although the *Richmond Whig* illustrated the apparent unity of Southern opinion on the political might of cotton, it clearly believed that the staple should march alongside free trade onto the international stage. Indeed, some Southerners had always been prepared to give this inducement to British recognition preeminence. Yet there was never any chance that it would be invested in the popular mind with the majesty of cotton, for Southern newspapers played incessantly on the cotton theme. Reports of the hurried convening of a large meeting in Manchester, the centre of the English textile industry, led the *Richmond Dispatch* to the conclusion that Britain was at last seeing both sides of the slavery question, the moral and that on which her "Bread is Buttered." "With but twelve weeks supply of cotton in the storehouses of Liverpool and Manchester, and a prospect of having the source of supply interfered with by a civil war, our English friends are beginning to desert and even to abuse their abolition allies."[7] But if economic self-interest reportedly showed every sign of triumphing over sentiment in Britain, just as they always insisted it would, many Southerners thought it prudent to make concessions to British antislavery sympathies.

It was in deference to foreign opinion that the committee named by the South Carolina Secession Convention to prepare an address to the people of the Southern states composed a document which played down slavery. A group of Louisiana secessionists called on the British consul at New Orleans to express the hope that a Southern Confederacy "would receive the aid and sympathy of European powers," and to assure him that there was no likelihood of the new Republic reopening the Atlantic slave trade.[8] Indeed, the states of Louisiana, Georgia, and Alabama quickly announced their opposition to this "infamous traffic," and the Montgomery Convention soon followed suit. On February 7 it forbade "The importation of African negroes from any foreign country other than the slaveholding states of the United States," and required the Confederate Congress "to pass such laws as shall effectually prevent the same."[9] The following day the Convention provided that "The Congress shall have power to levy and collect taxes, duties, imposts and excises for revenue necessary to pay the debts and carry on the government of the Confederacy; and all duties, imposts and excises shall be uniform throughout the States of the Confederacy."[10] On February 9 the Convention meeting as the Congress adopted temporarily the United States tariff of 1857.

These measures were the beginning of one devout secessionist's disillusionment with the conduct of the Convention and beyond it of the Confederacy it founded. Robert Barnwell Rhett had devoted himself to the tasks of fostering secession and defining a foreign policy that would in his opinion guarantee the permanency of the separation from the North. An integral part of that policy had been free trade, but this was not written into the Confederate constitution. Rhett had to be content with a general statement which, while it did not preclude free trade, simply indicated that any tariff adopted would be for revenue not protection. The explicit proposals banning bounties, establishing a maximum tariff rate that was tantamount to free trade, and providing for discriminatory duties as an instrument of economic coercion, all attractive to Rhett, were struck out during the debate on February 8. The trouble was that support for free trade was never as widespread in the South as Rhett thought it should be. At Montgomery it was opposed by those who saw

6

in direct taxation its inevitable handmaiden. "Direct taxation would ruin us," wrote one of Rhett's fellow delegates from South Carolina. "Each of our people would sooner give ten dollars which they have never seen, than one they have had in their pockets. We must have a revenue Tariff."[11] In addition, some delegates were increasingly aware, as Rhett was not, of the danger of war with the United States and thus proved amenable to the argument that a tariff was necessary to meet the costs of a large military establishment.

The Convention's decision to prohibit the African slave trade was another blow to Rhett. He was conscious of the widespread disapproval of its revival, even in the South, and was alive to the need to avoid alienating foreign opinion. However, he thought that this could be done through a constitutional provision giving to the Confederate Congress control over the subject. The Congress could then immediately prohibit the trade but at some later and more opportune date reopen it. Through this stratagem a constitutionally binding prohibition could be avoided. But when Rhett put this so-called South Carolina Plan to the Convention his was the only state to vote for it. The overwhelming rejection of his proposal was no doubt galling to him, but what particularly irked Rhett was the extent to which the slave trade provision seemed to have been drafted out of deference to the opinion and interests of the Upper South and the border states. For while it was often touted as a concession to foreign opinion, as indeed to some extent it was, the fact that it closed the transatlantic trade yet kept open the door to the continental indicated a desire to conciliate those slave states as yet still members of the Union. Rhett found this unacceptable, believing as he did that the constitution should represent the interests of the states sending delegates to Montgomery, not those that might at some future date join the new republic.

Yet of all the disappointments which the early days of the Confederacy held for Rhett, none was greater or fraught with more sinister implications than the choice of Jefferson Davis as provisional president. Perhaps he would have found it difficult initially to accept any man in this post, for he undoubtedly believed that by his long and sometimes lonely agitation for secession during the 1850s he had earned selection. However, although occasionally spoken of as the natural leader of the new nation, he must have known that this was an unrealizable

7

ambition. He could not command the backing of the entire South Carolina delegation at Montgomery, let alone general support within all six. Even those who privately regarded him with some sympathy, if not affection, considered him disqualified from the highest office. "Rhett is a generous-hearted and honest man with a vast quantity of cranks and a small proportion of commonsense,"[12] a fellow delegate remarked. But the inevitable personal disappointment was not the main source of Rhett's hostility to Davis. More important was his conviction that the provisional president was at heart a reconstructionist, one of those who saw in secession a device for extracting concessions from the Union, and the alarm that this engendered could not have been lessened by the selection of Alexander Stephens as vice-president. This cadaverous yet boyish-looking Georgian was a notoriously late convert to secession.

Rhett made no secret of his misgivings about Davis's loyalty to Southern independence and within a week of the election the "best friends" of the new republic were so troubled by these rumours that they were beginning to question the wisdom of the choice. To what extent Rhett was responsible for this is difficult if not impossible to say, but the result was the embarrassment of the president-elect whose friends struggled to allay suspicion by disclaiming "any idea of re-construction on his part."[13] "If he does not come out in his inaugural against this suicidal policy we shall have an explosion here," T. R. R. Cobb informed his wife on February 15, "he will be denounced by a large majority of this Congress who are almost unanimous against such a proposition."[14] However pleasing Davis's discomfiture was for Rhett, it did not represent the main thrust of his attack. He had concluded that he could best guarantee an enduring division of the Union by seizing control of the Confederacy's foreign policy. So he schemed to commit the new state to an irreversible course in its foreign relations before Davis was inaugurated.

Rhett's opportunity came with the announcement on February 12 that he had been named chairman of the Committee on Foreign Affairs. The potential influence of this position was greatly if briefly enhanced by the constitutional provision authorizing the Congress to exercise the executive powers until the president was inaugurated. Here was his chance to lead and it did not seem at all unlikely to him that his colleagues would follow. He moved rapidly to seize the initiative. Thus scarcely had the membership of his committee been announced than one of its members proposed "That the Committee on Foreign Affairs be instructed to inquire into the propriety of sending a commission to the Government of Great Britain and France and other European powers."[15]

Making no effort to disguise his sense of urgency, the South Carolinian reported out of his committee the very next day a resolution calling for the appointment of a three-man commission "forthwith by Congress in secret session, to proceed without delay to Great Britain, France and other European powers," and to act "under such instructions as may be given from time to time by Congress, or, after his inauguration by the President."[16] Evidently the purpose of this resolution was to prepare the ground for congressional instructions composed in Rhett's committee, while the inclusion of the president as an eventual participant may have been devised by Rhett as a screen to deflect any opposition to a too overt assumption of executive powers by the Congress. If indeed this was the motive for the concession it availed him little. Rhett's resolution was mutilated. The assault was led by a member of Rhett's committee, and one well acquainted with Davis, John Perkins of Louisiana. First, he moved that the provision under which the commissioners were to be appointed "forthwith by Congress in secret session" be amended to provide for their appointment by the president "as soon as practicable after his arrival" in Montgomery. Second, he proposed an amendment to the clause dealing with the commissioners' instructions. He suggested the deletion of the provision that they be given "by Congress, or after his inauguration, by the President," and the insertion, instead, of the words "by him."[17] Both amendments were adopted by the Congress, and amounted to complete defeat for Rhett. His ambition to initiate the Confederacy's foreign policy went unrealized, for all that remained of the original resolution was the provision for the appointment of a three-man commission. The date of its appointment, its composition, and its instructions had been reserved for President Davis. When it had come to the point Rhett had been unable to carry the Congress with him in his quest to bind the hands of the executive or usurp his functions. That was how the situation stood when the president-elect arrived in Montgomery on February 15.

Erect, courtly, proud, and resolute, Jefferson Davis seemed to be the embodiment of Southern civilization. To the office of president he brought a wealth of political, administrative, and military experience. A graduate of West Point, a hero of the Mexican War, a brilliantly successful secretary of war in the administration of Franklin Pierce, he had also distinguished himself in the United States Senate. Thus he not only looked and acted like a statesman but had many of the credentials of one. However, Davis was not without flaws. His public personality did not reflect the warmth of his close personal relations. Instead, he seemed humourless and aloof, he proved to be meddlesome and prickly, and he revealed a growing capacity to inure himself to advice as well as criticism. As for foreign affairs, that was a subject in which he was not well grounded, although his interests were not parochial. He had read widely and he subscribed to the London *Times*. He was able to offer the "very latest file" to Richard Cobden when they met as fellow passengers on a Mississippi river boat in the spring of 1859. But there was nothing in his background or experience to cause him to doubt that cotton was the key to Confederate foreign relations. Himself an example of cotton culture, he undoubtedly thought he was merely stating the obvious when in 1860 he declared that the exports of a united South would make for it "allies of all commercial and manufacturing powers."[18] In February 1861, when he was selected to preside over a Cotton Republic, a state overwhelmingly committed to the production of the staple for export, it was scarcely surprising that Davis reached out in his inaugural address to grasp the sceptre of King Cotton. The propaganda of secession was about to be embraced as the creed of the Confederacy.

The responsibility for Confederate foreign relations was not Davis's alone, however. It was shared by the other members of his administration. Naturally, the selection of his cabinet was the president's first concern on taking office. He quickly discovered that some of the men he wanted could not be had. Robert Barnwell of South Carolina declined the State Department, for that state's delegation was pressing for the appointment of Gustavus A. Memminger as secretary of the treasury. In his stead Barnwell suggested Howell Cobb or Robert Toombs, both of Georgia. But as Cobb had already expressed his unwillingness to enter the cabinet, what was by American tradition the senior post passed almost by default to Toombs.

Davis had always intended to offer a portfolio to Toombs, that of secretary of the treasury, for his understanding of the esoteric problems of finance was generally acknowledged and had led already to his selection as chairman of the Finance Committee of the Confederate Congress. Indeed this nomination seemed so obvious that it was being confidently predicted in Montgomery on February 20. Instead, it was the State Department that was proffered to him while Davis yielded to the pressure of the South Carolina delegation and nominated Memminger to the Treasury. Toombs, still brooding over his failure to be elected president, hesitated briefly before accepting the post. But ambition quickly got the better of pique and he appears to have entered office labouring under the delusion that he could still dominate the government, converting the lost presidency into a position of titular ascendancy only. Yet he was not the man to sustain, if ever he could have asserted, his dominance. Although intelligent, the Georgian lacked self-discipline. A ponderous figure whose petulantly creased features suggested years of self-indulgence, he exhibited a similar want of moderation in his speech. He had established a reputation as a "violent and impulsive" man endowed with considerable powers of oratory, but, as an English observer tartly remarked, that talent would be of little use in his dealings with foreign nations.[19]

The Confederate secretary of state was one of those ambivalent Southerners who were at one and the same time "Anglo-maniacs" and "Anglo-phobists." He proudly proclaimed his descent from "respectable English families"[20] and expressed a veneration for the British constitution which at times bordered on idolatry. He had visited Britain and after three days in London was writing ecstatically "of this capital of the world." "It is much greater than I had ever pictured to my imagination," he reported to an American friend, "and one is bewildered with the wealth, the magnificence, the beauty, and the thousand objects of grandeur and interest which arrest him at every turn."[21] But admiration was balanced by distaste for the "English policy." The owner of a large and profitable plantation, Toombs was an ardent defender of the peculiar institution as an instrument of civilization. Despising abolitionists, he was quick to give vent to his anger when early in 1858 the British searched some American merchantmen in the Caribbean, in an attempt to discourage the flourishing slave trade around Cuba. These incidents provided Toombs, as it did several of his colleagues, with a splendid opportunity to denounce the meddling transatlantic opponents of slavery, and he exploited it with characteristic intemperance. He demanded that an American squadron be sent into the Gulf of Mexico with orders to capture or sink the British vessels violating American sovereignty and hang the officers who commanded them. Happily, calmer heads prevailed.

Whatever his past suggestions for dealing with the British, Toombs seems to have made no such radical contribution to the formulation of a Confederate foreign policy in 1861. A former Whig with mildly protectionist sentiments he was never a likely advocate of free trade, so vociferously demanded by Robert Barnwell Rhett. As for the reliance on cotton, his position has been somewhat obscured by a belated attempt, long after the war, to escape responsibility for an unsuccessful policy. In 1881 the former secretary of state claimed that what he had wanted to do twenty years earlier "was to ship all the cotton to Europe and draw against it."[22] This proposal, which was evidence of a disagreement over how cotton should rule rather than a plot to dethrone it, was certainly made during the first meeting of the Confederate cabinet, but not it seems by Toombs. It was Judah P. Benjamin of Louisiana, the attorney-general, who urged that all the cotton on hand be shipped to England, and he was probably supported by Vice-President Stephens. But the majority of the cabinet remained faithful to the more orthodox canons of King Cotton. For one question the advocates of an "exportation policy" could never answer convincingly was, where were the vessels to come from to implement it? In fact this obstacle was insuperable as Davis and most of his colleagues, including no doubt the intelligent Toombs, were aware, and it was not long before Benjamin was proclaiming his adherence to the cotton diplomacy that commanded the support not only of the cabinet but also of the Congress and citizenry.

Although the Davis administration had quickly decided that Confederate foreign policy should be founded upon Britain's heavy dependence on Southern cotton, a dependence that would surely prompt her to recognize the Confederacy and if necessary intervene to prevent hostilities certain to disrupt that vital commerce, the president was still confronted with the task of selecting the men to carry it out. Predictably, Toombs soon tired of the humdrum work of the State Department. He proved neither diligent nor cooperative, so the post of assistant secretary assumed unusual importance. It was filled by William Montague Browne. Certainly British and perhaps even a gentleman by birth, he had travelled widely in Europe, acquired a facility in several foreign languages, and may have served in the British diplomatic service before emigrating to the United States in the mid-1850s. There he was reduced to journalism, joining the staff of the *New York Journal of Commerce*. But he possessed an ingratiating manner and rapidly earned a reputation as a loyal Democrat, with the result that in 1859 he was rewarded with the editorship of the Buchanan administration's organ, the *Washington Constitution*, and became a close friend of the president. Their relationship soured, however, during the winter of 1860 as Browne, through his editorials, first sympathized with secession and then exhorted all the slave states to follow South Carolina out of the Union. He became a Southerner by adoption. No supporter of the "English policy," despite his antecedents, he like other secessionists was confident that in the event of difficulties with the North the South could count upon the support of Britain and France. He was confident that abolition sentiment would never be permitted to endanger the commercial interests of those nations. The "absolute existence of a vast industry, the peace of densely-populated districts are considerations not to be overborne by the maudlin story of Uncle Tom," he proclaimed.[23] It was a conviction that the widely circulated report in the *Toronto Leader*, of imminent British recognition of a Confederacy, merely reinforced.

Given his avowed sympathies, it was not surprising that Browne began to search for alternative employment as the secession crisis deepened. A close friend of the highly respected Howell Cobb, who had been elected president of the Montgomery Convention, he was also well acquainted with Davis. These personal relations, the fact that he had served the South well from his important editorial desk, his diplomatic experience and knowledge of European affairs, and his wholehearted and public endorsement of what was emerging as the Davis administration's cotton diplomacy, all helped him win the post of assistant secretary of state. And while his appointment caused some muttering about Davis's "foreign pets,"[24] it was generally admitted that the choice was a sound one. Browne was intelligent, a man of "character with good sense, good temper and good manners,"[25] and the South was in his debt. Unhappily Davis's other major diplomatic appointments proved less successful.

There were those in the South who, fearing that the diplomatic task confronting the Confederacy was formidable, stressed the importance of restricting membership of the European commission to men "eminently qualified to perform it efficiently."[26] The proposition that the South send only its ablest sons abroad was one to which all could and did pay lip service, but Davis did not act upon it. He remained oblivious to the delicacy of the recognition negotiations, for nothing had occurred to shake the belief he shared with most Southerners that England and France would recognize their government as soon as it was properly organized. On the contrary, what straws there were in the wind heightened this optimism. It was still being widely reported that the London press was "gradually preparing the public mind for a fraternal embrace of the new Confederacy."[27] But confidence that the Confederate government would be promptly recognized did not rest solely upon a highly selective reading of the British press. The brief comments on the American crisis inserted in the Queen's speech opening Parliament early in February were eagerly misinterpreted as "unerring indications of the purpose to apply to the American case the rules of national policy enunciated by England so frequently and so strongly in regard to Italy, that a people, which has in a sufficiently authoritative form declared its will to erect a Government for itself, is entitled to have its decision respected by the world."[28] Further, there were reports in Northern newspapers that Lord Lyons, the British minister, had informed the United States government that Britain would decline to recognize any blockade that was not thorough and effectual. How could the modest United States Navy effectively blockade a coastline as extensive as that of the Confederacy? Clearly the British were carefully establishing legal grounds for the nullification of any measure that threatened to sever them from their suppliers of cotton.

This public evidence of British intentions was supported by the government's private information. John Slidell, the former Senator from Louisiana, informed Howell Cobb that he had "been much with the diplomatic corps" during the winter "with a view to ascertaining how European States would feel" about recognition. And on the basis of his intimacy with the French minister at Washington, Henri Mercier, he confidently predicted that Napoleon III would soon recognize the Confederacy. Also, that England would "not be slow to follow the example of France" if the North went ahead with its plan to enact a protective tariff.[29] There seemed then every reason for the optimism that abounded in Montgomery, in the face of which even the fear of war began to diminish daily. Satisfied that the securing of foreign recognition was little more than a formality, Davis did not choose the commissioners carefully. He used one of the positions as a convenient way of ridding himself of an unwanted colleague. Considering himself obliged to offer a cabinet portfolio to the secessionist firebrand William L. Yancey, he neatly discouraged acceptance. He held the minor post of attorney-general in one hand while thrusting forward membership of the commission to Europe with the other, and Yancey responded as he expected. He accepted the European mission.

To accompany Yancey the Confederate president seems to have quickly decided upon Slidell and Ambrose Dudley Mann. The need for a French-speaking member was obvious and Slidell possessed this and other qualifications. A United States senator from 1853 until the secession crisis, he was a man of formidable if somewhat sinister political reputation. His career had been marked by intrigue rather than statesmanship, reaching a fitting climax with his reputed role as Buchanan's *eminence grise*. He also boasted close relations with the French minister, and his offer to represent the Confederacy in Europe was difficult if not impossible to refuse. What better employment was there for such an artful political veteran than negotiating the recognition of the new state? And Davis's proffering of a place on the commission to Slidell may explain why Judah P. Benjamin, the latter's gifted former Senate colleague from Louisiana, was not appointed. For having extended an invitation which he had every reason to believe Slidell would accept, the president nominated Benjamin to the post Yancey had been persuaded to decline. Some days later, when Slidell declined the appointment, Davis discussed the matter with Benjamin. The attorney-general did not volunteer his own services; instead, the place went to one of his friends, Pierre Rost. A virtual nonentity, Rost had served in the Mississippi legislature before moving to Louisiana where he was eventually appointed an associate justice of the state's Supreme Court. By 1861 he was devoting most of his time to his sugar and cotton plantations. As for his diplomatic qualifications, they were his French birth and reported facility with the language, although Rost naively believed that he was sufficiently well informed to enlighten the Europeans on "topics connected with the prosperity of the Southern States."[30] Evidently, in appointing this "old and pleasant gentleman from New Orleans,"[31] neither Davis nor Benjamin gave much thought to the replacement of Slidell.

For his part Slidell gave two reasons for refusing an appointment he had sought. First, as he informed Davis, he disapproved of the collective nature of the mission. "I was willing to go to Paris alone," he wrote in a letter of explanation to Howell Cobb, through whom he had first offered his services, "because I knew that I could be useful but I am not willing to share either the responsibility of a failure or the credit of a success with others."[32] Second, and this he did not tell the president, he refused to serve with Mann.

Ambrose Dudley Mann had been born in Virginia and educated at West Point, although an aversion to military service prompted him to resign before graduation. He had had a successful career in the consular service before his appointment as assistant secretary of state. From his resignation in 1855 until the disruption of the Union he had campaigned for Southern rights and Southern economic independence. Thus his appointment "was not entirely illogical." He possessed an "expert knowledge of trade and shipping and experience in arranging commercial treaties."[33] Fully expecting recognition, Davis would have considered Mann's acknowledged qualifications peculiarly appropriate. But his commitment to Mann was as much personal as professional. The two men had become close friends during their service in the Pierce administration, and Davis believed that to "all the accomplishments of a trained diplomat" Mann "united every Christian virtue." For Jefferson Davis the Virginian was "this perfect man."[34]

With the pleasant Rost and the ideal Mann for colleagues Yancey must have expected to dominate the commission. Like his friend Rhett, he was such a notorious secessionist that he embarrassed the moderate elements who had organized and now dominated the Confederacy. This "most precipitate of precipitators"[35] bored them with his endless talk and may even have disturbed them with his uncontrolled emotions. His contemporaries had not forgotten nor had they forgiven his killing of his wife's uncle after an alleged verbal insult. He was voluble, vehement, ambitious, impressionable, and impressive. In 1848 he had played a major role in the drafting of the Alabama platform which demanded that the right of all citizens to enter every territory of the Union with all their property be recognized and protected. It was on this same platform that he organized the disruption of the Democratic party in 1860. Indisputably, he was a towering and frightening Southern personality who seemed a giant beside pygmies in the company of Rost and Mann. Also, with Congress voting the commissioners a very handsome salary, the post promised to be a comfortable one and when crowned by inevitable success it would serve as a platform strong enough to launch an even loftier political career.

Yet the wisdom of Yancey's selection was questioned by some of his contemporaries. His undisputed oratorical powers were considered harmfully irrelevant. "Who wants eloquence?" Mary Chesnut asked. "We want somebody who can hold his tongue. . . . No stump speeches will be possible, but only a little quiet conversation with slow, solid, commonsense people who begin to suspect as soon as any flourish of trumpets meet their ear."[36] Nor was the fact that Yancey had exercised his talent on behalf of the radical proslavery cause calculated to relieve this uneasiness. However, if he did not appear to be the kind of Confederate who would win British hearts, few Southerners thought British sentiment an important consideration. The need to ensure a continuous supply of cotton was considered more than enough inducement for Britain to pocket her scruples and recognize the Confederacy. And when Davis forwarded the nominations to Congress on February 27 it was not over Yancey or even Rost that that body lingered. Rhett's committee reported in favour of confirmation, but while Yancey and Rost were quickly and unanimously confirmed it was several days before the appointment of Mann was approved. Slidell was not alone in his poor opinion of "this perfect man," and others were irritated by the selection of a Virginian rather than a citizen of a state that had already seceded. Nevertheless, Mann's appointment was confirmed on March 7 and all that now remained was for him and his colleagues to be provided with their instructions. However, these were deferred and the commissioners' departure for Europe was postponed while Davis attempted to reach an understanding with the North.

That Davis should have first turned his eyes northward is

readily understandable. He desired a peaceful separation from the Union and if the North could be persuaded to accept the existence of an independent South foreign recognition would be more of a formality than it already appeared to be. Even if the negotiations failed the Confederacy could claim absolution from the sin of fratricide. This would not only stand the new nation in good stead abroad but also in the Upper South and the border states. These states had quickly grasped that a civil war was likely to be fought upon their territory, and were therefore more anxious than most for a peaceful solution to the crisis.

Jefferson Davis, no less than the leaders of the incoming Republican administration in Washington, appreciated the strategic and political importance of this region and was keen to placate its inhabitants. Undoubtedly he hoped to entice these fellow slave states into the Confederacy, but failing that they could still provide the new republic with an invaluable shield, so long as they opposed or refused to participate in any plan to coerce the South. Already the Confederate Convention and Congress had made ostentatious concessions to the citizens of these states. They had been guaranteed free navigation of the Mississippi, the vital artery of western commerce, and the door had been left open to the highly profitable domestic slave trade. But behind these two carrots there was also a stick, a contingent provision empowering Congress "to prohibit the introduction of slaves from any State not a member of the Confederacy."[37]

Not everyone in the Confederacy applauded the policy of placating the other slave states. Rhett continued to regard it with horror, for in it he still discerned the spectre of reconciliation. Equally appalled was his fellow South Carolinian, William Gilmore Simms, romantic poet, popular author, and rabid disunionist. He found particularly objectionable the thought of concessions to the North and Britain "on the score of negro slavery and the slave trade." "They have already voted us barbarians," he commented. "But we have them in our power."[38]

If many of his fellows would have greeted Simms's boast as no more than the statement of a self-evident truth, some were still speculating on how that unquestioned power could be most effectively exercised. Thus even as Davis appointed the members of the commission to Europe and briefly kept them waiting on developments at Washington the public discussion of Confederate foreign policy continued. Already in evidence were the supporters of cotton as an imperious ruler, those who believed that the most deliberate way in which the South could control its destiny was to place an embargo on the export of cotton. Such a course was soon broached in the Confederate Congress.

On February 21, Thomas Cobb, Howell's brother and fellow representative from Georgia, proposed that an export duty be imposed on cotton declaring, "we know that by an embargo we could soon place, not only the United States, but many of the European powers, under the necessity of electing between such a recognition of our independence, as we may require, or domestic convulsions at home."[39] The idea had not originated with Cobb but with his father-in-law, Chief Justice Lumpkin of Georgia, and Cobb raised it as a trial balloon to determine what support it would command in the Confederacy at large. Therefore, he was at pains to ensure that it received newspaper coverage. But those of his colleagues at Montgomery with whom he had discussed the scheme opposed any embargo at this time. It should be delayed at least until Britain had replied to the Confederate application for recognition, they reasoned, because to stop the supply of cotton at once would surely create unnecessary hostility toward the South. Unnecessary because, as Thomas Cobb reported to his wife, "The firm and universal conviction here is, that Great Britain, France, and Russia will acknowledge us at once in the family of nations."[40]

Cobb's remarks would have caused little embarrassment in Montgomery, for what was to be lost by this public flexing of Southern muscles? It served to remind the British that the South was fully aware of the power it possessed, and there seemed little danger of their taking offence. They stood to profit most from Congress's decision on February 25 to throw open the Confederate coasting trade to foreign competition. Also, Cobb quickly followed his talk of an embargo with a further concession to British interests. At his prompting the Confederate Congress agreed on March 7 that the president be authorized to instruct the commissioners "to enter into treaty obligations for the extension of international copyright privileges to all authors" of nations that provided for reciprocal arrangements.[41] Here was something certain to catch the eye of the British. Long indignant at the extensive practice of "literary piracy," they had negotiated a copyright convention with Sardinia in 1860 and were then negotiating with Hesse and Russia. America, with its large

English-speaking population, was a much greater prize; moreover, the new United States tariff bill had lately revived British accusations against the Union. Thus Cobb regarded the passage of his resolution as something of a masterstroke. "In my opinion," he wrote, "it will operate strongly to bring the literary world, especially of Great Britain, to sympathize with us against the Yankee literary pirates. Our cotton will bring the working people to the same point. . . . With these on our side we can bid defiance to potentates and powers."[42]

Meanwhile, others were seeking both to emphasize and advance Southern independence through direct trade and communication with Europe. The commercial advantages of cutting out Northern middlemen had long been obvious to Southern planters, but it was now recognized that direct steamship communication with Europe was as much a political as a commercial necessity. It would provide Britain with a "plausible" argument —"the protection of the ships and cargoes of her citizens"[43]—to frustrate any Northern attempt to regulate or to stifle Confederate commerce through floating customs houses or a blockade. As one newspaper confidently predicted, "England will take care of our rights on the water, while we have it all our own way on *terra firma.*" All in all the establishment of direct links with Europe would "tend greatly to friendly international relations." And on March 27, at the Cotton Planters Convention at Macon, Georgia, of which Howell Cobb was elected president, it was agreed that a commissioner be sent to Europe "charged with carrying out and consummating the Direct Trade movement."[44] But the success of this mission was clearly dependent upon that of the commissioners who had formally been provided with instructions on March 16.

Toombs's instructions to Yancey, Rost, and Mann reflected the general optimism about the Confederacy's foreign relations. To the support of the new nation's application for recognition he brought the familiar constitutional justification for secession, and he dwelt upon the provocations to which the South had been subjected. Naturally, he stressed the unity of British and Confederate interests in opposition to protective tariffs, and the commissioners were empowered, once they had been received officially, to "negotiate a treaty of friendship, commerce and navigation." Presumably, Mann's experience could be turned to good account in such negotiations. But Toombs's general comments about the commercial policy of the Confederacy, which he suggested would be tantamount to one of free trade, merely served as the preamble to a more specific discussion of the Confederacy's principal asset. The "Confederate States produce nearly nineteen-twentieths of all the cotton grown in the States which recently constituted the United States," he reminded the commissioners, and, he went on, "there is no extravagance in the assertion that the gross amount of the annual yield of the manufactories of Great Britain from the cotton of the Confederate States reaches $600,000,000." Therefore, the British government could be expected to "comprehend fully the condition to which the British realms would be reduced if the supply of our staple should suddenly fall or even be considerably diminished." Although a menace lurked here, Toombs believed that a "delicate allusion" to the probability of an interruption of supplies "might not be unkindly received" by the British foreign secretary.[45]

Clearly, nothing had occurred by the middle of March to dampen Southern optimism. Quite the reverse, the passage of a new United States tariff and the evidence of British irritation were gleefully seized upon as proof that the Confederate cause had taken yet another favourable turn. And no less significant than the tone of the British press was the news that William Gregory, the member of Parliament for Galway, had given notice of a motion calling for British recognition of the Confederacy. As the *Charleston Mercury* remarked, "a feather thrown up shows what way the wind blows."[46] Henry William Ravenel, a South Carolina planter and a botanist of international repute, wrote in his private journal, "Old prejudices against our misunderstood domestic institution of African servitude ... are giving way before the urgent calls of *Self Interest,* and we only need that they should become more intimately acquainted with it to dissipate their mistaken notions." Indeed, when Ravenel went on to define the choices presented to the European powers the logic of recognition seemed incontrovertible. On one side stood the Confederacy, which almost alone furnished the cotton that was so essential to Europe's commercial and manufacturing prosperity and offered them "a market for their goods on better terms than heretofore." Also, "We invite their vessels to do our carrying trade, or at any rate throw open the door of competition to them, which has been hitherto open only to U.S. vessels." On the other stood the United States, which with the secession of the South could furnish Europe with precious little cotton. In addition, the Union had just imposed a tariff which would "cut off trade in a great measure." Finally, the United States was "mainly a manufacturing and commercial nation, and must necessarily come into competition with them." The conclusion was inescapable—the United States' loss was Europe's gain, and this would determine British policy because "self interest is the ruling power among nations, no less than among individuals."[47]

Jefferson Davis had every reason for continuing to think so. From the governor of South Carolina he heard that Robert Bunch, the British consul at Charleston, had called upon him on April 16, "for the first time formally." The consul brought news of a meeting between the American minister in London and the British foreign secretary, at which the American had asked that Britain neither recognize the Confederacy nor do anything that might encourage hopes of recognition. Lord John Russell's reply had been noncommittal. He had said that it was impossible to foresee under what circumstances the application for recognition might be made and that he declined to give any pledge on the question. And while he had expressed the hope that the two sides might yet be reconciled, reconciliation had been placed beyond reach with the firing on Fort Sumter on April 12. In the aftermath of that momentous event Bunch's comments assumed even greater significance. For in addition to reporting the meeting in London, the consul informed Governor Pickens that he had been authorized to make it known to the Confederate authorities "that if the United States Government attempted a blockade of the Southern ports or if Congress at Washington declared the Southern ports were no longer ports of entry, etc., that it would immediately lead to the recognition of the Independence of the South by Great Britain," for free intercourse with the South "should" be maintained.[48] The success of the Confederate request for recognition seemed assured, for Pickens's letter was immediately followed by Lincoln's first Proclamation of Blockade. All Yancey and his colleagues were required to do was to present it.

As for Yancey, he had set out from Montgomery on March 15 bearing a "splendid gold cane" which had been presented to him by "his numerous lady friends."[49] Carrying $40 in cash and $6,500 in Treasury drafts he made his way to New Orleans, arriving there on March 18. He immediately fell ill. In poor general health and continually troubled by an arthritic condition of the spine, he was confined to his bed for ten days. However, he was fit enough to travel on March 31 when in the company of Rost he sailed for Cuba, landing at Havana on April 2. The flattering attention they received from the British there must have appeared a good omen to both men. They dined and attended a reception at the British consul's residence, and were given a tour of the British war steamer *Gladiator*. Then, on April 6, the two commissioners embarked upon a British mail steamer for St. Thomas. Arriving safely five days later, they sailed aboard another British steamer for Southampton on the fateful day of April 13.

Meanwhile, Mann had decided to travel to Europe via Washington and New York. Setting out on March 16, his unofficial, unauthorized, and ill-advised venture threatened to end sensationally when the new Republican secretary of state, William Henry Seward, urged that Mann be detained. He thought it would have a good effect on Northern public opinion, but Mann was permitted to get away. He appealed to a friend, Senator Lane of Indiana, for safe conduct, and Lane visited President Lincoln to urge that as Mann had not committed any treasonable act as yet, and as his arrest would not prevent the Confederacy being represented abroad, nothing was to be gained by his detention. The president agreed, but Mann, fearing a change of mind, rushed to New York and embarked on the first ship for Europe. He left the United States on March 30, never again to set foot on American soil. By the time his two colleagues joined him in England on April 27 the United States and the Confederacy were at war.

TWO

To preserve the Union

THROUGHOUT THE SECESSION WINTER the Northern press laboured to disturb Southern complacency. They harped upon Britain's abolitionist sympathies. Had she not forced slavery on the South during the colonial period only to wage war against it, openly and covertly, ever since? It was in Britain that Harriet Beecher Stowe had received her greatest ovation and John Brown's raid its loudest applause. Indeed, if anything was clear it was that the antislavery movement in the Northern States was "the small dust of the balance in comparison with the intense, bitter and universal hatred of slavery" which pervaded England.[1] Consequently, that country was "the last on the face of the earth to which the South should look for succor and assistance."[2] On the contrary, "England would not fail to use even the commercial dependence of the South upon her for purposes of agitation and eventual emancipation."[3] As for King Cotton, the boast that the South "might at any time starve not the North alone but Great Britain also into general bankruptcy, anarchy and communistic pillage,"[4] was denied and ridiculed in Congress and by the press. But secessionists seemed deaf to all argument, and as one Cotton State after another withdrew from the Union Northern newspapers issued the feeble caution that Britain could not, "with justice and safety," recognize the independence of the South before the United States did so.

Yet the extent to which Britain would be moved by "justice," particularly after the passage of the Morrill Tariff, was debatable. Some Northern voices were raised to join those of secessionists in describing it as an act of monumental ineptitude. Within and without Congress the tariff was denounced as ill-timed and ill-advised. It was a mordant Daniel Sickles who congratulated the chairman of the Ways and Means Committee for presiding over the "inception and elaboration of this measure." At a time, the

New York congressman continued, when the Union was faced with dismemberment and "all eyes are turned upon the policy which will control European States—whether it is to be the policy of non-interference, or the policy of recognition—the Chairman of the Committee of Ways and Means is offering the strongest provocation to England to precipitate recognition of the southern confederacy."[5]

But the tariff was not the only provocation. During the presidential election campaign, William Seward, "the high priest of the Republican party," had dwelt upon the republic's continental destiny, its inevitable expansion northwards to Hudson's Bay.[6] Then came the secession of South Carolina and the news that several other states were set on the same course, all of which prompted him to remark, perhaps in an effort to ease the tension in the North, "Let South Carolina, Alabama, Louisiana, or any other state go out, and while she is rushing out you will see Canada and all the Mexican States rushing in."[7] A few days later the *New York Times*, closely identified with Seward through its editor, Henry Raymond, reported the gratifying news that leading members of the Republican party were already preparing for the annexation of Mexico "as a ready means of at once indemnifying the North for the partial loss of Southern trade" and of countering the "schemes of slavery propagandism, which is one great incentive to disunion."[8] If international prudence dissuaded the *Times* from making any mention of Canada as an indemnity in December, the actual establishment of the Confederacy put an end to discretion. "Light follows the rising of the sun no more certainly than a dissolution of the American Union and the establishment of a Northern free Confederacy will bring about the acquisition of Canada," its Washington correspondent predicted on February 8. But the main agent for advertising what it was always careful to describe as the Seward plan was the Democratic *New York Herald*, which with its circulation of 80,000 claimed to be the world's largest daily newspaper.

From the last week of January to the first week of March the *Herald* was urging that the Southern states be allowed to go their own way peacefully and predicting an expansion of the Cotton South into Mexico and around the Gulf. Therefore the North should seek "a counterpoise to these acquisitions of its powerful neighbor by absorbing Canada."[9] The laws of nature and "the progress of political ideas have destined the annexation of Canada to the northern half of the United States," the *Herald* philosophized, "and now is the accepted time for its consummation." Canadians were congratulated that they were of the "same race, language and religion" as the people of the free states. They were informed that they were keen to join the Union, consequently the British government "should aid in the accomplishment of what it cannot possibly prevent." Indeed, there ought not to be "a moment's delay" in repairing the Union's loss of territory and population, "otherwise it would sink to a third or fourth rate power." If the Canadians failed to respond to the American invitation, if they denied the Republic its compensation, annexation was to be completed by force and Canada trained up as a territory.

While the *Herald* was busy annexing Canada and creating a new Union it fell to President Buchanan to attempt to preserve the old one. Anxious to escape from office on March 4 with the nation virtually intact, his main hope after Lincoln's election was to prevent the other Cotton States following South Carolina out of the Union. His chances, never good, were not improved by the weakness of his political position. The nominal leader of a divided and defeated party, his cabinet a microcosm of the nation, he temporized. He held the antislavery agitators responsible for the crisis, denied the right of secession, and rejected any policy of coercion. But the indecisive middle ground was a desolate place and from it a mournful Buchanan watched the rapid progress of disunion and the disintegration of his national cabinet.

Confronted by an apparently endless succession of domestic disasters, neither Buchanan nor his secretaries of state, first Lewis Cass and then Jeremiah Black, gave much thought or time to the foreign implications of the crisis. Relations with Britain were good, the president boasted in his last Annual Message to Congress on December 3, 1860. Differences over Britain's role in Central America, and difficulties over the visit and search of American merchant vessels by British cruisers had been settled in a way "entirely satisfactory" to the United States. The recent visit of the Prince of Wales to the Republic had been a great success and seemed certain "to increase the kindred and kindly feelings" of both governments and peoples "in their political and social intercourse with each other."[10] The only problem that remained was the dispute over the title to the island of San Juan but this could be settled through the "arbitration of some friendly and impartial power."[11] But no matter how friendly he believed relations with Britain to be, privately Buchanan doubted that she could afford to ignore the disaffected South. The Southerners "know that the world cannot do without their great staple and that England and France must have it,"[12] he wrote just before South Carolina seceded. Nevertheless, his administration did not resign itself to European recognition of the Confederacy, once it had been created. The news that Yancey, Rost, and Mann had been nominated as the Confederate commissioners to Europe prompted Jeremiah Black, four days before Lincoln's inauguration, to instruct all American ministers abroad to repeat Buchanan's denial of the right of secession and to ask all foreign powers to refrain from any act which might "encourage the revolutionary movement of the Seceding States, or increase the danger of disaffection" in those that had remained loyal. Any recognition of the "Confederated States," he warned, would "tend to disturb the friendly relations, diplomatic and commercial, now existing between those powers and the United States."[13] This was the policy Abraham Lincoln inherited on March 4.

The new president was unusual in appearance. Very tall, he shambled along in ill-fitting, funereal clothes, which in the spring of 1861 seemed suitable to the supposed undertaker for the dying Union. Visitors were struck by his long arms, large hands, huge feet, plain features, and high-pitched voice. Yet his face was marked by kindliness and he gave the impression of frankness. He also had "a certain pose and air,"[14] all of which made him neither unpleasant nor unattractive. However, he clearly lacked the grace and gentility of his Southern counterpart, with whom he was inevitably compared, and he lacked Davis's political and administrative experience as well. Several terms in the Illinois legislature and a single term in Congress were the extent of Lincoln's formal preparation for office. Nor could it be denied that he was more provincial than the Confederate president. He did not carry the latest issue of the London *Times* around with him. He was, as he himself was the first to admit, ignorant of the transatlantic world and international relations. "I don't know anything about diplomacy," he confessed to a foreign diplomat on the eve of his inauguration. "I will be apt to make blunders."[15]

To save the administration from serious mistakes he relied upon his secretary of state. "I shall have to depend upon you for taking care of the matters of foreign affairs of which I know so little, and with which I reckon you are so familiar," Lincoln informed him.[16]

Some of the president's political advisers feared that his first blunder was his nomination of William Henry Seward as secretary of state. The principal contender for the Republican nomination, only to be passed over for Lincoln, the disappointed New York senator had played little part in the election campaign until a group of Lincoln men negotiated his participation, perhaps with the promise of the State Department in the event of a Republican victory. Whether or not such an assurance was given, Lincoln quickly settled upon Seward as the senior member of his cabinet and he held fast to that decision despite a powerful lobby determined to prevent the appointment. In no doubt that Seward's strength within the party required recognition, he ignored those of his supporters who argued that this could be achieved by the offer of the mission to England. However, he was afraid of being snubbed, which would have been a humiliating and inauspicious opening to his administration, so he attempted to sound out Seward indirectly. When the canny New Yorker would not be drawn, Lincoln wrote formally on December 8 offering him the State Department. He also wrote privately and confidentially to describe as unfounded the rumours that he did not want Seward in the cabinet. On the contrary, "it has been my purpose, from the day of the nomination at Chicago," he assured him, "to assign you, by your leave, this place in the administration."[17]

Almost three weeks passed before Seward accepted the nomination. Conscious of the support he brought to the government, fully expecting to be its dominant figure, he held back in an effort to consolidate his position. He needed time, he explained to Lincoln, to consider whether he possessed "the qualifications and temper of a Minister" or should even "continue at all in the public service."[18] While he remained undecided, his political crony, Thurlow Weed, travelled to Illinois to discuss with Lincoln the remaining cabinet appointments. However, this deliberate indecision failed to disconcert the president-elect; he did not accept Seward's nominations. Unsuccessful in December, Seward made another attempt in March to secure control of the cabinet, and thus confirm what he was still sure would be his ascendancy. Shortly before the inauguration he suddenly asked "leave to withdraw" his acceptance of the State Department, but Lincoln, not to be panicked or outbluffed even on the hectic first day of his administration, asked Seward to reconsider his request, and mentioned also that William Dayton of New Jersey had been his second choice as secretary of state. The New Yorker could take a hint and immediately withdrew his letter of March 2.

For all his political deftness the new president remained a self-avowed novice in international relations. Consequently, the secretary's "qualifications and temper" would have interested most observers even if they had not shared his belief that he would dominate the government and shape its policy. Although small and slight, Seward was arresting in appearance. He had a thin, sallow face, a mop of greying hair which only partially covered his enormous ears, large eyes beneath heavy eyebrows, a great beak-like nose but an inconspicuous chin. Now approaching the end of his sixtieth year, he had been a politician for more than half his life. An Anti-Mason state senator, twice a Whig governor of New York, he had sat in the United States Senate since 1849, first as a Whig and then as the foremost Republican. Nothing if not adroit, he was considered even by his enemies to be "eminently qualified for the place, in talents, Knowledge, experience and urbanity of manners."[19] A member of the Senate Foreign Relations Committee since 1857, he had shown considerable interest in foreign affairs throughout the 1850s and had travelled to Europe for a second time in 1859. During this grand tour he had been fêted in Britain. Widely regarded as the next Republican presidential candidate, he was presented at Court and entertained by Lords Palmerston, Russell, and Derby. Revelling in this flattering attention, he delayed his departure from England as long as he could and left "with respect and kindness" for all he had met. For their part, the British had greeted him with more politeness than warmth. He had not impressed them personally and his career was not such that they would welcome his emergence as the head of an American government.

A devout nationalist, Seward had often declared that Britain— "the greatest, the most grasping and the most rapacious power" in the world[20]—was the obstacle that had to be removed from the path of America's rise to worldwide commercial supremacy and continental domination. For in the American firmament he detected the glimmer of Mexico, Central America, the Caribbean Islands, and Canada. A journey north of the border in 1857 caused him to doubt privately the inevitability of Canada being added to the Union, but in public he did not qualify his boast that American absorption of the British provinces was as certain as "that the stars will come out even if the moon delays its rising."[21] To the irritants of political astronomy and the terrestrial rhetoric of commercial rivalry, Seward added his support for the national aspirations of Ireland. As a New York politician he could scarcely ignore the Irish-American vote, but his criticisms of British policy went far beyond the call of expediency. A brief visit to the island during his first European tour in 1833 left him deeply impressed by the evidence of the suppression of Irish nationality. Perhaps the most disquieting of Seward's traits, however, was his tendency to exploit international problems for domestic gain. Thus he had been reasonable and unreasonable in turn, during the 1850s, in his interpretation of the Anglo-American arrangement in Central America, the Clayton-Bulwer Treaty, according to the partisan needs of the moment. Nor did his nomination as secretary of state bring any change of attitude. Instead, he was keener than ever to make foreign affairs a domestic servant. He spoke openly of a foreign war as "the best means of re-establishing internal peace,"[22] and bemoaned the absence of a dispute that would provide the excuse for a break with a foreign power. This was the man who was expected to determine the policy of the Lincoln administration.

Seward's first act as secretary was to institute a purge of the Department's employees, dismissing those whose loyalty was doubted. Next he had a list of the vacancies in the State Department drawn up and forwarded to Lincoln, and asked the other heads of department to do the same. He was seeking to establish his leadership and to expedite the distribution of patronage. But Lincoln required little prompting. Besieged by office seekers, many of whom had a claim to his favour, the president was alive to the need to have the foreign posts, especially those in England, France, Spain, and Mexico, "guarded as strongly and quickly as possible."[23] For the English mission he suggested William L. Dayton of New Jersey. At the Chicago Convention the full New Jersey delegation had supported Lincoln on the second ballot, having cast a favourite son vote for Dayton on the first. The New

Jersey Republicans now expected a reward for their nominal candidate. But Seward successfully diverted Dayton to Paris, and lauded Charles Francis Adams of Massachusetts as "far above all others adapted to British Court and society, infinitely more watchful capable efficient reliable everything." Anyway, New England was "an important point. What better can we do for her," he asked. "N. Jersey gives us little, and that grudgingly. I think Dayton's appointment would be as much too large for her as anything else we are likely to do for New England would be too small for her."[24]

Adams had already been urged upon Lincoln but as a cabinet member. His "eminent abilities," the "prestige of his name," even his private fortune "of one or two millions of dollars, which would give great confidence to the commercial and financial public,"[25] had all been cited as recommendations. He was also a friend of Seward's, with whom he had worked closely in search of a compromise solution to the secession crisis. But the New Englander's willingness to compromise, which some powerful members of his party interpreted as "a scheme of treason to Republicanism," and Lincoln's need for "a man of democratic antecedents from New England" conspired to deny him a portfolio.[26] And as soon as his appointment as minister to England was rumoured, the compromise spirit rose and threatened to haunt him again. His conciliatory attitude had cost him the close friendship of the inflexible and moralizing Charles Sumner, who belatedly attempted to deny him the mission and obtain it for himself. However, endorsed by the powerful Blairs, strongly sustained by Seward, even approved of by the secretary's principal antagonist in the cabinet, Salmon P. Chase, Adams was nominated on March 18. Sumner, meanwhile, obtained some consolation. He was selected as chairman of the Senate Committee on Foreign Relations and was granted "as free a hand as possible" in the distribution of diplomatic patronage.[27]

Of the new minister's peculiar fitness for the task of representing the United States in Great Britain there seemed no doubt. "Diplomacy and statesmanship run in his blood," commented one New England newspaper, "and have occupied no small portion of the studies of his life."[28] His father had served as American minister to the Court of St. James's, as indeed had his grandfather, and both had gone on to the presidency, while his mother had been the daughter of an American consul in the

British capital. It was as if he had been bred for the post. Then, as befitted an Adams, when Charles Francis grew to manhood and entered politics he did so as a moralist following the dictates of his developed conscience. "The first and greatest qualification of a statesman," he believed, was "the mastery of the whole theory of morals which makes the foundation of all human society." The second was "the application of the knowledge thus gained to the events of his time in a continuous and systematic way."[29] His consistent opposition to slavery not only met this test of statesmanship but it promised to make him as attractive to the English as his proslavery Southern counterpart Yancey was certain to prove repellent. Nor could two men be more unlike in their personalities, for the New Englander was almost English in his reserve and self-restraint.

Yet the puritan values to which the new minister so generously subscribed were not unequivocal advantages. Seriousness and sobriety command respect but they are not always accompanied by the social graces required of a diplomat. This "little bald-headed gentleman" with "clean-cut features and blue eyes,"[30] was neither a "pleasing after-dinner speaker nor a shining figure on festive occasions," and he lacked the "gifts of personal magnetism or sympathetic charm that would draw men to him."[31] Finally, the Adamses were not anglophiles. But if his inheritance, his education, and his training had left Charles Francis somewhat less than partial to the British he was quick to recognize the importance of the United States "keeping well with them" during her domestic crisis. Initially, he did not consider this a difficult problem. Called to Washington by Seward, he spent several hours at the State Department reading the correspondence that had passed between George Dallas in London and Lewis Cass. He considered the minister's letters dull and those of the former secretary impudent and surly, but emerged from the ordeal reassured that all questions of past difference with Britain had been settled or removed. All that was required of him was to keep on terms of good will during the "present difficulties." Satisfied that this task was undemanding, that there was no urgent need for his presence in London, Adams remained in Boston to attend the wedding of one of his sons on April 29. It was not until May 1, several weeks after the reported departure of the Confederate commissioners, that the new minister set sail for Britain.

For his part, Seward's attention was still fixed upon domestic not foreign politics. He did draft a circular to all American ministers abroad on March 9, but it did little more than echo Black's instructions of February 28. He gave more time and thought to relations with the Confederacy. As determined as ever to frame the policy of the administration, and convinced that through patience and the avoidance of hostilities lay the path to peaceful reunion, Seward struggled to prevent a confrontation over the remaining symbols of Federal authority in the seceded states—Forts Sumter and Pickens. Yet even as he undertook this forlorn task, the foreign implications of the worsening American crisis began to loom menacingly.

A growing uneasiness and uncertainty about European intentions found expression in the press. The Morrill Tariff stood in stark contrast to the commercial policies of the South. Against it the *New York Times* inveighed, as did the Democratic *New York Herald* which was now serving as a Northern retainer of King Cotton. Having interpreted Lincoln's inaugural address as an announcement of a coercive policy, by which it meant the reprovisioning of Forts Sumter and Pickens, the blockading of Southern ports, or the collection of customs revenues by vessels stationed outside, the *Herald* insisted that Britain and France would not tolerate any interference with their trade or damage to their industries. The British minister had already informed the American government that Britain would only recognize an effective blockade of the South, it revealed on March 5. As the United States Navy had insufficient ships to make a blockade effectual a collision with Britain was certain.

Public doubts about the attitude of the European powers were matched by private misgivings. From Paris came the disquieting information that the semi-official organs of the French government were clearly and strongly hostile toward the North, and that the entire Parisian press had been ordered to be sympathetic to the South. Also, the French capital was alive with rumours of a Franco-Confederate treaty, under the terms of which recognition was to be extended in return for the shipment of cotton "in French or Southern bottoms," and the freeing of imported French manufactures from all duties.[32] Back in Washington, such reports seemed anything but ill-founded. "I very much fear an early recognition on the part of France of the new Confederacy," commented Joseph Holt, the former postmaster-general in

34

the Buchanan administration, "which, followed as it would speedily be by others, would go far to consolidate the Southern republic. The bait for the material interests of Europe has been adroitly prepared, and cannot be long resisted."[33] Nor did Henri Mercier, the French minister, do anything to quieten these fears.

To the threat of European recognition of the Confederacy was soon added the danger of European intervention in the affairs of other American countries. For on March 29 came a report that an Anglo-French naval squadron had been organized for service in the Gulf of Mexico. Were the European powers preparing to enter Mexico, once again in a state of revolutionary turmoil, to obtain redress for the grievances of their subjects? The following day brought the news of the Spanish reoccupation of their former colony of Santo Domingo. "A year ago," the *Baltimore American and Commercial Advertiser* grieved, such demonstrations "would have aroused a storm of suspicion and patriotic excitement throughout the Union. Now we will have to accept it as part of the humiliation which is to be endured as the penalty of our national disruption." For the *New York Times*, the significance of the "ominous movements of European Powers" was even more profound. If "we do not speedily and vigorously commence the settlement of our own affairs, and the assertion of our existence," it warned, "a settlement may very speedily be commenced for us."[34]

These disturbing foreign developments found Seward deeply involved in indirect negotiations with the Confederate commissioners sent to Washington to secure the evacuation of Federal troops from Forts Sumter and Pickens. Acting on his own authority, he had reassured the Southerners on March 15, and again a week later, that Sumter would be evacuated. Then on March 29 Lincoln ordered an expedition to be readied for the reprovisioning of that fort, and on the last day of the month a similar order was made with respect to Pickens. Not surprisingly Seward quickly qualified his earlier assurances, informing the commissioners on April 1 that Lincoln might desire to supply Sumter but would not do so without first informing the governor of South Carolina. Dark as the future now appeared, the secretary still had hopes that Sumter would be abandoned and civil war avoided, but they rested upon the success of yet another of his attempts to assume responsibility for the administration's policies.

In his ill-timed "thoughts for the President's consideration," Seward presented himself as "the broad-shouldered Ajax that could alone sustain the weight then threatening to rend the Union asunder."[35] He would perform the miracle of reunion with the healing nostrum of foreign complications. What was needed, and what he could provide, he informed Lincoln, was a definite domestic and foreign policy. A policy that would *"Change the question before the Public from one upon Slavery . . . to one of Patriotism or Union."* As the continued occupation of Sumter was regarded as a slavery or partisan issue he would withdraw the Federal garrison from there but reinforce and defend the forts in the Gulf of Mexico. Also, the Navy should be "recalled from foreign stations to be prepared for a blockade." Abroad, explanations should be demanded from Spain and France, "categorically, at once," explanations should be sought from Great Britain and Russia, and agents sent into Canada, Mexico, and Central America, "to rouse a vigorous continental spirit of *Independence* in this continent against European intervention." And if satisfactory explanations were not received from Spain and France, he "Would convene Congress and declare war against them." Here was the Seward prescription for the revival of American nationalism—bellicosity and continentalism. That Lincoln would accept his right to prescribe Seward did not doubt. He may even have planned to announce his control of the administration as soon as the president abdicated his responsibilities to him. Instead, Lincoln gently put Seward in his place. But that was the State Department, and the president did concede that the news from Santo Domingo brought "a new item within the range of our foreign policy."[36] The following day Seward addressed a belligerent protest to the Spanish minister, and sent copies to Lyons and Mercier. Thus it served as an indirect warning to Britain and France not to meddle in American affairs.

As the possibility of a collision with the Confederacy over Sumter hardened into certainty during the first week of April, Seward's problems as secretary of state mounted. The Spanish intervention in Santo Domingo, the rumours of Anglo-French preparations for interference in Mexico and imminent French recognition of the Confederacy, were complicated by the danger of immediate difficulties with the British. A change in the tone of the British press was detected by some nervous observers. Disgust for a Slave Republic was being qualified by "approbation of the commercial platform" of the Confederacy.[37] A prominent Republican in New York confessed to Seward his alarm at the attitude of the London *Times*. "I am afraid that these articles are only the forerunners of a very strong and deep feeling against this country," Moses Grinnell wrote, "and that under the commercial feeling in England and France touching our recent Tariff act, they will ere long favor the recognition of this Southern ... Confederation."[38] In Washington also there was a belief that Britain and France would be guided by their commercial interests. As long as the United States abstained from any measure that would damage their commerce, Stoeckl, the Russian minister, advised Seward, it was unlikely that those two powers would do anything. A collision at Sumter, followed by civil war and Union attempts to sever commercial relations with the South, promised to provoke a response. Britain must have cotton, and she would obtain it one way or another, the British minister informed the secretary at a dinner party on March 25. To Stoeckl, a fellow guest, "there no longer remained any question what England would do in the event of a blockade of the cotton States."[39]

Seward poured out his deepening concern about British policy to William Howard Russell, the peripatetic correspondent of the London *Times*. Sent to the United States in March, Russell appeared in the American capital armed with letters of introduction and preceded by a formidable reputation made in the Crimea and India. Both president and secretary of state took time to court this man who seemed capable of creating a more favourable British opinion of the Union. At the Executive Mansion he was plainly but hospitably received by the Lincolns; he dined with Seward and also interviewed him. It was at one of these meetings, on April 4, that the secretary voiced his fear that even as the United States was at last preparing to suppress the rebellion the British might recognize the government at Montgomery. To prevent recognition, Seward warned, he was prepared to go to war. Four days later, when he asked the reporter to visit him again, Seward read to him "a very long, strong and able despatch" in which he sought to counter the dangers of British recognition with reason and "an undercurrent of menace."[40]

Seward argued that the demoralized state of the previous administration had enabled a minority of ardent secessionists to overwhelm a confused but loyal majority in the South. Now, however, the situation was different. Public property and institutions were being maintained and preserved with firmness and Federal authority would not again fall into abeyance. If this policy led to civil war the responsibility would clearly be that of the rebels. Should Charles Francis Adams, on his arrival in Britain, suspect the British government of being willing to grant recognition to the Confederacy he was instructed to leave it in no doubt that it could not take this step and remain on friendly terms with the Union. Indeed, the minister was authorized to inform the British that if they recognized the enemies of the Union they should also prepare to enter into an alliance with them. As for the Confederate appeals to "the cupidity and caprice of Great Britain," Seward warned against staking too much on the differing commercial policies of the North and the South. If the Morrill Act was as injurious to Northern interests as some of its opponents, domestic and foreign, insisted it was, then it would surely be repealed. Meanwhile, how long would the liberal commercial policy of the South last? With no other sources of revenue than duties on goods entering and leaving the Confederacy, faced with the "emergency of a military revolution," it was unlikely that the South would "be able to persevere in practicing the commercial liberality they proffer as an equivalent for recognition." Nor should the British fail to consider whether the new Southern government was "likely to be inaugurated without war," and whether their commerce with the United States "would be likely to be improved by flagrant war between the southern and northern states."[41]

As he listened to Seward reading this despatch, Russell concluded that even war with Britain "may not be out of the list of those means which would be available for re-fusing the broken union into a mass once more."[42] But this distant echo of the call for foreign complications was less distinct than the other sounds of Seward's foreign policy. The despatch would have an excellent effect when it came to light in Congress and the American public would think highly of the writer, the perceptive reporter remarked to the secretary. Of course, Russell had grasped here a fundamental Seward maxim. The first business of an American statesman was "to keep the confidence of his countrymen."[43] To do this he had constantly to exhibit "energetic and vigorous resistance to English injustice" no matter the damage to his reputation abroad.[44] But Seward's determination to retain the confidence of his countrymen was matched by his conviction that a show of absolute confidence in the permanence of the Union was indispensable. "You will make no admissions of the weakness of our constitution or any apprehensions on the part of the Government," he instructed Adams. On the contrary, by comparing the United States with other nations he would easily be able to prove that its constitution and government were the "strongest and surest" ever erected for the safety of any people.[45]

Convinced of the Union's basic strength, Seward was satisfied that it could only be seriously endangered by foreign intervention. This was sure to come "just as soon as the American people made up their minds to submit to it."[46] Consequently, he was quick to repudiate any suggestion of foreign mediation. Adams was ordered not to listen to any proposal of compromise "under foreign auspices."[47] Proposals that the Washington diplomatic corps mediate, and the suggestion of Governor Hicks of Maryland, that Lord Lyons be nominated as mediator, brought a scornful public response from Seward. He rejected the "arbitrament of any European monarchy."[48] Yet the danger that remained was of an uninvited European mediation or intervention. For Seward, the way to avoid that disaster was to warn foreign powers of the dire consequences of any interference. Against Britain the threat of war promised to be most effective. It permitted him to play upon her interrelated concerns for the balance of power in Europe and the security of her empire. Conservation of the empire was the one guiding thought of British statesmen, Seward had concluded during his visit to England in 1859. All "questions of morality, humanity, social progress are subordinated to the one policy of keeping the balance of power in Europe adjusted, that England and her colonies may be safe."[49] The British Empire was an "aggregation of diverse communities" covering a large portion of the earth and embracing one fifth of its entire population, he reminded Adams on April 10. But some of those communities were "held to their places in that system by bonds as fragile as the obligations of our own federal Union." Under the circumstances, would it be wise for Britain, by aiding in the dissolution of the United States, "to set a dangerous precedent, or provoke retaliation?" Had she no "dependency, island or province left exposed along the whole circle of her empire?" The danger to Canada, whose annexation Seward had long desired, was all too obvious. It was re-emphasized by the Ashmun affair.

On April 12 the cabinet agreed to Seward's suggestion that

George Ashmun be sent to Canada "as a special (secret) agent &
to keep political feelings right."[50] Rumours of the appointment
soon reached Lord Lyons, the British minister at Washington,
who suspected that the purpose of the mission "was to ascertain
the state of feeling in the Province with regard to annexing itself
to the United States."[51] Then on April 17, a few days after the
outbreak of war, the *New York Herald* announced that Ashmun
was to be sent to Canada "to explain our political position under
the present state of things." It was an improper proceeding, even
if this was all that Ashmun's task amounted to, for communications between the United States and Canada were supposed to
pass through the British legation in Washington. Embarrassed by
the public disclosure, Seward promptly terminated the mission
but did not discourage Ashmun from going ahead on his own.
In any event, when Lyons questioned him about the report in
the *Herald*, the secretary felt obliged to deny that any agent had
been sent "with any object affecting the present colonial relations" of Canada to Britain. What made the denial necessary and
not entirely convincing were Seward's remarks during the recent
election compaign. As the British minister remembered them,
the secretary "had alluded to the eventual acquisition of Canada
as a compensation to the Northern States for any loss they might
sustain in consequence of the disaffection of the Southern part
of the Union."[52]

In Canada, news of Ashmun's mission was doubly unwelcome
to the governor general, Sir Edmund Head. To natural suspicion
of the Americans' intentions was added personal embarrassment
at the selection of a man with whom Head had already had
several confidential discussions. For Ashmun had appeared
earlier in the province as the agent of the American creditors of
Canada's chronically insolvent Grand Trunk Railway. When
he returned early in May, the governor general took the precaution of meeting him only in the presence of two members of his
council. And when the American stated that he had been asked to
visit Canada to explain "the true position of the United States"
in the present crisis,[53] Head remarked that he could not deal
with him or any other agent because all communications with
the United States had to pass through the minister at Washington. Although that put an end to his avowed mission, Ashmun
did let it be known as he left Canada that the American government "would make the recognition of the Southern Confederacy

a *casus belli.*"[54] In the event of a war with Britain there was no doubt where the Americans would strike.

The outbreak of civil war heightened the Union's need to reawaken British concern for their empire, and thus dispel any thought of intervention. The Russian minister in Washington was surely not alone in believing that England would seize the first opportunity to recognize the Confederacy, or that France would follow suit. The loss of Sumter had prompted Lincoln to call for 75,000 men to suppress the illegal "combinations" in the South. Davis responded with a proclamation inviting applications for letters of marque and reprisal, only to have Lincoln issue his own proclamation on April 19, ordering a blockade of the Confederate ports. Eight days later it was extended to the ports of Virginia and North Carolina, for those states, along with the rest of the Upper South, now deserted the Union for the Confederacy. Britain's commercial and manufacturing interests were clearly in jeopardy.

Yet there were members of the Lincoln administration, including Seward, who believed or hoped that a blockade would not sever Europe from Southern cotton, but merely redirect this vital trade through Northern ports. Southerners were an agricultural people who could not rely upon the products of their own labour but were dependent upon the export and sale of their staples, therefore they *"must sell* or sink into poverty and ruin," Attorney-General Edward Bates reasoned. If their own ports were closed they would have to send "their products northwards to the ports of the States yet faithful."[55] Indeed, all their trade, both imports and exports, would pass through the ports of the Union. As a result, all the duties would be collected by the Union and all the profits of the trade would go to loyal citizens. The South, denied revenue from duties, would be forced to resort to the direct taxation that its people would not long endure. Here was the prospect of reunion with a minimum of suffering.

There was also hope that a renunciation of privateering on the part of the Union would induce Britain and other maritime powers not only to withhold recognition of Confederate belligerency but also to suppress Southern attempts to utilize this instrument of war. Therefore, American ministers abroad were quickly instructed to propose American accession to the Declaration of Paris of 1856, outlawing privateering. Lincoln, Seward, and

Charles Sumner all considered this a masterstroke of policy. Not everyone agreed. "They will not catch a fly by it," predicted Adam Gurowski,[56] who was soon to find employment in the State Department. Such scepticism should have been more widespread following the suspicious British rejection of another of Seward's proposals.

Still concerned about the flourishing slave trade around Cuba, the British government had instructed Lyons to revive a proposal made earlier to the Buchanan administration of joint Anglo-American antislaving patrols. The fact that the North was almost free of the slave states gave the British reason to hope that the traditional American reluctance to cooperate would now be overcome. But Seward's response was to argue that Spanish control of Santo Domingo would greatly increase the slave trade; therefore, what was required was an agreement to suppress the Cuban slave trade and to guarantee the independence of Santo Domingo. Clearly, Lyons commented, the former was merely the peg upon which to hang the latter. The advantages for Seward in such an alliance with Britain were obvious, at least to the British minister. It would enable him to use one European monarchy to give effect to his strong language protesting the interference of another in the affairs of the Western Hemisphere. At the same time it would give moral encouragement to the war party of the North and erect an additional barrier to Britain "ever entering into commercial and political relations with the South."[57] Finally, the French might join the alliance, thereby increasing the pressure upon Spain and the confidence of the war party, or they might support the Spanish and take Haiti for themselves. This would set Britain and France at odds, greatly reducing the danger of their intervention in the American war. "That motives of this kind have been Mr. Seward's inducement to propose the convention I have no doubt," Lyons concluded. "I mention them because they afford a clue to the course he will take in any negotiation into which he may enter respecting the Slave Trade proposals or other similar matters."[58]

Seward's gnawing fear of British meddling in the war had been increased by a report from Dallas in London. On April 8 he had called upon Lord John Russell to discuss Seward's circular of March 9. During the interview the foreign secretary had assured him that there was not "the slightest disposition in the British Government to grasp at any advantage which might be supposed to arise from the unpleasant domestic difficulties in the United States." However, when the American minister went on to emphasize the importance of Britain and France abstaining, "at least for a considerable time, from doing what, by encouraging groundless hopes, would widen a breach thought capable of being closed," Russell replied that he had said "all that at present it was in his power to say." The arrival of Dallas's successor, he went on, would be the "appropriate and natural occasion" for settling other matters.[59] To Seward these words sounded ominous. Was the British government thinking of extending aid of some kind to the Confederacy? "You will lose no time in making known to her Britannic Majesty's government," he instructed Charles Francis Adams, "that the President regards the answer of his lordship as possibly indicating a policy that this government would be obliged to deem injurious to its rights and derogating from its dignity."[60] Nor did he wait for the new minister to arrive in London to make his uneasiness known to the British. A copy of the despatch was sent to Lyons and was forwarded by him to Russell.

It was into this sea of misgivings about British intentions that the *Peerless* suddenly sailed. Several Northern states had already appealed unsuccessfully to the British North American authorities for permission to borrow or purchase Canadian arms when the governor of Massachusetts, John Andrew, was informed that a Canadian steamer, the *Peerless*, had been purchased for the rebels. Fearing that she was about to be commissioned as a Confederate privateer, and might escape from Lake Ontario to the sea, Andrew telegraphed the governor-general on April 27: "We rely upon you to take all possible steps to stop this piratical cruiser at the canals or elsewhere."[61] But Head refused to detain the vessel without evidence of her "piratical character." "The transfer of ownership, however suspicious in itself," he replied, "would not be sufficient to justify such a step in British waters."[62] Correct as it was, this response was unlikely to satisfy the Americans and Head feared that they would take matters into their own hands, perhaps damaging Canadian waterways in an effort to ensure that the *Peerless* did not escape. With this fear in mind he immediately ordered the stationing of troops on the Beauharnois and Cornwall canals. Four days later, on May 1, Seward took up the case of the *Peerless* with Lord Lyons and their encounter brought no easing of the tension.

43

The British minister, Richard Bickerton Pemell Lyons, was at 44 an experienced if undistinguished diplomat. His career, beginning in 1839, had been marked by painfully slow promotion from the ranks of the unpaid to paid attachés and then to the post of secretary of legation. After so many years in minor positions he had grown gloomy about his prospects of further advancement when, in 1857, he was appointed minister at Florence and then in November of the following year was offered the Washington legation. However, the appointment of this nonentity was not well-received in the United States. President Buchanan protested that the importance he attached to friendly Anglo-American relations did not appear to be fully reciprocated. The mission "ought always to be filled by a first rate man whose character is known in this country and whose acts and opinions will command respect and influence in England," he complained to an influential English friend.[63] Richard Cobden agreed. Lyons was not a man of "large experience," he was a "Lord without any antecedents," the Radical scornfully remarked.[64] Yet the new minister soon impressed others as a "most diligent, clear-headed and straightforward" man.[65]

Lyons made full allowance for the fact that he had not come to a country where "statesmen" decided the community's interest and guided public opinion by their superior wisdom, talents, and ability. Instead, he had to deal with "politicians," second-rate in station and ability, whose aim was first to divine then to pander to the feelings of the mob.[66] Also, he quickly realized how "very much pleased by attentions and civilities, and very prone to fancy themselves slighted" Americans were. From this he concluded that "one cannot be too careful with such very susceptible people."[67] In short, natively cautious, perhaps a little afraid of responsibility after so many years in lesser positions, Lyons proved taciturn and reserved; he listened more than he spoke. As for the outbreak of the civil war, he found that "peculiarly painful." Abhorrence of slavery and respect for law, as well as "a more complete unity of race and language," enlisted an Englishman's sympathies on the side of the North, he believed. However, he refrained from offering any encouragement to the Union, for war would injure both sides and Britain. Convinced that there was no hope either of reunion or of the reduction of the South "to the condition of a tolerably contented or at all events obedient dependency," sure that hostilities would result only in great loss of Northern life and money, the utter devastation of the South, and a suspension of cotton cultivation "calamitous even more to England than to the Northern States," Lyons favoured peaceful disunion.[68] But if this most sphinxlike of Washington diplomats kept his opinions to himself and his government, he was neither silent nor enigmatic when he met Seward on May 1.

The secretary informed the British minister that he had received reports that the *Peerless*, although on Lake Ontario carrying British papers and flying the British flag, was really in rebel hands. He requested that the Canadian government detain the vessel. But that was impossible, Lyons replied, without direct proof of the steamer's unlawful purposes. Apparently unwilling to wait upon such legal niceties, the American warned that the United States would not tolerate the fitting out and departure of piratical vessels. Orders would be sent to American naval officers instructing them to seize the steamer, whatever its papers and flag, he went on, as soon as they obtained "reliable information" that she had been sold or "contracted to be delivered" to the South.[69] This threat provoked even the reserved minister and he repeatedly protested against such an act, reminding Seward how sensitive the United States was to any interference with vessels flying her colours. Nevertheless, that evening Lyons learnt from Seward that his urgent protests had been of no avail, the orders had been sent to the naval officers. Happily, the storm that had threatened to burst around the *Peerless* quietly blew itself out. American officers failed to get the "reliable information" of Southern ownership because the steamer's purchaser proved to be a Northerner. As an American he required a sea letter from the consul-general at Montreal before he could obtain customs clearance. Still fearful that the vessel would fall into the wrong hands, the consul refused to issue that letter unless he selected the commander. The owner agreed, for there was no profit in a ship tied up in port, and the *Peerless* sailed for New York in June.

For Lyons, the significance of this episode was its confirmation of "the arrogant spirit and disregard of the rights and feelings of Foreign Nations" with which the Union seemed willing to conduct the civil war.[70] That same spirit and disregard pervaded Seward's despatch of May 3 to the American minister in Paris. The secretary had learnt that the French foreign minister had

45

inquired, during an interview with the American representative on April 15, about dissensions within the Lincoln cabinet. He seized upon this news to state, in "decided and haughty language,"[71] the essence of his foreign policy. The American people would not tolerate any intrusion into their affairs by European powers and were prepared to go to war to prevent foreign recognition of the Confederacy. Determined to parade the Union's position, thereby giving not only the French but also the British renewed cause to reassess their position before they responded to any Southern blandishments, Seward had this despatch published in the New York press on May 5.

Publication served a double purpose. Seward had taken his chance to reveal himself as an advocate of energetic measures against the rebellious South and all who would sustain her, thereby sloughing off his reputation as a compromiser. He wanted to gain the confidence of his countrymen, and in this he appears to have been successful. There was widespread applause of "one of the ablest, most vigorous and admirable" documents of American diplomacy.[72] But if the publication of the French correspondence was an adroit political move, what effect would it have on the Union's foreign relations? Had Seward, with this and his earlier note to Adams, intimidated the British and the French? Had he dissuaded them from any action that might sustain the Confederacy?

THREE

Looking to London

IF NEWSPAPERS PROVIDE ANY GUIDE to public opinion, it would seem that the events in the United States at first cheered and then alarmed more Canadians than they saddened. Nor is this surprising, for in 1861 the anti-Americanism that had been an emotional and institutional legacy of the American Revolution was still a potent force in the province. Initial resentment of the new American nation had been unavoidable, not least because its establishment had been achieved only at the cost of much social dislocation. Thousands of refugees from the triumphant rebellion emigrated to British territories. Some of these loyalists settled an area of Quebec west of the Ottawa river which was then organized as the province of Upper Canada. Yet even the deep wells of their bitterness seemed certain to dry up with time, while the sentiment of the province as a whole promised to warm to the Republic as Americans entered it in search of cheap land. Nonetheless the aversion for things American did not weaken, having been in some measure institutionalized in the form of government framed for the Canadas.

A post mortem on the loss of the American colonies had satisfied the British that imperial authority had died of governmental imbalance. The representative branches in the American colonial governments had expanded their powers at the expense of the executive until, unchecked, they had overreached themselves. Determined not to repeat this mistake, in 1791 the British government instituted an elaborate scheme of correction that looked to the creation of an aristocratic class and the conversion of the legislative council into a provincial equivalent of the House of Lords. Although some of its more fanciful aspects failed to survive, the tradition of a conservative Canadian government standing out in sharp relief against the backdrop of an ever more radical system in the United States had been established.

47

Institutional distinctiveness was sustained by ideological hostility. Instability and anarchy were confidently predicted as the inevitable fates awaiting the United States, a belief which the continual broadening of the base of the American government did nothing to dispel. Of course, during the 1830s and 1840s reform movements, seeking to root out entrenched institutions and dilute the conservatism that nourished them in Canada, found inspiration in the example of Jacksonian America. But the reformers quickly discovered that for the majority of Canadians there could be no ideological rapprochement with the Republic. Instead, the loyalist spirit of Upper Canada was constantly refortified by evidence of American predatory interest in the colony and the loyalist ranks were continually swollen by fresh inductions. Retired British army officers were encouraged, through generous land grants, to settle in Canada and substantial numbers of them did so. They were accompanied and followed by thousands of other immigrants, until by 1850 more than four hundred thousand out of a total population of less than two millions had been born in the British Isles. It was little wonder that in 1859 Richard Cobden "thought that the men looked more English," by which he meant British, "than those on the other side of the American frontier."[1] Meanwhile in Lower Canada the fear that Americanization would lead to assimilation and the disappearance of the distinctive French-Canadian identity, in short that Quebec would follow the path of Louisiana, easily overwhelmed the occasional expression of sentiment there in favour of closer association with the United States.

The smoldering fires of Canadian mistrust were all too frequently restoked and fanned by the Americans themselves. Their declaration of war on Great Britain in 1812 had been followed by an attempt to engulf Canada which, while it was farcically mismanaged, replenished the fund of bitter memories. The experiences of this war, with its raids and burnings, may well have broadened the base of Canadian hostility from dislike "of a particular form of government to dislike of the people who lived under it."[2] This dislike was intensified by the subsequent American raids and burnings along the border in support of the otherwise ineffectual Mackenzie rebellion. Nor did it lessen during the 1840s when the Manifest Destiny that seemed to guide the Republic into a confrontation with Britain over Oregon and rationalized the ravaging of Mexico appeared to threaten Canada. Hopes for better relations were strengthened by the signing of the Reciprocity Treaty of 1854. But distrust of the United States was never permitted to slumber for long. A war crisis in the following year, arising out of British efforts to recruit for the Crimea in the United States, played upon the old fears in a more dramatic way. Unsettling also was the threat of American penetration in the west. In 1840 Canadians had been worried by the danger of the rapidly expanding population of Michigan moving into the vast, unpopulated area between Lakes Ontario and Huron. By the 1850s the arrival of American gold miners in New Caledonia created tension there, while the conduct of a United States general in ordering the military occupation of the disputed San Juan island almost elevated a minor border problem into a grave international incident. Then there was the evidence of Minnesota's pursuit of what it considered its Manifest Destiny in the North West. In the loss of that region, the *Toronto Globe* warned, lay the prospect of the inevitable absorption of the remainder of British North America by the Republic. Meanwhile, the economic benefits of reciprocity were endangered by the increasing agitation in the Northeastern states for the treaty's abrogation. The protective tariff policy upon which Canada had embarked in 1858 provided American protectionists with fresh arguments when they carried to Congress their demand for an end to the treaty. Such demands seemed certain to be strengthened by the triumph of the Republicans in 1860, for their platform endorsed the principle of protection. Finally, loose talk during and after the election of the North "compensating" itself for the loss of the South by expanding northwards was calculated to inspire even less affection than Seward's rhetorical flights on the future of continentalism in speeches delivered at, among other places, St. Paul, Minnesota.

It was in the light of this abrasive and uneasy relationship that elements of the Canadian press quickly concluded that American disunion was something less than an unmitigated disaster for North America. Even before the secession of the South the post-election political turmoil in the Republic was greeted as a welcome check "at least for a while," to its further expansion.[3] Once the withdrawal of the Southern states was under way and there was talk of a new American confederation the *Toronto Leader* announced contentedly that the "ideal of territorial expansion will have to be given up."[4] Confident of their security, the Canadian press mocked and ridiculed the fatuous and threatening leading articles in the *New York Herald*. Any annexation which took place would be in the opposite direction from that espoused by the *Herald*, they suggested. The reported organization of a petition in Maine in support of that state's admission to British North America was widely publicized, while the *Leader* generously informed the Northern states that all applications would receive "a fair and candid consideration."[5] And when the seemingly indecisive course not only of the Buchanan administration but also, briefly, of its successor suggested that the right of secession had been tacitly conceded, there was a further elaboration of Canadian territorial daydreams. An emboldened *Quebec Morning Chronicle* reminded its readers of Seward's campaign remarks, "encouraging Canada to prepare for statehood," as justification for its playing of this game in reverse. "Would not the Western States make fine constituents of a great vice-regal Confederation?" it asked.[6] In fact it soon answered its own question, proposing that a vast new confederacy, composed of Maine, New York, Ohio, Indiana, Michigan, Wisconsin, Iowa, Minnesota, the Canadas, and the Maritime Provinces, be created and that it accept an English prince as its executive officer. New Jersey, Pennsylvania, and much of New England were to be arbitrarily excluded from this new union because they were "repellent states."

One of the principal benefits that the *Chronicle* expected Lower Canada to derive from the creation of a new nation of sixteen millions of people was that "she would become as well as New York and Maine the carrier and manufacturer for the rest of the federation."[7] But the commercial profits of the American crisis did not depend upon the formation of a new federation. The peace and stability of Canada, and the turmoil in the United States, promised to divert capital and enterprise to the province, producing a vast expansion of commerce as Canadian lakes, canals, rivers and roads were utilized by cautious merchants. In short, after years of disappointment, it seemed probable to the excited Canadians that the trade of the American Middle West would at last be redirected from the Erie canal system to the St. Lawrence waterway. No less likely was a turning of the tide of immigration northwards. For even though nearly a million British immigrants had landed at British North American ports between 1815 and 1855, these were but a fraction of those who entered the United States. Between 1815 and 1860 the Republic attracted three times as many British subjects as the provinces, indeed many of those who landed north of the border quickly moved on to the United States. But the American annual totals were swollen further by the arrival of vast numbers of Germans and other Europeans.

In Canada, however, the settlers were almost exclusively British, as the chief emigration agent detailed in his report for 1860. He revealed that of just over ten thousand immigrants in that year no more than a quarter were of non-British origins and fully four-fifths of these travelled directly to the United States, along with the same proportion of much the same number of Irish. Faced with these continual losses the Canadian government had initiated a modest advertising campaign in 1856, designed to deflect British immigrants from the Union and to encourage more Europeans to settle in the province. The uninviting commotion in the United States now held out a far stronger hope not only that this drain would be plugged but that the comparative imbalance in American and North American statistics would be reversed. The immigrants' search for peace, freedom, and stability was certain to lead them to Canada.

If some of these speculations had a dreamlike quality about them, particularly the vision of a Vice-Regal Confederacy (which may have been the product of a devious annexationist mind),[8] they did reflect the excitement of some Canadians at the sudden and by no means unrealistic prospect of establishing at long last a balance of power, commercial as well as political, in North America, one that would enable Canada to emerge from the ever-lengthening shadow of her neighbour. "Alongside of a colossal power like the United States we should be liable to be snubbed and bullied and invaded, whenever such a course of conduct was dictated by our strong neighbour," the *Leader* commented.[9] But the division of the Republic into two nations meant that a third great power in North America "would not only become possible but necessary." In short, it seemed that one of the aims of British policy since 1815 was about to be achieved, for it was "manifest" that British North America was now destined to "play no unimportant part in maintaining the equilibrium of power" there.[10]

This calculating and ironic response to the events in the United States was primarily the work of newspapers tied to the Liberal-Conservative government by the bond of patronage.

This is not to suggest that they never expressed sympathy for the Union or ever applauded disunion. On the contrary, they had initially dismissed talk of secession as nothing more than Southern brag and bluster, and subsequently they had piously deprecated the disruption of institutions that after Britain's were the most perfect in the world. However, as the ties of union loosened so the sympathy of these Canadian newspapers weakened. The conflict at Sumter was accepted as proof of the Union's permanent disruption and it inspired the frankly nationalist comment: "How to benefit our own country from the changes which are likely to follow should be our study."[11]

Less calculating and more consistently sympathetic than the organs identified with the government was the *Toronto Globe*. Owned and chiefly edited by the earnest George Brown, leader of the opposition Reform party in Canada West, the *Globe* was the province's most influential newspaper. Claiming a circulation of 30,000 in 1860, it was read by far more Canadians than any of its competitors. What determined the *Globe*'s initial response to the crisis of the Republic was Brown's detestation of the institution of slavery. Of course in this he was not alone. Slavery was anathema in Canada West which had long provided refuge for fugitive slaves. Indeed, the prevalence of antislavery sentiment there was undoubtedly one reason why that section of the province showed a greater interest in American affairs than did Lower Canada, or Canada East. French-Canadians reportedly knew little of slavery and had small opportunity to learn from runaways because there were less than 200 negroes in all of Lower Canada in 1860. But the fortress mentality that encouraged this ignorance also preserved a cultural distinctiveness in an otherwise British America and generated a dislike of American institutions and of Yankees. This sentiment, mixed with pleasure at "the relative importance" which events had tended to give the Creole population of Louisiana, led French-Canadians to view with indifference if not satisfaction the prospect of the dissolution of the United States.

Their hostility to the institution of slavery did not prevent the growth of racial prejudice among Upper Canadians. Although fugitive slaves were sheltered and sites provided for experimental black settlements, opposition to the newcomers, who amounted to no more than a tiny fraction of the population in 1860, rapidly developed in those areas where they congregated. Nevertheless,

Canada West was not quite a microcosm of the Northern states. There was no systematic and legislative curtailment of the political rights of blacks. The gulf separating words and deeds on the issues of slavery and the negro remained wider in the Northern states than in Canada, and for that reason the Liberal-Conservative press continued to challenge the Republican party's claim to be the party of freedom. There was no enthusiasm in Canada for the proslavery movement inaugurated by South Carolina, the *Toronto Leader* declared, but Canadians had not forgotten that while abolition "has been preached in the North," its "American apostles have not had the honesty to take the British way of doing the thing, and show their readiness to prove their devotion to their doctrines by providing those means by which England got rid of slavery in the West Indies."[12] The fact that the British solution was constitutionally inapplicable to the United States either escaped or was ignored by the *Leader*, which continued to imply that Canadians need not sympathize with the Union cause for reasons of humanitarianism. Other Liberal-Conservative newspapers also questioned whether slavery was the principal cause of secession. The *Montreal Gazette*, not only an organ of the commercial interests of Lower Canada but the traditional voice of the Tories there, emphasized the part played by commercial rivalry in the development of sectional differences. Once the Union and the Confederacy had adopted their contrasting tariffs the *Gazette* was joined by the *Quebec Morning Chronicle*, which was increasingly identified as a vehicle for the views of John A. Macdonald, one of the twin pillars of the governing Liberal-Conservative coalition.

Far less dubious about the issues at stake in the United States, the *Globe* hailed the Republican victory in 1860 as a great triumph of freedom over slavery. When South Carolina led the Cotton South out of the Union the Republicans were applauded for their adoption of a "strong position against secession"[13] and for their refusal to compromise "on dishonourable terms."[14] News of the formation of the Confederacy and of Jefferson Davis's inaugural made the *Globe* call a halt to a frantic campaign for peaceful separation and justify a sweeping endorsement of the North by tying the cause of that section to the interests of civilization and humanity. "The existence of a professedly Christian and civilized nation of manstealers would be a disgrace not only to America, but to the world," it proclaimed, "and however strong the measures the men of the North take for breaking it down, they will be justified in the opinion of all civilized communities, and will confer an inestimable benefit upon the human race at large."[15] The fall of Fort Sumter persuaded the *Globe* that concessions on the part of the North to the South were impossible.

The prospect of a fundamental reordering of continental power and influence which so affected Liberal-Conservative thinking was at best only indistinctly alluded to by the *Globe*, when it dallied with the fantasy of the South returning to British allegiance. And the disinclination of Brown's newspaper to consider this most exciting of all the benefits Canada might derive from a division of the Republic was illustrative of its complete disagreement with the government press on the consequences of the American crisis for the province. Far from stressing the prospective commercial advantages of disunion it emphasized the immediate commercial dislocation, an inevitable result of the interdependence of the economies of the Republic and the province. The failure of American banks and commercial houses during the political upheaval in the United States exacted a toll in Canada, and of this the *Globe* was careful to inform its readers. And while it also mocked the *New York Herald*, it cautioned against over-confidence on the sensitive subject of annexation. Rather than putting an end to American schemes, disunion would revive them "under more favourable auspices,"[16] for the withdrawal of the Slave South from the Union would remove the force that for obvious reasons checked Northern ambitions to annex the free territories of British North America. Evidently, the *Globe* was seeking to convince Canadians that their interests no less than the cause of humanity would best be served if the Union was maintained. Talk in the United States of "compensations" for the loss of the South, although aggravating, did nothing to weaken the *Globe*'s argument. Yet the moral issue remained for it the crucial question posed by the American crisis. However, its answer, which was to marry the cause of the Union to that of humanity, exposed it and all others who founded their Unionist sympathies upon this ground to a devastating rejoinder. Any failure of the Union to live up to the noble purpose being ascribed to it threatened to confirm what the Liberal-Conservative press was already charging, namely, that this was a marriage of convenience not love.

Although the *Globe*'s was the most powerful voice in English Canada its overriding and sympathetic emphasis upon the Northern states' opposition to slavery was not endorsed by all Reform newspapers. Certainly the *Montreal Witness* saw slavery as the root of the American "humiliation," while the *Sarnia Observer* found the cause of secession in the growing determination of humane and enlightened Northerners to limit the brutal and barbaric slave power. But the *St. Catharines Journal*, with an eye to a great increase in the use of the nearby Welland Canal, was as willing as the government organs to tally the commercial profit. As for the seeds of dissolution, it believed that they had been nurtured not by slavery but by universal suffrage and the practice of electing officers of every description. Indeed on this point, that the United States had foundered on the rock of excess democracy, there was a measure of bipartisan agreement. No advocate of universal suffrage, George Brown would surely have accepted the *Sarnia Observer*'s implied criticism of the Union when it boasted that "The measure of liberty, freedom and protection we now enjoy under British rule, we look upon as far in advance of that enjoyed by our neighbours."[17] Naturally, the Liberal-Conservative press was far more self-indulgent on the subject of universal suffrage—a system whereby "The brainless man who is hail-fellow-well-met with tavern loafers rises ... while the retiring man of merit is neglected."[18] But the hone on which the edge of such comments had been sharpened was the decade of sectional antagonism in Canada.

Just as the 1850s had seen growing discord between North and South in the United States so had these years witnessed mounting strife within the Union of the Canadas. A high tariff, compensation for withdrawal of French-Canadian seigneurial rights, and church involvement in education were all grievances of the majority of English in Canada West. But underlying all other problems was the over-representation of the predominantly French-Canadian East in the Assembly. The irony was that when the Canadian Union had been put together in 1841 the two provinces had been given equal representation because the population of Lower Canada far outnumbered that of Upper Canada. Determined to reduce the more populous French-Canadians to a subordinate political role, the Imperial government gave equal representation in the assembly to Canada West (Upper Canada). The expectation was that the members from Canada West would combine with the English minority in Canada East to dominate the affairs of the Union. But the scheme backfired. The French clung together far more successfully than the fractious English, and there occurred an unforeseen and dramatic growth of the population of English Canada. The census of 1851 revealed that the population of the West had overtaken that of the East and, what was more, showed every indication of continuing to increase at a faster rate. In short, what in the 1840s had been a French-Canadian grievance became during the 1850s an English one; what had been designed to secure English dominance of the Province of Canada was now seen by the French as a bulwark for the preservation of their identity. And playing their advantage to the full, the dominant group of conservative French-Canadians, the *Bleus*, made common cause with a minority of moderate Conservatives in the West to form the Liberal-Conservative governments that controlled the administration of the province after 1855.

Of course, the fact that a minority in the more populous West were maintained in office through an alliance with a majority in the East, a state of affairs possible only for as long as the system of equal representation was continued, intensified Western demands for change. At times the discontented spoke of dissolution of the Canadian Union, but the main thrust of the Reform agitation was the modification rather than the dismantling of the existing constitutional structure. In 1859, led by George Brown, they proposed a federation of the two Canadas, thus relegating sectional issues to sectional governments while "some joint authority" would control those matters common to both. The defeat of this proposal in the Assembly in 1860 forced Brown and his party to concentrate once again on what had been the most consistent demand of the more populous West during the 1850s—representation by population.

The Liberal-Conservatives had responded to the demands for constitutional change with the time-honoured and as yet not time-worn charge that their Reform opponents were the advance agents of American democracy or, what was even worse, of annexation. Separation of the Canadas "would lead to the annexation to the States of Canada, west of Toronto."[19] Federation was an American solution for Canada's problems and was being pressed upon Canadians by Yankees. "The experiment has worked so wondrously well with themselves," the *Ottawa Citizen*

56

sardonically observed early in 1861, "that we are not surprised that they should wish to extend the benefits to their neighbours."[20] As for representation by population, conveniently forgetting that Western Conservatives had endorsed it before they gained office, the Liberal-Conservative organs damned it as being tantamount to the universal manhood suffrage established across the border.

To charge George Brown and the Reform party with the crime of Americanism was blatantly unfair. They were as attached to the British connection and British responsible government as any man. Through the *Globe*, Brown had fought strenuously against the annexationists of 1848, against the Upper Canadian radicals or 'Yankee Grits' of the early 1850s, who expressed a preference for American elective institutions, and he was in the vanguard of those warning of the dangers of American absorption of the North West. Nevertheless, the force of the accusation was not weakened by his frank admission that the example set by the United States had been "of infinite value to the cause of liberty the world over,"[21] by the incorporation of the "Yankee Grits" into the Reform party following Brown's purchase of their principal organ, the *North American*, and by his employment of its editor, William McDougall, on the editorial staff of the *Globe*. Also, worn down by repeated setbacks, Brown did permit the *Globe* early in the summer of 1859 to dally with the idea of dissolution of the Union and the "remodelling of government along American lines."[22] However, he quickly recovered his political composure and through the Great Reform Convention of September 1859, which endorsed the federation scheme, he helped to check the demand for dissolution, to preserve the Reform party from radical control, and to ensure that it would "profess the mid-Victorian Parliamentary Liberalism" he favoured, "not the elective democracy of the neighbouring American republic."[23]

Although the federation proposal was overwhelmingly defeated in Parliament in May 1860, Brown and his supporters gained rather than lost by their revival of the cry for representation by population. It always promised to be a far more effective call, for it was one that even some Liberal-Conservatives in Canada West were finding it difficult to ignore. The publication of the 1861 census returns revealed that the West now outnumbered the East by as many as 285,000 persons, a statistic which gave renewed vitality to the agitation. Disturbing enough in itself, the outcry became far more serious for the government when it was joined by some western Conservatives who shared the Reformers' resentment at the continued Lower Canadian domination of the Union. Under these circumstances, with his parliamentary support weakening on this fundamental issue, Macdonald and his ministerial colleagues must have greeted the American crisis as a godsend.

It seems unlikely that the difficulties of the American Union evoked any more sympathy within the government than among its supporters. Neither of the leaders of the Liberal-Conservative coalition were admirers of the Republic. Although George-Etienne Cartier, the premier, had sought refuge across the border after the Papineau uprising in 1837 he acquired no fondness for the United States. Returning to Canada a few months later he quickly forsook political radicalism for the practice of law. Elected to the legislature as a Liberal in 1849, he opposed the call for annexation to the United States and expressed the belief that the existing form of government, and the Union, offered the best solution of Canada's problems. By the mid-1850s he was a leading member of the Liberal-Conservative coalition, and while he denied that he had been converted to Toryism he found the company of the more progressive Tories from the West far from uncongenial. They could agree on the need to preserve the equality of representation for the two sections, on the desirability of supporting separate schools, and on opposition to what they considered excessively democratic innovations. For, as Cartier prospered as a lawyer and as a lobbyist for railroads, he gave voice to a view of society that was founded upon a reverential respect for property, to him the source of all civic virtue and a bulwark against civic vice. The possession of property was an indispensable qualification for suffrage and thus for social stability. Naturally, this conviction encouraged disdain for the United States. But scorn for American democracy was coloured by fearful respect, and Cartier's attachment to the British monarchy was sustained not only by the belief that it was a more stable form of government than republicanism but also by the certainty that it offered the best guarantee for the preservation of French-Canadian nationality in North America. To such a man secession and civil war in the United States were by no means unwelcome.

No less anti-American and even more pro-British was his sharp-witted political partner, John A. Macdonald, whose coarse features and unruly hair were the cartoonists' delight. Born in Scotland and carried to Canada as an infant, he had grown up in Kingston where he eventually practised law. A conservative community, the real capital of the Upper Canadian loyalists, Kingston helped to shape his political and social attitudes. The experience of the 1837 rebellion, or more properly the raids by American filibusters and American-based rebels during that and the following year, left him with a "lingering anxiety for the problem of North American defence."[24] And for him, as for the constituents who elected him to the Assembly in 1844, the integrity of Canada depended upon "its permanent connection" with Britain. In his first election address Macdonald made a promise that his electors wanted to hear, but also one that he kept throughout his life. He declared that he would "resist to the utmost, any attempt, (from whatever quarter it may come)," which might tend to weaken the union with the mother country.[25] Consequently, he fought annexation in 1849 and resisted through much of the following decade any proposal that to his mind threatened to Americanize Canadian political institutions. Of the superiority of British institutions over those of the United States, of the supremacy of limited constitutional monarchy over Yankee democracy, Macdonald never had any doubt. He did support representation by population early in the 1850s, as a means of breaking the Reformers' hold on power, but he could not have found it an attractive doctrine to embrace. Anyway, once in power himself, through an alliance with the *Bleus*, he had several reasons for his adamant opposition. Beyond the obvious one, the threat it posed to his minority party's continued exercise of power, he was influenced by French-Canadian warnings that to abandon sectional equality was to dissolve the Union. Also, like his fellow conservative, Cartier, he came to regard representation by population as a long step along the path that led to the enfeebling American practice of universal suffrage. Undoubtedly, he shared Cartier's belief that the violent disruption of the American Union was the inevitable consequence of mob rule. It marked "the final stage in the discredit, not merely of federation, but also of democracy and republicanism."[26]

The traditional Canadian hostility towards the United States was reinforced in 1861 by a number of contemporary irritants. Denial of equal participation in the coastal and lake trade of the United States, which they interpreted as a violation of the Reciprocity Treaty, aroused Canadian ire. The Canadians were even more annoyed by the prospect of reciprocity being destroyed by the triumphant Republican party. Writing on the eve of Lincoln's election, Lord Lyons gloomily predicted that the Republicans, committed to protection, anxious to increase revenues and goaded by earlier tariff increases by Canada, would find a way of nullifying the Reciprocity Treaty. He fancied that a Republican Congress, unable to abrogate the treaty unilaterally before 1865, would simply repeal the acts that had admitted, duty free, the articles enumerated in the treaty. And his pessimism was deepened by the opinion that the British position was almost helpless. He could not conceive of "any retaliatory measures which would not disastrously affect the interests of the Empire at large, and those of Canada in particular."[27]

Although the fears that Lyons voiced in November failed to materialize immediately, it was a measure of Canadian uneasiness about the future of reciprocity that the wording of the Morrill Tariff was suddenly seen as the instrument of American abrogation. Reports that it referred to the "late, so-called Reciprocity Treaty" greatly agitated the Canadian government. They were "very angry" with Lord Lyons, holding him responsible for the fact that they had not been warned that the tariff "touched" the treaty, and in their anger they were quite willing to remind the Americans what they stood to lose. "The approaching opening of Navigation and of the Fishery season," Lyons was informed, "makes it especially necessary that we should be informed on the point whether the Treaty exists, or whether according to the Tariff act, it is to be considered wholly set aside."[28] The threat of exclusion from the Bay of Chaleur and the Gulf of St. Lawrence was not one which American fishermen would treat lightly.

The British minister at Washington, now far less pessimistic, replied quickly and reassuringly to the Canadian inquiry. He reminded them that treaties are the supreme law of the land in the United States, and from this they derived some comfort. Macdonald instructed the editor of the *Toronto Leader* to contradict the public reports that the Morrill Tariff was prejudicial to reciprocity. No doubt he also spoke to the editor of the *Quebec Morning Chronicle*, for it followed suit the very next day. Meanwhile, the opposition *Globe* had already attempted to persuade

Canadians that the Morrill Tariff was of little concern to them "because the manufacturing interest in Canada is as yet in its infancy, and we produce so few manufactured goods that it matters little to us whether the United States market is open to them or not."[29] And once the Canadians had begun to calm down Lyons drew their attention to the last United States tariff, that of 1857, which had imposed duties upon articles enumerated in the Reciprocity Treaty but had not led to the duty being actually levied on trade with the province. Instead Canadian-American commerce had continued unencumbered. But if there were constitutional and historic reasons for calm, even the wording of the Morrill Act would not have appeared at all alarming had the Canadians stopped to consider it in context. The clause in which the words "late, so-called" were used, Lyons informed Lord John Russell, tended to confirm rather than invalidate the treaty. All of which served to emphasize the intensity of the Canadian government's distrust of American intentions.

It was against this background, not only of dislike and distrust of the United States but also mounting domestic agitation for constitutional change, that Cartier, Macdonald, and their colleagues faced the Provincial Parliament in March. From the outset it was clear that they intended to capitalize upon the American difficulties in an effort to frustrate the demands for change. As one government supporter put it on March 18, one lesson to be learned from the dissolution of the American Union was the need for mutual and reasonable concessions and for the withdrawal of unreasonable demands. Representation by population was such a demand requiring just such concessions, Cartier argued on April 5. He chided those from the West who had introduced and were supporting this proposal. Had not Lower Canada had the far larger population in 1841, but had it pressed the issue to the point of causing serious trouble? He dismissed the claims of those who had thought it necessary to endorse the doctrine as one of English origin, and he seized the opportunity to ridicule his opposition in Canada East, the *Rouges*, who in 1849 had called for the acceptance of American political institutions as a means of implementing a radical transformation of French-Canadian society. "I do not like the American system," he announced to the surprise of no one. "I like the system of responsibility practised in England [and] if to-day the Americans are on the eve of deplorable struggles that is due entirely to the irresponsibility of the leaders of the administration."[30]

While the premier used the American crisis to good political advantage in Canada East, it was left to Macdonald to convert it into a birch with which to flog the western Reformers. He had already decided that the forthcoming election should be fought on the issue of whether Canada "will be a limited constitutional monarchy or a Yankee democracy,"[31] when a member of the opposition committed a grave verbal blunder. On April 17 the debate on representation by population was still continuing. D'Arcy McGee protested the way in which "the recent sad experience of the United States has been frequently held up to us as a warning, against extending the power of the people in this House, during this debate."[32] But it was William McDougall, the former "Yankee Grit," the former editor of the *North American* and a present member of the editorial staff of the *Globe*, who uttered the fateful words. Having dwelt upon the bonds of sympathy and commercial interest that united the peoples of Western Canada and the Northern states, he suggested that in the event of the call for constitutional reform going unheeded the residents of Canada West would look to the United States "for relief from a domination which oppresses and degrades them, and which threatens to become even more intolerable."[33]

For a politician as adept as Macdonald the opening that McDougall had offered to him was enormous. In his reply he quickly coined an election slogan. "If there was a loyal people in the world, it was the people of Upper Canada," he proclaimed, "and he was confident that they would not look to Washington [cheers] notwithstanding that they were invited" by McDougall. If "Looking to Washington" was the unpatriotic motto now to be fastened upon the Reformers, Macdonald took care to provide his own supporters with further ammunition to fight off the calls for constitutional change. Brown's moribund federation scheme was dragged out to be paraded and criticized as an invitation to a repetition in Canada of the American disaster. The fatal mistake of the United States, Macdonald informed the House, "was in making each State a distinct sovereignty, and giving to each distinct sovereign powers, except in those instances where they were specially reserved in the Constitution. The true principle of confederation lay in giving to the general government all the principles of sovereignty." As for representation by population, that also was American. Population was only one of the elements upon which representation should be founded, "and the true principle by which representation should be regulated, was that all interests should be represented." That was the system, he continued, pointedly, under which "England had flourished and had withstood the storms of revolution, of foreign war and domestic dissension."[34]

Macdonald then turned to the enjoyable task of berating the opposition as petty men who were willing to jeopardize the great national destiny beckoning Canada. Following the path well marked by the government organs, he reminded his countrymen of Seward's talk of annexing Canada as compensation for the loss of the Southern states. This served to reawaken traditional Canadian fears, to imply that McDougall and his colleagues were agents of the American secretary of state, and to provoke irritated Canadians into unabashed calculations of the benefits of American disunion. The opposition knew, he charged, that "in consequence of the unhappy war which was now raging in the United States, there was every prospect of the emigration and wealth of the old world—the great bulk of which found its way to the Western Prairies of a foreign country—now finding a home in Canada." They knew also, he continued, "that in consequence of this fratricidal war, and this inevitable disruption, Canada had every prospect of being the great nation of this continent." Nevertheless, "for factious and party purposes," they were "ready and willing to blight all this fair prospect, to prejudice if not ruin our hopes, our well grounded hopes, just at the moment of fruition, by the factious insanity of their course."[35]

That Macdonald had stolen the initiative and thrown the opposition onto the defensive with his brilliant speech there was never any doubt. The proposal to enact representation by population was subsequently defeated, twelve members from Canada West uniting with all but one of the representatives from Canada East. But this speech was a strategic triumph as well as a tactical victory. As the governor general reported home, it left the opposition scrambling to disavow the meaning that Macdonald had gleefully attributed to them. They were clearly afraid that the charge of disloyalty was going to tell upon them heavily at the polls. The mob had ruled the politics of the United States for years, the *St. Catharines Journal* reminded its readers, and the outbreak of the civil war proved that "none but the principles held and practised under the British Constitution are those

63

which can insure permanence." Canadians should feel thankful "for the glorious privileges they enjoy of living under this Constitution" and should "take every peaceable and honourable means to bring it to bear" on their neighbours.[36] Forced to prove that it was as pro-British and as un-American as any other organ, the *Globe* recalled that in the past the United States had invariably sought to take full advantage of British difficulties. If Britain now gave tit for tat "our near neighbours would be taught a lesson that would live some years in their democratic recollection." Thus while British opinion hoped that the rebellion would be subdued and slavery ended "We are not altogether displeased at finding them in a fix which will compel them to abate their pretensions, and trust that the lesson they are now receiving may prove salutary in its effects."[37]

These professions of loyal sentiment and protestations of opposition to the establishment of universal suffrage in Canada were never likely to deter the government organs from embellishing Macdonald's charges. Their course had been set and they pursued it relentlessly. The Canadian people would not look to Washington "for the cure to their political maladies,"[38] particularly when "the evils" of Republican institutions were being made "terribly apparent."[39] They would not permit Canada West to be "handed over to the Northern States as compensation for the loss of territory incident to the formation of the Southern Confederacy."[40] Nor would they endorse the *Globe*'s attempts to commit Canada as a partisan of the North, for this might lead to British involvement in the war and was but the second string of the annexation fiddle.

Although the disruption of the American Union was a satisfying political windfall for the somewhat beleaguered Canadian government early in 1861, not all of the fruits of that crisis were as palatable. Expressions of concern for the security of the province were not always political cant. Sir Edmund Head, the erudite and experienced governor general, who returned to Canada in February after a leave in Britain, soon grew uneasy about the consequences of American events. The talk of annexing Canada he interpreted "either as a threat to the South showing the resources on which the North would fall back—or as a real movement, to be taken advantage of, if the secession is ultimately carried out."[41] Seward's prominence in the Republican administration about to take office provided no reassurance, for the annexation talk was in accordance with his previous "dodges."[42] Indeed, the secretary of state-designate excited so much distrust that Head even suspected that the wording of the Morrill Act was yet another of his schemes "to show the Canadians the practical inconvenience of belonging to Great Britain still."[43] Then, once Seward had taken control of the Department of State, there came the Ashmun and *Peerless* affairs and a reminder from Lyons that Canada was looked upon as Britain's weak point; that in the event of hostilities the American blow would fall there. All of this bred insecurity in the Canadian government, which became something of an ally to Seward in his campaign to check Britain by threatening the colony.

Head warned the Imperial government that if Britain took any step likely to annoy the United States "The spite of the Yankees might be vented here."[44] Therefore, any recognition of the Southern States ought to be accompanied or preceded by a large increase in British military and naval power in North America. However, the main worry of the colonial government was not the threat of immediate invasion but the conduct of the Americans once their civil war was over. The likelihood that the war's end would find tens of thousands of men "kicking their heels with arms in their hands" was serious enough, because if they were out of "humour with England" they might easily be disposed "to give trouble in Canada."[45] What made this prospect even more disturbing for the Canadians was the sinister figure of Seward. To Head it was plain that the secretary's belligerent attitude toward Britain had been struck in order to convince the American people that they had been grievously injured by British recognition of Southern belligerency. As soon as terms had been arranged with the Confederacy the warlike ardour and preparations of the Union could be turned against Canada quickly and without warning. Instead of falling victim to random filibustering the province would be claimed as the Northern indemnity.

In this frame of mind Head pondered how best to cope with the American danger. With his own term of office expiring, and with the Imperial government searching for a successor, he suggested that a distinguished soldier be appointed. Such an appointment would be far from unpopular in Canada, he argued, and it would impress upon the Americans the need to maintain peace. More that this, he believed that it would be worth 4,000 troops. If these military implications were at best problematical, there could be no doubt of the urgent necessity to put the province's militia in better order. The Militia Bill of 1855 had provided for an "Active Militia" of some 5,000 men, uniformed, armed, and at least partially trained. But when a new act was passed in 1859, the authorized strength was slightly reduced while the annual drill period and annual appropriations were greatly reduced. The result was a marked decline in the strength, enthusiasm, and efficiency of the force. Under any circumstances then the militia stood in need of improvement but the American crisis made it doubly necessary. Accused by the governor general of a breach of faith in allowing the defence of the colony to lapse in this manner, Head's ministers decided to include an increased vote for the militia in the supplementary estimates. And during the debate in the legislature, Macdonald made the most of the threat of filibustering after the civil war, warning that it would be very unwise to permit the "volunteer force of 5,000 men to be altogether dissipated or rendered useless."[46] In fact the ministers were prepared to do more, they were willing to ask for "a vote of credit in case of emergencies," but the governor-general demurred. The Canadian posture "ought to be one of total unsus-piciousness," he reasoned, "until we are actually and really prepared which must be done from England."[47]

In March of 1861 there were no more than 4,300 British regulars in the North American provinces and only 2,200 of them were in Canada. That the Canadians would expect a substantial increase in the Imperial establishment was certain, given their tradition of seeking to impose upon the British government as much of the burden of colonial defence as they could. Before the month of April was out the *Toronto Leader*, the government's principal organ in Canada West, was calling for the arming of Canadian neutrality, a neutrality the province had been in-structed to adopt in January. "Our neighbours are arming for war," it observed. "Let us be armed that we may enjoy an assurance of peace," and by arming the *Leader* meant a show of regular soldiery sufficient "to produce an impression of prepared-ness, and lay the basis of more vigorous and successful action than all the volunteers in the province unassisted could hope to accomplish."[48] Six to eight British regiments would have the desired effect, it was estimated.

The conviction that British reinforcements were indispensable strengthened as suspicion of American intentions deepened.

Before the end of May Head was warning the Imperial government that Canadian unease had combined with the settled belief that any difficulties with the United States would stem solely from the connection with Britain to produce a dangerous temper. "There is certainly a notion that the English Government are leaving them to take their chances," the governor reported.[49] And while he denied the justice of this opinion he did dwell upon the deficiency of the military equipment of the province. In 1856, 10,000 rifled muskets, camp equipages for 10,000 men, and some 4 million ball cartridges had been sent to Canada, but since that time these supplies had been redistributed. General Fenwick Williams, the officer commanding the British troops in Canada, reported in May that there were 7,000 Enfield rifles and 10,000 muskets in the province but only 446 sets of accoutrements for the former and 5,600 pouches and cross belts for the latter, most of them thirty years old. Indeed this enormous discrepancy between rifles and accoutrements rendered the weapons that were on hand virtually useless, Williams added. Head soon discovered that many of the rifles had been sent without his knowledge let alone approval to the Lower Provinces. "I do not think it desirable at a time so many thousand men are in arms on our frontier," he wrote home, "that there should be any want of means for arming a large number of men on our side in case of emergency."[50]

An increase in the Imperial military establishment and supplies was not all that Head recommended. Of first importance for Canadian security was command of Lake Ontario, and while the Rush-Bagot Convention with the United States prevented the stationing of armed vessels on the lakes it was possible to evade these restrictions by keeping gunboats on the St. Lawrence. With this in mind Head had taken the precaution, as early as April 26, to send home the "dimensions and depth of water in all the Canal locks."[51] Their recommendations made, Head and his government waited for a response from London. Satisfied that a strong defence was "the best sedative" but that any measures adopted by the province would be largely ineffectual, or at worst provocative, convinced that the real strength had to come from Britain, for the militia was "worth very little," the governor general decided that there was little more to be done but "to wait quietly" for reinforcements from home.[52] Thus all eyes in North America were turned to Britain, the South in hope, the North with misgiving, and Canada in search of protection.

FOUR

The Proclamation of Neutrality

THE DRAMATIC GROWTH AND DEVELOPMENT of the United States during the first half of the nineteenth century excited both interest and concern in Britain. The depth of that interest encouraged two hundred and thirty of the uncounted British visitors to the Republic between 1836 and 1860 to publish accounts of their travels, and it was reflected in the immediate translation and success of Alexis de Tocqueville's *Democracy in America*, and in the appointment of J. C. Bancroft Davis as the American correspondent of the influential London *Times* in 1854. As a result, while the great majority of Englishmen remained "as ignorant of American history since the revolution as of the Chinese Empire, and of American geography as of the geography of Central Africa,"[1] among the upper classes ignorance was less profound. They could read and marvel at the prosperity, and cavil at the habits of Americans. They deplored slavery and devoured *Uncle Tom's Cabin*. Yet as compelling a subject as this institution was, even it could not rival the attraction of democracy. For American democracy was an issue in British politics.

Richard Cobden and John Bright, the principal and the pedagogue of the Manchester School, were known as the two members of Parliament for the United States. These two Radicals were a striking and formidable pair. Cobden, pale and slender, lacked physical robustness but not intellectual and moral strength. Bright, whose taurine appearance gave a misleading impression of sound health, was an eloquent spokesman for economic licence and political rectitude. He was also forceful, abrasive, and impatient, as he struggled to overcome the political liability of his religious nonconformity and to speed the pace of reform. Both men corresponded with Americans, read American newspapers, and entertained distinguished American visitors to Britain, but only Cobden braved the Atlantic. First in 1835, and again

69

twenty-four years later, he journeyed to North America and from each visit returned home convinced of the Republic's "inherent greatness."[2] The American experience was cited in support of a host of reform causes, from universal education at public expense to the abolition of the stamp duty which effectively priced newspapers beyond the means of many people. Soon in harness behind him was Bright, and in the repeal of some of the "taxes upon knowledge" in 1855 they saw hope of important public questions being removed from the control of "cliques and coteries of political jobbers."[3] In the following year they helped to found an inexpensive Radical organ, the *Morning Star*, and Bright's brother-in-law was appointed editor.

In their battle for "peace, retrenchment and reform," the two Radicals continually pointed to the United States as an inspiring example. It was a foreign policy of nonintervention in the troubles of Europe, they declared, that permitted the Union to escape a heavy burden of military expenditures and thus to prosper. They made much of the fact that Britain's annual budget was five times that of the republic. But if the cost of British government was exorbitant it also rested on a narrow popular base, and fusing these two complaints Bright denounced his nation's foreign policy as a giant scheme of outdoor relief for the privileged classes. In 1858 he launched a characteristically vigorous campaign for parliamentary reform, demanding a broad suffrage and a redistribution of seats that would reflect the distribution of population. Again he cited the American precedent.

Whatever their achievements, Cobden and Bright did little to inspire warmer British feelings for the United States. They affronted the pride and complacency with which Englishmen regarded their nation, as the exemplar of a "harmonious and orderly modern society."[4] Incessant praise of the United States as the fount of political and social wisdom, even to the use of American flags at election rallies to represent freedom, excited more rancour than envy. Bright attracted the greater censure, not least because he personified for some of his countrymen "the headlong downward course by which we are daily approximating an American form of government and (what is worse) an American tone in politics."[5] The British, as even the young William Seward had quickly recognized when he first travelled among them in 1833, had no wish to be Americanized.

Recalling the bitter memories of 1776 and the "knife in the back" of 1812, fearful of democracy as a challenge to privilege and scornful of it as a basis of government, Conservatives decried the American example and damned the Radicals as un-British. For them America was "Crude at the surface, rotten at the core." Instead of a nation in which all interests were in harmony, they portrayed a country in which sectionalism was prevalent, politicians incompetent, and corruption rife. They also denounced it for its materialist and bourgeois values, and with this indictment probably won working class approval. "English working-men often shared with the Tory landed gentry feelings of recoil from new economic and social forms, and looked back nostalgically to an era of rural patriarchy."[6]

Between the poles of Cobdenite praise and Conservative abuse lay the Whig-Liberals. Many Liberals found in Tocqueville a persuasive interpreter of the United States. The strength of the Frenchman, as John Stuart Mill pointed out, was his accounting of both the assets and liabilities of American democracy. Its great virtue was the constant involvement of much of the population in politics, and its most dangerous vice the inherent threat of mass tyranny. Thus the task confronting those who saw the American system as the wave of the future was to erect dykes to protect the vulnerable areas in popular government. As for the Whigs, slowly giving way to Liberals by the 1850s, they had used the American example during the agitation for reform that climaxed in 1832 and until mid-century considered America's faults less significant than her merits. But by 1850 they were losing confidence in and sympathy for the Union. Their thirst for reform quenched by the limited results of the 1832 bill, some old Whigs opposed the later agitation and became anti-American in the process. Others disparaged the quality of American leadership, claiming that statesmen had been succeeded by demagogues or nonentities, while the growth of sectionalism brought into doubt the effectiveness and permanence of the federal system. In short, the low political opinion of the Republic that was traditionally associated with Conservatives gained new adherents from the ranks of those who reacted adversely to Radical praise, responded positively to Conservative criticism, or simply surrendered to Whig pessimism about majority rule.

But the wedges of Anglo-American discord were manifold. The years between the end of the War of 1812 and the beginning of the civil war saw almost three millions of British subjects endure the hardships of the Atlantic crossing to settle in the United States. Yet this social link proved more of a fetter than a bond. The great majority were Irish animated by a savage hatred of Britain. Concentrated in the northeastern states, permitted by slipshod and corrupt naturalization procedures to participate quickly in political life, they were a disruptive force in Anglo-American relations. Politicians with a substantial number of Irish constituents felt obliged to rail against Britain whilst American governments became more sensitive than ever to the charge of truckling to the British. For their part, the British were irritated by the periodic political outbursts and angered by the efforts of "Yankee Irish" to liberate their native land, either by direct action, as in 1848 and 1854, or through the shipment of money and munitions to Irish nationalists.

Economically, the interests of Britain and the United States were also diverging. It was true that the liberalization of the American tariff in 1833, 1846, and 1857, together with the extension to Americans of full trading privileges with the British West Indies, the repeal of the Corn Laws, and the dismantling of the Navigation Code created "a climate of relatively free trade"[7] as British manufactures were exchanged for American raw products. Indeed, for a time, it seemed that the two economies were complementary. But there was heavy British investment in the United States and these funds helped to finance the transportation revolution and to release domestic capital for industrial development. Thus the British assisted the growth of an industrial America and by so doing contributed to the emancipation of the American economy from its colonial status and to its elevation to the rank of a competitor.

Although the rivalry was not formalized until the enactment of the Morrill Tariff, the economic clouds had been gathering over the Atlantic for some time. Many of the British visitors to the Republic were struck by the evidence of her rapid industrial development. Cobden and Bright, businessmen both, voiced fear of as well as admiration for the United States. Unless Britain took a leaf out of America's book and adopted policies that permitted her to concentrate on economic growth she would forfeit the economic leadership of the world, they warned. While the prescient Radicals failed to stampede their countrymen into reform that does not mean that all of these warnings fell on deaf ears. Englishmen may not have realized in 1860 that the United States was an industrial nation second only to their own, but there was reason enough for uneasiness. As early as the 1840s manufacturers were complaining of the exodus of valuable workmen to the United States, having seen their exports to that market more than halved since 1832. Mid-century found the two nations competing for commerce on the west coast of Africa and in Latin America, and brought evidence of superior American technology. The Americans' exhibits at the Crystal Palace in 1851 attracted much attention, and before long their sewing machines and reapers were being imported into Britain or manufactured there from patents. Finally, the 1850s witnessed Lancashire's loss to New England of the lucrative American market for coarse cottons. By 1860 American mills were consuming a third of the quantity of cotton needed to supply those in Britain.

Worried by the growth of the American textile industry; irritated by the demands of the Southern planters for higher profits and by their schemes to force up prices artificially through false reports of crop failures; afraid that their American supplies would be cut off, perhaps as a result of a slave insurrection, a breach in Anglo-American relations, a natural disaster, or the Union's political troubles, some Manchester textile men struggled to lessen their dependence upon American cotton. In 1857 they formed the Cotton Supply Association, and soon convinced of India's cotton-producing potential they began to urge the Indian government to undertake the massive program of public works that would enable them to exploit this source. Yet by 1860 the Association's achievements had been slight, and this failure together with the evidence of increasing turmoil in the United States, and the prospect of the Indian government building a road that would provide access to the valued Dharwar-American cotton prompted the formation of the Manchester Cotton Company. Closely identified with the Association, it endorsed the older organization's call for public works. However, both groups encountered a powerful opponent in Sir Charles Wood, who had taken over the India Office in 1859. He proved to be a far more loyal adherent to *laissez-faire* economics than the men from Manchester. He found irksome their demands that the government do what he believed they should properly do for themselves. Also, he was anxious to defend the Indian *ryots* from the danger of abuse. As a result, 1860 found the British textile industry as nervously dependent as ever on Southern cotton.

No less disturbing was the American challenge to the supremacy of the British mercantile marine. For a full decade after 1847 the United States was the world's leading shipbuilding nation. American-built vessels won the best cargoes and most of the passenger business in the lucrative North Atlantic trade, while the total tonnage of the American commercial marine almost equalled that of Britain. Such statistics made unpleasant reading for British commercial interests, as did the sharp decline between 1847 and 1860 in the proportion of British tonnage using British ports. Their response was to question the wisdom of the repeal of the Navigation Laws and to press for the opening of the United States coasting trade to British vessels.

Just as the 1850s saw the economic interests of Britain and the United States diverge and then collide, so it witnessed the slackening of humanitarian ties. The British and American peace movements that met in convention in London in 1843 and provided the model for several international meetings between 1848 and 1851 waned rather than waxed during the rest of the decade. Yet nowhere was the failure of cooperation more marked than in the struggle against slavery. The promise of joint action was never truly fulfilled. Although British and American abolitionists met as the World Anti-Slavery Convention in 1841, and again in 1843, a schism within the ranks of the American movement and the decision of British societies to take sides in the quarrel led to bitterness. Consequently, while cooperation was never nonexistent, it became increasingly difficult as relations grew strained. Nor was the situation improved by the decline of British interest in antislavery work by midcentury, as evidenced in dwindling membership, shrinking funds, and public indifference.

Even more pronounced was the failure of Anglo-American cooperation against the Atlantic slave trade. Having abolished the trade in 1807, the British were moved by humanitarianism and self-interest to secure international acceptance and enforcement of the ban. Through difficult bargaining and simple bribery they negotiated treaties with other nations, outlawing the trade and empowering British naval officers to detain violators. But the United States refused to be a party to such an arrangement. Although her own abolition took effect in 1808 and Congress condemned the trade as piracy in 1820 she consistently rejected any proposal to concede to British officers the right to visit and search vessels sailing under the American flag. Memories of her colonial status, of British interference with her commerce during the Napoleonic Wars, and of the War of 1812, all prompted this refusal. So too did an unwillingness to antagonize Southern states into which African slaves were being smuggled, and the suspicion that Britain's true purpose was to monopolize the trade of West Africa. And while under the terms of the Webster-Ashburton Treaty of 1842 the Americans agreed to station a cruising squadron off the African coast for at least five years, the vessels sent were insufficient and inappropriate for the task and they were based too far away from the coast. One result was that the thriving slave trade with Cuba during the 1850s was "financed by American capital, carried in American ships, manned by American seamen and protected by the American flag."[8] When the British Navy attempted to suppress it there were howls of protest from the American press and an outburst of belligerent ranting in Congress against any interference with American commerce. In the face of this concerted indignation, the British government first ordered its vessels to respect the American flag "under all circumstances" and then withdrew them.[9]

This humiliating retreat could only have served to remind Englishmen of the sorry figure their nation had cut in its diplomatic dealings with the republic. It was additional evidence for the charge that forbearance and concessions were the perpetual price of friendship with the United States. The Webster-Ashburton Treaty had conceded the larger portion of the disputed territory along the Maine border to the Union. The Oregon settlement, in spite of the wild American talk of 54° 40′, saw the British concede all that the United States had originally demanded and been refused—the land south of the 49th parallel. Not surprisingly, to nationalists both treaties had about them the taint of capitulation. Unhappily, further affronts awaited John Bull. The expulsion in 1856 of John Crampton, the British minister to the United States, along with three consuls, for a breach of the neutrality laws added to the British sense of grievance. Nor was it diminished by the withdrawal of the slave squadron from the Caribbean and then by the surrender to American demands in Central America after a decade of resistance. Perhaps the galling character of this policy of appeasement helps to explain the determination to draw the line at San Juan. For the news that an American general had attempted to resolve the dispute over this island off the British Columbian coast by landing troops there inflamed public opinion. London shopkeepers placed maps in their windows showing the island as British territory. "John Bull's habit is to take things quietly," an influential Englishman cautioned President Buchanan, "but his anger has been roused by the high-handed proceedings of General Harney more than I ever remember upon occasions of the kind, and this miserable business might be productive of disastrous consequences."[10]

It was with unfriendly eyes, therefore, that Britannia watched Brother Jonathan in 1860. The natural bonds of origin and language had proven ineffective restraints upon ill-feeling. Dislike of the American political system, resentment of Radical proposals to remake Britain in the image of America, irritation at the consequences of Irish emigration, anxiety over the dependence of Lancashire on Southern cotton, concern with the growth of American economic and commercial competition, indignation at the Americans' frustration of British efforts to suppress the slave trade, and anger at the drubbing they had administered to British pride in a series of diplomatic confrontations, could all be reduced to disapproval, distrust, and apprehension of the United States. Even the splendid reception accorded the Prince of Wales during his tour of North America in 1860 seems to have given Anglo-American relations no more than a thin veneer of amiability. Certainly it failed to shake one old Tory's conviction that "the Yankees are a damned lot and republican institutions are all rot."[11] As Charles Francis Adams quickly discerned, the "grim spectre of democracy, the ingrained jealousy of American power, and the natural pugnacity of John Bull" discoloured the British view of the United States.[12]

Inevitably, this antipathy influenced the British reaction to the breakup of the Union. It encouraged a steadfast preoccupation with their own interests. But sentiment and interest aside, the British were obliged to examine the American crisis within the larger context of their foreign relations. This meant that the startling events in the Western Hemisphere had to compete for their attention with dramatic developments in Europe. In 1859 and 1860 the gaze of the British public was fixed on France and Italy. Napoleon III had conspired with Cavour to unify Northern Italy, but inadvertently he initiated the unification of the peninsula and strengthened British distrust of him. His annexation of Savoy and Nice brought to a pitch fears that the Italian adventure was merely the prelude to a campaign of conquest destined to end in an invasion of Britain. Why else was the French emperor constructing a revolutionary ironclad fleet which jeopardized the wooden-hulled naval supremacy of Britain? The response of the government was to embark upon a frantic naval race and call for elaborate defensive works, while the public feverishly prepared to throw back the invaders. In their tens of thousands men enrolled in the Volunteer Rifle Movement.

Yet this reaction to the French was clearly defensive, and together with the general approval of the government's nonintervention in Italian affairs it seemed to confirm that support was mounting in the country for a less intrusive foreign policy. Without being converted by Cobden and Bright, the public was prepared to take up their slogan. At the very least, the belligerent interventionism of the Crimean period had given way to a more insular outlook.

Preoccupied with the enigmatic behaviour of Napoleon, the British initially gave little thought to the momentous events across the Atlantic. Many Englishmen realized that the dangerous French emperor was anxious to conciliate them. The Cobden-Chevalier Treaty, signed in January 1860, greatly benefited British industry and freer trade was soon followed by greater freedom of movement. Englishmen were permitted to enter France without passports. November saw decrees granting greater debating privileges to the *Corps Legislatif* and the Senate, and this halting step away from authoritarianism won approval in England. Nevertheless, the public's suspicion of Napoleon remained strong. French obstruction of the Sardinian campaign in Italy, French intervention in Syria, and rumours of French backing of Hungarian dissidents in the Austrian Empire all nourished British fears, as did the unabated pace of French naval construction. The emperor remained an untrustworthy neighbour. Perhaps he no longer threatened Britain herself but he could be expected to grasp every opportunity to reorder the map of Europe. As the *Times* put it, "No man seems to watch more keenly for accidents and trusts more to combinations which may spontaneously arise."[18]

One journal that deplored this preoccupation with Europe was the *Edinburgh Review*. It complained in October 1860, that

77

a "movement in Italy, a word spoken in Switzerland, a sign of mutual confidence among the German Powers, or a change in mood of the French newspapers, excites and occupies more attention in England than events of the greatest moment and indications of the deepest significance in the United States." The future of the American experiment in self-government and the livelihood of the four millions of Britons dependent upon the textile industry were at stake, warned the *Review*, whose editor, Henry Reeve, was Tocqueville's English translator. However, it admitted that "we have to overcome a sensation of weariness and distaste before we can throw our minds into the study of American affairs, even during a crisis like the present." But as the American crisis deepened the British mastered their aversion.

The major newspapers were generally agreed that in one way or another slavery was the root of the Union's troubles, but this did not stifle unsympathetic comment. As Walter Bagehot, the newly appointed editor of the world's "first commercial paper,"[14] wrote in the *Economist* on January 12, the North was spurning an opportunity to rid itself peacefully of the Southern incubus because of a conviction that "the greatness of the American Republic is bound up with the continuance of the Federation." Northerners have become prisoners of their own rhetoric, he charged. "They have flung themselves and their institutions insultingly and bombastically in the face of Europe, requiring everyone to avow that no nation of the old world could match their power, or rival their constitution, or hold a candle to them as regarded the well-being, the capability for self-government and the political wisdom of their people."

The call for a peaceful separation also came from Radical organs. Secession would vindicate democracy, *Reynolds's Newspaper* and the *Morning Star* both asserted, if peacefully achieved. After all, what was at stake was nothing less than the principle upon which the Americans had made good their independence from Britain. More conservative newspapers agreed that the crisis was a test of democratic institutions, but they found them wanting. Turmoil was the inescapable result of the quadrennial election of a head of state and the subsequent interregnum between election and inauguration, the *Times* affirmed. Thus a dispute that could have been resolved in another nation was in America widening into a "breach which it is evident no compromise or concession is destined to bridge over."[15]

78

For Britain, the consequences of the failure of American democracy promised to be far-reaching. In North America, Canada now stood as an example of the prosperity and contentment that monarchical institutions alone guaranteed and she might well emerge as the dominant power. What was certain was that disunion would leave the United States "less aggressive, less insolent, and less irritable than she had been." The division of one large, encroaching, and bullying state into two meant that each would be "more occupied with its immediate neighbour, and therefore less inclined to pick quarrels with more distant nations."[16] But the republic's difficulties had domestic repercussions for Britain as well. Those conservatives who earlier had writhed under the Radicals' lash now heaped ridicule upon Bright and other "unthinking and unprincipled demagogues" who had been pressing "revolutionary demands for reform." The British people had been given a timely reminder that the "widest enjoyment of the electoral franchise" was more akin "to tyranny than true liberty."[17]

Whatever the political gains and lessons of the Union's troubles, Englishmen could never forget the commercial perils. How would the American turbulence affect Britain's supply of cotton? On January 19 Bagehot attempted to reassure his readers. He insisted that the quantities obtainable from the West Indies, Brazil, Egypt, and India could be greatly increased and new areas of supply developed in Australia, Natal, and the west coast of Africa. In effect, he was assuring them that cotton need not dominate their response to the American crisis if they turned immediately to the task of freeing themselves from their reliance on the Southern States. And this call for prompt action was taken up by a number of journals including the *Times*. It urged the Lancashire manufacturers to finance cotton cultivation in India, Africa, and Australia. In fact the Manchester Chamber of Commerce had already organized a meeting in their city, which was held on January 31. Those in attendance, and they included representatives of other chambers, members of Parliament, and local manufacturers, endorsed a familiar proposal. India had the ability to make up any deficiency in the American supply if a program of internal improvements was initiated by the colonial government. But this call received a chilly reception in the *Times*. "The Indian government has difficulties of its own," the *Times* protested, "and it is unreasonable to demand that those difficulties should be aggravated in order to do for Manchester that which she ought long ago to have done for herself."[18]

It was against such examples of "so-called liberalism" that the *Morning Herald* inveighed. If ever there was a time for the government to develop the colonies it was now, the Conservative organ asserted. Sound as the doctrine was "that trade and commerce should, so far as possible, be left to take care of themselves," there are contingencies "when this rule must be set aside."[19] Meanwhile, "the most celebrated and widely circulated radical newspaper" of that time,[20] *Reynolds's*, which claimed to speak for the working class, was demanding government intervention at home. What was going to be required, it declared, was assistance for the operatives thrown out of work when the cotton supply failed, either in the form of direct relief or state financed emigration to colonies where labour was scarce.

The signs of the mounting anxiety over cotton were everywhere, in "Pamphlets, leading articles and letters to the leading newspapers," and they prompted Bagehot's return to the problem in the *Economist* on February 2. He insisted that the danger had been exaggerated and cited the immutable law of economics that as long as a commodity was produced it would find its way to where it was demanded. He stressed what the Manchester men had already done to develop new supplies, and drew attention to the vast stocks of the fibre in Britain. There was "six months supply in hand to meet casualties and to gain time," he calculated.

Walter Bagehot's efforts to calm his fellow countrymen's fears were accompanied by warnings to the South that materialism was not the mainspring of British policy. Neither the threat of losing cotton nor the promise of free trade could drag or tempt Britain into aiding a revolt she believed to be "utterly unprovoked." Also, her hatred of slavery and her "rule of non-intervention between revolted subjects and the Government to which they are supposed to owe allegiance" would prevent her from supporting the Southern states. Do "these sharp Southerners really believe," an incredulous Bagehot asked, "that England will not only break the rule in their case, and break through it against the whole current of their political sympathies, but avow to the world that they do it for the sake of gain and gain alone. Where would England's political influence in Europe be after such an act as this?"[21]

The British press greeted in the same critical spirit the news that the seceded states had linked arms. The forming of the Confederacy produced little excitement and excited less enthusiasm. It had already been dubbed "Slaveownia."[22] The constitutional prohibition of the slave trade made no difference for it was interpreted as nothing more than a gambit in the contest with the North for the allegiance of the border states. Nevertheless, as even the ardently antislavery *Spectator* was soon forced to admit, "The danger of the moment is not now so much slavery as the prevalence of a false political economy."[23]

The Morrill Tarriff provoked the British into an angry outburst against the Union, but it did not work to the South's advantage. Instead, the news of Yancey's appointment as a Confederate commissioner, which brought a bitter denunciation of those "American fanatics" who believed that in Britain "the coarsest self-interest overrules every consideration,"[24] the Southern talk of an export duty on cotton, and the passage of the Northern protective tariff, gave British newspapers an opportunity to adopt an attitude of impartial dislike. As the *Times* remarked, "both sides, agreeing on nothing else, are quite unanimous on two things; first, the avoidance of direct taxes on themselves, and secondly, the desire to fix upon England the expenses of their inglorious and unnatural combat."[25]

The news of Sumter's fall brought no change of attitude. The outbreak of war merely served to discredit further those given to eulogizing the American system. Not that the matter had ever been in doubt, for "Equal citizenship, popular supremacy, vote by ballot and universal suffrage may do well for a while, but they invariably fail in the day of trial." Those who would alter the English constitution would do well to ask why the republics of Greece, Rome, Venice, France, and America had "all suffered and died from intestine disorders."[26] Yet however much they continued to savour the opportunity to interpret American disasters as vindication of their own political system, and however much they had welcomed the destruction of "the diplomatic influence and external power of the United States," and the diminution of American "insolence and swagger,"[27] the English press did not welcome civil war. Whether friend or foe of the Union they had their reasons for supporting its peaceful dissolution. Not the least of these was the belief that coercion was futile. It was an "almost inconceivable idea" that the North, for all its unquestioned military advantages, could subdue "a dozen great territories with some eight millions of inhabitants as active and warlike as any on the globe."[28] Anyway even conquest could not restore the Union, for war would intensify the mutual hatreds, leaving the North with no alternative but indefinite occupation of the South.

Coercion might be a policy devoid of hope but its probable consequences for them continued to alarm the British. Talk of obtaining cotton from elsewhere had not stilled their fears that the sudden loss of American supplies would bring disaster to the textile regions. Yet it was certain that the North would resort to a blockade of the Southern ports, and no British remonstrance was likely to deter them. "They have bullied and overreached us on all occasions for many years," growled the *Herald*, "and a powerful party among the supporters of Mr. Lincoln make no secret at the moment of laying hands on Canada."[29] Therefore, Britain should prepare for the worst. Meanwhile, the *Times* urged that any blockade be carefully scrutinized to ensure that it was effective and hence legal. But neither of these suggestions challenged the prevailing sentiment for nonintervention. "All we can do is keep aloof,"[30] the *Times* concluded, and *Punch* admonished the prime minister to keep Britain neutral. Great "as is our interest," announced the *Morning Post*, widely regarded as the prime minister's mouthpiece, "it behooves the government of this country to maintain a position of strict and impartial neutrality."[31]

In 1861 the British government was led by a man of unmatched experience in foreign affairs. Henry John Temple, Lord Palmerston, had celebrated his seventy-sixth birthday on October 20, 1860. He disappointed some foreign visitors, for his physical size did not match his giant reputation. He was not as tall as they expected and bore the inevitable marks of physical decay. His sight was failing, his white hair was thin, and his back slightly stooped. However, the former Prince Cupid's face was still "handsome, and his address very gentle, soft and winning,"[32] while his mind was as alert and agile as ever. Indeed, he possessed all the sly appeal of an old reprobate and exhibited all the vigour and breezy self-confidence of a young one. Born into the world of privilege, he had held public office for so long that he might well have regarded it as his birthright. He had served one government after another, almost without interruption, first as a Tory and then as a Whig, from 1807 until first called upon to form an administration of his own in 1855. But it was during his fifteen years at the Foreign Office between 1830 and 1851 that Palmerston made his mark.

First as foreign secretary and later as prime minister Palmerston personified much of the British nation. Proud and masterful, he was an unswerving nationalist who apparently saw little room for morality in international politics. Thus he agreed with Cobden and Bright on the need for free trade, but not from any common conviction that it was a "moral power" in diplomacy. Palmerston was convinced "of its superior profitableness and expediency."[33] His "polar star and guiding principle" was his nation's interests, political and commercial.[34] For him, foreign policy was a matter of checking and balancing great powers whose interests might conflict with those of Britain, and intimidating small or weak nations which violated treaty obligations, mistreated British subjects, discriminated against British interests, or refused to open themselves to trade.

Palmerston's attitude towards the United States was plain enough: he disliked Americans and distrusted their Republic. "In the first place you must recollect that he was launched into public life when the feeling of the whole country was still bitter against them as rebellious colonists," a cabinet colleague once explained, "and no man quite gets rid of his early impressions."[35] Then, as befitted a former Tory, he had only contempt for American democracy, and when he called Bright an "Americanizer" he intended no compliment. The only political lesson the Americans could teach the British, he asserted, was the foolishness of extending the franchise to the lower classes. But Palmerston's disdain was heightened by American obstruction of British efforts to destroy the slave trade. For although no ardent champion of the negro he was unimpeachably zealous when it came to the suppression of the trade. Finally, his "feeling toward them" was further "aggravated" by their "success and prosperity together with a tone of insolence."[36] In the Americans' behaviour, in their swallowing of Texas and devouring of half of Mexico, in their attempts to obtain Cuba and talk of annexing Canada, he found ample evidence for his contention that large republics were "essentially and inherently aggressive."[37] Then again, Palmerston believed that all nations, but especially republican nations, "in which the masses influence or direct the destinies of the Country are swayed much more by Passion than Interest" because "Passion is a single feeling which aims directly at the object, while Interest is a calculation of relative good and evil, and is liable to hesitation and doubt; moreover Passion sways the Masses, while Interest acts comparatively on the few." Therefore, while he did not reject completely the "liberal" notion "that Commercial Intercourse is the best security for Peace, because it creates interests which would be damaged by war,"[38] Palmerston placed little store in the moderating or pacific influence of Anglo-American trade. Against the aggressive and irrational Americans firm and persevering resistance was the only sensible policy, otherwise there would be no end to their encroachments. Conciliation and moderation would be interpreted as "weakness and Gullibility," and would ultimately encourage them to demand Canada. Thus the first Palmerston administration, which fell in 1858, was marked by an attempt to challenge them in Central America, to hold them in check until "the Swarms are prepared to separate from the Parent Hive."[39]

Remembering his hostility, Americans had not welcomed Palmerston's return to power in 1859. They fancied that any government led by him "would be unfavourable to the maintenance of friendly relations between England and America."[40] Yet the foreign policy of Britain remained unpredictable for Palmerston had appointed Lord John Russell to the Foreign Office. Not that he wanted him there. Born to rule, Russell had had a career that rivalled the prime minister's both in length and distinction. They had served together in the Whig cabinets of the 1830s and when Russell formed a government in 1846 Palmerston went to the Foreign Office. Russell dismissed him in 1851 only to be toppled from power shortly afterwards on the tit for tat motion of the former foreign secretary. For the next few years they manoeuvred for the leadership of the Whig party, and though the contest was won by Palmerston in 1859 he could not form a government without the support of Russell. The latter's price was the Foreign Office, a post he had held only once and then very briefly, and his hope was to advance the cause of Italian unity. He had given little thought to the problem of dealing with the United States, but like Palmerston he was committed to the destruction of the slave trade and he bitterly resented its continuation under the American flag. Unlike the prime minister, he did not see any reason to prevent American penetration of Central

America. However, once he was convinced that British interests were threatened, he was determined in his defence of them, and a potentially volatile mixture of impulsiveness and belligerence was stirred in Russell by the San Juan affair. Fortunately, the American government had disavowed the action of General Harney.

But Russell failed to establish his authority over foreign relations. Although he was impulsive and had a reputation for being headstrong, his personality was no match for that of the debonair prime minister. Reserved, his shyness mistaken for Whig hauteur, he was something of a recluse. Nor could he match the older man's vigour, for he was small and frail. Finally, deficient in "subtlety and scope,"[41] a novice in international politics, he never escaped from Palmerston's long shadow. He turned to him for advice, sent foreign diplomats to see him, and forwarded draft despatches which Palmerston criticized and changed freely. Before long it was being put about that "John Russell has neither policy nor principles of his own, and is in the hands of Palmerston, who is an artful old dodger."[42] Even with respect to Italy, the one region of which he did have greater knowledge, Russell followed the prime minister. As for relations with the United States, "The policy of the government does not seem to be at all guided by him," Charles Francis Adams wrote of Russell after a year's observation. "It is rather that of Lord Palmerston, and for that reason not to be trusted by us."[43]

Although Palmerston dominated the foreign secretary, who was cruelly but not inaccurately caricatured by *Punch* as a diminutive flunkey of the great man, he did not always succeed in getting his way with the cabinet. Some members had only agreed to join it on the understanding that they would be "kept informed of everything that was done in foreign policy,"[44] and with the support of the Crown they prevented any meddling in the affairs of Italy. Chastened or not by this setback, Palmerston had good reason to keep well clear of the American crisis.

He had returned to office at the head of a motley collection of Whigs, Liberals, Peelites, and Radicals. With the inclusion of Thomas Milner Gibson and Charles Villiers among his ministers he had hoped to attract Radical support, for the former had sat for Manchester along with Bright until 1857 and the latter had been prominent in the free trade movement. W. E. Gladstone, a Peelite, also joined the cabinet, as chancellor of the exchequer, and his advocacy of free trade, the repeal of the remaining "taxes on knowledge," and cheap, efficient government endeared him to the Cobdenites. Yet nothing short of the implementation of their policies could guarantee their allegiance to a government led by a man they considered a dangerous anachronism, and few acts were more certain to antagonize them than interference in the affairs of the American Republic.

Secession was a heavy blow to Cobden and Bright, but they found solace in the "grandeur of the free states, free from political brotherhood with the South," in the hope that democracy would be vindicated by a peaceful separation, and in the inevitable triumph of retrenchment.[45] "The crisis in the United States *may have* a tremendous influence on this county," Bright commented to Gladstone, in a letter from Lancashire on New Year's Day, "and any great check to trade here is felt over the whole country, and will affect the revenue."[46] Clearly, the existing rate of taxation and expenditure could not be long continued. Yet the prospect of a serious recession in the textile industry was disturbing. There had been an "enormous increase of building for spinning and manufacturing purposes," with many new companies founded on the "cooperative principle." This development promised to "revolutionize" the cotton trade, but success was dependent on "fair weather" and failure threatened unusually bitter disappointment.[47] It was this knowledge that reinforced Cobden's yearning for peaceful separation, his hope that the Americans "separate without bloodshed and a negro insurrection, so as to give time to obtain a supply of cotton from other quarters."[48]

Despite this Radical political tail whose wagging he could never hope to control, Palmerston managed to maintain his government's stability with the aid of the Conservatives. Although the largest homogeneous party in Parliament they failed to ally with some of the smaller groups that held the balance of power, and in Palmerston encountered "an adept at the politics of consensus." Also, they had few grounds of difference with this former Tory, against whom "they could play neither the constitutional nor the patriotic card." Both the Earl of Derby, the party's leader, and Benjamin Disraeli, the leader in the Commons, were hard pressed to avoid being "not a voice but an echo."[49] Instead of scheming to oust Palmerston they often made common cause with him against his Radical wing. But however compatible Palmerston and Derby were in domestic affairs, the Conservative leader had an "isolationist's disgust with the Troubles of other nations."[50] Thus a division resulting from any meddling in the Republic's troubles was likely to find Derby urging his followers into the same lobby as the Cobdenites.

Hampered by the strength of noninterventionist sentiment, in Parliament and the country, the prime minister's style was also cramped by the French. The distrust born of Napoleon's naval building and Italian adventure was nourished by a steady diet of suspicion. Suspicion that he was seeking fortified points on both sides of the Straits of Gibraltar, that the construction of the Suez Canal was another part of a scheme to convert the Mediterranean into a French lake, and to expose India to attack, that he planned mischief in the Turkish Empire and had designs on Iceland. Then the new year of 1861 was heralded by reports of "some secret understanding and plotting between France and Russia."[51] Clearly, British embroilment in the Union's difficulties would be an invitation to French and Russian opportunism elsewhere.

Reports from the United States re-emphasized the need for caution in approaching the crisis there. Even before the presidential election Lyons had warned that "a Foreign war finds favour, as a remedy for intestine divisions."[52] Lincoln's success and the South's response made the minister "very nervous" about the incoming administration. To Russell, he stressed the importance of their avoiding "anything likely to give the Americans a pretext for quarrelling with us," for a foreign war was still "the remedy very generally prescribed" for the Union's troubles.[53] And no act, Lyons concluded, was more certain to be grasped as a pretext than one that could be interpreted as British interference in the crisis. Yet he was also anxious to avoid antagonizing Southerners, who "would in all probability establish a low Tariff and throw themselves fraternally into our arms, if we let them."[54] Not that they would be pleasant to embrace, with their preposterous notions about the influence of cotton, talk of reopening the slave trade, and commitment to the perpetuation of slavery. "It is to be apprehended that we shall have considerable difficulty in planning our relations commercial or political on a satisfactory footing with a people imbued with such sentiments," Lyons concluded, "immense as is the importance to us of procuring a cheap and abundant supply of their staple commodity." What he suggested, therefore, was that Britain exercise "caution and Watchfulness to avoid giving serious offence to either party."[55]

Palmerston and Russell readily agreed with the minister that "Nothing could be more unadvisable" than for Britain to interfere in any American conflict,[56] and they took care to guard against the charge of intervention. Rear Admiral Milne, commander of the North American Station, was ordered to abstain "from any measure or demonstration likely to give umbrage to any party in the United States, or to have the appearance of partisanship on either side."[57] Similar instructions were sent to Canada, while Lyons and the British consuls were ordered to do no more than urge that bloodshed be avoided if their advice was sought by federal or state officials. It was the "fervent prayer" of an impartial Britain, Palmerston declared during a speech at Southampton on January 8, that the "world may be spared the afflicting spectacle of a hostile conflict between brother and brother."[58]

Of course, the fervency of these prayers owed much to the anxiety about cotton. "Any war will be almost sure to interfere with the cotton crops, and this is what really affects us, and what we care about,"[59] wrote one man who moved on the periphery of the cabinet. The cotton market was already rising on speculation that the Union would collapse into civil war. That prospect convinced Palmerston "that no Time should be lost in securing a supply of cotton from other quarters than America."[60] But the Board of Trade would not condone the economic heresy of government action to stimulate cotton production. It insisted that the "ordinary response of supply and demand" could be relied upon in the case of cotton as in that of every other article. It stressed that it was the duty "of those interested in that result to make every becoming assertion on their part to communicate the facts of their wants, and to facilitate through suitable agencies the prompt transmission of those supplies that may be anticipated."[61] However, the Board did endorse Russell's reply to a request for help from the Liverpool and Manchester Chambers of Commerce, in which he authorized agents of the Cotton Supply Association to call upon consuls for estimates of the cotton producing potential of their areas. Then, on the last day of February, the government of India responded to the continuing agitation in Manchester for action. It suggested that private agents be sent into the interior to ensure that the natives were aware that Indian cotton would soon be in great demand. Also, it offered to provide banking facilities where none existed and to make simple grants for the improvement of trails and carts; but this was a far cry from the program of public works the Manchester men were pressing for. Clearly, the Union's troubles had not stampeded the government into a change of economic policy, but as the political crisis in the Republic deepened Palmerston and Russell moved to define their policy of cautious watchfulness in more positive terms.

The Union's passing went unmourned within the government, as without. Palmerston's pleasure at the appearance of the "disunited States of America" was only to be expected,[62] but even the Duke of Argyll, whose ardent opposition to slavery was soon to sustain his support of the North, initially could not "pretend much sorrow about the break up of the Union."[63] Along with many Englishmen he believed that once slavery was denied the protection of the United States it would prove vulnerable to world opinion. Others felt that the North had connived too long at slavery to deserve sympathy. But there was no sympathy either for the Confederacy. The banning of the African slave trade was regarded as a concession to the border states and to European opinion which was likely to be flouted immediately and eventually withdrawn. Palmerston feared that the South would resort to filibustering in Central America and annex parts of Mexico as soon as the "dread of war" with the North receded.[64] The Confederate tariff was not all that the British had been led to expect. Yet the most objectionable aspect of Southern policy was the assumption that the Confederacy could dictate Britain's course of action. Robert Bunch, who from his consular post at Charleston served as the government's principal observer of Confederate affairs, dwelt upon Southern exultation at Britain's dependence on their pleasure. They disliked the British violently for their hostility to slavery and would take any opportunity to humiliate them, the consul reported home. He pointed to the Confederate Commission as an example. Thus Yancey was "a rabid Secessionist, a favourer of the revival of the Slave Trade and a Filibuster of the extremest type of manifest destiny." Mann was the "son of a bankrupt grocer in the Eastern part of Virginia," while Rost was unknown to everyone.[65] Yet as politically objectionable or socially insignificant as these men were, Lyons urged Russell not to rebuff them. To do so, he warned, might encourage the "violent party" at Washington "who maintain that any measures whatever may be taken by this Government against Foreign Commerce," without provoking the resistance of the British, "or inducing them to improve their commercial position by a recognition of the Southern Confederacy."[66]

Lyons's fears about the policy of the incoming Republican administration had been heightened by the nomination of Seward. The minister thought little of the president and was one of the many observers who believed that the secretary of state would dominate the government. It was a disturbing prospect. Seward's career provided ample evidence of his readiness to court domestic popularity by displaying "insolence" towards Britain. He was certain to tap the reservoir of anglophobia in America, which was refilled continually by the streams of envy, fear, and scorn. "I am afraid he takes no other view of Foreign Relations than as safe levers to work with upon public opinion here," Lyons warned.[67] But Seward was only one of the dark clouds gathering on the horizon. The Morrill Tariff and proposals for the coercion of the South, either by blockade or a declaration closing its ports of entry, were commercial storm warnings. The British did not stand inert. Russell agreed with Palmerston that a British regiment should be sent to Vancouver, presumably to be on hand if the San Juan dispute was revived. In Washington, Lyons unsuccessfully sought to reach an understanding with Buchanan about the island before March 4. Also, he strove to protect British commercial interests. He lobbied quietly against the tariff, pressing upon Northerners the "imprudence of driving the trading and manufacturing interests of Europe into sympathy with the Secession Party," but failed to gain more than an amendment removing a discriminatory duty on British books. The trouble was that many Southerners were absent from Washington and those who did remain refused to oppose the tariff. "They rejoice in thinking that additional value will be given to the offers of Free Trade which the South is supposed to be ready to make to European nations," he explained to Russell.[68] For his part the foreign secretary fanned Union fears regarding Britain's future conduct. He refused to give any assurance that the British government would never recognize the Confederacy, and he decided to see the Confederate commissioners unofficially when they arrived. Beyond this, he attempted to disabuse the North of the notion that Britain would acquiesce in any exclusion of her vessels from Southern ports.

A declaration that the Southern ports were no longer ports of entry might force on the question of recognition, Russell wrote to Lyons. It would amount to nothing less than a paper blockade and would leave the European nations with the choice of submitting to an illegal interference with their commerce or recognizing the Confederacy and requiring the United States to treat their vessels as neutral. Yet the British quickly reconciled themselves to a formal blockade. Although it would produce "misery, discord and enmity incalculable,"[69] there was promise of relief in the traditional American doctrine that to be lawful a blockade had to be effective. British vessels would therefore be able to use any port "before which the United States did not establish a regular effective Blockade,"[70] and the length of Confederate coast and the inadequacy of the Union navy suggested that a number of ports would be left open.

Making the most of the one high card he held, the threat of recognition, Lyons argued against any interference with foreign commerce. It would be a fatal step, he warned Americans, because it would bring the European powers into the dispute and encourage them to throw "their weight into the other scale."[71] This attempt at a finesse was not without results. On March 20 Seward called on Lyons to voice his apprehension of any recognition of the South. The minister naturally pressed home the point that no "European Power was likely to quit" an attitude of expectation "provided that in practice its commerce was not interfered with,"[72] and for the next three weeks he clung to the hope that the Americans could be frightened out of any action that would damage British trade. But then came the fall of Sumter, Lincoln's call for troops, Davis's authorization of letters of marque, and the Proclamation of Blockade. It was a response Lyons accepted as "less likely to be injurious or to raise awkward questions, than any of the irregular modes of closing the Southern Ports which were proposed."[73]

In England, news of the outbreak of the civil war quickened the search for peaceful ways of minimizing the damage to British commerce. At the first report of Lincoln's proposed blockade Russell asked Dallas to call at the Foreign Office, and during their interview on May 1 he intimated that this step might spur British recognition of the Confederacy. His satisfaction with the minister's assurance that his information about a blockade was inaccurate was shortlived, and he became "rather grumpy" when he learned that it was Dallas who was mistaken. But ministerial ill-temper was a far cry from recognition of the South. Britain had foreign difficulties enough without adding the United States to them, particularly as no support for that step had emerged in the nation. The press had treated any talk of recognition as premature, and antislavery societies were organizing a campaign of opposition. And although William Gregory had given notice in Parliament of a motion for "an early acknowledgement of the Southern American Confederation," this had been followed by a notice of amendment from W. E. Forster, that "the House does not at present desire to express any opinion in favour of such recognition, and trusts that the Government will at no time make it without obtaining due security against the renewal of the African Slave Trade."[74] Both Palmerston and Russell repeatedly urged Gregory not to press his motion. As the prime minister warned, each party to the American dispute would be offended by what was said against them and would care little for what was said for them, and all Americans would say that Parliament had "no business to meddle with American affairs."[75] Perhaps convinced that a debate could only do harm Gregory agreed to postpone his motion, while Russell announced Britain's determination to stand aloof in the Commons on May 2. "Nothing but the imperative duty of protecting British interests if they should be attacked justifies the Government in at all interfering," he said in answer to a question. "We have not been involved in any way in that contest by any act or giving any advice in the matter, and, for God's sake, let us if possible keep out of it."[76]

Yet the Union and Confederate proclamations had re-emphasized the problem of protecting British interests from injury rather than attack. The day he made his impassioned remarks in the House Russell turned to the law officers for advice. The lord chancellor considered the questions raised by the American war "strange" and "unprecedented," and found Grotius and Vattel "no assistance."[77] However, he and his colleagues agreed that the "best solution would be for the European nations to determine that the war between the two Confederacies shall be carried on on the principle of *justum bellum* and shall be conducted according to the rules of the Treaty of Paris."[78] Specifically, they proposed that recognition of Confederate belligerency be tied to acceptance of the principles that free ships make free goods and that privateering be abolished. If in this way British trade would be protected from Southern depredations, so also would the effects of the Union blockade be vitiated. The declaration that "the whole line of coast" was not accessible could not be maintained for it was a recognized rule of a regular war that a blockade had to be efficient to be lawful. That had been one of the terms of the Declaration of Paris, and while the Americans had not been a party to the 1856 agreement they had long supported that principle, Russell reminded the Commons on May 6. Therefore, the war in America must be considered a regular war and Britain would "apply to it all the rules respecting blockade, letters of marque etc. which belong to neutrals during a war," he informed Lyons.[79] Evidently, Russell had not accepted the law officers' suggestion that recognition of Confederate belligerency be made conditional on her acceptance of the Paris Declaration. No doubt he saw Confederate privateering as less of a danger to British commerce, particularly, the vital cotton trade, than a blockade. Anyway, the United States had never relinquished the right to issue letters of marque and Russell had already taken the precaution of asking the Admiralty to reinforce the North American Squadron. By its very presence it would impose some restraint on privateers. Consequently what Russell wrote to Lyons was that the law officers thought "it would be desirable if both parties would agree to accept the Declaration of Paris regarding the flag covering the goods and the prohibition of privateering."[80]

The strengthening of the North American Squadron was soon followed by an announcement that recognition of Confederate belligerency was imminent. Lyons was given "timely notice" of the government's decision on May 6 and instructed not to keep the news to himself. But there was little likelihood of it being kept secret because the foreign secretary gave just as timely notice to the Commons. That same day, in reply to a question from Gregory, he said that "the Southern Confederate states must be recognized by Great Britain as belligerents."[81] A more formal expression of British policy was postponed while the law officers pondered the legal niceties. Then on May 9 a spokesman revealed that the government was thinking of issuing a proclamation based on the Foreign Enlistment Act, which prohibited any British subject from engaging "in any hostilities that may be carried on between any two foreign States."[82] However, its appearance was delayed by the problem of an exact wording, "a matter of considerable importance and difficulty," Earl Granville explained to the Lords on May 10. The government was "anxious to make it as plain and emphatic as possible."[83]

Dated May 13 and officially printed on May 14, the proclamation prohibited British enlistments, efforts to encourage the enlistment of others, and the equipment of ships of war for either side in America. Any vessel equipped in a British port would be confiscated while belligerent vessels visiting British ports were forbidden to change or increase their equipment. Violators of these provisions faced punishment in British courts and the forfeiture of any claim to British protection. The proclamation was forwarded to Lyons on May 15 and then to British consuls. They were instructed to exhibit it in their offices and to make sure that it was known to British subjects residing within their jurisdiction, "taking care however to do so in the manner best calculated to avoid wounding the susceptibilities of the authorities or the people of the place where they reside."[84]

In Britain, the Proclamation of Neutrality was welcomed by the press and approved of in Parliament, but it did not still all uneasiness. Although involvement in the war would mean forfeiture of protection, there was every reason to believe that if the Union carried out its threat to treat privateers as pirates and in so doing condemned a British subject the British government would not show indifference. A British subject taken on board a privateer licensed by a government whose belligerent rights Britain had recognized could not be rightfully treated as a pirate. Also, as Lord Derby put it, "The Northern States, on the one hand, cannot be entitled to claim the rights of belligerents for themselves" with a blockade, "and, on the other, to treat the Southern States not as belligerents, but as rebels." Then again, the British knew that it was not in the power of the Union effectively to blockade all the Southern ports. They were prepared for the government to recognize the blockade before those ports where it was enforced, the Conservative leader declared in the Lords, but it was important that the British government make it clear "that a mere paper blockade, or a blockade extending over a space to which it is physically impossible that an effectual blockade can be applied" would not be recognized.[85] Of course that ground had been prepared. The proclamation was intended not only to regularize relations with the Confederacy but also to ensure that the blockade would be subjected to the exacting test

94

of legitimacy, a test it soon seemed more incapable than ever of passing.

The secession of the Upper South following Lincoln's militant response to the fall of Sumter had brought a second Proclamation of Blockade. Lord Lyons quickly expressed to Seward his doubt that the United States possessed the necessary vessels to close 3,000 miles of coast, but the secretary insisted "that the whole would be blockaded, and blockaded effectively."[86] This assurance notwithstanding, the task was regarded by British observers as manifestly beyond the power of the United States. Presumably, the moment had come to refuse recognition and Admiral Milne was ordered "to report fully on the question how far the Blockade of the Southern Ports now undertaken by the United States Government is an effective one." However, he was not to disregard the blockade wherever he considered it ineffective. Instead, he was to bring his views to the attention of the commander of the blockading squadron, in "courteous but precise terms," so that British subjects might cite his "reclamations" when seeking redress for injury.[87] This cautious and evidential approach was the work of John Harding, the Queen's advocate, a "clever but flighty and intractable man,"[88] to whom Russell had referred the question of the blockade's legality.

In his report, which was adopted as government policy, Harding held that opinions about a blockade's effectiveness were not evidence and until failure was proven "beyond all doubt" the British government could not intervene. He had no taste for a debate on abstract principles of international law at the outset of a civil war. If British vessels were seized for breaking an illegal blockade, or warned off ports that were not properly closed, then there would be cause for complaint. But complaints should be founded on actual cases and interference only undertaken when British subjects had "clearly sustained losses or actual wrongs, for which neither the Prize Court nor any other Courts" would afford them redress.[89]

In support of his recommendations Harding marshalled the arguments of prudence and expediency. British protests against the blockade's inefficiency would surely "stimulate the vigilance and rigour" of the Unionists and "excite some irritation" in their "highly sensitive temperament" without any "sufficient, adequate or direct advantage."[90] Lyons had made much the same point. At a time of the year when Britain had little trade with the South, what purpose was there in infuriating the North by refusing to recognize the blockade? However, he showed no enthusiasm either for Mercier's proposal that the French and British governments should announce that they would not recognize the blockade after September. Such a declaration "would hardly produce less commotion here than a refusal to recognize it *ab initio*," he warned, and might tempt the Lincoln administration into "some violent proceeding with regard to England and France."[91]

If the British had long been "prepared to be anxious" about Seward's policy, their anxiety soon went "beyond all expectation."[92] Poor Lyons lived in constant dread of "some foolish violent proceeding."[93] The secretary's dissatisfaction with Russell's response to his circular of March 9 and his handling of the *Peerless* episode were "painful" reminders of his "strong inclination" to seek domestic profit in "high-handed conduct and violent language toward Britain."[94] Also, Lyons suspected that Seward was so unimpressed with the importance of conciliating other nations and so unconscious of the relative weakness of the now dismembered Union that he still believed in the reunifying powers of foreign war. Nor did Lyons place much faith in the cabinet's restraining influence. Its members were more ignorant of foreign affairs than Seward, he reported, and they were being hounded by an "ignorant mob" howling for energetic measures. Thus the sequel to the *Peerless* affair might be the seizure of a suspected privateer in Canadian waters, or some other violation of Canadian territory. Sure that Britain's chances of avoiding difficulties depended on her being firm from the outset, Lyons thought it "worthy of consideration whether means should not be provided for effectually defending Canada against any inroad from this Country, made with or without the sanction of the Government here."[95]

The British cabinet had already accepted the colonial secretary's recommendation that a regiment be ordered to Canada before the reports and assessments of Seward's behaviour began to arrive. But to the extent that he helped to discourage a confrontation over the blockade and had prompted the increase in their North American military establishment, the secretary had influenced British conduct. Yet irritation mixed with apprehension about the future rather than present fear was the predominant sentiment within the cabinet. At the Colonial Office,

the Duke of Newcastle thought that Edmund Head made insufficient allowance for Seward's "hyper-American use of the policy
of bully and bluster." He had met the American during the
Prince of Wales's visit to the United States and recalled that
Seward had "fairly" told him that he would insult Britain to
secure his domestic position. However, he had shown no anxiety
for a war, indeed he had professed the belief that Britain would
never go to war with the United States. Now, six months later,
Seward's first idea was plainly to appeal to the mob by forcing
insults down the throat of Britain. His second was to prepare
that same mob for a war with Britain "if the result of the quarrel
with the Southern states should render an inroad into Canada a
measure of political advantage to his position." But the end of
the American war would bring another danger, Newcastle
believed. The Union was certain to raise an army "composed of
the scum of all nations—Germans, Irish and others who fear
neither God nor man—who are imbued with hatred of all
Government and whose aspirations are for a Red Republic."
Once international peace had been restored American politicians, desperate to protect their own institutions, would divert
"this blood red stream" into British territory.[96] Sidney Herbert,
the war secretary, without recognizing the revolutionary consequences of the struggle, was of like mind. "This American
effervescence will pass away," he predicted, but the end of the
Americans' difficulties "will be the beginning of our own."[97]

Also, there was disbelief within the cabinet that "any Government of ordinary prudence" would gratuitously increase the
number of its enemies and "incur the hostility of so formidable
a power as England" at the outbreak of civil war.[98] Even Seward
was not that insane, and if he was his colleagues would surely
not encourage him "in a game of brag with England."[99] Thus
Russell did not expect an attack on Canada but he did foresee
continual provocation by Seward. "It seems to me we ought
quietly to strengthen ourselves in British America," he wrote to
Palmerston.[100] He was preaching to the converted. No one was
keener to order reinforcements to North America than the prime
minister, who was a firm believer in the effectiveness of costly
deterrents. However, he had to contend with an economy-minded
chancellor and the unpopularity of colonial military expenditures. The imperial authorities had long sought a more coherent
and equitable policy of colonial defence, certainly one that

would cost the British taxpayer less. Throughout the spring a parliamentary committee chaired by Arthur Mills, an advocate of colonial self-defence, had been gathering evidence on this very subject. Among the witnesses called was Newcastle, who on May 16 had been subjected to a searching examination. Having just recommended to the cabinet that a regiment of regulars be sent to Canada it was not surprising that he stoutly maintained that this was not the time to leave the defence of British North America to the colonists. It was not at all unlikely, he warned, "that in the present state of a neighbouring country, Canada might be the scene of hostile incursions by filibustering parties," and "for the purpose of meeting aggressions of that kind, an organized regular force is better, and more trustworthy than a volunteer force."[101] More significant was the attitude of Gladstone. Although convinced that the defence of colonies by the parent state had "rather an enervating effect" upon them, the chancellor admitted, when he was called before the committee on June 6, that the possibility of difficulties with the United States "introduced a great number of important limiting considerations as to the time and mode of proceedings to the establishment of general principles."[102]

In broad agreement that Seward was "a vapouring, blustering, ignorant man," who had got it into his head that England could be insulted with impunity and was therefore capable of stumbling into a war with her, the cabinet suspected that if he found the Confederacy "too hard a morsel for his teeth" he might "try to make up for ill-success against the South by picking a quarrel with and attacking what he may believe to be a less strong and less prepared neighbour to the North."[103] Thus there was little dissent from Palmerston's proposal that three regiments, not one, be sent to Canada, along with a field battery of Armstrong guns. Head's suggestion that gunboats be stationed on the St. Lawrence was referred to the Admiralty. In proposing and carrying through these measures, Palmerston took care to pay lip service to the principle of colonial self-defence. The "main force for Defence must be local," he conceded, and 8,000 rifles, 10,000 sets of accoutrements, and 2,500,000 rounds of ammunition were also shipped to North America. But everybody knew "the advantage of a regular force as foundation for an irregular army." The presence of British regulars "would inspire confidence and stimulate and organize local exertion."[104] Indeed, political embarrassment loomed if they did not, and Newcastle informed

Head that the purpose of "this manifestation of our determination to defend Canada" was to make the Americans "a little more cautious" and to encourage the Canadians to adopt "corresponding efforts for their self-defence."[105]

Initially, the intention had been to send the troops and supplies to Canada quietly and "without parade." Then came reports from the United States of the angry public reaction to British neutrality, and the government responded dramatically. The largest ship in the world, the *Great Eastern*, was hurriedly chartered by the War Office. Carrying more than 2,000 troops and almost 500 women and children, in fact twice as many people as had ever sailed in one vessel before, the voyage enlivened by a mutiny among the impressed members of the crew and the discovery of five female stowaways, she crossed the Atlantic in record time. When she arrived at Quebec it took the ferries two days to empty her of men, women, children, animals, and supplies. This was the kind of theatrical demonstration Palmerston relished.

American displeasure with British policy had been foreshadowed during the first interview between Russell and Charles Francis Adams on May 18. The new American minister had landed at Liverpool five days earlier after nearly two weeks at sea. He had not dallied there but travelled down to London the same afternoon and had planned to call on the foreign secretary the very next morning. However, Russell had been called to Woburn where his brother was fatally ill. While waiting for an opportunity to meet him, Adams completed the formalities of accepting responsibility for the mission from Dallas and presenting his credentials to Queen Victoria. Yet he already doubted that he would be staying long in England. The tone of the press, the "leading idea" that peaceful disunion was best for all concerned, not least for the British themselves, and the comments in Parliament worried him. Then came the publication of the Proclamation of Neutrality. "The inference seemed almost inevitable," he reported to Seward, "that there existed a disposition at least not to chill the hopes of those who are now drawing the very breath of life only from the expectation of sympathy in Great Britain."[106] That same day, May 17, he received Seward's note of April 27, expressing "no little indignation" at the behaviour of the Palmerston government and so he immediately requested an interview with Russell.[107]

As the foreign secretary was now in mourning for his brother,

Adams drove down to his country retreat in Richmond Park, Pembroke Lodge, on May 18. The Englishman proved "provokingly diplomatic."[108] He remarked that his earlier comments to Dallas had been misinterpreted, and that he had simply meant to say that Britain was not disposed to interfere in any way in the American war. Turning to the proclamation, he explained that the British needed to define their attitude toward the conflict and a *justum bellum* recognized "a war of two sides, without in any way implying an opinion on its justice." Nor did he accept Adams's contention that the proclamation had been precipitate. The American government had acted just as quickly in the past, he retorted. He then went on to inquire sceptically whether the United States intended to live up to its traditional doctrine that blockades be effective. Sensibly, Adams replied that even though the blockade "might not be perfect, it would be sufficient so to come within the legitimate construction of the term." He also deflected a question about the tariff by claiming that it was "mainly passed as a revenue measure, with incidental protection."[109]

Although the interview passed amiably enough, Adams returned to London no less glum about the future of his mission. Doubtful that this explanation of the British government's policy would prove satisfactory to his own, by no means immune himself from the suspicion that the British were playing false with his country, this prudent Yankee decided that it would not be sound business to rent a house in London for any length of time. Nevertheless, there was soon some brightening of these gloomy skies and Adams was able to report to Seward "a considerable amelioration of sentiment" towards the United States.[110] Both Russell and Gladstone castigated a Conservative member of Parliament who had welcomed the bursting of the "great Republican bubble." Indeed, there was a call in the Commons for a neutrality in speech to match the government's neutral conduct and Gregory was persuaded not to force a discussion of his oft-postponed motion to recognize the Confederacy. The great majority of members were agreed that they should abstain as much as possible from the discussion of American affairs. Even more cheering for Adams was the announcement on June 3 that belligerent vessels would not be permitted to bring their prizes into British ports.

This decision may have been inspired by Lyons's warning that if Southern privateers were allowed to carry their prizes into British ports it would be necessary to provide against Union attempts to cut them out. However, if it was one more cautious move to prevent Britain being dragged into the conflict, it had the added attraction of striking a blow against a practice the British had long deplored. Whatever the motive, the effectiveness of one of the Confederacy's weapons had been seriously impaired. Only the North had the commercial marine that could be menaced by privateers. And when members of the American legation complained that the order "placed the true and spurious Governments on the same footing," that ardent pro-Unionist W. E. Forster replied that they "must not be nice about such little matters," as Britain had done all she could to aid them.[111]

FIVE

A strict concert with France

THE NEWS FROM BRITAIN caused an uproar in the North. Russell's private interview with the Confederate commissioners on May 3, his comments in Parliament on May 6, followed by the Proclamation of Neutrality a week later, seemed an alarming sequence of events to many Unionists. Clearly the "shopkeeping spirit" had triumphed over "any interest in the maintenance of free institutions." Moved by sordid motives—the protection of her cotton supply, the injury of a naval and commercial rival, and the removal of the democratic threat to "Kingcraft and aristocracy"—Britain was favouring the Confederacy. Thus her "half recognition" of the insurgents was bound to confirm them "in the mistaken notion" that the world was "at their feet for cotton." But this policy was not only mean and misleading, it was also perilous. If persisted in it would lead to war with the United States—a war that would see rebellion fomented in Ireland and Canada annexed. Of course there was some questioning of the wisdom of these fulminations and threats of retaliation, yet the browbeating continued in the press for many Northerners were confident that Britain could ill-afford embroilment in the hostilities. Not only had the British to worry about the security of Canada, the belligerent *New York Herald* frequently remarked, but they had to keep in mind the danger of Napoleon III being given a free hand in Europe.

The *Herald*'s confidence in the awkwardness of Britain's international position was fully shared by Seward, indeed he may have inspired the reassuring articles of its diplomatic correspondent. The secretary also shared the newspaper's opinion that the "duplicity and arrogance" of British statesmen was "directly traceable" to the belief that the United States was "in too feeble and distracted a condition to resent indignities."[1] Great Britain and France "have lost their fear, and with it their respect for this country," he wrote to his daughter.[2] However, he was neither going to tolerate a state of affairs in which "Adams and Dayton have audiences and compliments in the Minister's Audience Chamber, and Toombs's emissaries have access to his Bedroom," nor accept meekly British recognition of Confederate belligerency.[3] "God damn them, I'll give them hell," he shouted during a visit from Charles Sumner.[4] The time had come for a bold, even bellicose remonstrance, which would "roll back the demoralizing tide" from Europe.[5] Fearing the loss of Canada and distrusting Napoleon, the British would have to draw back if threatened with involvement in the American conflict. Thus in his "bold and decisive instructions" to Adams on May 21, Seward insisted that as "Intercourse of any kind with the so-called Commissioners is liable to be construed as recognition" the minister should "desist from all intercourse whatever" with the British government so long as it continued to have dealings with the Confederates. As for formal British recognition of the South, that would be intervention in the civil war, and "When this act of intervention is distinctly performed, we from that hour, shall cease to be friends and become once more, as we have twice before been forced to be, enemies of Great Britain."[6]

But Seward's prospects of overawing the British "by threatening conduct" faded in the face of opposition to his policy within the administration. Although he succeeded in forcing the despatch past critical colleagues and ignored Lincoln's suggestions for toning it down, he did follow the president's direction and marked it confidential. The paper was not "to be read or shown to the British secretary of state," nor were any of its positions "to be prematurely, unnecessarily, or indiscreetly made known," he informed Adams, but its spirit was to be his guide.[7] Of dubious value, therefore, at least until it was sent to Congress and published at the end of the year, the effectiveness of this bold remonstrance was further impaired by the conduct of Charles Sumner. The chairman of the Senate Foreign Relations Committee believed in a conciliatory foreign policy. He was for inconveniencing British manufacturing interests as little as possible and for allying the North to the antislavery forces in England, establishing "a counterpoise to the allurements held out by the South to the trading and manufacturing interests."[8] Shown Seward's despatch by a worried president, Sumner hurried to the British and French legations to tell Lyons and

Mercier that this latest missive had not been approved by the cabinet and had only been authorized by Lincoln on the understanding that its communication to Russell would be left to Adams's discretion. But the senator did not rest there in his efforts to undermine Seward.

Sumner's faith in conciliation was reinforced by John Lothrop Motley, the historian, who returned to the United States early in June after a lengthy residence in London. Determined to combat "irritation towards England" and restore "the old kindness," Motley assured his influential friends of Britain's honest intent. One of these was Sumner who admitted to being "happy in the assurance that all will go right in England."[9] In this mood of certainty, he began to disparage both Seward and his policy, talking openly of his being "distrusted and overruled in the Cabinet, and disliked and distrusted by the diplomats."[10] Indeed, the chairman of the Foreign Relations Committee was hoping to replace the secretary of state as the president's principal adviser on foreign affairs, and he must have been encouraged by Lincoln's evident misgivings about Seward's course.

Having failed to persuade Seward to amend his despatch of May 21, Lincoln publicly admitted on June 4 that the United States had little reason to complain of the conduct of any European power. At a dinner for the diplomatic corps he remarked to the minister for Bremen that all the European nations had "by the long continuing want of any distinct policy on the part of the United States been induced, more or less, to believe the Union weaker and the seceded States stronger than was really the fact."[11] In private, he admitted the disadvantages of being forced to rely upon other people's judgment in foreign affairs. He made no attempt to conceal his ignorance, disarming critics with his candour and humility, but he had recognized "the necessity of 'studying up' on the subject as much as his opportunities permitted him."[12] Yet there was no immediate invasion of Seward's province. When Motley visited Lincoln, to repeat his heartening monologue on Britain's attitude, the president listened attentively and approvingly before observing that "it does not so much signify what I think, you must persuade Seward to think as you do." He welcomed the historian's reply that he had "found Seward much mitigated in his feelings compared with what" he had expected.[13]

Perhaps responding to the criticism of his policy of "decision and demonstration," certainly feeling the unpleasantness of his position,[14] Seward quickly softened the tone of his instructions to Adams. With the cabinet satisfied by the minister's report of his first meeting with Russell, with the stock market rising in response to "the reported tenor" of the despatches from Britain, Seward informed Adams early in June that "This government has no disposition to lift questions of national pride or sensibility up to the level of diplomatic controversy, because it earnestly and ardently desires to maintain peace, harmony, and cordial friendship with Great Britain."[15] Further mollified by reports of Russell's rebuke of a member of Parliament who had gloated over America's difficulties, and by the British decision to close their ports to prizes, the secretary wrote to his wife on June 13 that he was able to see a "pacific solution" to America's affairs in Europe.[16]

Ironically, as Seward was waxing conciliatory Lord Lyons grew increasingly fearful. He knew that the secretary's colleagues had checked his bellicose course, but lacked confidence in their ability to restrain him for any length of time. Convinced that Seward's insolent treatment of foreign powers was "much to the taste of the American public," doubly apprehensive following conversations with politicians who boasted that the temper of Congress when it met in July would be belligerent, the British minister concluded that a sudden declaration of war against Britain was "by no means impossible so long as Canada seems open to invasion."[17] He telegraphed this warning to Russell on June 5. He also alerted Admiral Milne with whom he had already agreed that British vessels off the American coast should remain as unobtrusive as possible, to lessen the likelihood of an American officer succumbing to the temptation "to obtain for himself popular applause by violent proceedings against Great Britain."[18] On June 10 he arranged with the admiral that the telegram, "Could you forward a letter for me to Antigua?" would be the signal that hostilities were imminent.[19] Of course, Lyons had also taken the precaution of preparing the Canadians.

The gloomy tidings from Washington found the colonial government committed to putting the militia in better order, waiting for reinforcements from Britain, and determined to adopt a public posture of "total unsuspiciousness" until "actually and really prepared" by the mother country. It was equally determined to make clear its complete neutrality in the American conflict. On May 25 the *Canada Gazette* published the Foreign Enlistment Act, which, as the *Montreal Gazette* remarked, "requires that British subjects, whatever may be their sympathies, will refrain from enlisting" in the service of either side.[20] In the same spirit Canadians welcomed the prospect of a British recognition of Confederate belligerency. If Britain did not recognize the Confederate States as belligerents, the *Globe* warned, she would have to treat all privateers as pirates, "in fact she would have to go to war with the South."[21] The only neutral ground was that chosen by Russell. As for the cries from the United States that this step amounted to interference and would provoke retaliation, they were dismissed as nonsense and evidence that the "genius of bullying" had possessed "the whole tribe of journalists." Whatever Britain's course "her actions are sure to be misconstrued and her people libelled," the *Globe* concluded.[22]

For the Cartier-Macdonald administration the American outburst was far from unwelcome. It readily lent itself to a partisan interpretation. "The threat of revenging upon Canada imaginary wrongs or insults received at the hands of the British government," the *Toronto Leader* charged, "has several times been repeated by American journals, since a member of the Canadian Opposition uttered the foolish threat of appealing to Washington for assistance. This threat has misled the *New York Herald* and other American journals."[23] Meanwhile the administration's English mouthpiece in Canada East, the *Quebec Morning Chronicle*, was arguing that the "hastiness and irritability" that prompted the abuse and menaces was a "characteristic of all democracies."[24] And as all the Liberal-Conservative organs had laboured to establish, representation by population, for which the Reformers were campaigning, was tantamount to universal suffrage and democracy.

Quick to capitalize upon its advantages, which included the illness of George Brown as well as the menacing tone of the American press, the government decided to dissolve the provincial Parliament and call a general election. The issues on which it intended to fight were announced by Macdonald in his election address on June 10. Learning from the obvious defects of the American constitution, Canadians should provide for an efficient central government when they sought to unite the North American provinces. As for the Americanizing proposal of representation by population, Macdonald insisted that "with the present feeling in Lower Canada, no government could be formed from either side of the House to carry out that principle." Anyway, the civil war demonstrated the superiority of British institutions and of the principle on which they were founded. "Long may that principle—the Monarchical principle—prevail in this land," he proclaimed. "Let there be no 'looking to Washington', as was threatened by a leading member of the opposition last session; but let the cry, with the moderate party, be 'Canada United, as one Province, and under One Sovereign'."[25] The rewards of unity, government organs reminded Canadians, would be immense. The civil war was certain to leave the North and the South "weakened commercially, weakened financially, and lowered in the scale of nations." Thus if Canada avoided internal dissension, put down effectually the few men who were looking to Washington, and when she undertook constitutional change did so by consolidating the various British colonies into one, she would "be a power among nations," and would soon become a rival "to either of the confederacies which will be carved out of the *debris* of the once proud American Republic."[26] Her prospects were breathtaking. Covering an enormous territory, rich in natural resources, she would be populated by millions and was destined to be the envy of Americans.

Optimism about the future also abounded in the Confederacy, where the press welcomed both the ridicule which Canadians heaped upon Northern projects of annexation and the announcement that neither Canadian men nor arms would be made available for service with the Union. Those "mad fanatics" of the North who had been counting upon British assistance had now learnt that Canadians did not respond with alacrity to the appeal for aid and comfort, while it was certain that Britain would not long tolerate the Union's attempted blockade of the Confederacy's ports. The English press, which was so carefully scrutinized by Southerners, seemed to be leaning to the Southern side. It denounced the Northern tariff, welcomed the Confederate, and betrayed understandable concern for free and uninterrupted commercial relations with the Southern states. Then on May 15 came the exciting news of Russell's comments in the House of Commons nine days earlier. His reiteration of the principle that blockades had to be effective to be valid was hailed as a public warning to the North that the paper blockade announced by

Lincoln would be ignored. Even more thrilling was his opinion that the Confederacy must be recognized as a belligerent. That the first step of Great Britain had been "a long and firm one in exactly the direction which the people of the Southern States expected" was evident.[27] As a prominent member of the Confederate Congress wrote on May 15, "Our foreign relations are propitious."[28]

In this confident mood there was little likelihood of Congress supporting Robert Barnwell Rhett when he revived his challenge to the Davis administration's foreign policy. On May 13 he repeated his call for the offer of virtual free trade with any nation that would recognize the Confederacy. The Confederate commissioners should be authorized by Congress "to propose a maximum of duties not higher than twenty per cent *ad valorem* on all articles of manufacture or production imported from any nation which shall make a treaty with the Confederate States satisfactory in other respects."[29] Framed in the form of a resolution, this proposal was referred to the Committee on Foreign Affairs. There, even though Rhett was chairman, it was altered from an instruction to an expression of Congressional opinion. His colleagues were no more willing than they had been in February to force Rhett's views upon the president, especially now that further concessions to Britain and France were evidently unnecessary. That point, as well as the danger of free trade to infant industries in the Confederacy, was stressed by nascent protectionists when the modified resolution was debated on May 20. And when they successfully amended the already meaningless resolution, cutting the duration of any treaty from twenty to five years, the disappointed South Carolinian moved to have it tabled.

The failure of Rhett's attempt to reshape Confederate foreign policy left the instructions to the commissioners in Europe unaltered. Cotton remained their principal argument for recognition, and the Confederate government quickly tightened its grip on this all-important weapon. On May 21 Davis signed into law an act which prohibited the export of Southern cotton except through Confederate ports. There was going to be no shipment of cotton north, either for Northern industries or for export to Europe. If Europeans wanted cotton they would have to get it from Southern ports. Here was an additional reason for Britain to ignore the Proclamation of Blockade. As soon as she realized that the Confederates had dug in behind their cotton bales she would warn the besieging North out of her path. Of course, there was a danger that this policy would not take effect for several months, that the weight of the cotton argument would not be felt until the shipping season opened. However, most Southerners were reluctant to admit publicly that they expected such a lengthy delay. They spoke of sixty days as the limit of Britain's patience. The need to protect the immense sums invested in the textile industry, the attractions of Southern commercial liberality, and the opportunity to effect the dismemberment of her great commercial and manufacturing rival were inducements all too powerful to be long ignored. It was equally certain that the violent Northern denunciations of British policy would merely strengthen their desire to curb the insolence and crush the power of the "Yankee States."

The one check to Confederate confidence was the British decision to prohibit vessels from carrying prizes into their ports. Although the ban applied to both belligerents its practical effect would be to hamper the activities of Confederate privateers. Recognizing this, Rhett's *Charleston Mercury* denounced the measure as one of quasi-hostility and called for an embargo upon the export of cotton and tobacco. This would teach the British the power of Confederate statesmanship, it insisted, suddenly overcoming earlier doubts of the diplomatic power of Southern staples. For the most part, however, the Confederate public was encouraged to take the news calmly. British recognition was still only a matter of time, much of the press declared reassuringly. All that was required was for the need for cotton to become more acute and for the Confederacy to prove her ability to defend herself on the battlefield. This same belief was being fostered within the Davis administration by the commissioners in Europe.

At the end of May, after more than a month in Britain, Yancey and his colleagues had little to show for their labours but they saw no reason to be despondent. They had been visited by a number of British politicians and had been granted two private interviews with Lord John Russell, while Rost had travelled to Paris where he had had a meeting with Count de Morny, Napoleon III's half-brother. The Proclamation of Neutrality had recognized the Confederacy as a belligerent, and the commissioners believed that a public sentiment more favourable to the South was emerging in Britain. As for the recognition of

Confederate independence, they quickly concluded that it was certain "unless the fortunes of war should be against us to such an extent as to destroy all reasonable hope of our permanency," and would come either when Britain saw the chance to secure "some decided advantage," or when the "necessity for having cotton becomes pressing."[30] Even the less cheering events of early June, the closing of British ports and the withdrawal of Gregory's motion, failed to dampen their spirits. They remained convinced that England and France were merely waiting for evidence of the Confederacy's ability and strength to maintain herself. Indeed, as soon as the European powers were satisfied that the North and the South were "irremediably separated," Yancey and Rost reported from Paris on June 10, they would be easily persuaded of that ability. In any case, whenever the cotton crop was ready for market necessity would force the British and the French "to conclusions favorable to the South." In short, recognition would be extended within a few months. The certainty of this encouraged the commissioners to persevere with the policy one of them described as "attentive observation and 'masterly inactivity'," attempting to mould public opinion in as unobtrusive a way as possible, at least until "some favorable event" enabled them to press the Confederate case for recognition.

The discreet and conciliatory conduct of the Southern emissaries, who provided assurances that the slave trade would never be revived and that neutral flags and goods would be respected by Confederate privateers, must have been welcome to the British government, which was permitted as a result to give its attention to the troublesome North. Lyons's recommendations for dealing with the fractious Union had either been anticipated or were endorsed by his government. His theory that to prevent war it was sometimes necessary to be prepared for it was suitably Palmerstonian, as was his proposal that British forces in North America be strengthened. Thus the North American squadron had been reinforced and the garrison in Canada substantially increased. His suggestion that Charles Sumner be cultivated, that he be made aware of the perils to which Seward and the Lincoln cabinet were exposing the United States, was pursued. The Duke of Argyll, lord privy seal and a correspondent of the senator's, soon wrote "a few lines very earnestly to entreat" that he use his influence and official authority to induce his government, "and especially Mr. Seward, to act in a more liberal, and a less reckless spirit." There was a very real danger, Argyll warned, that through miscalculation or ignorance Seward might stumble into a war. "I rejoice that at such a critical time *you* are at the head of the Body which on Foreign Relations is able to control the government," the Duke wrote flatteringly, feeding Sumner's voracious vanity, "because I know how anxious you will be to be just and considerate in your dealings. I only wish you had been in Seward's place."[31]

But of all the moves he suggested for holding Seward and the North in check, Lyons insisted that none was more important than a close identity of British and French policies. Time and again he repeated the advice that "Our best chance of avoiding extremities would undoubtedly be to act in entire concert with France." If the two nations were divided in their attitude toward the war he feared that the United States government would "be encouraged to try any amount of violence against one separately, probably against England," as that would arouse "the greatest excitement" in the Union. "But even Mr. Seward could hardly be violent against England and France united, especially if their decisions were urged firmly and judiciously."[32] Russell required little coaxing in this direction. At the beginning of April he had pointed out to a receptive French foreign minister, Thouvenel, the "advantages which would result from frank explanations between the two governments on every report and every alarm tending to disquiet Europe."[33] Indeed, from a joint decision to receive the Confederate commissioners unofficially the policy of "frank explanations" rapidly developed. The British recognition of Confederate belligerency was endorsed by Thouvenel, although the French equivalent of the Proclamation of Neutrality did not appear for another month. The British ban of prizes from their ports was followed by a similar French prohibition. Yet joint activity could prove mutually restrictive, as the Anglo-French efforts to secure the belligerents' acceptance of the principles of the Declaration of Paris emphasized.

At the root of the problems that beset this attempt at cooperative diplomacy lay distrust, not merely a healthy scepticism of the purity of American motives in offering to adhere to the declaration, but an intense suspicion which was the inevitable result of Seward's policy of intimidation. Lyons's conviction that a close identity of British and French attitudes was essential if the bellicose secretary was to be restrained, drove the worried minister to search unceasingly for evidence of ploys to separate the two nations. But the British government's anxiety not to be separated from France was intensified and complicated by its continuing distrust of Napoleon III.

Serious difficulties with the United States were as inopportune in May as they had been earlier in the year, for Europe appeared to be on the verge of another convulsion. The one man ready to seize any opportunity was the emperor and British involvement in the American war would free him from their inhibiting influence. Therefore, the restraint of Seward was vital. Preparedness and the concert with France were accepted as the most effective means of exercising this control, but in their anxiety to work closely with Napoleon the British did not forget to take care that he did not play them false. The danger, which the "anti-English party" in the United States understood and exploited, was that France would lead Britain into an American dispute only to desert her. Certainly, Lord Cowley, the British ambassador in Paris, suspected that behind Napoleon's occasional suggestions of Anglo-French intervention on behalf of the South there lurked a wish "to get us into hot water with the North, which France would of course consider as so much gain to her—that is, we should be attacked, while she would look on."[34] With the balance of power in Europe and the security of their North American possessions to be kept in mind, and distrusting the other parties to the negotiations, the British soon let their suspicions get the better of their desire to formalize the protection of neutral commerce.

On May 6, as yet unaware of the United States government's willingness to accede to the full declaration, Lord John Russell sought to rally the French to the cause of minimizing the damaging effects of the American war on neutrals. Although the North had proclaimed its intention to institute a blockade and the South its intention to invite applications for privateering commissions, neither side had declared its position with respect to Articles II and III of the Declaration—that a neutral flag covers an enemy's goods, except contraband, and that neutral goods, bar contraband, are not liable to capture under an enemy's flag. Perhaps for that reason Russell first proposed to the French that they ask both belligerents to abide by these provisions. The French approved. But on May 11 Russell forwarded to Paris the draft of a despatch to Lyons in which the Americans were invited to accede to all four articles. No doubt he was encouraged to seek full accession by Lyons's private report that Seward was talking in Washington of the United States adhering to the entire declaration. Yet the catch to the American proposal was plain. "It would no doubt be very convenient if the Navies of Europe would put down the Privateers," Lyons wrote on April 27.[35]

Thouvenel doubted the wisdom of Russell's latest proposal. He was afraid that the Americans might interpret it as an attempt to take advantage of their predicament to extract concessions they had formerly refused, or that it would lead to Anglo-French involvement in the war. For even if the North accepted the South surely would not. As a result Britain and France might find themselves forcing the Confederacy to agree to the limitation on privateering. And when on May 14 he learned from Mercier of Seward's willingness to accede to the full declaration Thouvenel's fears grew. His first objection to Russell's course had been removed but not the second. Convinced that a trap had been set and baited to make the European nations treat Southern privateers as pirates, he instructed the French ambassador in London to caution the British. However, the French could not dissuade Russell from seeking the full adoption of the Paris Declaration.

In his instructions to Lyons of May 18, Russell pointed out that the Americans and the British had long been agreed on the last three articles of the declaration. Turning to the first, which dealt with privateering, and which the United States had in previous years refused to accept as it stood, he remarked that commanders and crews of privateers must, "by the law of nations," conduct themselves "according to the established laws of war." Therefore, the British government would hold any government that issued letters of marque "responsible for and liable to make good any losses sustained by Her Majesty's subjects in consequence of wrongful proceedings" of vessels sailing under them. "In this way," he concluded, "the object of the Declaration of Paris may, to a certain extent, be attained without the adoption of any new principle." Quite clearly Russell had not given up hope of securing a renunciation of privateering. But the Foreign Office was alive to the danger that the North might renounce this weapon in an attempt to lure the British into suppressing Confederate "pirates."[36] Consequently, in an accompanying despatch, drafted by Edmund Hammond, the permanent under-secretary, Lyons was informed that the government could not accept a renunciation if it was coupled with a condition that the British enforce it on the Confederate States, either by denying them the right to issue letters of marque or by interfering with the operations of vessels that held them and acted "according to the recognized principles and under the admitted liabilities of the Law of Nations."

Yet it remained Russell's hope to see privateering abolished, and to this end he was far less reluctant than his French counterpart to exert "a little moral pressure" on the South. It was too late to follow the earlier suggestion of the law officers and make Confederate relinquishment the price for a recognition of belligerency, but if the North accepted the declaration "bodily," he was willing to "tell the South that we make their acceptance a *sine qua non* of our friendship—I will not say of our neutrality."[37] In this context, another reason for the cabinet's decision a few days later to close British ports to prizes may have been a desire to weaken the predictable Confederate reluctance to surrender privateering, by seriously limiting its effectiveness. In any event, Lyons had his instructions, which were to be communicated to the South as well as the North. Meanwhile, the French had adopted the whole of Russell's despatch of May 18, "excepting the demand for the abolition of privateering in general." However, Mercier had been given "some latitude of action on this point"[38] and Russell was able to reassure Lyons that the French minister would receive instructions "analogous" to his own.

The task of negotiating with the Confederates and with Seward was one that Lyons had not sought and did not relish. The likelihood that the South would make much of an approach from the European nations, coupled with the knowledge that Seward would not tolerate any communication between the European governments and the Confederacy, induced caution. Fearing dismissal if compromised by overtures to the South, Lyons decided to remain as remote as possible from the discussions. Also, both he and Mercier were agreed that the Davis administration should not be approached until they had spoken to Seward. That was not a meeting they were anxious to arrange, however. The secretary was certain to be "furious" when he discovered that acceptance of the declaration by the United States would not commit Britain and France to the suppression of Confederate privateering. They concluded that their best hope of restraining him was to make their courses "as nearly as possible identical." Of course, for Lyons this union was doubly important. It would keep within bounds "the game of the violent party" to find some "shade of difference" between France and England "in order to use violent language, or to take violent measures against England, without necessarily involving themselves with France also."[39] Moreover, it suited his purpose to let Mercier take the lead.

As American tempers cooled, after the first inflamed outburst against Britain, the two ministers decided that an approach should be made to Seward, and Mercier went to the State Department to arrange a joint interview. He quickly learnt that Seward did not favour joint diplomacy and was not keen to discuss the Declaration of Paris. Above all, it was clear that the American wanted "to avoid having the fact established" that he had "official cognizance" of the recognition of Confederate belligerency by France and Britain. To the suspicious Lyons this smacked of an attempt to draw a distinction between the two nations in the matter of belligerency. Seward was out to create the impression that France had not really taken the same course as Britain, perhaps even hoping, the Englishman concluded, that she would retract recognition if she had not already committed herself by some official act. This would enable him "to be violent against England, without being obliged to adopt the same course with France." How to counteract this scheme was Lyons's immediate problem. He decided that it was essential that Mercier accompany him to the State Department, so that it was established "beyond contradiction" that France occupied "precisely the same position" as England,[40] and on June 15 the two men called on the secretary together. Although he repeated his objections to this joint approach and his unwillingness to accept any communication "founded upon the assumption that the Rebels of the South be regarded as Belligerents," Seward's "language and demeanour throughout the interview were calm, friendly and good humoured."[41] To a direct question from Mercier he affirmed that he wanted the matter of the declaration settled in Europe. However, he promised to give the ministers copies of his instructions to Adams and Dayton and asked if he might see their instructions so that he could frame his own note in a way that would "not misapprehend the views" of their governments.

Lyons emerged from the interview well satisfied. The identity of French and British policies had been established and Seward had repeated his readiness to adhere to the declaration. His satisfaction was enhanced by relief that he was not obliged to conduct the negotiations, and thus would not have to inform Seward that adherence to the first article did not affect the Confederate right to issue letters of marque. As for the equally delicate problem of approaching the South, the ministers agreed to put it off until they had seen Seward's instructions to Adams and Dayton.

Candid about his own reasons for welcoming this escape from an unenviable duty, Lyons gave some thought to Seward's motives for transferring the discussions to London and Paris. He deduced that the secretary was caught between fear that Congress, when it met, would join those who held him responsible for bad relations with Europe, and apprehension that any moderation of his tone would cost him his "mob popularity." His refusal to receive the British and French communications was "just one of those safe half-measures, which may be represented in one light or the other according to circumstances."[42] But his main aim was to gain time. Seward was hoping, the Englishman guessed, that the Anglo-French attitude towards the war had changed in the weeks since the instructions had been sent to Lyons and Mercier. Certainly, the prospects of the Union looked brighter than they had a month earlier, as Lyons admitted in a report to Russell; nevertheless, the future was far from clear. The South had threatened Washington from time to time, while the North was at best only inching forward in Virginia. Unless one side decided to make a dash for the other's capital—for the Confederates had moved to Richmond—the haze promised to last all summer, if not longer. In that case the uncertainty surrounding the Lincoln administration's attitude towards Britain was also likely to persist. For that condition a "strict concert with France" remained the best treatment. In fact, Russell's concern for that concert prompted him to recall to London the negotiations concerning the first article of the declaration, long before he heard of Seward's decision to shift the entire discussion to Europe.

At their first meeting, on May 18, Russell and Adams said little about the Declaration of Paris. The American mentioned that he was empowered to negotiate and Russell revealed that he had already sent instructions on this subject to Lyons. Believing that it would be better to leave the negotiations to Seward, Adams did not press them in London. However, in Paris Dayton did go ahead and initiate discussions with Thouvenel. On May 29 he proposed the adherence of the United States, not to the declaration as it stood but with the amendment first proposed by Secretary of State Marcy in 1856. This would have exempted from seizure the private property of subjects and citizens of belligerents, except contraband. Dayton's reasons for reviving this proposal in 1861 were complex, but it proved no more acceptable to the great maritime powers than it had been five years earlier. Certainly England did not intend to forgo such an "effective mode" of employing her naval strength. But if the amendment was unacceptable it soon acquired for Russell a sinister character. Informed by the French of what Dayton was proposing in Paris he raised the matter with Adams on June 12. When he learned that Adams had not been instructed to press the Marcy amendment, the foreign secretary concluded that he had caught Seward attempting to separate Britain and France and set them at odds. And shallow as he considered this particular ploy, it did persuade him to revise his instructions to Lyons. The minister was to press on with any negotiations for United States adoption of Articles II, III, and IV but refer to London any proposal to adopt the first article.

The significance of Russell's question about the Marcy amendment naturally escaped Adams, who had every reason to believe that the negotiations for American accession to the declaration would be conducted in Washington. He was preoccupied anyway with Seward's despatch of May 21. Its arrival, coupled with the news that his personal income had suffered as a result of a decline in business activity, depressed him. The confidence that he had gained from the events of the first week of June was shaken during the second. To challenge the British was madness. It would throw "the game into the hands of the enemy," impoverish that nation, and reduce the Adamses to beggary. Clearly it was his duty "to prevent mutual irritation from coming to a downright quarrel,"[43] so he exercised the discretion he had been given. At his meeting with Russell on June 12 Adams mentioned the dissatisfaction that the foreign secretary's two meetings with the Confederates had caused in the United States. "I added, as moderately as I could," he reported to Seward, "that in all frankness any further protraction of this relation could scarcely fail to be viewed by us as hostile in spirit and to require some corresponding action accordingly." In reply Russell first took care to inform the American that the British had acted in concert with the French in this matter, but then remarked that "he had no expectation" of seeing the Confederates "any more." He turned aside yet again Adams's complaint that the proclamation of British neutrality had been hasty. And when the American referred to the recent despatch of troops to Canada, which he said "would naturally excite attention" in the United States, Russell explained that the province had "been denuded of troops for some time back," and that they were "a proper measure of precaution, in the present disordered condition of things in the United States."[44] To lend weight to this explanation he pointedly mentioned the Ashmun and *Peerless* affairs.

Adams had performed his delicate task well, and at the American legation there was renewed confidence after the interview. Relations with Britain "are more satisfactory than they were a week ago," Benjamin Moran wrote in his journal.[45] Nevertheless, the fundamental problem remained, how to keep them running smoothly? Closer personal relations with the ministry would help, Adams concluded. Satisfied that the greater part of the administration were "well disposed," that as a body they were more friendly to the United States than the Conservatives, he was as gregarious as his austere character permitted. He invariably accepted invitations to the dinners and receptions that members of the government frequently gave and the shy Russell quickly grew to like him "very much."[46] Useful as this was, Adams realized that it was more important that Seward win the confidence of the British government. Disturbed by British suspicion of the secretary of state, and attributing it to the malign influence of Charles Sumner, he wrote to Seward advising him to draw Lyons "a little out of that association and nearer to yourself." Equally helpful would be a softening of the tone of Seward's despatches, and with this in mind Adams composed a lengthy analysis of British opinion. He admitted that for political or material reasons "a very large proportion of the active population" favoured the peaceful dissolution of the Union, but reported that he was "earnestly assured" that the British desired "only to be perfectly neutral." "I believe that this sentiment is now growing to be universal," he wrote reassuringly.[47] Yet no matter how hard he strove to improve relations with Britain, Adams never doubted that events entirely beyond his influence would finally determine the British attitude. A positive pro-Union spirit would depend "far more" upon the extent to which the American government enforced obedience, "than upon an absolute affinity in sentiment."[48] Thus by mid-June both Union and Confederate diplomats in London were looking for assistance to the Northern and Southern armies.

As he waited anxiously for military news from home, Adams received his instructions to undertake the negotiations for accession to the declaration. He did so in a mental state of flux, as his faith in Britain's neutral intentions ebbed and flowed. By mid-July he considered relations with her sufficiently stable to rent a house for a year, instead of on a monthly basis. Yet the obstacles to smooth relations remained. Seward, after his favourable response to Adams's report of his first meeting with Russell, had turned querulous again. In a private note to Adams he wrote of the shock, offence, and disgust with which the American people had reacted to the news of the British Proclamation of Neutrality, to "its arrangements with the French Government to deny the sovereignty of the United States, and its countenance of the insurrection."[49] He complained that all the powers of Europe except Britain had "expressed sympathy for the integrity of the American Republic." Nor did Adams consider Seward's language unjustified. Privately, he admitted to "feeling every day that the secret wish of almost all classes is to see us permanently divided."[50] To W. E. Forster, whom he considered the best friend of the Union that he had met, he sadly cited the British press as proof of the "earnestness of the feeling in favor of a division of the Union."[51]

The leading English newspapers had approved of Parliament's decision to forgo discussion of the American crisis, and if they were not prepared to take a vow of silence themselves they did treat the war with caution and restraint during much of June. Then came the reports of the bitter American criticism of British policy. These were angrily dismissed as unjustified. At a public meeting in London on July 24, called to discuss the American war, the chairman, the Earl of Shaftesbury, that distinguished humanitarian and son-in-law of Palmerston, won general approval for his claim that "there was no sympathy in this country for either one side or the other, simply because we believed there was no sincerity in either of them."[52] To secure the South the North would willingly have compromised on slavery, *Black-*

wood's charged. However, secession made slave property far less secure, for once he had escaped to the free States the fugitive would now indeed be free. Thus the interests of humanity as well as the national interest of Great Britain would best be served by the Union's dissolution. The existence of two confederacies, each exerting a "salutary check" upon the other, would at last produce in North America "a courteous and considerate diplomacy." No longer would the British have to face "the unpleasant alternative of admitting arrogant pretensions or engaging in a senseless quarrel." Finally, there was the comforting knowledge that the Union's troubles had already exercised a "salutary check" upon British democrats. "Democracy on its Trial," was the title of a lengthy article in the July *Quarterly Review* written by Lord Robert Cecil, and the Tory author was well satisfied that it had been convicted. Founded on the ignorant mob, the American government had "exhibited a pitiable mixture of inopportune apathy and inopportune fury." Taking heed of this lesson Parliament had refused to consider any Reform bill.

It was against this disquieting background of public comment that Adams approached Russell about the Declaration of Paris. He did so distrustfully. His recollection of what had been said at their meeting on May 18 and the account he had received from Seward of what had taken place at Washington, particularly the secretary's report that Lyons did not consider himself authorized to enter into a convention, fed the minister's suspicions not of "absolute double dealing," but that British "practice works pretty much to the same effect."[53] He decided that it would be unwise to trust to conversation. So on July 11 he wrote to Russell to inform him that he was empowered to negotiate and when he met with the foreign secretary two days later he presented him with a proposed arrangement which was the same as the declaration. Russell seems to have assumed that negotiations had been resumed in Paris, for Adams mentioned that Dayton had similar instructions. He promised to submit the proposal to his colleagues and when he spoke to the French ambassador on July 15 Russell was thinking of signing a convention with Adams the following day. But the negotiations had not been resumed in Paris. Dayton was questioning the wisdom of continuing with them and had remained mute on this topic while waiting for further instructions from Seward.

The French were alarmed. Russell was urged to delay by

Flahault, the French ambassador in London, and he was further cautioned by Lord Cowley. The sensitive French had been wounded and the suspicion roused that Russell was willing to go on alone with the Americans, Cowley reported from Paris. It was desirable that he ask Adams to include "France in the bargain." For it was not only Britain's interest to let the Americans see that she was "acting cordially with France," but it was "also of great importance not to give France any excuse, however trivial, to take a line of her own."[54] Still keen to reach a settlement, Russell thought that all of this could be achieved through an assurance from Adams that the United States was willing to enter into a similar engagement with France and other maritime powers, and did not propose to make a separate convention with Britain alone. However, the French had carried their misgivings about the survival of the concert to Palmerston and he advised Russell to be even more cautious. "It is obvious that for evident reasons the United States Government wishes to separate England from France," he wrote, "and it is our interest to defeat this policy." Therefore, the Americans should be informed that Britain would sign a convention as soon as they were informed that a similar convention had been agreed and was ready for signature with France. "It might not be amiss," he concluded, "that both Conventions should be signed at Paris simultaneously."[55] That was the gist of the reply that Russell gave Adams on July 18. Clearly, the British were more determined than ever not to be separated from the French. And they had good reason, for they were faced by the prospect of a serious confrontation with the United States over a measure to declare the Southern ports no longer ports of entry.

Forewarned by Lyons in May of the likelihood of the Congress reviving this unacceptable proposal, the British government had ample time in which to prepare its response. The first step was to call for the opinion of the law officers. No belligerent power "has the right, by mere prohibitory enactment," they replied, "to require neutral nations to abstain from all commercial dealings" with another belligerent power. "Such a right can extend only to ports of which the belligerent is in actual possession and into which he can therefore not only forbid entry, but by competent force on the spot, give effect to such prohibition." The Union exercised no such control over the Southern ports, therefore any act of Congress to declare them closed "may be treated as nugatory by the Law of Nations, and an attempt to enforce it by the seizure and confiscation of a neutral ship may be justly regarded as an act of hostility." The law officers also suggested that the government seek the support of other maritime powers, particularly France, "in not acknowledging the right of Congress to shut up the Southern ports."[56]

Before asking the French to join them "in any Declaration" about the right of the North to shut the ports, Russell and Palmerston agreed to wait and see what shape the American proposition took. Nevertheless, it was only sound policy to head off a crisis if that was possible, so Russell decided to drop a few broad hints of British opposition. He welcomed the opportunity given to him by a Commons question on June 27, about a similar law enacted by New Granada, then struggling to control Panamanian rebels, to announce publicly that the British government could not recognize this authority when the ports were in the hands of insurgents. The very next day he quizzed Adams about the possibility of Congress passing a similar measure. Although the minister doubted the constitutionality of such an act, implying presumably that it could not be enforced even if it was enacted, Russell remarked that "a strict adherence" to the law of nations would be "the best method of preserving friendly relations." In his own words he had given Adams "fair warning," and the minister duly informed Seward.[57]

Russell then turned to France, in search not of a joint declaration but of support for his policy and common instructions to the ministers in Washington. Cowley was instructed to raise the problem with Thouvenel. He found him unprepared, for Mercier had not kept him informed of the Northern intention, and while the foreign minister was of the personal opinion that this proposal was tantamount to a paper blockade he would make no official comment until he had consulted his legal advisers. However, he did question the expediency of Russell's suggestion that "some hint" be given "which might prevent the obnoxious measure from being brought forward."[58] The Frenchman feared that this policy would defeat its own object, that in the state of Northern opinion at that moment it was more likely to encourage than prevent passage of the measure. Yet he did endorse the British policy, sending the appropriate instructions to Mercier, when the French law officers formally condemned any closure of the ports by decree, and when the British were joined by

Flahault in London in urging the policy of "fair warning." But Thouvenel's hesitation had an effect upon Russell. When he wrote to Lyons on July 6 to inform him that the British and French governments would consider any act closing the ports illegal, the foreign secretary instructed him not to "raise the question at all with Mr. Seward unless, in consultation with M. Mercier, you shall deem it expedient to do so." The British government wish to act "in complete accordance" with France, he concluded.[59]

A few days later Russell decided that a more positive instruction to Lyons was required. He had received from the minister the unwelcome news that the passage of the measure was certain when Congress met. His initial response was forceful. The British government "cannot allow the Queen's subjects to be deprived of any of the rights of neutrals," he warned in his draft despatch. "They would consider a decree closing the ports of the South actually in the possession of the insurgents or Confederate States as null and void and they would deem it their duty to resist its execution by force if necessary."[60] But these stern words were tempered by Palmerston. "Cannot" became "will not," and the words "by force if necessary" were excised.[61] Left untouched was the heart of the instruction. "You will concert with M. Mercier as to the best mode of communicating this decision to the President and the Secretary of State," Russell ordered Lyons. "But at all events you will take care not to leave him [Seward] in ignorance of the decision of Her Majesty's Government."

A copy of the proposed despatch was sent to Paris, to ensure that the ministers in Washington received common instructions. However, Thouvenel had left Paris, and while Cowley did forward it to a senior member of the Ministry of Foreign Affairs, he was sure that the question was of too great an importance, "involving as it may do peace or war with the United States," for him to decide without consulting the foreign minister. Indeed, Cowley thought that Thouvenel would want "to take the Emperor's orders."[62] As a result, several days elapsed before Russell was informed that the French had agreed to send instructions to Mercier analogous to those drafted for Lyons. The British note was sent out on July 20, and four days later Russell reiterated Britain's refusal to allow her ships "to be stopped and overhauled, unless there is a suspicion of contraband of war, or an attempt to enter a blockaded port."[63] Forbidding as these warning were, the British were not seeking difficulties with the Americans. "It is of course desirable not to get into a quarrel sooner than we can help, nor at all if we can help it," Russell wrote to Lyons.[64] In this spirit, he ordered the minister not to initiate the negotiations for Confederate adherence to the declaration, that is, if he had not already taken that step. (He had.) Lyons was also instructed not to protest cases of inconvenience to British merchant vessels in American waters unless the necessity for doing so was both strong and urgent. Similarly, problems arising out of any law declaring the ports closed were to be referred home. Lyons was "not to act without previous instructions, fitted to the case."[65]

All of this had been written before the news reached England of the passage of the law closing the ports. Its arrival there on July 26 obviously signalled the failure of the Anglo-French efforts to dissuade the Americans from taking this course. Not that this failure had been unforeseen. Even if the Americans declined to take his hints or respond to his warnings not to enact this legislation Russell had always hoped that Lincoln could be persuaded not to enforce it. Anxious to hurry the president along this path, he drafted another forceful despatch to Lyons. Denying that the measure was lawful, he warned that the British "reserve to themselves, therefore, in case it should be exercised, the right of acting in concert with other nations in opposition to so violent an attack on the rights of commercial countries and so flagrant a violation of international law."[66]

Drafted on July 26, this despatch was circulated among the members of the cabinet along with the correspondence from Lyons. They were divided in their reaction and the despatch went through four ever more moderate drafts before it was sent on August 8. Most members were reluctant to commit themselves to a position that might lead to war with the Union, a war in which Britain would be "obliged to take part apparently with the party of Slavery Extension, to expose Canada to invasion, and to enter into a mighty contest with 20 millions" of her own race. Yet she could "hardly submit to pretensions in violation of the Law of Nations." It would be an invitation to aggression to submit tamely to an obvious wrong from an "arrogant and encroaching people."[67] No less important, the Northern measure would further impair British chances of obtaining the cotton then maturing in the South, cotton essential for the prosperity of the textile industry and the welfare of people dependent upon it. Reluctant to face the consequences either of resistance or submission to the American law, the cabinet relied upon Lincoln's prudence. In the despatch that was finally approved and sent, the British government announced that it did not acknowledge the power to close the ports as belonging to the American president by international law "or as consistent with the friendly and commercial relations at present subsisting," and that it would "consider its exercise as a violation of the unquestioned rights of neutral nations." However, it trusted that Lincoln would not exercise this power when he had "in his own hands the rights of Blockading the Southern Ports in conformity with international law, without raising objections on the part of other Maritime Powers."[68] In case he did Milne's squadron was quietly strengthened and further reinforcements prepared, but the admiral was ordered to caution his officers "so that the calm and deliberate measures of the government may not be frustrated by any premature act, which would further complicate a state of affairs already most embarrassing." The government was willing to wait for "explanations" from the United States and considered friendly relations with the Union too important to risk a "chance collision or any preventive action."[69] A few days later Russell heard from Lyons that it was very unlikely that Lincoln would issue a proclamation closing the Southern ports.

If the encouraging news from the United States brought a sigh of relief from the British government it was lost in the finale of the negotiations for American adherence to the Paris Declaration. Dayton's silence on the subject was broken before the end of July. He was instructed to proceed by Seward who was not deterred by the minister's fears of French and British reservations that would countenance Confederate privateering. On July 24 Dayton travelled to London to consult with Adams, and he agreed to revive the negotiations in Paris once Adams had provided evidence of the British government's unwillingness to adopt the Marcy amendment. On July 31 the minister obtained from Russell the proof Dayton demanded. Britain was only interested in a convention with the United States that accepted the declaration as it stood, Russell wrote, and she would continue with the negotiations as soon as the necessary arrangements could be perfected in London and Paris "so that the Convention may be signed simultaneously at those capitals." But to these familiar conditions the foreign secretary now added his first clear warning "that on the part of Great Britain the engagement will be prospective, and will not invalidate anything already done."[70] The reservation that Lyons had been instructed to make at the very beginning of the negotiations had finally been made. And while its meaning was clear, an uncharacteristically obtuse Adams "frankly" admitted to Seward and Dayton that he did not understand this condition. Yet he must surely have guessed. "What dirty object is aimed at we don't exactly know," Benjamin Moran commented, "but there is something favorable to Southern Piracy contemplated by the condition."[71] Nor was Dayton puzzled. He interpreted Russell's comment as proof that he had been right to warn Seward that Britain and France would hedge any agreement with conditions designed to save them from treating Confederate privateers as pirates.

The distrust of Britain that Russell's note heightened among the members of the American legation in London was matched by the continuing British suspicion of the United States. A report from Paris that only in London had the proposals for a convention been different, that in St. Petersburg, Berlin, and the French capital they had all been the same, strengthened the conviction that the principal American aim was to draw a distinction between Britain and the other European nations, especially France. Of course, that scheme could be thwarted by British care "to act on the same plan as the French Government." What remained to be avoided was the other pitfall prepared by Seward. The secretary's purpose "was to force the Western powers to treat the Southern privateers as pirates," Dayton let slip to the French.[72] To defeat it, Russell had drafted a rider to the declaration. Adopted by both France and Britain, it was presented to Adams and Dayton. Thus Adams was informed that in signing a convention "Her Majesty does not intend thereby to undertake any engagement which shall have a bearing direct or indirect, on the internal difficulties now prevailing in the United States."[73] Not that Russell expected him to sign a document bearing this reservation. The American was furious and found it difficult to suppress his "indignation at the miserable shuffling practised throughout this negotiation."[74] He wrote to Russell on August 23 to express his resentment at the implication that the United States government "might be desirous at this time to take a part in the Declaration not from any high purpose or durable policy, but with the view of securing some temporary object in the unhappy struggle which is going on at home." If the parties were not to sign the instrument on terms of perfect reciprocity and without equivocation and obligation of any kind on any side," he added, "then it is plain that the proper season for such an engagement has not yet arrived."[75]

For Britain, the conclusion to the negotiations was to be far less unsatisfactory than it was for the Union. Although a formal accession by the United States to the declaration was now out of the question, Articles II, III, and IV, over which there was no dispute, were soon acknowledged. There was also the satisfaction of having evaded the traps the British were certain that Seward had set for them. Most important, the Anglo-French concert had weathered its first crisis. This instrument of restraint, curbing the foolhardy Americans in North America and thus checking the opportunistic French in Europe, remained intact. Indeed, the conduct of the French had allayed some of Cowley's fears that they were seeking to involve Britain with the United States, only to leave her in the lurch. "I am exceedingly satisfied with the desire he evinces not to separate in any way from us on the American crisis," the ambassador wrote of Thouvenel.[76]

SIX

The blockade begins

THE SUMMER OF 1861 proved to be a dispiriting time for the Union. The Proclamation of Neutrality still rankled, not least because it placed the Union "on the level of the men of Montgomery." The same indignant objection was made to the British decision to close their ports to prizes, as soon as it was realized that the ban applied to Federal as well as Confederate vessels. Then came the news of the troop reinforcements for Canada and the reported despatch of British frigates to monitor the blockade. Here was more evidence of perfidious Albion. She did not mean to adhere long "to the neutrality dodge." Once again the topical question was, "How to keep England straight?" *Harper's Weekly* would have placed an embargo on the $140 millions of British manufactured goods imported by the United States. The *New York Herald*, with characteristic disregard for the realities of the situation, revived the foreign war panacea. Less disputable was the need to improve the efficiency of the blockade. The sealing of the Confederate ports was doubly essential, for it would deny the Confederacy the means of continuing the struggle and deny the cotton-hungry British an excuse to intervene. An alternative course, and one that avoided the hard test of efficiency, was for the nation to assert its right to name its own ports of entry. "The first thing Congress should do," the *New York Times* proclaimed on the eve of its special session, "is to declare that the rebel ports are closed as ports of entry until they have resumed allegiance to the Government."[1]

The government shared this concern about the blockade. Some time after Lincoln's proclamation a joint board of the Coast Survey and the Navy Department had been appointed to study the problems and make recommendations. This Blockade Board issued its first report at the end of May. It called for the creation of three squadrons, Atlantic, Home, and Gulf, and this was done, although the Atlantic and Home squadrons soon merged and operated as one. However, the blockade squadrons were not immediately effective and there were those within the administration, of whom Lincoln and Gideon Welles, the secretary of the navy, were two, who doubted whether an effective blockade could be mounted at all the ports along the extensive American coast. Inevitably, they as much as the public were attracted to the other course. If the ports were decreed to be closed they could be guarded sufficiently to cut off commerce "pretty effectually," and the British denied an excuse to frustrate the Union's economic coercion of the South.

Whatever its attractions this course was not free of difficulties. Could a government close ports that it had ceased to control? Only a few months earlier the United States had informed New Granada that a "government has the perfect right to close any of its ports, provided such ports be in the possession of the authorities." If they were not "the Decree must be considered as tantamount to a blockade by proclamation."[2] The fact that Lincoln had already proclaimed a regular blockade in no way simplified the problem. By that act the Union had itself conceded belligerent status to the South and invoked the law of nations. How could it now declare the Confederate ports closed on the basis of municipal law? The only possible answer, however unconvincing, was to deny that the South was a belligerent.

Seward issued this denial when he refused to negotiate with Lyons and Mercier on the Declaration of Paris because their instructions were founded upon the recognition of Confederate belligerency. The United States, he wrote in his instructions to Adams, transferring the negotiations to Europe, could not debate the "novel and extraordinary positions" that it was divided into belligerent parties and that Britain had assumed the attitude of a neutral between them. Nor did he fail to claim that nothing had been done which impaired the right of the Union to suppress the insurrection by excluding all commerce from the ports controlled by insurgents, "either by closing the ports directly or by the more lenient means of a blockade."[3] If this was assertion not argument, it did place the Union's position on record and the transfer of the negotiations to London and Paris did borrow time. In fact a month elapsed between the date of Seward's refusal to negotiate with Lyons and Mercier in Washington and the arrival of his instructions in London on July 11. By his dilatory conduct Seward at least ensured that he could not be compelled to receive official notice of British and French recognition of Confederate belligerency before the United States had reasserted her claim to exercise authority in the South.

When Congress met on July 4 it received from Lincoln a message unexpectedly optimistic in its view of foreign relations. The president claimed "that the sovereignty, and rights of the United States, are now everywhere practically respected by foreign powers; and a general sympathy with the country is manifested throughout the world."[4] These were Seward's words. He deleted from the first draft the president's statement that he found "no cause of complaint against the present course of any foreign power" on the subject of American sovereignty.[5] No doubt Seward made this amendment in order to vindicate his conduct of foreign relations and forestall Sumner, who was rumoured to be preparing an indictment of him for mishandling relations with Britain, but he was also mindful of the dispute in the offing over Southern belligerency. Thus he also deleted Lincoln's potentially embarrassing admission that foreign nations could claim that between them and the United States "the strict law of blockades shall apply." Six days later a bill was reported to the House which provided "for the collection of duties on imports and for other purposes." Wherever the president found that the revenue laws could not be executed and duties collected regularly at Southern ports, he was authorized to provide for their execution and collection by vessels at sea. He was also empowered to close such ports as ports of entry, and any vessel that attempted to enter one of them was to be forfeited to the United States, "together with its tackle, apparel, furniture and cargo."[6] Only ten dissenting votes were recorded in the House and six in the Senate, and the bill passed without any serious discussion of its international consequences.

Yet Congress had not taken this decision in ignorance of the danger of foreign opposition. Lord John Russell's comments about New Granada had arrived "most opportunely," shortly before the bill came before the Senate. And while they had no effect there the cabinet made no move to exercise this new authority. Emboldened by this unexpected delay, Lyons and Mercier bestirred themselves. They had kept silent before, agreeing with Thouvenel that protests would speed not prevent the bill's passage. Mercier now called on Seward to inform him that the French government would not consider such a closure of the ports justifiable and to warn that any attempt to enforce it was likely to lead to serious consequences. The secretary's reply was encouraging. He announced that he was disinclined to see the measure implemented. He even asked the Frenchman for sections of his instructions, to help to strengthen his hand, and together with Lyons the French minister decided which passages to let him have. On the morning of July 20 the secretary asked the British minister to call at the State Department. His purpose was twofold. First, he was seeking to follow Adams's advice to draw Lyons closer to himself. He had always been inclined to peaceful and moderate counsels, Seward confided, but he could not afford to lessen his means of usefulness "by going against the current of public feeling." This predicament should be kept in mind when his conduct was judged by foreign ministers. If he had used strong language in his earlier communications to foreign powers "it was from the necessity of making them clearly understand" the state of American public opinion "and the results it might produce."[7]

However sceptical he was of Seward's self-analysis, and however dubious he remained of there being any lasting improvement in the secretary's attitude toward Britain, Lyons was convinced by the meeting on July 20 that the American's present mood was prudent and pacific. Seward's subsequent refusal to comply with a request from the House for the correspondence between the United States and foreign powers "with reference to maritime rights," and his opposition to the issuance of a proclamation closing the Southern ports as ports of entry, strengthened the British minister's conviction. For it was clear to Lyons that the secretary's main purpose in calling him to the State Department had been to discuss the international consequences of the enabling act. Seward referred to the reports of Russell's remarks about New Granada and mentioned that he was preparing an "exposition" which would be sent to Adams and Dayton. More important, he was anxious that the British avoid "decided language" and "strong measures." Personally opposed to the measure being applied, he "could not be sure that he might not be overruled in the Cabinet." If public opinion was inflamed by news from Britain it might prove impossible to postpone bringing the bill into operation, he warned. And when Lyons emphasized that his government did not accept that the

United States had the right to declare closed ports not in her possession, Seward asked him for extracts from his instructions, hinting that he could make good use of them "in deliberating with the President."[8] With the help of the French minister Lyons went over his instructions of July 6, to decide which portions to forward.

Seward's "exposition" was dated July 21 but was not sent until the beginning of August. In it concessions to European opinion were accompanied by flourishes calculated to comfort if not distract the American public when the despatch was published. The claim that the integrity of the republic remained unbroken was paraded, as was the insistence that Britain should in no way intervene in the struggle or communicate with the Confederates. He trumpeted the unique merits of the Union's cause. Its policy was not "a creature of the government but an inspiration of the people." It was "based on interests of the greatest importance, and sentiments of the highest virtue," whereas that of foreign states rested on "ephemeral interests of commerce or of ambition merely." With such high principles to defend, the course of the Union could not be changed either by the fortunes of war at home or the action of foreign states. Here was the root of Seward's anxiety that the British refrain from peremptory conduct. He had no wish to find himself exposed to the accusation that he had backed down before British threats. But amidst the bold declarations were instructions to Adams to prevent "misconceptions" of the bill. It gave the president powers to be exercised at his discretion. It did not indicate a Congressional conviction that the ports ought to be closed as ports of entry, simply a concern that if that step became necessary it would "not fail for want of power explicitly conferred by law." Nor would the existing policy be changed without consideration of the foreign and domestic circumstances "bearing upon the question," Seward wrote reassuringly.[9] But he had stopped short of a commitment and he withheld the despatch until his colleagues reluctantly agreed not to apply the measure.

By July 23 a majority of the cabinet were pressing for the implementation of the act "forthwith," but Seward held firm in opposition. He soon won the support of Lincoln. The events of late July put the president in a melancholy mood. The defeat and humiliating panic at Bull Run were depressing enough without the prospect of difficulties with the British. Convinced of Britain's determination to have the cotton crop just as soon as it matured, certain that the Southern coast was too extensive to be effectually blockaded and that to resort to the powers Congress had given him would result in another war, Lincoln found ample reason to be melancholy. All that could be done, he decided, was to increase the navy as quickly as possible, to blockade as many ports as the available force permitted, and to "say nothing about the rest."[10]

One puzzling aspect of the debate on the enabling act was the role of Seward. Why had he moderated his tone? Lyons soon found a satisfactory explanation. The secretary had failed in his bid for the leadership of the "violent party," while it was his enemies in Congress and the cabinet who were pressing for a proclamation declaring the ports closed. Their intention was to make him the scapegoat if the measure brought troubles with Britain and France. Here was reason enough for caution, but it was strengthened by the evident failure of his blustering attempt to alter the course of Britain or separate her from France. Undoubtedly, as Lyons surmised, Seward's motives were complex. He had resented Sumner's attacks on him as a warmonger and must have enjoyed the irony of this situation, for Sumner had sponsored the enabling act in the Senate. Also, he was still anxious to overcome much of the foreign distrust of him. Thus he went to some lengths to assure Lyons of his pacific motives and he used his despatch to Adams to place before the British, and the American public when it was published, his own view of his conduct. However he may at any time have been understood, Seward wrote, he had acted from "an earnest and profound solicitude to avert foreign war; that alone has prompted the emphatic and sometimes, perhaps, impassioned remonstrances I have hitherto made against any form or measures of recognition of the insurgents by the government of Great Britain."[11] Finally, he had reason to fear serious difficulties with Britain after he heard of Russell's remarks in the Commons. But he could not count on being confronted by her alone.

Seward's early hopes of being able to browbeat the British had been dimmed by a number of setbacks, not least the "strict" Anglo-French concert. It was "hardly to be contemplated" that in the midst of an insurrection the American government "would be willing to face also the combined power of the two great empires of Western Europe."[12] Nor could the economic arguments for appeasement be ignored. The war was proving expensive and the government's reluctance to raise the large sums required by taxation left it with the sole alternative of borrowing. The money was there to be had. Frightened by the economic consequences of disunion, American businessmen had reduced both their activities and investments. Also, severe crop failures in Europe had created an unusual demand for American foodstuffs. The result was that bank reserves, already enlarged by the business community's unwillingness to borrow and to purchase, were swollen by the inflow of British and European gold to pay for the farm products. Thus the government's task was to persuade potential lenders to advance the $240 millions Secretary Chase sought from them. The danger of a war with Britain, let alone with her and France combined, was certain to discourage cautious American capitalists from parting with their money and it would extinguish the flickering hope that Europeans would buy United States bonds. But the importance of keeping relations with Britain on an even keel was greater still after July 21. As he looked down from the windows of the State Department on "a motley crowd of demoralized soldiers and curious citizens" thronging Washington's streets for a day or two after Bull Run, Seward worried about "the certain effect that the event would have upon opinion in Europe."[13] This was no time to give the Europeans any excuse to intervene or possible investors fresh reason to hold back their money. No wonder Lyons was able to write home on July 30 that it was now unlikely that the president would exercise his powers to close the ports.

By mid-August the domestic situation had improved. The panic following Bull Run had passed and on August 15 Chase completed an arrangement with banks in New York, Boston, and Philadelphia, under which they would make a series of advances in coin to the government. Abroad, developments had been less satisfactory. Seward had received word from Adams of Russell's first warning that any agreement on the Declaration of Paris would be prospective only and could not invalidate anything already done. He must have realized that the game was up, and Britain's refusal to play was particularly galling because all the other maritime nations had been watching her for a lead. Yet to have "understood" Russell's comments would have been tantamount to an admission that the Union's offer to accede had not been straightforward. Consequently, Seward wrote an artful despatch that was earmarked for publication. Adams was instructed to seek an explanation of Russell's comments, but not in a querulous or hypercritical spirit. The United States did not see the need for such a reservation, Seward wrote, but moved by the interests of commerce and civilization, she would refuse "nothing which shall be really just or even non-essential and non-injurious" to herself. Of course, she could not be expected to compromise in any way her "national integrity, safety, or honor."[14]

Already Britain and France had been moved by their commercial interests to communicate with the Confederacy about the declaration. This Seward knew because he had been permitted to read unofficially Mercier's instructions, but the news attracted a "somewhat inconvenient amount" of public attention when a Southern messenger was detained in New York. British by birth but American by choice, a colonel in the South Carolina militia, Robert Mure had been issued a passport by the British consul at Charleston, in which he was misleadingly described as a "British merchant residing in Charleston." He carried not only a sealed consular bag, whose contents were so voluminous that Seward doubted that it was all official correspondence—after all the port was blockaded—but also a number of private letters. Among these was at least one which reported that Consul Bunch had described the Anglo-French dealings with the Confederacy on the declaration as the first step toward "direct treating."[15] Seward could ill-afford to ignore these activities now that they had been drawn publicly to his notice. He did not tamper with the consular bag but it was forwarded to London by special messenger with a request that any material treasonable to the United States be returned. In addition, he instructed Adams to request the recall of Bunch.

That Seward sought the recall of the British consul but not the Frenchman implicated with him in the negotiations is readily understandable. To draw a distinction between Bunch and his French counterpart might fracture that inhibiting "strict concert," and was easily justified on official grounds. Not only was it the Englishman's messenger who had been detained but the documents found upon him confirmed the suspicion which Union authorities harboured about this British consul.

One of the abiding problems of the Confederacy was communications. The blockade and then the suspension of postal arrangements impeded the flow of information between the South and Europe. British newspapers were delayed for weeks, Northern newspapers became the principal source of European news, and public confidence was shaken as one optimistic rumour after another proved to be false. For the government this problem was a serious diplomatic handicap. Delivery of despatches from and instructions to the commissioners in Europe was infuriatingly slow and uncertain. However, the fact that Robert Bunch had agreed to include a letter from a prominent Confederate congressman to William Gregory in his consular pouch in May led William M. Browne, the assistant secretary of state, to suggest that the consul be invited to serve as the Confederacy's postman. Bunch declined the position but he continued to forward some letters and his messengers carried the correspondence of Southerners. The consul's cooperativeness did not go undetected in the North, and Seward forwarded to Lyons a police report charging Bunch with making "use of his office for facilitating the transmission of treasonable correspondence."[16] Although he denied the accusation, the British minister immediately took steps to avoid difficulties. He drew the attention of all the consuls in the South to an order from Seward that any passport issued to a person to pass through Union lines, or travel to a foreign country, be countersigned by the secretary. Furthermore, Lyons called for the exercise of extreme caution in the forwarding of correspondence of British subjects. Letters containing "allusions to political or military events" were not to be accepted. "And you will take care that no person bearing a passport from you stating him to be charged with despatches," Lyons concluded, "convey any letters which have not been entrusted to him by you."[17] Thus, in issuing a passport to Mure, Bunch not only ignored Seward's order but also failed to practise the extreme caution Lyons demanded. He stood indicted for insubordination or convicted of incompetence. But he was protected from the consequences of his folly by the fact that the demand for his recall was tied to the negotiations concerning the Declaration of Paris.

Lyons and Mercier had finally plucked up enough courage to initiate the discussions with the South at the beginning of July. A copy of Russell's instructions of May 18 was sent to Bunch on July 5 while Thouvenel's similar orders were forwarded to the French consul, Belligny. They were advised not to go in person to Richmond or negotiate directly with the Confederate government, and above all they were to avoid raising the question of recognition. Bunch was also warned that any disclosure of his involvement might lead to "some inconvenient outbreak" in Washington, such as the withdrawal of his exequatur.[18] Finally, Lyons made clear his own determination to remain as remote as possible from the negotiations. Bunch was to look upon his instructions as coming from London, the minister wrote, and he was to say as little as possible about the channel by which they had been communicated.

Requiring an intermediary, Bunch and Belligny selected William Henry Trescot, who had retired from public service and was now managing his plantation. Together with Durant St. André, who was about to replace Belligny, they met with Trescot on the evening of July 19. The three Europeans repeatedly stressed the need for complete secrecy, suggesting that the Confederacy make a "spontaneous" announcement of its acceptance of the second and third articles of the Declaration of Paris. The only bait they could dangle before the Davis administration was "the very great significance and importance" of this indirect negotiation. It did not imply recognition, but the consuls indicated "that the consequences would be most agreeable and beneficial to the Confederate Government."[19] After some discussion Trescot accepted the commission. It was agreed that he would travel to Richmond to inform Jefferson Davis that he was the bearer of an important communication from Bunch and Belligny, which had to be made in strictest confidence. Only if Davis was willing to accept this condition was Trescot to go ahead. On July 20 the South Carolinian set out from Charleston armed with copies of Bunch's instructions and reached Richmond two days later. There, he learnt that Davis was with the victorious troops at Bull Run. Although he must have been weary of travelling by this time Trescot decided to go on and the following morning found him on a train for Manassas Junction, near the battlefield. On the way his train met one carrying the wounded, and hearing that Davis was on board Trescot joined him. They arranged an interview for the next day, at which Trescot reported his mission and presented the papers entrusted to him. The president said that he would call a meeting of the cabinet to discuss the proposal and its decision would be communicated by the secretary of state.

Davis called the members of his cabinet together on the evening of July 25, but his messenger "erred in the notice" to them so only Stephen Mallory appeared.[20] They were all present the following morning, however, when they agreed to introduce a resolution into the Congress to give effect to Articles II, III, and IV of the declaration. Introduced on July 30 it passed on August 8, but on August 13 it was repassed in an amended form which emphasized the Confederacy's determination to exercise the right of privateering "as established by practice and recognized by the law of nations."[21]

The task of introducing both resolutions had fallen to a new secretary of state. Toombs had resigned his office on July 24. A high opinion of his own abilities and an ever lower one of those of several of his colleagues helped to make an unhappy position unbearable. Bull Run probably settled the question of resignation. He had failed to dominate the administration and the State Department was an obscure place compared with the battlefield. To a vaulting ambition the popular adulation heaped upon the military hero of Manassas revealed the path to glory and the road to the Executive Mansion. Toombs joined the army, but before he had even been measured for his uniform Robert Hunter had replaced him as secretary of state. To this position the Virginian brought the same attitudes and much the same experience as the Georgian. A lawyer by training, Hunter was another prosperous planter and successful politician. A decade in the House of Representatives, over which he had presided as speaker, had been followed by fourteen years in the Senate. Though by no means a hasty secessionist he had proven inflexibly Southern in his sympathies and attitudes, and his commitment to Southern independence was total. An ambitious and forceful man, "he planned for the possible advancement of his political fortunes which victory for the Confederacy would make possible."[22] Like Toombs he seemed miscast. As Louis Wigfall remarked, "I don't know what we Southern men would do without Hunter; he is the only one among us who knows anything about finance."[23] Certainly he did not bring any fresh ideas to the management of foreign relations, for here again he differed little from his predecessors, who had left office convinced that cotton would not fail the South. "France and England will acknowledge our independence this fall unless we are overcome before that time," he had assured Vice-President Stephens on July 5, "simply holding things as they are will secure that, any decided success will hasten it."[24] Entering office in the exuberant aftermath of the victory at Bull Run, Hunter saw no cause to dispute this opinion. The battle had demonstrated the South's ability to sustain itself, he wrote to Yancey, Rost, and Mann in his first despatch, and "I see no reason to make any change in the instructions you have already received from this Department. The purpose and general policy of the Government of the Confederate States remain unchanged."[25]

Although its confidence in the power of cotton remained unshaken, the Confederate government was growing aggrieved at the conduct of the British. Britain's closing of her ports to prizes was festering in Southern minds, and if that decision had been intended to exert a "little moral pressure" on the Confederacy to abandon privateering it had proved unsuccessful. As for Confederate compliance with the Anglo-French request for a "spontaneous" acknowledgement of the other principles of the declaration, that was marked by resentment. Coming so soon after Bull Run, which had seemed certain to exercise "a decided influence" on foreign relations,[26] these secret and indirect negotiations were objectionable if not demoralizing. Through Trescot, Davis informed the consuls of all these grievances. The closing of British ports was unfair and unneutral. The "irregular" form of communication on the declaration was wanting in the respect to which the Confederacy considered herself "fully entitled," and was "calculated rather to embarrass than to assist the final adjustment of important questions." Nor did the president disguise his government's growing impatience for recognition. It was in the interests of all the nations of Europe, he declared, that the vast industrial, commercial, and moral interests at stake in the American war be put without delay under the "charge and guardianship of recognized and recognizable national representatives."[27]

Impatience spread like a contagion through the Confederacy during the hot summer months of July and August. That soothing assurance, "recognition is only a matter of time," was heard less often. News of the withdrawal of Gregory's motion and the closure of British ports, and W. H. Russell's rigorously impartial letters, republished from the *Times* and Northern newspapers, added to the general discomfort of the season. It was clear that Britain had not been waiting for the first opportunity to recognize the South and was willing to postpone that step for as long as possible. The military success at Bull Run suddenly seemed less decisive. "The Lord help us, since England and France won't —or don't," Mary Chesnut despairingly wrote in her diary on July 27.[28] Yet few Southerners admitted to any loss of faith in cotton. Their loyalty to this monarch was as strong as the government's but they were impatient to see him crowned. Britain had to be convinced once and for all that nothing short of recognition and a denial of the blockade's legality would secure the precious cotton for her industry. Recognition alone would not suffice. A declaration of the blockade's ineffectiveness was also necessary if the South was to obtain "credit in the money markets of the world" and be given "the means of amply sustaining that credit" by the shipment and sale of her products. Furthermore it would enable her to secure "arms and munitions of war, and if the Lincoln government attempted to maintain its blockade would, indirectly," bring her powerful allies in the persons of Britain and even France.[29] But to impress these requirements upon the British a more coercive foreign policy was needed, and no organ demanded it with more persistence or vehemence than the *Charleston Mercury*.

Rhett's newspaper had concluded that the commissioners had failed. For this the Davis administration was held primarily responsible. It had neglected to dangle the supposedly irresistible bait of commercial advantage before Britain and France. As a result the Confederate States were now obliged to resort "to other instrumentalities than negotiation to make themselves respected and their independence acknowledged."[30] Three "obvious" steps should now be taken—the recall of the commissioners, the dismissal of all foreign consuls still accredited to the United States, and a trade embargo. The time had come to carry out the ultimate threat, a ban on the export of cotton, and thus make Britain understand that she could not count upon leaks in the blockade or the Union's lifting of it at some port to obtain the cotton she so desperately required. She should be offered a choice between denunciation of the blockade and recognition of Confederate independence on the one hand and the loss of cotton on the other.

When Congress met in mid-July Rhett was ready with his either-or policy. He revived an emasculated version of his earlier proposal "to extend for a limited period commercial and tonnage advantages to those nations earliest recognizing" Confederate independence,[31] while Louis Wigfall proposed that Congress take the three "obvious" steps that would compel Britain and France to nibble on this small carrot. But the Committee on Foreign Affairs ignored Rhett's promptings yet again, and Congress accepted its recommendation that Wigfall's resolutions be tabled. With the loss of the goad Rhett quickly lost interest in the carrot, which was eventually reported to the house, placed on the calendar, and there withered from inattention.

By the session's end the advocates of a more coercive foreign policy had little to show for their agitation, other than the extension of the earlier bill that had prohibited the export of cotton through any but Southern ports. First tobacco, and then sugar, rice, molasses, and syrup were brought under this ban. Frustrated, the hardliners rounded on the administration and assailed it for their failure. Certainly, it opposed any legislative embargo. Davis was still unwilling to surrender to Rhett the control of foreign policy, and he had to consider not only the vocal minority within Congress and the business community without who dissented from this measure, but also the inadvisability of making the economic ruin of Britain and France an avowed aim of the Confederacy. Yet anxiety not to be compromised internationally had to be weighed against the danger of antagonizing the growing body of domestic support for a ban on the export of cotton. In this predicament the administration undoubtedly welcomed the voluntary embargo quickly organized by the coercionists and widely supported by the press. Here was a release for the pent-up public desire to see the power of cotton exercised, here was an opportunity to present Britain and France with the choice of breaking the blockade or risking economic disaster, but not as the official policy of the Confederacy.

Beginning in New Orleans, where the cotton factors urged the planters to keep back their cotton, the embargo rapidly spread to Mobile, Savannah, and Charleston. Encouraged by such mundane considerations as the cost of bagging, which had tripled in a few months, by the higher insurance premiums charged at seaports where the cotton was most vulnerable to Northern raids, and then by the refusal of insurance brokers to provide any coverage at all, planters across the Confederacy held back their crop. Meanwhile, the Confederate government launched a more orthodox diplomatic campaign against the blockade. The British were provided with an excuse to denounce it, and thereby fore-stall the humiliating charge that they had been coerced by the Southern planters. Through Trescot, Hunter had made known to Bunch the Confederacy's expectation that the same Anglo-French concern "which led to the desire on their part for the accession of the Confederate States" to the principles of the Declaration of Paris "would induce them to watch with utmost strictness the violation of the rule in relation to blockade by the United States." To this the British consul replied that he had reported to Lord John Russell how "utterly and ludicrously ineffectual" the blockade of North and South Carolina was.[32] He also suggested a tactic to the South. If the Confederate collectors of customs would furnish a history of the blockade at each port he would forward it privately to the foreign secretary. When he informed Hunter of this suggestion, Trescot advised the new secretary of state to embody such a report in his instructions to the Confederate commissioners, while a copy could be sent to Bunch. Three weeks later, on August 24, Hunter forwarded to Yancey, Rost, and Mann reports from the collectors at Charleston, Savannah, Wilmington, and Pensacola. "These reports furnish conclusive evidence that the blockade of the coast of the Confederate States is nominal, not real," he commented. Therefore it was "in contravention of the now universally accepted law of nations," and every seizure, every hindrance of foreign vessels was "illegal and void."[33]

This decision to concentrate on the blockade coincided with the disbanding of the Confederate Commission. The three commissioners had not escaped criticism for the Confederacy's failure to secure recognition and to bring an end to the blockade. Toombs left office grumbling privately that the newspapers gave "better accounts of the state of things in Europe" and were "much better informed,"[34] and Rhett's *Mercury* took them publicly to task. European confidence in the South was not to be won "by humble entreaty" and "back door diplomacy."[35] Yet most observers conceded that there were mitigating factors—the failure of the Davis administration to provide them with the proper instructions and the weakness inherent in a collective mission. What was required were individual representatives at the courts of the major powers, and on July 31 a resolution was introduced into the Confederate Congress instructing the Committee on Foreign Affairs "to inquire into the expediency of providing by law for sending and accrediting ministers of the Confederate States to the several governments of England, France and Spain."[36] By August 21 Davis had signed a bill that authorized him to appoint two additional commissioners to Europe and to determine to what nations they and the men already in Europe should be accredited. On August 24 Hunter wrote to inform the commission that Rost had been selected to represent the Confederacy in Spain. Four days later James M. Mason was nominated as commissioner to England and John Slidell as commissioner to France. The following month saw Mann instructed to undertake the mission to Belgium. In the meantime Yancey had decided to resign.

Temperamentally unsuited for the patient, discreet, and obscure role to which the realities of international politics condemned him, Yancey had become increasingly aware that he would not be returning home quickly, sporting the feather of British recognition in his political cap. The task was proving far more difficult than either he or the government had bargained for. "Had I known the trouble and delay involved in this mission," he confided to a friend early in July, "I should never have accepted it."[37] The plain truth was that cotton was not King in Europe, merely "one of the greatest of commercial elements." Unfortunately for the South, Britain and France had no immediate need of it. Estimating that their existing stocks would carry them through until December or January, he saw little hope of any change in their policy of strict neutrality before then. Increasingly he and his fellow commissioners turned to the blockade as "the great lever" which would eventually "decide the relations between Europe and the South." They were convinced that it would be "watched closely and with increasing interest" by the British, who would apply "the most rigid interpretations of international law" to the test of its legitimacy.[38] Nor did news of Bull Run cause them to change their stance. Although this victory was the "favourable event" for which they had long been holding themselves in readiness, although as recently as July 15 they had agreed to seize just such an opportunity to demand official recognition of their presence and to push the question "to a determination," by August 7 they entertained "no hope" that the British were ready to acknowledge Confederate independence. It was still Britain's intention to declare the blockade ineffectual, they believed, but after this step she would be "more decidedly neutral" than ever in order to furnish no further cause of offence to the United States. Therefore, she would hold the question of recognition in abeyance "until it had been practically settled between the two belligerent powers, by such an over-whelming military success upon one side or the other, as to render it a matter of no doubt in European eyes which will eventually triumph."[39]

Their doubts about the diplomatic significance of Bull Run did not prevent the commissioners from trying to exploit the Confederate victory. Their spirits were lifted by a constant stream of callers offering congratulations. "I could not imagine that there was such an amount of ardent sympathy for the cause of my country as has manifested itself," wrote the exultant Mann to his friend William Gregory.[40] So they decided to seek another informal interview with Russell before settling whether to ask "for a public and official acknowledgment of their character." Refused permission to call upon him, they were obliged to communicate in writing and on August 14 they addressed a long note to the foreign secretary. They expressed pleasure at the recognition of Confederate belligerency and pain at the closing of British ports to prizes. They emphasized their earlier forbear-ance in not pressing for diplomatic recognition, thereby saving Britain from a crisis with the United States. They denied that the cause of the North was the cause of human freedom, citing as proof the resolutions passed by the United States Congress after Bull Run, which declared that the war was being fought to up-hold the constitution and to enforce the laws. Many of these laws were proslavery, they reminded Russell. Consequently, anti-slavery sentiment in Britain could have no sympathy with the Union. On the contrary, it had ample reason to be disgusted with the "canting hypocrisy" of the North, which was acting out of base feelings of self-aggrandizement and revenge rather than the "high philanthropic considerations" beating in the hearts of many Englishmen.

These critical yet flattering remarks merely served as a lengthy preamble to the note's substance, a tentative request for recog-nition and a confident reminder that the time was fast approach-ing for a denial of the blockade's legality. The cotton-picking season had already begun and a fair crop would be prepared for market but not delivered to Southern wharves until there was a prospect of the blockade being raised. Raise the blockade or do without cotton was the message here, although the commissioners stressed that ample legal grounds existed to justify this action publicly. The Union was guilty at worst of proclaiming a paper blockade and at best of establishing an ineffective one, they charged. Thus the blockade of all the ports of the South "was declared to have commenced by the blockading officer off Charleston, when in truth, at that time and for weeks after there was no pretense of a blockade of the gulf." In effect, then, the commission and the Confederate government, quite independently of one another, had reached the same conclusion and founded much the same policy upon it. The South should concentrate on the blockade rather than on recognition, for the threat of a cotton famine was certain to induce the hungry British to raise the former but not necessarily to grant the latter.

The certainty of the blockade being raised by the beginning of the new year was an inducement not strong enough to hold Yancey in his place as a commissioner. There was little chance of any immediate change in the British government's attitude, as Russell's reply to the commissioner's note quickly made plain, and Yancey was reluctant to wait either for the inevitable exhaustion of the cotton stocks or a series of Confederate military victories. He was restless and he began to brood upon the difficulties of his position. He and the other commissioners were acutely conscious of their isolation. They were isolated from the Confederate government, from whom they had not even received an acknowledgement of the receipt of any of their despatches. They had no "regular mode of communicating" with the Department of State and had "no funds with which to organize the means of forwarding despatches."[41] The lack of instructions from home led to disagreements over what they should do. Should they wait in Britain for recognition or should they press their claim for it to the point of a British refusal and then go on to other European nations? Such disagreements emphasized the weakness of a collective mission. A "Commission of three persons can act effectually only when entirely agreed," they admitted in a despatch, and they asked for "full instructions from the President, under the altered condition of affairs," to help them reach a "concord of views."[42] Unknown to them this difficulty had been recognized in Richmond and was about to be remedied by the dissolution of the commission.

Isolated from their own government the Confederate commissioners were kept at arm's length by that of Britain. "It is perhaps proper also to state that the Commission has not received the least notice or attention, official or social, from any member of the Government since its arrival in England," they reported.[43] That same day, August 7, they learnt that they would no longer be admitted to informal interviews with Russell. For the restless, ambitious Yancey, this sense of being far from the centre of affairs was a particularly heavy burden. Unlike Mann, he was not used to long periods of diplomatic service overseas, nor was he a political nonentity like Rost, for whom appointment to the commission had come as an entirely unexpected distinction. He had been an influential politician, a man who was a mover of affairs, who inspired and drew inspiration from the crowd. He longed to hear about "public matters—men and politics and their combinations." He missed his family and heard from them very infrequently. He was concerned about his finances and his health. He was "fattening and growing gray" in London, his bowels were "not right" and his back continually pained him.[44] Lonely, unhappy, unwell, worried and homesick, seeing little hope of his brief diplomatic career being crowned by some rapid triumph, perhaps feeling more than a little useless, Yancey wanted to go home and he decided to resign and return to Alabama as soon as he could be replaced.

The calculation of Britain's cotton stocks which enabled even the unhappy Yancey to regard the blockade's days as numbered was accepted as accurate by Charles Francis Adams. But the American minister was not at all settled in his mind whether December would see an attempt to "impeach the laws of blockade."[45] He could take some comfort from the fact that the British had always shown more interest in providing for the threatened dearth by encouraging cotton production in other parts of the world than in raising the blockade. Nor did the prospect of a Southern embargo produce any marked change in this public attitude. Discussing the "Threatened Famine of Cotton," the *Economist* continued to deny that Britain and France could be driven by distress in their manufacturing districts to raise the blockade. This would amount to a declaration of war on the Union, it warned in July. Anyway, it remained convinced that so long as cotton was grown it would find its way to market. Southern cotton would seep through leaks in the blockade, while the rise in the price of the fibre, as the Southern supply fell off, would stimulate production in India, Egypt, and elsewhere.

This midsummer concern with the bleak winter that threatened the textile industry was shared by Palmerston, who thought it wise "to put one's house in wind and water tight condition against the time when foul weather may come on." In a letter to the president of the Board of Trade he asked whether that or any other Department had "any means of procuring or of helping to procure any where in the wide world a subsidiary supply of cotton?" The prime minister expected little of the manufacturers themselves, for they were some of "the most helpless and short-sighted of men—They are like the people who held out their dishes and prayed that it might rain plum puddings." They had been looking to India as an alternative source of supply for years, "but their looks seem to have had only the first effect of the rattlesnake viz: to paralyse the object looked at, and as yet it has shewn no signs of falling into their jaws." What had the Board of Trade done, or what could it do, he asked, to stimulate supply from Africa, India, Australia, Fiji Islands, Syria, and Egypt? "If active measures were taken in time to draw from these places such quantities of cotton as might be procured, some portion at least of the probable falling off of this next year might be made good, and our demand this year would make a better supply spring up for future years."[46]

Thomas Milner Gibson quickly informed Palmerston that his department was awake to this problem. The Board of Trade was doing all that it could, he replied. Of course, as one of the original pupils of the Manchester School, he saw no way in which the Board could "take any direct part in procuring an additional supply of cotton beyond that which the manufacturers and merchants can get for themselves." Yet Gibson acknowledged that these men could not be counted on to provide the cotton that was soon going to be required. The Cotton Supply Association had failed to take up Lord John Russell's earlier offer of the services of British consuls, nor had it suggested any way in which "the agency of the Government could be made directly useful to them," he reported.[47] In fact neither the Association nor the government was quite as inert as Gibson thought. A mission organized by the Association was already preparing to leave for Egypt and India, and its visit to Egypt resulted in the despatch of superior seed and detailed instructions for planting and cultivation to the producers there. As for India, Sir Charles Wood promised in the Commons on July 25 that the government would do its utmost to improve communications between the cotton growing interior and the coast. Yet this did not amount to a significant change of policy, for the approved program of public works was a modest one, it had been long delayed, and was to be delayed long into 1862. Nor did Wood give any commitment to stimulate directly cotton cultivation. Indeed, all that the Indian government felt able to do was to offer prizes for the quality and quantity of cotton produced. Nevertheless, Palmerston's loyal *Morning Post* had to defend even this modest measure from "Economists of a certain school" who objected in principle "to State interference of this description."[48]

Although Gibson was convinced that the government could do little and believed that the merchants had done less to ensure that cotton continued to reach Britain in quantity, he found reason to hope that Lancashire would weather the crisis. He was sure that news of an event as momentous as the American war would quickly spread around the world, stimulating "to the highest degree" the activity of everyone interested in the growth or trade of cotton. They would respond to the prospects of high prices and great gains. Indeed, India had already increased her shipments to Britain. There were reported to be 310,000 bales on their way from the subcontinent, he informed Palmerston on July 9, which was 75,000 bales more than the quantity at the same period in 1860. Substantial as this increase was, it was no more than a drop in the ocean of Britain's need. The answer to the problem lay in America, and Gibson, no less than the other members of the government, doubted that the United States could mount an effectual blockade. Presumably, cotton would find its way to Europe through the many leaks and these, moreover, would provide Britain with the grounds on which to challenge the blockade's legality.

Meanwhile Robert Bunch was busy feeding the British government's scepticism about the blockade. In a despatch that reached England on July 11 he reported that vessels had been warned off Savannah although no blockade had been established at the Georgia port, and that the blockade off Charleston had been lifted between May 15 and May 29. During that period six vessels had entered the port and five of them had cleared it again. Whatever the intention of the United States government, the consul concluded, "it is perfectly clear that the Blockade was utterly and entirely ineffective and null for nearly fifteen days."[49] From Milne came the news that a British vessel had been warned off all the ports south of Chesapeake Bay. Turning once again to the Queen's advocate for an opinion, the Foreign Office asked whether such a warning was proper, in the light of the reported imperfections of the blockade, and whether the British government should request from the United States a declaration of the existence of an effective blockade.

The reply that Harding gave was as cautious as his earlier advice in May. He found no serious cause of complaint against the enforcement of the blockade. On the contrary, he was of the opinion that the blockading officers had performed their duties liberally and courteously. Nor did he see any advantage in a general declaration, for the practice the United States was following, in giving each individual vessel notice, was far more beneficial to neutral interests. As for the vessel warned off all the ports south of Chesapeake Bay, she had been en route for the West Indies, therefore he saw no reason to complain, for she had not been injured even by an incorrect notice of blockade. In short, he continued to stress the desirability of avoiding irritating discussions with the United States, at least until there was some strong case of wrong to a British subject for which there was no other redress except intervention. These were the only conditions, he believed, on which Britain should impeach "the validity of the blockade either generally or in any particular instance."[50] There were prize courts in the United States that claimed to administer the law of nations correctly and impartially, he reminded Russell. Thus any British subject who considered the seizure of or interference with his vessel illegal should take his complaint there in the first instance. Above all, Harding called for more information. Regular and accurate reports on the condition of the blockade were vital, he insisted, if the government was to be in a position to support those British subjects who claimed to have been injured by an illegal blockade.

Submitted on July 27, at the height of the crisis created by the news that Congress had empowered Lincoln to declare the Southern ports closed, Harding's dispassionate opinion was promptly endorsed. That same day Russell instructed Lyons to call the attention of consuls in the South to the need for particular information on the state of the blockade in their area, information that would supplement the reports that the Admiralty was receiving from Milne. And neither the easing of tension over the act declaring the Southern ports closed nor the Confederate success at Bull Run brought any change of policy. Writing to Lyons on August 9, Russell instructed the minister "to make every enquiry short of an application to the United States Government, with the view of ascertaining the manner in which the blockade is conducted."[51] However, the danger of an Anglo-American collision over the blockade's effectiveness was still present. The Union's attempt to remove this contentious issue, by claiming authority over the Southern ports, had failed. The South meanwhile was doing all that it could to bring on a crisis by preventing cotton escaping through the leaks. As for Britain, Charles Francis Adams was sure that she would welcome an excuse to violate the blockade and this her consuls could be expected to provide. Their reports on the blockade's effectiveness would arrive in a Britain where the stocks of cotton had begun to fall at an alarming rate, just as the traditional cotton shipping season opened.

SEVEN

Britain rests on her oars

CHARLES FRANCIS ADAMS RECEIVED THE NEWS of the defeat and panic at Bull Run on August 4. It came as a hard blow and he briefly gave way to despair. "The division of the country is now certain," he wrote in his diary for August 8. "The question only remains to decide whether slavery shall be abolished in Maryland, Virginia and Missouri while there is time." He quickly found his way out of this dark pit, by following the glimmer of his nation's providential destiny, but he still had to suffer the amused contempt of the English. A brave and dogged people themselves, they had "little mercy for weakness, physical or moral," and they were encouraged to ridicule the Union army's conduct by the reports of William Howard Russell. The correspondent of the *Times* graphically portrayed and pungently analysed the collapse of the Northern forces into "miserable, causeless panic." But the English derided the Union's political system as much as its sorry military performance. It was clearer than ever that democracy and republican government were not synonymous with peace and prosperity. The United States had embarked on a war that she intended to finance by loans not taxation, which would leave her in five years with a larger national debt than that of Britain. Judging the future by the present, the *Times* commented sardonically, "it will not surprise us if we live to hear our cousins boasting that their Budgets are the most exorbitant and their National Debt the biggest and the most rapid growth in creation."[1] Yet much of this derision was vicarious. It was at Bright and his fellow Americanizers that elements of the press were really taking aim.

Word of Bull Run reached Britain as a parliamentary by-election, in which Bright was campaigning on behalf of a fellow Radical, was being held in South Lancashire. In a speech at Rochdale Town Hall on August 1, he had broken a public silence to defend and praise the Union. The American Republic had "never fought for the 'balance of power' in Europe," or to keep up "a decaying Empire," it had not squandered the money of its people, while the amount it was raising "in the great emergency of this grievous war" was no greater than what Britain raised "every year during a time of peace." The American war, successful or not, Christian or not, wise or not, was a war to "sustain the government and to sustain the authority of a great nation," and if the British were true to their own sympathies and history they would withhold sympathy from those who wished "to build up a great empire on the perpetual bondage of millions of their countrymen."[2] This provocative language, with its implication that the Jefferson Bricks were at their usual place "in the van of human civilization and moral purity," did not aid the Radical candidate. He was tarred with the brush of Americanizer and his Conservative opponent was returned for the constituency.

But American democracy and John Bright were not bereft of sympathizers and friends. The *Spectator*'s expressions of sympathy for the Union after Bull Run were genuine, and the *Morning Star and Dial*, having forsaken peace at any price to follow Bright in calling for a Northern victory, took other organs to task for their "columns of scornful comment." *Reynolds's Newspaper* vigorously disputed that Bull Run could be interpreted as evidence of the incompetence of democracy. The victors were as democratic as the vanquished, it reminded the "English Middle Class." Yet neither these dissenting voices nor the frank admission by the *Times* that many of its criticisms were provoked by the "panegyrics" of America's friends, changed Adams's opinion "that as a whole the English are pleased with our misfortunes." There never had been any "real goodwill" toward the United States, he fretted, "and the appearance of it of late years was only the effect of their fears of our prosperity and our growing strength." The feeling that prevailed in Britain was "unfriendly and jealous."[3]

The minister found ample evidence of this unfriendliness in the British government's tolerance of the activities of the Southern military and naval purchasing agents. Soon after the organization of the Confederacy, Caleb Huse had been sent to England to purchase arms and he was followed by James Bulloch and James North who it was hoped would purchase or have constructed a Confederate navy. Of these agents and those who came after them Bulloch was with good reason the most feared by the Union. He disembarked at Liverpool on June 4 and within a month, aided by the Liverpool firm of Fraser, Trenholm and Company, which soon became the South's British banker, had purchased "a fair quantity of naval supplies on their credit," and had "laid the keel of the first foreign built Confederate cruiser."[4] All of this was perfectly legal, Bulloch had learned. Eminent legal counsel provided the Confederate agent with the loopholes in the Foreign Enlistment Act through which a Southern navy could sail. It was neither the purchase nor the building of vessels that the law prohibited, the lawyers reported, but their being equipped "with the intent to cruise against a friendly state."[5] By taking care to conceal his purpose Bulloch quickly threatened to reduce the Act to a nullity.

Union agents and representatives did their utmost to keep track of the Confederates, hoping to expose their activities and defeat their object. The ubiquitous Henry Shelton Sanford, the United States minister to Belgium, revelled in his other duties as the head of secret service operations in Europe. He recruited a force of private detectives to spy on the Southerners, which they did with as little stealth as success. Indignant at these supposedly surreptitious operations, embarrassed by the publicity given to them by the English press, annoyed by Sanford's flitting in and out of Britain, and critical of the expense, Adams was successful in having this organization disbanded early in 1862. Instead of spies the minister preferred to rely upon the regular agents of the government—the consuls. At Liverpool the acting consul, Henry Wilding, maintained a close watch on the port, the docks, and Fraser, Trenholm and Company. He obtained an assurance of the vigilance of the customs collectors and the dock police in watching for any violation of the Proclamation of Neutrality, and he employed his own private detective. It was from Wilding that the American legation heard on August 14 of the loading of an armed vessel with munitions at West Hartlepool. This report brought Adams hurrying back to London from a tour in the country with his family.

In a note to Russell, he called his attention to the vessel, the *Bermuda*. It was "ostensibly owned" by Fraser, Trenholm, "well known to consist in part of Americans in sympathy with the insurgents," was armed with four guns, and had been taking on "crates and barrels suspected of being munitions" for the South.

The cargo was "nominally entered or destined to Havana" but the armament and cargo plainly indicated that the vessel was on an errand neither of mercy nor peace. And as she was believed to be about to sail Adams called for a "prompt and effective investigation" whilst there was time.[6] The United States asked for nothing more than the simple enforcement of the law, he remarked. He soon discovered that the task of frustrating Bulloch and his colleagues was going to be anything but simple. Although Russell promptly answered that he had "lost no time" in forwarding the information to the proper department, a full week passed before the British government gave its reply. By that time the *Bermuda* had sailed, but Adams's disappointment in this particular instance was less overwhelming than his sense of the hopelessness of ever securing effective British action. The law officers, Russell informed the American on August 22, had advised him that there was insufficient evidence to interfere with the sailing of the *Bermuda* and that the Foreign Enlistment Act had "no reference to the mere nature of the cargo on board."[7]

To the minister the meaning of this refusal to seize the vessel was clear. No assistance could be expected from the British in preventing military supplies reaching the South. Nor was he wrong. The Home Office was being kept informed of the extensive arms sales to both belligerents by the police. It forwarded the reports to the Foreign Office along with the opinion that there was no distinction in the law between munitions and other articles of merchandise. When Britain was at peace they could be sent to any part of the world; it was up to belligerents to protect themselves. Deducing this, Adams decided that all he could hope to do was to gather information and send it home in time for the vessels carrying munitions to be intercepted. In this resigned mood he refrained from any protest at the fitting out of a second vessel laden with arms, the *Fingal*, early in October. Russell was "so completely inclined to repose on the arms of the Law Officers," the minister explained to Seward, "that I shall despair of every attempt to wake him up hereafter by any appeal of my making."[8] The news that the *Bermuda* had successfully run the blockade with her cargo of weapons made him despair also of the Union navy's ability to put a stop to the trade.

This air of discouragement met Captain Alexander Schultz when he strode into the American legation on September 2. He carried Bunch's consular bag and bore Seward's instructions requesting the consul's recall. The revelation that the British and French consuls had been negotiating with the Confederacy did little to lift Adams's spirits. Sure that they would not have taken this step on their own initiative, he feared that this episode would soon lead to "grave results." He spent almost a full day preparing two notes to Russell, in which he followed Seward's instructions closely. He explained how the consular bag had come into the possession of the United States, asked for the return of any treasonable correspondence, and detailed the reasons why Bunch should be recalled. In the mid-afternoon of September 3 the notes and the bag were delivered at the Foreign Office and Adams waited anxiously for a reply. It came ten days later, and was a flat refusal.

Russell admitted that the bag had contained private correspondence of British subjects, but retorted that this service had been provided as a "palliative" for the "inconvenience" and "evil" caused by the suspension of American postal arrangements, a suspension that contravened the treaty obligations of the United States. As for the consul's recall, the foreign secretary explained that Bunch had merely been following his instructions when he dealt with the Confederacy and for this the British government could not remove him. He ignored the complaints that Bunch had violated the requirement that all passports be countersigned by Seward and had issued one to a courier of Mure's questionable history. However, Russell did offer the United States some consolation. He disclaimed all responsibility for the alleged comment that the approach to the South on the declaration was the first step to recognition, and stated emphatically that the British government had not recognized the independence of the "so-called" Confederate States and was not prepared to do so. "This is the pith of the note," one member of the legation commented, "and is worth more than all the rest."[9] Yet explicit and welcome as Russell's statement was, for it helped to allay fears of recognition roused by press reports, it had not settled the Bunch affair. Seward was unlikely to let the matter rest, particularly as he had in his hand the means of forcing Bunch's withdrawal. He could revoke the consul's exequatur.

The American request for the removal of Bunch found Palmerston and Russell at odds with senior members of the cabinet on how to respond to the developments in the United States. The two "old ringleaders" wanted to increase yet again the military and naval forces in North America. They remained convinced that demonstrations were the most effective way of restraining the "swaggering bullies" across the Atlantic. Worried that Seward would "blow up the coals again" when he discovered that the British had not walked into the trap he had baited with the Declaration of Paris, the foreign secretary urged in mid-August that five line-of-battle ships be sent out to Milne during the autumn. With Russell behaving like a diminutive Palmerston, proposing to move a squadron rather than fleets, the prime minister concentrated on military reinforcements. He urged that the regulars' strength in Canada should be raised to "ten thousand troops of the line, with proportional artillery," for anything less would leave the province "in a State of Insecurity" during the months when communication was cut off by ice.[10] Indeed, he hoped to repeat the earlier dramatic exercise of using the *Great Eastern* as the troopship. But both men encountered stiff opposition from the service ministers concerned.

At the Admiralty, the Duke of Somerset did not see any political necessity for more vessels on the North American station and he provided Russell and Palmerston with a list of practical objections. He opposed the "diminishment" of the Home Squadron then practising "evolutions" at sea. Line-of-battle ships could not get into the shallow harbour at Bermuda. Milne's vessels were clearly sufficient to cope with anything that the Americans could put out against him, for while many of theirs were "sailers" his had the "weather gage [*sic*] below decks in the shape of the steam engines" which worked their screws.[11] Nor did Somerset forget to raise the spectres of desertion and inadequate supplies, but above all he protested the expense. He would have to commission ships to replace any sent to Milne, which would necessarily increase expenditures. "I am desirous of keeping down expenditures under other heads of expense," he wrote to the prime minister, "as we shall need to augment expenditure for iron-ships in our next budget."[12] Committed to the task of defeating France in the naval race, he was not keen to fight more battles than were absolutely necessary with the parsimonious chancellor of the exchequer, Gladstone. However, when pressed by Russell and Palmerston, he did agree to send to Milne an additional "Strong Frigate or perhaps two," vessels he described as equivalent to American sailing line-of-battle ships.

The prime minister's own plan, which Russell endorsed, to

raise British troop strength in Canada to ten thousand men was received without enthusiasm at the War Office. There, Sir George Cornewall Lewis had replaced the failing Sidney Herbert in July. Civilized, intellectual, more scholar than politician, Lewis was by temperament "sedate, cool and dispassionate," while his mind "was critical, slow to accept opinions or theories which he thought insufficiently verified."[13] On August 26 Palmerston wrote to him expressing the opinion that although there was no immediate danger of a European war relations with the United States were in a "ticklish condition." No reliance could be placed on Seward and Lincoln and the only security against "wrong insult and aggression on their part" was strength in Canada and off the American coast. The naval force was nearly sufficient and was about to be added to, he informed the war secretary, but the military force in the North American provinces was "far from sufficient." Ten thousand men should be stationed in Canada during the winter and they could be carried there by the *Great Eastern* before the St. Lawrence was closed to navigation. "If we are known to be ready and prepared we shall not be attacked," he concluded, "if we are thought to be weak and imperfectly prepared we shall be infallibly brought to grief."[14]

Lewis was sceptical of Palmerston's analysis of the situation. He considered the danger of a rebellion in Hungary and a war with Austria "more pressing" than that of war with the United States. After the debacle at Bull Run he was convinced that Northerners were preoccupied with the grim desire to give the South a good drubbing. "Their eyes will be turned southward, not northward," he replied. Yet he had to admit "that the men who get into power at Washington are a singularly reckless and unscrupulous set," and that it would be "a most unwise economy on our part to afford any temptation for an aggressive and insolent policy by appearing to be unprepared on our Canadian frontier."[15] Consequently, he ordered enquiries to be made at the Horse Guards to ascertain which regiments they would propose sending, and at the Admiralty to find out what transports would be available. This last enquiry brought an immediate protest from Somerset, who was no more willing to send military reinforcements than naval. The reasons he gave were climatic. The winter was the season when the Union must act vigorously against the South, presumably because it would then be cool, but was not the time of the year it would select for an invasion of frigid Canada. In full agreement with Lewis that there was no immediate danger to British North America, he was satisfied that the force already sent there was "sufficient to prove that England intends to protect that territory" and saw no reason "for sending more regiments at present."[16]

To the support of the dubious Lewis and the more adamant Somerset came a "more than doubtful" Newcastle. The colonial secretary had just secured a successor to Sir Edmund Head. He had not followed the retiring governor general's advice to appoint a military man, for the record of generals as governors was not a happy one. Nevertheless, Newcastle may have wished from time to time during the summer of 1861, as one civilian after another declined his offer of the post, that a military man could be ordered to accept. However, his persistence was eventually rewarded. On August 27 he was able to write to Head, who was growing anxious that his successor might not appear before the onset of winter, and his family had no wish to confront the Atlantic then, that Viscount Monck had accepted and would be leaving for Quebec at the beginning of October.

Suggested for the post by John Delane, the editor of the *Times*, the new governor did not lend distinction to what was the most important colonial post. An Anglo-Irish aristocrat, although Newcastle hastened to reassure Head that his geniality was "almost the only part of the Irish character he shows,"[17] Monck had held minor offices in the Aberdeen and the first Palmerston governments. He had lost his parliamentary seat in the 1857 election and his treasury post with Palmerston's fall in 1858, and he failed in a bid for re-election in 1859. At best he appeared to be a man marked for junior positions. He had impressed those under whom he served as "a man of good sense and judgement, and of fair abilities and application,"[18] and Palmerston intended to offer him the comparatively insignificant office of Irish lord of the treasury. For his part, Monck accepted the governor-generalship because he was "very tired of doing nothing at home" and did not see "much chance" of an immediate return to office in England. Had he known that he could have had the Irish treasury he would probably still have chosen to go out to Canada. Not only was the office far more important but his tenure of it promised to be far more secure. He doubted the Palmerston government's ability to survive the forthcoming parliamentary session. John Bright had so damaged the Liberal cause in England, he wrote to a friend, that "even with Pam's great popularity" the government would "find it difficult to keep their legs after Parliament meets."[19]

Neither his appointment of an inexperienced and undistinguished successor to Head, for which he was sharply taken to task by the Radical and Conservative press alike, nor his earlier support for the sending of military reinforcements to Canada prevented Newcastle from adding his voice to those of Somerset and Lewis. He, like everyone else, was quick to deny that he placed any reliance "on the temper and disposition" of Seward and the Lincoln cabinet, but he was willing to rely upon the security provided by the course of events in the United States since June. It was now next to impossible, he thought, for the Union to divert its "warlike tendencies to Canada during the next 7 or 8 months," and it certainly could not do so until it had made a compromise with the Confederacy. Then there was the comforting lesson of Bull Run. Such an "ill-appointed" army could never invade Canada during the winter. "All the horrors of Moscow would be repeated." Telling as he considered these arguments to be, Newcastle must have realized that they might not prove weighty enough to restrain a prime minister of Palmerston's experience and skill in foreign affairs. Some less easily disputed objection was required, and this was what the colonial secretary provided. There were no barracks for more troops, he claimed, while to billet them in towns would be fatal. As most of the towns were close to the frontier, on the other side of which British soldiers could expect less discipline and more money, the "temptation to desertion" would be great and "the facilities more frequent" during the winter. The result would be a general demoralization of the British forces in North America. "If in the Spring matters look threatening," he added, "the Great Eastern will soon carry out as many Regiments as we want, and those Regiments will be in high order and fit for anything."[20]

To all these reasons for his opposition Newcastle might have added another. He had not forgotten the hostile reception given to the decision in June to send three regiments to Canada. Widely condemned as an unnecessary provocation to the United States, it had prompted "a nasty article" in the normally Palmerstonian *Times* and exposed him to Conservative assaults in

Parliament. The expedition was not powerful enough to defend the frontier nor necessary to garrison the towns, Benjamin Disraeli had charged, and the Americans would infer that there was on the part of the British cabinet suspicion, fear, and preparation for hostilities. As for the admitted danger of filibustering raids, "are there no inhabitants in Canada," he had gone on to ask, "are there not a numerous and gallant people there, accustomed to military discipline?" In sending troops the government had taken "this early opportunity of letting the people of Canada know that we are prepared to assume the monopoly of defending them," which was "rather calculated to damp their ardour and make them feel that it is not their business to protect their hearths and homes and national honour, and that they may pursue their profitable callings without coming forward in an emergency of this character." As colonial secretary, Newcastle bore a large measure of the responsibility for this violation of what Disraeli had termed the "tone and spirit of colonial policy adopted by Parliament" and "approved by the country."[21] Not surprisingly, he was anxious for the vindication that would be his if the British reinforcements served as a nucleus and inspiration for an army of Canadian volunteers.

By August there were encouraging reports from the province. The "miserably small" force of militia was at last growing in numbers and Newcastle's concern was that the arrival of more regulars would dampen the volunteering spirit. He had evidence enough of colonial opposition to any attempt to charge them "with a large portion of the burthen of defence in a war caused by interest in no degree of a local or Colonial character,"[22] by which the Canadians meant any war with the United States, to risk strengthening it. That the departure of regulars would be trumpeted as proof of the government's acceptance of the colonial position, not only in Canada but also in England, was never in doubt. For when someone leaked to the *Times* the news that plans were afoot to order another three regiments to Canada, it responded with another "nasty article." As a demonstration, the newspaper asked, what would these reinforcements demonstrate? It could not plausibly be argued that the provision of two men for every mile of Canadian frontier would overawe the Americans. On the other hand, if intended as a pledge to the Canadians that they could rely on Britain, "It is the enunciation of a principle that Quebec and Toronto and Montreal have nothing to do with a Canadian war, and that they may buy and sell and live at ease, for that Yorkshire and Lancashire and Middlesex will work for their defence."[23]

Yet this opposition within and outside the government did not immediately convince Palmerston to withdraw his proposal. His concern was less with the inexpediency of appearing to concede British responsibility for Canadian defence and more with the damage to Britain's prestige and power should the province be lost. "Theoretical political Economists may discuss at their leisure the question as to the value of Colonies to the Mother Country," he remarked scornfully in a note to his one firm supporter, Russell, "but no man with half an eye in his head, or half an idea in his brain could fail to perceive what a lowering of the position of England in the world would follow the conquest of our North American Provinces by the North Americans, especially after Bulls Run Races."[24] For the prime minister the essence of the problem was simple: Canada must be defended and to defend it Britain had to have troops there, not to throw the Americans back but to discourage them from attack. It was quite impossible for "European ingenuity to foresee the countless tricks and subtleties upon which the North Americans might contrive to pick a quarrel" with Britain, he warned Lewis and Newcastle. The defeat at Bull Run might cool the Northerners' ardour "and lower their hopes as against the South" but it would "rather tend to turn their thoughts of compensation towards the north," while the subsequent reorganization of the Union army by General McClellan would "afford them the belief that they have better means of accomplishing their desires." And if the North was unlikely to attack Canada during the bitter winter months there were periods during autumn and spring when it would be far easier for the North to campaign than for Britain to maintain communication with the province. There was only one way to ensure peace with men who had "no sense of honour" and who were "swayed by the passions of irresponsible masses and by a reckless desire to hold their Positions by all and any means," and that was to be manifestly strong and determined.[25]

Palmerston also challenged the argument that the regulars sent out in June had been sufficient to demonstrate Britain's resolution. It was not simply the "small force" actually despatched but the "expectation that more would follow" that had had such "a wholesome effect upon the tone and temper of Lincoln and Seward," he countered. The fears that more British troops would mean less Canadian self-defence were brushed aside. He continued to insist that reinforcements would "give spirit and confidence" to the Canadians, thereby encouraging the formation of militia companies. Finally, the prime minister found no security for Canada in the "strict concert" with France. He accepted that the United States wanted to avoid a quarrel with Britain and France combined or the French alone. France could hit them hard at sea, he reasoned, while they had "no arm long enough to reach France in return." But the Northerners' attitude toward Britain was quite different. They believed that they could "indemnify themselves in Canada" for any damage that Britain inflicted on them at sea, and "we are not to suppose that our dear friend and ally at the Tuileries would take up the cudgels for us in any dispute in which we might have been singled out for attack," Palmerston concluded.[26] These were the political grounds on which he continued to press for a substantial increase in the number of British regulars in North America. Yet he had not answered Newcastle's one practical objection, and this he admitted. If there were no barracks available that might be a reason for not sending any more men, Palmerston conceded. This was the weakness in his case and it was quickly exploited by Lewis and Newcastle.

The war secretary had received fresh ammunition from Canada, where a shortage of barracks had already forced one regiment to remain under canvas for some time. This news strengthened Newcastle's opposition to the sending of reinforcements and he continued to plug away at the danger of "loss by desertion and the demoralizing effects of imperfect accommodation during a long winter."[27] However, on the other side Palmerston and Russell were rearmed by the Bunch affair.

As both Russell and Palmerston were out of London, the American request for the consul's recall went to the permanent under-secretary, Edmund Hammond. He lost no time in sounding the alarm. The United States intended to pick a quarrel with Britain, he wrote to them both, for Seward could hardly have supposed that it would be complied with. Was the next step going to be the dismissal of Lyons? With this thought in mind and at Palmerston's suggestion, Russell wrote privately to the minister instructing him to go to Canada in the event that he was presented with his passports. "This would look like giving the Washingtonians an opportunity to settle matters in a friendly way," the prime minister explained, "and Lyons might be able to give our People in Canada Information about matters in the States, which might be useful."[28] Of course, the only sure way of persuading the Americans to be reasonable was to strengthen the British forces in North America. Russell, savouring vindication, expressed regret that Somerset had opposed his plan to send a squadron to Milne. "It would have inspired respect," he asserted, "and we might have been saved this trouble."[29] Palmerston responded characteristically. The government "must immediately send more troops to Canada and more ships to Milne."[30] But both men quickly discovered that the spectre of another Crampton affair was not enough to thin the ranks of their ministerial opponents. On the contrary, they were swollen by a number of fresh recruits.

A report in the *Times* on September 2, that an additional three regiments were about to be ordered to Canada, served as a recruitment notice to ministers not involved in the original discussions and still relaxing in the country. Sir George Grey, the Duke of Argyll, and Gladstone all signalled their disapproval of what they regarded as an unnecessary, expensive irritant to Anglo-American relations. Before this growing opposition Russell and Palmerston at last undertook a strategic withdrawal. The foreign secretary was the first to give ground. On September 14 he admitted to Palmerston that Newcastle's objections had made "some impression" on him. The prime minister soon fell back to join him. He conceded that Somerset had impressed him with his argument that to send more ships to Milne was to invite desertions. One of the royal princes had recently returned from North America on a vessel that had lost many men while on station. And however dubious he remained of the merit of Newcastle's objections, for the redeployment of the troops in Canada had been proposed as a solution to the barracks problem, Palmerston was willing to postpone any decision on reinforcements until word had been received of Seward's reaction to the refusal to remove Bunch. "If they take our answer quietly well and good, and we may perhaps wait till the spring," he wrote to Russell. "The next Fortnight or three weeks will probably throw light on the subject."[31]

At least one minister's anxiety that the United States not be provoked, even if that meant sacrificing Bunch, was rooted in the fear that a far more serious difficulty than that of the consul was looming. If it came, Gladstone did not want to have "the decks encumbered with the relics of former and perhaps frivolous quarrels." The "very ugly question" that he saw in the offing was whether "to respect the American Blockade up to the point of enduring for its sake not only heavy losses in a general sense but great public evils and possibly political and social dangers."[32] From the tone of the press it seemed unlikely that it could be avoided for as long as the chancellor hoped.

The claims of Harriet Beecher Stowe, that abolition was the cause of the war and the eradication of slavery justified it, drew a scornful public response and were dismissed as a "mischievous misrepresentation" of the facts. The Americans' frustration of British efforts to suppress the slave trade was recalled, as was the persecution of the abolitionists in the North, the detestation and oppression of the blacks there, and the Northern willingness to compromise with the South during the secession crisis. The Civil War was being fought by the South for independence and by the North for Union, and while it readily conceded that abolition would eventually become an issue in the conflict, the *Times* declared that the time had long passed for any appeal for sympathy based upon Britain's humanitarianism. Only a declaration of war on slavery at the outset of the crisis could have won British sympathy. Thus delivered from moral qualms, the press turned the public's attention to material considerations. Rising fears of the exhaustion of the cotton stocks, as short time spread in Lancashire, led to an increasing emphasis on the blockade's ineffectiveness. Among the members of American legation in London there was little doubt that the "suffering interests" were organizing a "violent push" to solve their problems through a government announcement of the blockade's illegality and a promise of protection for British merchants who ran it.

No major organ was more direct in its approach to the problem of the cotton supply and the blockade than *Reynolds's Newspaper*, which claimed to speak for those who would suffer most during a cotton famine. Having satisfied itself that the cause of the North was not the cause of freedom, it put the issue simply enough on September 29—"England must break the Blockade, or Her Millions will starve." Insufficiently effective to be recognized in international law, the blockade was not "sufficiently ineffective to render it innocuous to Britain's commerce and manufactures." And to those who said that to break the blockade was to provoke war with the United States, *Reynolds's* retorted that the Northerners were not such idiots as to embark on a foreign war as well as a Civil one, and that even if they were it was "Better to fight the Yankees than starve our operatives." Nor was this newspaper as unrepresentative of working-class opinion in Lancashire as has traditionally been implied. It was not under the control of workers, but its solution for the problems of the textile regions was endorsed by those that were, such as the *Bee-Hive* and *The Working Man.*

The truth was that the reality of short time and the prospect of unemployment brought working-class calls for the breaking of the blockade and the recognition of the South. This was not surprising. Those operatives in and around the Yorkshire textile town of Halifax, who had invested in cooperative mills over the previous year or two, mills that seemed certain to be some of the first to go bankrupt, were threatened not only with unemployment but the loss of their life's savings. In Lancashire, where as many as two million people subsisted all but exclusively on cotton, public opinion was "almost unanimously adverse to the Northern cause," the American consul at Manchester, Henry Lord, reported.[33] Only in Rochdale, where Bright had his mill, could the operatives be relied upon to support it. Yet Bright's very commitment to that cause, which he had publicly affirmed at Rochdale Town Hall on August 1, helped to alienate some influential trades union leaders from it. Men who remembered the Chartist movement, who recalled the opposition of Bright and Cobden to the factory reform movement, were convinced of the Radicals' perfidy. But union leaders were joined in their opposition to the Northern cause by those who were unreconciled to capitalism, who looked upon the manufacturing capitalists of the North as a greater enemy of the workingman than the landowning oligarchy portrayed as the dominant force in the Confederacy.

Suspecting that the Palmerston government "would not be unwilling to see a demand from Lancashire for some interference with the blockade,"[34] Bright strove to still the agitation of the "suffering interests." It was to the operatives that he had addressed his warning at Rochdale that to break the blockade meant a war with the United States, from which few working

people would profit, "to say nothing at all of the manifest injustice and wrong against all international law, that a legal and
effective blockade should be interfered with by another country."[35] The safety of the cotton on which Lancashire depended
rested on the success of the United States government, he
declared. Cheered in Rochdale, this argument proved less persuasive elsewhere. Yet Bright's was not a lone voice. The Bradford
member of Parliament and textile manufacturer, W. E. Forster,
that "strangely uncouth, large-limbed" man whose manners were
"as little cultivated as his appearance,"[36] delivered a lecture on
the war at the local mechanics' institute on October 1, having
first ensured that it would be reported in the *Times* and thus
be widely read by the more influential sections of the nation.
Perhaps there was some truth to the charge that he spoke out so
boldly on this topic in order to make his political mark quickly,
for he had been elected to Parliament only in February. Nor
were his constituents suffering as a result of the war. The French
demand for their worsteds, thanks to Cobden's treaty, more than
made up for the loss of the American market. Certainly none of
Forster's listeners on October 1 disputed his opinion that it
would be to every Englishman's eternal disgrace to interfere on
behalf of the South and slavery. Any breach of international law
"by infraction of a legitimate blockade, or by premature recognition of the Southern Confederacy, contrary to the international
rules which we ourselves have laid down," he charged, "would be
such intervention."[37]

In less overt activities, Bright was joined by Cobden. They
were not as one in their attitude toward the war, for the older
man's main concern was peace not a Northern victory. He hoped
that the awful price, in men and monies, would induce the com-
batants to come to terms with one another, and was most anxious
to prevent Britain becoming involved in the struggle. He pressed
Bright to draw closer to men such as Forster who was well-
connected with the chambers of commerce. It was vital to organize among other branches of manufacturing a countervailing
force to the cotton dealers and brokers who were certain to hound
the government into hostile measures against the North. Without their support on questions like America, he argued, "We
shall be nothing but the voice in the wilderness."[38] But Bright
was sceptical of his ability to harness the chambers. They were
admirers of Palmerston and Russell. "There is an inveterate

flunkeyism which pervades nearly all the newly rich or the money-making men in these districts and I have little faith in their latent powers," he replied sourly.[39] Nor was Forster much more optimistic when Cobden approached him. The chambers would be difficult to handle, he warned, "the purely commercial interests being so strong."[40] Yet both he and Bright agreed to do what they could, even though they feared it would be little.

Bright also gave thought to what Cobden could do, beyond being a liberal with advice. He urged him to take advantage of the close relationship established with Gladstone during negotiation of the Anglo-French commercial treaty. It was important that the chancellor should not keep to his own department and leave the "fire-brands of the Foreign Office" to pile up "material for a future conflagration."[41] Cobden was reluctant. Their confidential relations had been confined to the one subject and Gladstone had not encouraged him to break fresh ground, he replied. There was "the gulf of separation which always prevents one from holding very familiar intercourse with a *Cabinet Minister*, and which makes me feel estranged even from Gibson, whilst towards [Charles] Villiers I seem to feel as if we had never a thought in common instead of our having been for seven years in constant correspondence." Indeed, in Gladstone's case the gulf was all the wider because of his "fastidious," "conscientious," even "pedantic," character. He was just as fastidious himself, Cobden admitted, "and perhaps even more sensitive" when it came to the question of forcing himself upon others.[42]

Whatever the cause, whether inhibitions or inability, Bright and Cobden were clearly having little success in creating a counterweight to any pressure for intervention in the American war. Meanwhile, the "suffering interests" continued to suffer and more deeply. By the beginning of October almost the entire cotton trade was on short time, the mills working no more than four days each week. "Multitudes are agitating for a recognition of the Confederates," Consul Lord reported home from Manchester, "but as that would have no favorable effect upon the supply of cotton, of course they mean the forcible interference with the blockadge [*sic*]."[43] Even the Potteries had begun to suffer, where works closed as trade with the Americans declined. And the satisfaction Bright derived from the knowledge that the recession would compel retrenchment was outweighed by worry about the immediate consequences for foreign relations. His distrust and contempt for Palmerston and Russell—"the one is without heart for any good, and the other is so capricious as to be almost without head"—left no room for doubt that "they would be ready for any mischief, if they were sure that public clamour would back them."[44] In this opinion he did them less than justice. Palmerston and Russell responded with far more caution than Bright would have thought possible to the clamour to do something about the looming cotton crisis.

Neither reason nor excuse for the breaking of the blockade appeared to be wanting in October. The gravity of the crisis had been investigated the month before by Austen Henry Layard, the under-secretary of state for foreign affairs. He had sought the opinions of "persons connected with the cotton trade and shipping with the United States."[45] While one of these, Forster, had minimized the dangers, another, William Lindsay, predicted dire times ahead. The Confederates were in deadly earnest with their embargo, he warned. The only way Britain could obtain Southern cotton was to go and get it, ignoring the blockade. Unknown to Lindsay, the government had accumulated ample evidence to justify that action. The reports of Milne's officers and the Southern consuls had clearly established the blockade's many imperfections. Nevertheless, Palmerston and Russell held back. They accepted that the cotton question would assume a "serious character" by the opening of the new year, and would be an "ugly" one by the time Parliament met in February. Yet that was one sound reason for postponing action. It was possible, if unlikely, that the war would be settled by February. If not, Palmerston admitted, the British government would then be obliged "either singly or conjointly with France to tell the Northerners that we cannot allow some millions of our people to perish to please the Northern States, and that the Blockade of the South must be so far released as to allow cotton laded ships to come out."[46] But there was another reason for procrastination, and that was a natural abhorrence of being seen to act at the bidding of the South. To recognize the Southerners "because they keep cotton from us," Russell commented, "would be ignominious beyond measure" and "no English Parliament could do so base a thing."[47]

No sooner had Palmerston and Russell decided to postpone a decision on the "delicate" and "difficult" American question than they were approached by the French. The textile industry of France was also suffering. Declining production brought short time and unemployment; the resulting unrest was fed by an increase in bread prices following a poor harvest. The government attempted to limit unemployment and mitigate distress by expanding its program of public works and importing foreign wheat, but the answer to France's industrial problems lay waiting in the Southern states. Trade with the South had to be reopened, manufacturers and chambers of commerce insisted, either through mediation or recognition of the Confederacy and the raising of the blockade. In fact, Thouvenel had already authorized Mercier to press for the release of the cotton. Following the minister's advice, he had provided him with instructions empowering him to use the implied threat of any or all of these steps to induce the Union to permit cotton to reach Europe. At the emperor's suggestion he sent a copy of these instructions to England and no doubt expected her full support. The British need was as great as if not greater than that of France, and Palmerston had been talking of joint action to secure cotton. Yet within a few days the prime minister emerged as a firm opponent of any attempt to coerce the North.

By October 17 the Foreign Office had learned, probably both from France and Lyons, of the direction in which Mercier would lead Anglo-French policy. The French minister realized that his nation needed British backing, that "she would not and could not go faster than England." It was his opinion that they should settle "precisely what was to be done" and then "execute the measures determined upon promptly and resolutely." Specifically, they should take the "first good opportunity" to recognize the South and then inform the United States that they could not allow their trade with a friendly nation "to be any longer interrupted." Such a bold and decided policy would "be less likely to lead to a conflict than attempts to open the trade by 'chicanes' about the validity of the Blockade, or by any small expedients."[48]

Russell thought there was "much good sense" in the Frenchman's observations. He remained sensitive about Britain being seen to break the blockade "for the sake of getting cotton," but her motives could be cloaked in some grand humanitarian gesture.[49] During a speech at Newcastle a few days earlier, in which he had described a war fought on one side for empire and on the other for power, Russell had asked whether it was not the duty of men "who profess a regard for the principles of Christianity,"

171

men "who wish to preserve in perpetuity the sacred inheritance of liberty, to endeavour to see whether this sanguinary conflict cannot be put an end to?"[50] This language was unguarded, ambiguous, and unsympathetic, the *Morning Star and Dial* complained, for it encouraged "the hope of something being done by our diplomatists and warships to relieve the cotton crisis."[51] Indeed, what the foreign secretary had in mind was an Anglo-French declaration to the belligerents, "make up your quarrels; we propose to you terms of pacification which we think fair and equitable. If you accept them well and good—But if your adversary accepts them, and you refuse them, our mediation is at an end, and you may expect to see us your enemies!"[52] However, he still believed that the proper time for issuing such an ultimatum was early in the new year. By then the threat to Lancashire would be acute and the government's need for a policy that promised relief urgent. For the Conservatives could be expected to exploit the cotton problem when Parliament met early in February. As for the restraining doctrine of nonintervention, that would undoubtedly lose favour with all but the Cobdenites as distress among the textile operatives grew.

Palmerston immediately rejected Russell's proposed course of action. Quarrelling and fighting were inherent in man, and to prevent its indulgence was "to impose Restraints on natural liberty," he philosophized. A "state may shackle its own subjects, but it is an infringement on national independence so to restrain other nations." As for cotton, he now minimized that problem. He saw little prospect of distress in the mill towns becoming so severe that British policy would have to be changed. Larger than usual supplies could be expected from "other quarters," and some would find its way from America. The Northern cruisers might not be able to maintain the blockade throughout the winter months, and cotton ships would therefore be free to come out of the South. "If this should be so it is scarcely likely that the Southerners would refuse to realize the value of their cotton by selling it at good Prices to England and France," he reasoned. "They cannot be so flush of money as to forego such means for defraying the expenses of their war." No hint here of the demand that the North allow cotton to be taken out of the Confederacy. Now "true policy" was "to go on as we have begun, and to keep quite clear of the conflict between North and South."[53]

For the prime minister's caution Lyons could claim some

credit. He warned that nothing less than an overwhelming Anglo-French naval force off the United States coast could prevent the North going to war rather than submitting to any interference. Even then he was not sure that they would not fight. Swaggering bullies they were, but Americans were not to be easily bullied. Palmerston wanted no war with the United States. A rupture "would at all times be an evil," he wrote to Russell, "but it would be more inconvenient to us in winter than in summer, because our Communication with Canada would be cut off, and we have not there a garrison sufficient for war time."[54] Yet had he had in North America the 10,000 men he had wanted it is by no means certain that Palmerston would have supported a bolder course. There was the familiar, limiting distrust of France. The French could afford to be more aggressive because they had no point of contact with the United States, they possessed a stronger navy than the Americans, and had a smaller commercial marine than Britain to protect or lose. It would be against British possessions that the United States would carry on a war, and that raised the question of how reliable and useful an ally the French would be. Could they be trusted? There would have been little doubt in Palmerston's mind that they could not. He believed that Napoleon detested Austria, and at the bottom of his heart hated England, because they were "European obstacles impeding the execution of great schemes of conquest and aggrandisement for France."[55] An Austrian move into Herzegovina had kept the European pot simmering, while Napoleon's continued occupation of Rome kept him well placed to turn the flank of the Austrians in Venetia or to press on to Dalmatia whenever it suited him. Spring might well be the time the emperor would choose to implement this strategy, Palmerston suggested to Russell. Of course that would be shortly after the proposed Anglo-French intervention in the American conflict.

The danger that could still not be ignored was that Napoleon, having led them into a war with the United States, would desert the British, even making his own peace with the Americans. They could be expected to welcome the withdrawal of one opponent for they would be absorbed with the task of seizing the North American possessions of the other. From Paris Cowley voiced his old fear, revived by the Bunch affair, that the French would play Britain false in America. Seward's failure to request the recall of the French consul, news of the withdrawal of Belligny and his replacement by St. André as a consular agent, which avoided the question of an exequatur, Thouvenel's lack of sympathy for the plight of Bunch, and the emperor's hostile reaction to what he considered the mistrust and misrepresentation of him by the English press, all alarmed the British ambassador. In short the "whole question" was much more delicate and difficult than Russell apparently realized. "The only thing to do seems to be to lie on our oars," Palmerston decided, "and to give no pretext to the Washingtonians to quarrel with us, while on the other hand we maintain our Rights and those of our Fellow Countrymen."[56]

Much the same advice continued to be given by John Harding. He was asked to comment on the consuls' reports of the blockade's inefficiency, sent to him by the Foreign Office. The Queen's advocate did not dispute that "the uncertain and imperfect maintenance of the very extensive Blockade of 'all Southern ports' announced by the United States may be very injurious to British interests, and may form a proper subject for international remonstrance," but he still thought it desirable "to establish by evidence in any prize court the inefficiency of any nominal blockade." He also repeated his practical reason for Britain continuing to rest on her oars. British interests profited to some extent from the imperfect way in which the blockade was maintained and he did not see how they would be advanced by calling the attention of the United States government to its inefficiency. Anyway, "the mere fact that several vessels have succeeded in evading a blockade will not of itself establish its invalidity," he declared, adding "that a port may often be effectually blockaded, although the blockading force is altogether out of sight, or is even supposed by those at the port to be absent."[57] Thus, having called a few weeks earlier for more evidence, the exacting advocate was now suggesting that the evidence from the consuls was inconclusive. He was as doubtful of the legality of any attempt to break the blockade as Palmerston was of its political wisdom, and his report confirmed Russell's decision to follow the prime minister's lead. Before October was out the foreign secretary had publicly refused to accede to the request of a Liverpool merchant that British ships of war aid merchant vessels to secure access to the blockaded Confederate ports. The Union "may rest assured that England will not be tempted by the hunger for cotton to embroil herself in the war," the Radical *Morning Star* concluded.[58]

Charles Francis Adams had already deduced as much. He had been watching anxiously for any moderation of British opinion or change in British policy and endeavouring to limit friction. He drew for Seward a by no means unsympathetic portrait of the economic conditions that prompted the call in England for an end to the blockade. He sought to stem any ill effects that might flow from Russell's remarks in Newcastle, reporting that several other ministers had touched on American affairs in speeches and had called for the maintenance of a rigid neutrality. He forwarded an article from the London *Times* of October 17, which he carefully identified with Palmerston's views, as evidence that there was "no intention to interfere with the blockade or to pronounce judgement in any way upon the merits of the American question." He had no reason to suppose that Russell did not "entirely concur in the justice of this policy," Adams added. "I believe him to be at heart more friendly to the United States than many who profess a great deal more."[59] Here was Adams at his anodyne best. He remained alive to the importance of "keeping well" with the British during the American crisis. This effort to forestall any outburst from Seward on one side of the Atlantic was matched by his own patience, civility, and soft speech on the other. But as he admitted to friends, "I should like of all things to say what I think of them." Privately, he was as indignant in October as he had been in August at the "ill-suppressed satisfaction in the continuance of our difficulties, the eager prognostication of the permanence of our division, the arrogant self-sufficiency" of the British bearing toward Americans.[60] Nor did the perceptive minister doubt that what prevented this sentiment from being reflected in a more challenging policy was the political outlook in Europe, where there were commotions in Austria, Hungary, Italy, and Poland, and the profound distrust of Napoleon. The English volunteers continued to parade while the emperor pressed on with his program of naval construction and maintained what Adams called a "colossal" military organization.

What these patriotic Englishmen did not know was that Napoleon was turning to Mexico for a solution to his European problems. Still opposed to the unification of Italy, he wanted the peninsula trifurcated—the Kingdom of the Two Sicilies restored, the remnants of the Papal States enlarged, and the Italian king compensated with the acquisition of Venetia. Unfortunately, the Austrians would not consider the cession of part of their territory to a new north Italian kingdom. Caught in this impasse, Napoleon listened more attentively to those around him who had been urging the establishment of a Mexican monarchy. That nation was in turmoil and the United States too preoccupied with its domestic troubles to offer any serious challenge to intervention. Napoleon had long been interested in Central America and he now saw an opportunity to create a stable "Latin State" capable of balancing the power of the United States. And by placing an Austrian on a Mexican throne he hoped to establish the closer relations he sought with Austria and eventually to persuade her to relinquish Venetia. In September 1861, Archduke Ferdinand Maximilian, the former viceroy of Lombardy-Venetia, was approached and by the beginning of October he had responded favourably. "Le dessein napoléonien" had taken shape and the news that the Mexican government had suspended all payments on foreign debts provided the excuse to set it in motion. Together with Britain and Spain, a joint expedition was organized to force the Mexicans to honour their obligations.

In the convention which they signed in London on October 31 the three European powers disclaimed any intention to violate the integrity, sovereignty, or independence of the Mexican Republic. As it did no apparent violence to the British doctrine of nonintervention the joint expedition was welcomed on the stock exchange and was popular in the press. However, continued cooperation among the powers soon ceased to be possible. Russell was informed by Cowley in January that the rumours of Napoleon's scheme to enthrone the Austrian archduke were all too well founded, while in Mexico the French quickly repudiated the Preliminaries of La Soledad, signed by the Allies and a representative of the Mexican government on February 19, 1862, in which they repeated the earlier disclaimers. On April 9 the joint intervention was dissolved and the French left to press on alone with the imperial design. But the British government did not follow this public disassociation from the Mexican venture with private endeavours to end it. Although Russell opposed the French action, it won Palmerston's quiet endorsement and he prevented the foreign secretary both from protesting the French violation of the London Convention and from urging the Austrians to forbid Maximilian's participation. Also, when the British representative in Mexico signed an agreement with the Mexicans on April 29, which gave his government what it sought, strenuous French protests prevented its ratification.

Palmerston had long been concerned with the containment of any southward advance by the Union, and he saw in the creation of a stable Mexican monarchy the means of stopping "the North Americans, whether of the Federal or Confederate States, in their projected absorption of Mexico."[61] He had rejected Seward's belated attempt to forestall European intervention by offering to assume the payment of the Mexican debt for five years in return for a mortgage on Lower California and three other provinces. To the prime minister this proposal merely prepared the ground for a foreclosure. And while Palmerston did suggest that the United States be invited to join the European expedition, he knew that this was an offer she would never accept. But his interest in the French intervention was not limited to its American consequences. The implications for Europe were no less important. Involvement in Central America would temper Napoleon's opportunism elsewhere. This prospect, together with the likelihood of an ever more deafening clamour for the abandonment of nonintervention as the distress in Lancashire grew more severe, suggested that the foreign and domestic shackles on British policy toward the American war were loosening. Only the colonial fetter remained as tight. Canada was still inadequately prepared to resist any American attack.

The reaction of the Canadian press to the news from Bull Run had been one of undisguised satisfaction. Among Liberal-Conservatives still celebrating the success of the Cartier-Macdonald coalition in the provincial election, the personal defeat of George Brown and his resignation as leader of the Reform party, and the repudiation of the "looking to Washington" policy, the "temporary defeat and humiliation of the most insolent and overbearing power in the world" was scarcely to be regretted.[62] It was a lesson "of which the Northern States and people stood greatly in need."[63] The time had come for the Americans "to moderate their pretensions and in their intercourse with other nations to adopt a courtesy to which they have hitherto been strangers."[64] No one expected the South to conquer the North but there was a conviction that "the ultimate independence" of the South was not improbable. It was "for the interest of both parties, as well as beneficial to the commerce of the world to agree to a peaceable separation."[65] Not forgotten either were the benefits to Canada. American capital was pouring into the province for investment, government newspapers claimed, crowds of families were flocking across the border in search of peaceful homes, while European immigrants were bound to prefer the stability, liberty, and security of property that existed in Canada to the anarchy and despotism of the Republic.

Even the opposition *Globe*, while it continued to insist that every Canadian "who desires to see his country prosperous should pray for the speedy success of Northern arms and the prompt suppression of the slave power,"[66] expressed pleasure that a "knock-down rebuke" had been given to the "arrogant braggart tone" of a considerable section of the American press.[67] More important, it believed that the Union would at last be obliged to make a genuine appeal to British sympathies by declaring war on slavery, and by mid-August the *Globe* detected signs that the struggle was rapidly becoming one for emancipation. A confiscation Act passed by Congress and a letter from Secretary of War Cameron to General Butler, concerning the policy of returning fugitives to their Southern masters, were greeted as evidence "that the slaves once escaped will thenceforward be free."[68] Fortified by the assurance that the cause of the Union was that of freedom, the *Globe* returned with renewed vigour to the task of attacking those who welcomed its dissolution.

The righteous *Globe* was struck by the "existence of strong affinities between a certain political party in Canada and the slave-holders of the Southern States."[69] It was the "Ministerialist and Corruptionist party" that sympathized with the proslavery Confederacy. In reply the patriotic *Leader* impugned the *Globe*'s loyalty. The Reform newspaper's concern for humanity was dismissed as a trick to mask its looking to Washington, and Lincoln's countermanding of General Frémont's proclamation freeing the slaves of rebels in Missouri came at a convenient moment. The president was more interested in holding the allegiance of the border slave states than ending slavery in Missouri. Clearly, the American war was still being fought for union not emancipation. Thus the *Globe*'s "pretence of philanthropy" was ridiculous, its true purpose was to conciliate American politicians and stock jobbers "and to build up an annexationist party."[70]

Whatever pleasure the news from the Republic gave Canadians was lessened by reports from England. The hostile response of the influential *Times* to the proposal that more British troops be sent to the province and its insistence that the colonists provide for their own defence, naturally attracted attention. Canadians reassured themselves that the mother country would never leave them in the lurch, but there were murmurings that the colony's defences had not been placed in proper order. On September 23 the Executive Council drew up a minute expressing "serious apprehension" at the inadequate means at the disposal of the imperial and colonial forces in the province to resist an American attack. With only 15,000 stand of arms and without any provision for modern field artillery, less than eight weeks before the close of navigation on the St. Lawrence, the council complained that hostilities during the winter would find the colony "almost wholly defenceless." What it sought was 100,000 stand of arms, plus sufficient ammunition and artillery, before the onset of winter. The bait it dangled before the Colonial Office was the encouragement such supplies would give to the next session of the Provincial Parliament to organize a more efficient militia. The message was plain enough. If the British expected the Canadians to improve the quality of their self-defence they should provide abundant weapons.

The Duke of Newcastle considered it neither necessary nor prudent to send out 100,000 stand of arms immediately. He saw no imminent danger of an American attack on Canada. Yet there was "quite enough danger and uncertainty in the future to justify and even require every precaution and necessary step for arming the militia" and providing for regulars that might be sent out in the spring.[71] He was nibbling on the colonial bait. He forwarded the minute to the War Office, and recommended that the store of arms in Canada be considerably increased, for that would "greatly encourage the spirit of self-defence."[72] It was decided that three batteries of artillery, 10,000 rifled muskets, and 15,000 short rifles should be sent. However by then it was already late October and the last sailing of the season for Quebec was November 5. To charter a steamship would have been expensive. So Newcastle ordered that all but a few thousand weapons be held in Britain until the spring. This meant that the colony would remain, in the Executive Council's words, "almost wholly defenceless" until May.

EIGHT

Mason and Slidell

IN THE UNION, there had been a predictably violent public reaction to the British response to the fiasco at Bull Run. William Howard Russell, whose letters to the *Times* were widely reprinted in America, was so abused and denounced that he wanted to return home but he was persuaded to remain by Mowbrey Morris, the newspaper's parsimonious manager. Too much money had been invested in Russell's trip for him to return, particularly now that the season for hostilities was just opening. Then there was the personal humiliation of being hounded out of the United States. "Surely you would not like to face all those sarcasms and insinuations," Morris wrote slyly. "So pray stay where you are—avoid all unnecessary risk to health and limb—but don't leave your post."[1] Believing himself condemned to provide a "material guarantee" for the good behaviour of the *Times*, Russell appealed to Dasent, the assistant editor. He did not ask that the paper be muzzled, simply that it be less acerbic in tone. "They are in such a sore irritable state here," he explained, "that a drop of acid plays the devil and makes them leap like dervishes."[2]

Sheltered from personal abuse, Lyons was less perturbed by the angry outcry. Admittedly he did not "feel at ease," for he did not discount "the effect of Public Cry" on American policy,[3] but he looked to the government's continuing need to raise money from cautious bankers to keep foreign relations on an even keel and he rightly deduced that it was preoccupied with the task of making the blockade more effective. It was anxiety to satisfy England and France on this crucial point that had deterred the Navy Department from detaching light and fast steamers to cruise after Confederate privateers. And while Seward stoutly maintained in his diplomatic correspondence that the blockade was effective and "must be respected," evidence of inefficiency led to embarrassing public criticism of the Navy. That department's response was traditional—a change of commanders. By the end of September Samuel Du Pont, a member of the Blockade Board, had been ordered to take command of the South Atlantic Squadron. He brought to the post an acute awareness of the international implications of his squadron's performance. There were "much greater interests involved in leaving a port uncovered than the getting in and out of vessels," he wrote to a friend. "If Lord Lyons finds out what has happened, Mr. Seward will have a hard road to hoe."[4] But efforts to plug the leaks and thereby deny the British and the French an excuse to break the blockade were coupled with schemes designed to mitigate its ill-effects in those nations.

The seizure of one or more cotton ports was certain to be "attended by immediate and great results." It would harass and alarm the Confederates, forcing them to call back for "home defence" troops campaigning against the Union armies. It would lift Northern spirits and make the task of raising loans easier. Also, it would enable the Union to "get out enough cotton to make a full supply for home consumption, and some for Europe." Once satisfied not only that the United States had both the will and the ability to win the war, but that the cotton famine would soon be eased, foreign nations would give "little trouble about *Blockade*."[5] Like any hopeful policy this one quickly won supporters. Among them was Seward. By October 12 he was excitedly talking to Lyons of the imminent seizure of a Southern port, releasing cotton which he was sure "would materially change the views of the European Powers."[6] The international benefits also attracted Lincoln's support for the "seaside excursionists." Although sceptical, as was Lyons, that Southerners would carry their cotton to any port under Union control, the president thought "it would be well to show Europe that it was secession that distressed them" not the United States.[7]

As well as manoeuvring to lessen foreign hostility toward the blockade, the Lincoln administration attempted to allay British irritation at its arbitrary methods in dealing with domestic foes. Lyons had watched in amazement as the American public "very recklessly" applauded the suspension, "without law, of all their liberties."[8] Lincoln's suspension of habeas corpus even though the chief justice of the Supreme Court "declared emphatically against it," the subsequent arrests, the refusal of military officers "to make any return to writs of Habeas Corpus," the stopping of opposition newspapers at post offices, convinced the British minister that the United States had abandoned the rule of law. Inevitably some British subjects were detained. When these cases were brought to Seward's attention the minister found him conciliatory. The secretary maintained his government's right to arrest foreigners as well as citizens, and to confine them "indefinitely without cause assigned," but he always speedily ordered the release of British subjects. This "line of civility and moderation towards Europe" gave Lyons grounds for hope that even the Bunch affair would pass off quietly. He was confident that the American government would not respond with "strong measures" to the news that the British had refused to recall the consul. He thought that Seward's vigour would carry him no further than a withdrawal of exequatur, and he intended "to try to make him see the absurdity of that."

When he met with Seward on October 12 to discuss the matter Lyons found him still toeing the civil and moderate line. The secretary's position was difficult, as the minister appreciated, now that Britain had made "a plain official declaration" that she recognized the rebels as belligerents and had been in communication with them. Nevertheless, Seward appeared to be taxing his ingenuity to find a way of avoiding a quarrel with Britain on the one hand, and domestic censure for "having pusillanimously retreated from the high position he originally took up" on the other. One way out of this predicament was to make the most of the fact that the British government had instructed Bunch to approach the South long before Seward had warned off the European powers. And determined "to assist not to thwart Mr. Seward's endeavours to treat the question amicably," Lyons readily fell in behind him on this point. However, the Englishman stressed that his country and France had openly recognized the South as belligerents and that it would be impossible for them to carry on diplomatic business with the United States "on the false hypothesis that the United States Government had not cognizance of this." Their recognition and its consequences had to be accepted "as the only basis which remained for sincere and satisfactory relations."[9] As for Bunch, Lyons did his best to convince Seward that he had no grounds of complaint against the consul personally.

Although he recognized the continuing danger of Bunch's

exequatur being withdrawn as a "sop to public opinion," Lyons must have felt confident after the meeting on October 12 that Seward would at least refrain from any immediate demonstrations. The American had repeatedly declared "that it was all important to gain time," and they both saw the wisdom of maintaining "a confidential intercourse" with a view to making their "official communications as conducive as possible to goodwill between the two Countries."[10] Yet within a few days Seward was cavorting before the gallery in his familiar role, inspiring neither confidence nor goodwill.

First, he exploited Lyons's official protest at the arbitrary arrest of British subjects. In Britain, the American government's resort "to passports and espionage and letter-opening and press-gagging and imprisonment on suspicion of being suspected, in fact exagerating all the paraphernalia of old world despotisms which they have always derided and abused," was a source of sardonic amusement.[11] But Palmerston was not the man to watch silently the Americans "following fast the example of Spanish Americans and the Continental Despots" when British subjects were among those imprisoned on "mere suspicion."[12] Russell was soon informing Lyons that the law officers had "pronounced" against Seward's depriving British subjects of their liberty upon the reports of spies and informers. This "despotic and arbitrary power" was inconsistent with the constitution of the United States and at "variance with the Treaties of Amity subsisting between the two nations," and the minister was instructed "to remonstrate against such wanton proceedings" and to say to Seward that it was the British government's opinion that the authority of Congress was necessary to justify such conduct.[13]

Lyons had verbally prepared the secretary for the remonstrance at their meeting on October 12. At that time the American had reacted calmly, saying that he would probably answer that he had arrested British subjects with the greatest reluctance but not without strong necessity, and had liberated them at the earliest moment compatible with public safety. That was before he read Lyons's note, which obediently followed his instructions. Seward's reply was marked by characteristic flourishes. He sarcastically rejected the British interpretation of the American constitution, which would leave upon the president "the sole executive responsibility of suppressing the existing insurrection, while it would transfer to Congress the most material and indispensable power to be employed for that purpose." Instead, Lincoln preferred to be governed by the view of American organic national law which enabled him to "execute his great trust with complete success, receives the sanction of the highest authorities of our own country and is sustained by the general consent of the people for whom alone the Constitution was established."[14] It was a reply clearly written for publication and Seward informed Lyons that he intended to publish the correspondence immediately. This would have a good effect on public opinion at home and abroad, he explained to the disbelieving minister, for the position taken by the American government would be made manifest to the world.

Here was Seward at his old game of turning an international problem to domestic advantage. He was courting personal popularity by publicly administering a rebuke to the British, against whom ill-feeling was still running high in the North. With his position in need of bolstering, for he was being damned as "Sir Forcible Feeble" and there were persistent rumours of conspiracies to drive him from the cabinet, Seward had returned to first principles. He took his chance to regain the confidence of his countrymen. But he was also summoning all anglophobes to the support of the administration's abridgment of civil liberties. Could a true American side with the detested British in their impertinent intrusion into American affairs? Surely all patriots would champion the president's right to suspend habeas corpus against the British contention that it rested with Congress? Nor had Seward misjudged the public response, and Lyons decided not to pursue a suggestion of Edmund Hammond that the arbitrary arrest of a British subject be used to test before the American courts the constitutionality of Lincoln's conduct. Seward would relish the prospect, he explained. Indeed, were he to get wind of this, he was quite capable of seizing a British subject just to bring the matter on, confident that under these circumstances he could be sure of a favourable judicial decision.

Lyons was soon confronted with additional evidence of the secretary's abandonment of the "civil and moderate line." On October 17 Northern newspapers published a startling circular letter from Seward to the governors of seaboard and Great Lakes states, in which he first drew attention to "disloyal citizens" who were seeking to embroil foreign powers in the insurrection, then claimed that the danger of intervention was less serious than it had been at any previous time during the war, and concluded that it was still necessary to take every precaution to avert "the evils of foreign war" at a time of civil disturbance. One obvious precaution was to put the nation's harbours and ports in "a condition of complete defence, for any nation may be said to invite aggression in stirring periods when it fails to show that it sets its guard on every side from which invasion might possibly come." Completely unexpected, the circular raised fears of foreign war, depressed the stock market, and left observers perplexed. "If its language is to be taken literally," the *Boston Evening Transcript* remarked, "nothing in the situation of our foreign relations called for a public notification, causing public distrust and a fall in Government securities."[15]

Nine days later Lyons was informed that Bunch's exequatur had been revoked. He viewed this "high-handed proceeding" as another sop to public opinion, and privately fumed "that never were serious charges brought upon slighter foundation."[16] But he misjudged Seward's motives, while his loyalty to Bunch was misplaced. The secretary's sudden return to his "old ways" was not simply a case of popularity-hunting. Just as his public rebuke of Lyons over habeas corpus had been perfectly consistent with his policy of never tolerating any European interference in American affairs, so the publication of the circular and the revocation of the exequatur were desperate attempts to warn off both Britain and France from dealing with the two newly-appointed Confederate commissioners.

The news that James M. Mason and John Slidell were on their way to Europe alarmed Northerners, for there was an uneasy feeling that the South had selected the best possible time and men for this mission. Thousands of workers were reported to be unemployed in France and on short time in England. The long-awaited cotton crisis was clearly close at hand, and who knew what fresh inducements to interfere in the war Mason and Slidell had been authorized to offer? What was certain was that they would have the best chance yet of a friendly reception. From John Bigelow, the new consul at Paris, Seward received a depressing assessment of French and English public opinion. The United States "has nothing to hope from the forbearance of the French government," he warned. Only an exhibition of power and determination could check unfriendly movements. "If they see that they have got to have a serious contest with us England

186

will not participate," Bigelow believed, because Palmerston would not dare arm the opposition "with such a bludgeon as a war with America to sustain the independence of the Slave States would be."[17]

This was a time of "intense anxiety" for Seward. "The pressure of interests and ambitions in Europe, which disunionists have procured to operate on the Cabinets of London and Paris," he wrote to his wife, "have made it doubtful whether we can escape the yet deeper and darker abyss of foreign war."[18] His response was almost instinctive. The dismissal of Bunch confirmed that the United States would treat as "offensive" any communication with the South while the publication of the circular was "an intimation anew" that any intervention was being provided for. More particularly, it served to remind Britain of the proximity of Canada. With the inhibiting Anglo-French concert still holding together, denying him opportunities to play one off against the other, Seward was abiding by his conviction that the security of their colonies was a fundamental maxim of British policy. Not that they had given him any cause to doubt it, by sending troop reinforcements to Canada and strengthening the militia.

Seward's anxiety about European intentions could scarcely have been lessened by a visit from the French minister on October 24. Observing the growing concern within the American government as the economic pressures on the European powers steadily increased, Mercier chose this moment to read to Seward the instructions he had secured from Thouvenel. He dwelt upon the dire straits of the textile industry of France and stressed the need to find some way of enabling the manufacturers to get cotton from the South. It was an account that left Seward unsympathetic. In his mind the Europeans had brought the suffering down upon themselves. The insurrection "would never have obtained its present development," he steadfastly believed, "but for the injudicious toleration of its appeals in Europe."[19] However, he kept this opinion to himself on October 24, simply taking a copy of Thouvenal's despatch which he said he wished to show to the president. Two days later he visited the French legation to discuss the note. To the Frenchman it seemed as if Seward was willing to open the blockade in return for a withdrawal of French recognition of Confederate belligerency. How it was to be opened was not made perfectly clear, although Seward was still counting heavily on the capture of a cotton port and the power to

issue licences to trade. That he would have welcomed an opportunity to license Frenchmen only, thereby separating France
from Britain, Mercier did not doubt. There was even less doubt
about Seward's intentions should any nation intervene in the
war. The United States would fight, he warned. Those countries
that needed cotton would have to come to some arrangement
with the North. This "high tone," coming as a climax to Seward's
fortnight of activity, worried the British minister when he heard
of it from Mercier. The United States had returned "to an incon-
siderate and unconciliatory policy towards the Powers of
Europe."[20] "The weather here is looking squally again," he
wrote to Admiral Milne on October 28, "but I hope not to have
to ask you immediately 'whether you can forward a letter for me
to Antigua'."[21]

Seward's return to his "old ways," his indulging of his "fondness for *coups-d'etat* and startling manifestoes"[22] was as unwelcome to some of his colleagues as it was to Lyons. But he brooked
no interference with his conduct of foreign affairs. "My asso-
ciates, of course, can differ with me about what I ought to do or
say," he commented, "but not advise me what to do and say."[23]
Yet it was not unreasonable to question whether threats, direct
or implied, were the best or only way of heading off Mason and
Slidell, and this Seward himself conceded with his decision
late in October to send "collateral missions" to Europe. These
agents were to be "gentlemen of intelligence and experience,
possessing a good knowledge of all the circumstances which
preceded and occasioned the Rebellion," and were to "disabuse
the public" of England and France of "misunderstandings."[24]
For this daunting task Seward wanted Edward Everett, J. P.
Kennedy of Baltimore, Archbishop Hughes of New York, and
Bishop McIlvaine of Ohio. Everett, a distinguished former minister to Britain with many prominent friends in that country,
declined this unofficial position, as did Kennedy, though for
pecuniary reasons rather than, as in Everett's case, reasons of
pride and personal convenience. Even Seward's friend Hughes
would only go if accompanied by Thurlow Weed. Already
besieged, Seward had no wish to provide his numerous and vocal
enemies with fresh ammunition by appointing an old crony
whose enemies outnumbered his own. But he had no choice, for
he was determined to send the Catholic Archbishop to France.
He took the precaution, however, of allowing Weed to go abroad

as a "volunteer" at his own expense. An astute political manager and experienced newspaperman, Weed was expected to gain for the Union a better press in Britain; it was hoped that his "sincere, if not polished ways" would not be "too repulsive to English refinement."

The choice of McIlvaine was a shrewd one, for the bishop was a close friend of Seward's principal adversary in the cabinet, Salmon Chase. Also, of the three emissaries he was the only one "so well known and respected in England" as to require no introduction from Lyons.[25] A frequent visitor there, an intimate of highly placed Englishmen, closely associated with the evangelical leaders of the Church of England, and honoured with the D.C.L. degree by both Oxford and Cambridge, McIlvaine was expected to mix with the "higher classes" and encourage them and the Anglican clergy to pronounce against the Confederacy. Convinced that he could not exert this "quiet, natural and conversational influence" if his stay in England was confined to eight weeks, as Seward proposed, or if it got abroad that he was a paid agent of the government, the bishop postponed his departure and even talked of declining the mission. In this way he extracted the concessions he sought, regarding expenses and the length of his visit, and avoided some of the publicity that attended the departure of the others.

Meanwhile, the two Southern emissaries Seward was struggling to head off had been turned back. Mason and Slidell had slipped out of the Confederacy in mid-October, leaving behind a "nation" that had recovered some of its earlier assurance about foreign relations. William Russell's infuriating description of Bull Run, which gave the impression that the battle "was a regular Chinese engagement on both sides," soon seemed less important than the comment of the *Morning Post*, "the mouthpiece of the men in power," that the Southern states "have achieved their independence." This authoritative observation plainly foreshadowed "the recognition of the South and the disregard of the blockade."[26] It seemed just as obvious that Bull Run would doom Union attempts to raise loans in Europe. News of the failure of Seward's attempt to cripple Confederate efforts to wage war at sea by adhering to the Declaration of Paris made pleasant reading in the press and there were cheering rumours that Admiral Milne had officially described the blockade as totally inefficient, and that Sir James Ferguson, a Conservative member of Parliament, had arrived in Richmond bearing "official communications."[27] Finally, there came reports of Britain's determination to strengthen her forces in Canada.

Southerners had quickly grasped the meaning of Seward's "interest" in Canada, and they admitted the awkwardness of Britain's position. Yet Canada was not plagued by "a revolutionary party sufficiently strong to overthrow the government, and hand the province over to the authority at Washington."[28] Therefore, all the British needed to do was to put the province in a thorough state of defence, and by the end of September it seemed clear that the defensive measures were "well nigh completed." With Canada loyal and adequately defended, Britain could ignore Seward's threats and the South count upon the blockade being raised as soon as Manchester ran short of cotton. Thus the revival of Southern confidence meant no weakening of the resolve to halt the export of the staple. To the "Bright Genius" who had warned the operatives of Rochdale that to break the blockade was to declare war on the United States, and that war would bring half wages for "a very considerable time," the *Richmond Dispatch* answered that half a loaf was better than none. "The welfare of England and France—their commercial safety—the food of millions of their subjects—are all dependent upon this blockade."[29] When the two powers discovered that not a bale of cotton nor a pound of tobacco would reach them except from Confederate harbours they would raise the blockade. Maintain and perfect the voluntary embargo, that was the cry Southern newspapers set up. To do so was to "win the crowning victory of the Southern cause."

Responding to these exhortations, some Southerners prevented the departure of vessels that had successfully run the blockade and taken on a cargo of cotton. And when Robert Bunch wrote to the governor of North Carolina to complain "that evil-disposed people" were preventing the departure of a British vessel with her cargo, his letter was forwarded to Richmond with a request for advice. The Davis administration saw an opportunity and took it. The governor was instructed to inform the consul that the subject of foreign commerce "was under the control of the Confederate Government and that he must address his complaints here."[30] The only way to obtain relief from the voluntary embargo was through direct treating with the Confederacy, with all that that implied.

But opposition to the embargo was not confined to Bunch, as the letters to the editors of newspapers indicated. No graver mistake could be made, some writers warned, than to suppose that England could be frightened into intervening by the threat to withhold cotton. Instead, she would look for alternative supplies. How was the Confederacy to raise the money needed to purchase weapons and munitions, others asked, if she did not sell cotton? Was it not foolhardy of the South to assist Lincoln by making his ineffectual blockade fully effective? Yet rational questions failed to shake the argument of the embargo's advocates, for whom it was a matter of faith and pride, and they made much of the rumour that Lincoln had promised Britain and France that a cotton port would soon be open for business. "Is it our duty or interest to carry out the pledges of Lincoln," the *Charleston Daily Courier* asked.[31] The only honourable reply was to hold the cotton in the interior, even to burn it to prevent it falling into Union hands. If England dreamt that she could depend on the North for cotton the time had come to "open her eyes by the light of a vast conflagration" to the fact that Southerners were "prepared and determined" to convert their land into "a desert rather than permit it to become the victim of Northern subjugation."[32]

Reconciliation to the prospect of such deeds of heroic self-sacrifice was eased by the certainty that they would not have to be endured for long. By mid-October the South was buzzing with the news that short time was becoming more general in Lancashire. Before long Britain's stocks of American cotton would be exhausted, and she "will have changed her policy from all her past history," the *Richmond Whig* remarked, "if she permits her people to suffer by reason of a blockade as illegal in its character as it is atrocious in its objects."[33] Already agog, the South hailed the publication of Seward's circular letter as "one of the most auspicious events since the war began."[34] It was further proof that a crisis was imminent. Had Seward taken fright at "some secret information of the designs of England"? Had the great powers signified their resolve "not to suffer beyond some brief period"? Unquestionably, the circular was "an unofficial, indirect, irresponsible" threat of war. It would be ignored. Britain was the only power that could be threatened by the order to the governors of the lake states, but she could rely on the loyal Canadian population and her defensive military preparations were rapidly nearing completion. In short, Seward's despairing effort to counteract the influence of Mason and Slidell in Europe was doomed.

Confederates were as confident that they had selected the best time and men to renew their approaches to the European powers as Unionists were fearful. John Slidell, who had accepted Davis's second offer of a diplomatic appointment now that the responsibility was individual not collective and Mann had been exiled to Belgium, was a man who had impressed the discerning correspondent of the *Times*. He was "an excellent judge of mankind, adroit, persevering, and subtle, full of device and fond of intrigue," being something more than the Thurlow Weed of the South.[35] His colleague James M. Mason was quite different, being as bluff as Slidell was vulpine. The English would like him, Southerners believed, because he was "so manly, so straightforward, so truthful and bold."[36] He was a Virginia "aristocrat" who traced his ancestry to the ubiquitous Cavalier, and was the grandson of a hero of the Revolution. Another lawyer by training and politician by vocation, a member of the Senate from 1847 to 1861, he had served as chairman of the Foreign Relations Committee for the last ten of those years. He could therefore claim a greater knowledge of foreign affairs than most of his fellows, and seemed well equipped to serve as a diplomat in England. The diarist Mary Chesnut mocks his dress, his pronunciation, his habit of chewing tobacco, his disdain for mountains, and his hypochondria, but he could be engaging. Richard Cobden had found him so during his visit to the United States in 1859, when Mason regaled him with depreciatory stories of the demigods of the Revolution. In all, and not least in appearance and demeanour, for he was "a thick-set, heavily built man" who could be supercilious and pompous, Mason was what Americans considered the model of an "old English gentleman." He was "peculiarly fitted" to represent the Confederacy in "the Mother country."[37] Even Rhett's *Charleston Mercury* agreed. "Mr. Mason and Mr. Slidell possess character, ability, and, what is no less important, eminent social fitness for their respective posts; and whatever be their instructions, we wish them prompt and perfect success."[38]

It was the judgment of Rhett's newspaper that the original mission to Europe had been premature. Neither Southern politics, statesmen, nor resources had been sufficiently understood in Europe "to secure an early confidence" in Confederate success. Amazed and confused by the spectacle of the dissolution of the Union, foreign statesmen had reacted understandably with "utmost wariness." But the situation had changed since Yancey and his colleagues set out in March. Confederate independence had been assured by the victory at Bull Run, the North had fallen under a "tyrannical and imbecile administration" while the South was governed by an orderly and constitutional regime. Then there was the precedent of British policy toward Italy. Recognition of the Confederacy would be "in strict conformity with that policy declared so recently as 1859 and 1860" and England and France had a "strong interest" to follow this precedent. "Cotton is not king in the absolute sense of the term," the *Mercury* conceded, marking a sharp break with its hysterical demands for an embargo only a few weeks earlier, "for, in the history of the world, no monopoly has secured absolute power; but it does give us a large and legitimate influence in the commercial and financial affairs of the world, and thus indirectly confers political power." All that the new commissioners had to do was negotiate an early recognition, and they required no larger authority than that.

The instructions Mason had already received from Hunter were what Rhett hoped they would be. The secretary emphasized the strengthened position of the Confederacy. Eleven states had confederated together, and they would probably be joined, eventually, by Maryland, Missouri, and Kentucky. Large enough "to become the seat of an immense power," the Confederate States had the added good fortune to boast "the best varieties of climate and production known to the temperate zone" and produced vital staples. It was obvious that the South could not be conquered, therefore the cause of peace and the interests of mankind demanded that the strife be ended. If Britain failed "to throw the great moral influence of such a recognition into the scale of peace," she would share the responsibility for the continuance of an unnecessary war. But her humanity was sustained by "deep political and commercial interests" in the establishment of an independent South. Division of the Union effectively checked a burgeoning rival in manufacturing and a full-grown one in navigation and commerce. A balance of power would be created in North America, and "fears of a disturbance of the peace of the world from the desire for the annexation of contiguous territory on the part of a vast and overshadowing political and military organization will be dissipated."[39] In offering these views to the British government Mason was authorized to quote chapter and verse of Russell's Italian correspondence, to illustrate that the Confederate case was "precisely and entirely" within the principles on which it then acted. Finally, he was instructed to press the issue of the blockade.

Mason was promised "abundant evidence" of the blockade's ineffectiveness. Reminding him of the provision of the Declaration of Paris, Hunter suggested that "it may perhaps be fairly urged that the five great powers owe it to their consistency, and to the world, to make good a declaration thus solemnly made." Of course, England and France had the added and powerful inducement of seeing "a ready and easy access to the cheapest and most abundant sources of cotton supply." And if the might of cotton was not constantly paraded in these instructions, it was still omnipresent. Cotton was the first of the South's staples and Hunter expressed the Southern confidence that within the Confederacy "must be found for years to come the great source of cotton supply." Evidently, the members of the Davis administration were clinging to cotton as their great weapon, but they were using it with diplomatic discretion. Although there had been no slackening of resentment over the working of European neutrality, which saw the declaration enforced to the letter on privateering but not on the blockade, Mason was instructed to correct the error that the Confederate government had "prohibited the exportation of cotton by sea to neutral and friendly nations." The laws of the Confederacy "warrant no such prohibition," William M. Browne wrote in a subsequent despatch.[40]

If the time was right, as were the men and their instructions, all that remained to be done was to get Mason and Slidell safely to Europe. The original plan was to charter the steamer *Nashville*. She was swift enough to run the blockade and large enough to cross the Atlantic without too much discomfort to her passengers, and her arrival in Liverpool or London with commissioners on board would "produce a good effect."[41] She could then return laden with munitions. But soon after their arrival at Charleston on October 2 Mason and Slidell abandoned the *Nashville*. They were persuaded that her draught was too deep to permit a safe passage over the harbour bar except under the most favourable conditions of wind and tide. Then, when the Federal blockade was strengthened by the arrival of a very trim-looking steamer, the two men thought of forsaking Charleston. They could travel overland to Mexico and pick up a British steamer there, but this route was quickly dismissed as "impracticable from delay."[42] Finally, their attention was directed to another steamer, the *Gordon*.

Although small, the *Gordon* was very fast, of so light a draught that she could pass over the bar at any time, and was well known to the blockading squadron. Often used to reconnoitre the Federal vessels, her speed had soon convinced them of the futility of chasing her. Mason and Slidell chartered her to carry them to Havana, where they could obtain passage on a British vessel. On the night of October 12 she was boarded by the Slidell entourage, which consisted of his three children and wife, George Eustis, his secretary of legation, and Mrs. Eustis. Mason and his secretary completed the party, the Virginian having decided to leave his family at home. After a brief and anxious farewell from friends, they were gone. Aided by a dark night and heavy rain, all lights including cigars extinguished, her passengers huddled on the deck and sworn to silence and stillness, the *Gordon* stole through the blockade. She stopped briefly off Nassau in case a connection could be made there with a British steamer, but learning that it could not the vessel hurried on to Cuba. Running short of coal she made for the nearest port on the island, some 100 miles up the coast from Havana. The commissioners soon discovered that they had just missed one British steamer and would have to wait three weeks for another. Uneasy about such a long residence on the fever-ridden island, and quickly debilitated by the heat, Mason and Slidell were at least comforted by the knowledge that they were safe. Having run the blockade successfully everything else was plain sailing, Mason wrote to his wife, "because under any foreign flag we are safe from molestation."[43]

The publicity given to their mission, including details of their proposed voyage, had provoked complaints that some Southern newspapers were playing into the hands of the Federal authorities. The suspicion that the Union would dearly love to get its hands on the two men had been strengthened by the sudden reinforcement of the Federal squadron off Charleston. The news that they had successfully run the blockade relieved these anxieties. However, some Southerners did question whether Mason and Slidell would be safe even on a British steamer. Did not neutrality forbid "the transportation of the dispatches and public personages, or of troops and contraband of war for either belligerent?" Could a Federal ship, by following the British principle of the right of search in time of war, "undertake to stop the British passenger vessel, and take out the unlawful passengers?" No, replied the *New Orleans Daily Picayune*. This would be "a reading of the law of nations entirely novel, and if Mr. Lincoln should undertake to act upon it, he would find himself confronted instantly with the power of Great Britain, resenting an act of war."[44]

Southern suspicions that the "Yankees" were striving to nab both Slidell and Mason were not ill-founded. As well as manoeuvring to head them off by diplomatic means, Seward reacted to the reports that they had run the blockade on the *Nashville* with a suggestion to Gideon Welles that Federal vessels waylay them. Welles ordered several warships off in pursuit, one of them, the *James Adger*, continuing all the way across the Atlantic. Meanwhile, Captain Charles Wilkes and the *San Jacinto* were prowling around Cuba. Wilkes had not been ordered to look for the two Confederates. He was bringing the *San Jacinto* back from the African slave trade patrol to participate in an expedition against Port Royal, and had joined a search in the Gulf for a Confederate privateer. Putting in to Cienfuegos to refuel he heard that Mason and Slidell were in Havana, and he steamed there determined to intercept the *Gordon*, or *Theodora* as she had been renamed, on her return voyage. When he arrived he found that she had gone but that the two commissioners were still there, waiting for the *Trent*, a British mail steamer, due to sail on November 7. They were tempting bait and Wilkes was not the man to resist it. A distinguished nautical scientist and explorer, he had not received the recognition be believed his achievements warranted. Impulsive, over-zealous, ambitious, ill-starred, he was hungry for the fame and promotion that awaited the man who captured the Confederates and thereby stopped "their diabolical scheme."[45]

Leaving Havana on November 2 the *San Jacinto* crossed to Key West. Wilkes was seeking help to patrol the narrow Bahama Channel through which the *Trent* would have to pass and where he planned to intercept the British steamer. None was available, so he set out alone. At this time he intended not only to seize Mason and Slidell but also to take the *Trent* as prize. After consulting the works of several legal authorities he was sure he had ample grounds on which to detain her. He even drafted a note to Welles announcing the seizure of the captain, officers, and engineer of the *Trent* as well as the Confederates, which he planned to forward with the commander of the prize crew put aboard the mail steamer. This was how matters stood on November 8, a day Wilkes greeted as "one of the most important in my naval life."[46] He stationed the *San Jacinto* in the middle of the Bahama Channel and waited. Just before mid-day the smoke of the *Trent* was sighted, and when she came up to the American sloop about an hour later a shot was fired across her bows. When she failed to heave to it was followed by a shell, the *Trent* immediately slackened speed and shut off steam.

First one, then a second boatload of men from the *San Jacinto* boarded the *Trent* to help enact a curiously stylized yet chaotic scene. By now Wilkes had changed his mind about taking the mail steamer as prize. Possibly his nerve had been shaken by the warnings of his executive officer that Britain was certain to react violently to the indignity, although as he explained it in his report, "the reduced number of my officers and crew and the large number of passengers on board bound to Europe who would be put to great inconvenience, decided me to allow them to proceed."[47] He sought only the commissioners and their secretaries. When the purpose of the boarding party became known the other passengers, perhaps eighty of them, and almost all British, began to mill around voicing their indignation while the captain and the naval officer in charge of the mails did not disguise their fury. Mason and Slidell then demanded a demonstration of force greater than they could resist, and when this was paraded they agreed to leave. The four men were taken to the Federal warship, to be followed by their baggage but not their instructions. Mason had had the presence of mind to entrust them to Commander Williams, the mail agent, for safekeeping.

It was the evening of November 23 before the *San Jacinto* anchored in Boston harbour, having stopped briefly at Fortress Monroe and New York on her way up the coast. The Confederates were incarcerated in Fort Warren while Wilkes began to sample the public adulation that his act had brought him. A national hero, he was fêted wherever he went, Congress passed a resolution of congratulation on December 2 and the American Museum issued an invitation. "We have at present many interesting curiosities," P. T. Barnum wrote, "and I trust that half an hour spent here would not be thrown away."[48]

There was nothing inexplicable about the tidal wave of public exultation that swept over the North bearing the triumphant Wilkes on its crest. For in the space of a few days the course of the Civil War appeared to have dramatically changed. First, on November 14, came word of the "brilliant victory" at Port Royal. A cotton port had at last been captured, and the implications of that success were obvious. Britain would be able to get cotton, thus the last ray lighting up Confederate hopes had been extinguished. Three days later the excited Northern public were reading of Wilkes's exploit. The two dangerous men thought to be capable of capitalizing upon European economic difficulties had been taken. This was a source of intense relief and together with the victory at Port Royal promised to "strike consternation among the rebels." But the tone of exultation also owed much to the fact that Mason and Slidell had been forcibly removed from a British vessel. There had been no slackening in recent weeks of the bitter public criticism of "British malignity and impudence."

In this atmosphere there was something intoxicating in the news of an American firing "his shot across the bows of the ship that bore the British Lion at its head."[49] And there was malicious satisfaction that Wilkes had followed "the rules of international law as laid down by British authorities and supported by British precedent."[50] Yet it was not long before the effects of this heady wine began to wear off. If the British were as anxious to destroy the Union as Northerners believed, then they were likely to use the capture of Mason and Slidell as an excuse for quarrelling with the United States. Was there a danger of war with Britain? The "fancy pigeons and lame ducks of Wall Street" plainly thought so, for stock prices again tumbled.[51] Many Southerners agreed with them.

There was an unmistakable air of anticipation in the Confederate capital, Richmond. The government, like the press and the public, had "great hopes" that Britain would "resent and punish the act." It was inconceivable that the British would "submit quietly to the insult,"[52] the exact nature of which Jefferson Davis described in his speech opening the fifth session of the Confederate Congress on November 18. "These gentlemen were as much under the jurisdiction of the British Government upon that ship and beneath its flag," he claimed, "as if they had been on its soil, and a claim on the part of the United States to seize them in the streets of London would have been as well founded as that to apprehend them where they were taken."[53] The British now had to live up to their "proud boast" to "maintain inviolate the right of asylum" wherever their jurisdiction extended. What better pretext could they have to intervene, by breaking the blockade and recognizing the Confederacy? Nor did Davis forget to remind them of what was at stake. He warned that if the "illegal blockade" was permitted to continue the South would be compelled to become self-sufficient. Labour and capital would be diverted from the production of staples to "other employments," not only making the Confederacy a rival instead of a customer of industrial nations, but so diminishing the supply of cotton "as to bring ruin upon all those interests of foreign countries" dependent upon it.

Confederate hopes and Union fears of a hostile British response to the *Trent* affair were strengthened by the Canadian reaction to the incident. Throughout October the provincial newspapers had continued to use the American war as a partisan whip with which to flog one another, either as an enemy of humanity or as a slave of American interests. The Rankin affair, in which an opposition member of the Legislature and militia officer had been charged with contravening the Foreign Enlistment Act by accepting an American commission to recruit Canadians for the Union armies, provided ammunition for the Liberal-Conservative organs. They not only vented their fury upon the Americans, recalling the Crampton episode five years earlier, but hastened to implicate Brown when the *Globe* stood up for Rankin. "He has got beyond 'looking to Washington'," the *Leader* screamed. "He has sold himself bodily to Washington, daily does the work of Washington, and will soon be driven to Washington for his reward."[54] Then came Seward's circular letter. Although the *Globe* bravely denied that any menace to Canada was intended, the "Ministerial Press" offered the circular, and the habeas corpus correspondence, as evidence of the depth of "bad feeling" in the United States. Morbidly sensitive to British opinion, the Americans had revealed fears of an "Approaching Crisis" with England and France over the "letter and spirit of the law of blockade."[55] Three weeks later the Canadian newspapers were full of the arrest of Mason and Slidell, and for the United States there was an ominous unity to their response. Even the *Globe* and the *Leader* were in broad agreement.

The action of Wilkes was widely denounced as an outrage to the British flag, an infraction of international law, "a gross wrong which can only be repaired by the offer of ample apologies by the United States Government, and the liberation of the captives." Not only was it wrong, the *Globe* charged, "it was also one of the most absurd and stupid acts which history records."[56] In seizing the Confederate commissioners Wilkes had "done more to accomplish their errand than anything they could possibly have done themselves." But while it joined with the Liberal-Conservative press in condemning this outrage, the *Globe* struggled valiantly to be more optimistic than they about the outcome. It did not agree with them that Anglo-American distrust would now give way to hostilities. Yet faith in the good sense of the United States was not easily maintained. The American government desired peace, a perplexed *Globe* insisted on November 26, so "why does it suffer its officer to become a medium for the display of anti-British feeling," thereby erecting a barrier of pride which might "prevent justice being done on one side or the other." Nor was the conduct of the Canadian authorities any more encouraging. General Fenwick Williams was rushing along the border throwing up defences, making what the *Globe* called "Warlike Movements." Clearly, the Canadian government was preparing for "difficulties" with the United States.

The *Trent* affair provided the inexperienced Monck with an unexpectedly demanding initiation as governor general. When he landed at Quebec he must have known that he had undertaken a difficult task made more so by the American war. There was the irritant of Northern attempts to recruit in Canada, against which Head had already made a very dry protest through Lyons. In reply the United States had denied the charge. There was the renewed colonial request, for aid to construct a railroad between Halifax and Quebec. Here the colonists saw the opportunity that was now open to them. They had stressed the strategic considerations before, the fact that in the event of a war with the United States imperial promises of protection from aggression would be impossible to fulfil during the winter months without a railway linking Canada to the Maritimes. The Civil War and the deterioration in Anglo-American relations greatly strengthened their case and although they knew that

Gladstone was certain to oppose their application Canada, Nova Scotia, and New Brunswick appointed a delegation to visit England. Head strongly supported the mission, as did Arthur Gordon, the lieutenant-governor of New Brunswick. Monck soon added his voice to theirs. "The condition and possible future action of the Northern States renders the arguments in favour of the proposal stronger at present than at any former period," he wrote to Newcastle.[57] But important as this question was, at least to the colony and for imperial relations, it was a problem on which Monck had certainly been briefed by Head during their two days of conversations. Neither his talk with Head nor his instructions from Newcastle could have prepared him for the crisis that erupted less than a month after he took office. After all, both men had been satisfied that there was little danger of an imminent confrontation with the United States.

At Head's suggestion Monck had acted quickly to maintain the confidential relationship the retiring governor had enjoyed with Lord Lyons, and it was from the minister that he received the ominous opinion that the *Trent* incident was a "very serious matter." His reaction was admirably level-headed. He cautiously set about putting the province's defences in better order. He was convinced that ostentatious measures of preparation were dangerous. They would cause "undue excitement of alarm" within the province, where anti-American sentiment was "already powerful enough," and an "exasperation of feeling" across the border.[58] An excited population on one side and an irritated one on the other was a recipe for border incidents which the United States might welcome as an excuse to take offence. Monck therefore gave a "good deal of anxious thought" to the problem of preparing in the least provocative way for a possible rupture with the North during the winter. An essential step was to strengthen the Active Militia. By November 1861, there were not more than 5,500 men enrolled in its two classes. Those in Class A had some rudimentary training, being paid for drilling, but their numbers were limited by law. There was no legal limit to the size of Class B whose members were not paid unless they were called out to service. Nevertheless, enrolments had been effectively limited by colonial parsimony. The province was responsible for equipping the militia and it failed to appropriate the funds needed to provide weapons for the men of Class B. The crisis with the United States now promised to loosen the colonial purse

strings, but Monck could not obtain a larger militia appropria-
tion without the consent of the legislature and to call it into
special session would defeat his quiet policy. Yet he was determined to take advantage of the "good spirit" and he secured
from the ministry a promise to pay for any arms issued to the
militia by the imperial authorities. Thus the way had been
cleared for a quick, quiet, and substantial increase in the size of
the militia without "resort to extraordinary measures and agencies which would attract attention and foment excitement."[59]

Although he had agreed to equip volunteers from his own
stores, on the understanding that the colony would pay for them
later, Fenwick Williams had little faith in the militia. Too small
a proportion of the able-bodied volunteered, he charged, and
too few of those enrolled turned out for drill. He had the professional soldier's contempt for this sorry and inefficient civilian
force. The only trained and reliable men at his disposal were
the 5,000 regulars in the province. Clearly his means were
insufficient to defend the entire colony and he concentrated on
the task of defending strategic points. Monck made no objection
to Williams's proposals, for he was keen to use the "great uneasiness and alarm" in Canada to get defensive works executed that
would otherwise have continued to be neglected.[60] However, he
quickly discovered that Fenwick Williams was too difficult an
old war horse to be held on a tight rein. The general raced along
the border making ostentatious preparations to resist attack, and
his activities excited comment on both sides. While he was
pleased by the news that Lyons also thought "quiet" the best
policy, Monck had to admit in his reply that he had "sometimes
a little difficulty here in keeping it present to the minds of some
in this Province."[61]

The seizure of the Confederate commissioners and the insult
to the British flag were no more than a glum Lyons had feared
since Seward's return to his old ways. But he resolved to maintain
"entire reserve on the question,"[62] to be more sphinx-like than
ever. Although "frightened" by the defencelessness of Canada,
which was reported to him by Alexander Galt, the province's
finance minister, who arrived in Washington at the beginning of
December, Lyons maintained his mask of impassivity as he
waited for instructions from home. Seward had also decided to
say nothing until he heard from the British government, but
while he waited he attempted to prevent the administration from

committing itself to the support of Wilkes. It was not an easy task. Attorney-General Bates considered the forcible removal of Mason and Slidell from the *Trent* lawful, and Gideon Welles, relishing the popularity the Navy had at last won with the success at Port Royal and the capture of the Confederates, wrote a letter of congratulation to Wilkes which was immediately published.

Seward anticipated an outpouring of British sympathy for Mason and Slidell, and if this induced caution so did the conduct of the diplomatic corps. Unlike Lyons, they made no secret of their opinion. Almost to a man they declared that Wilkes's action was an outrage which would rouse Britain to the point of war. The increasingly apprehensive Seward belatedly authorized Adams to inform Palmerston and Russell that Wilkes had acted "without instructions, and even without the knowledge of the Government." Consequently, the subject was "free of embarrassment which might have resulted if the act had been specifically directed by us."[63] He was already preparing the ground for a formal repudiation of the act if that became necessary, and he was doing it at home as well as abroad. The faithful *New York Times* reminded the Northern population that the capture of the commissioners had been "entirely spontaneous and unauthorized,"[64] and Lincoln's first annual message to Congress made no mention of the incident. Once again Seward had preserved his freedom of action, making possible a full reparation without too much loss of dignity. Yet it was still by no means certain that he would be able to carry the public and the administration with him if Britain demanded the return of Mason and Slidell.

NINE

One war at a time

LONG BEFORE THE NEWS of the *Trent* incident reached England Adams had been contemplating a demoralizing accumulation of setbacks and difficulties. These included the destruction of a Northern merchantman off the British coast by a Confederate steamer, the *Nashville*; the failure of the Union navy to intercept vessels leaving Britain for the South laden with arms; the confidence every success engendered among Confederates in Britain, already disturbingly "indefatigable in their labors to operate on public opinion through the newspapers, and by private channels;"[1] finally, the ever-deepening cotton crisis.

A published survey of 836 mills, employing some 172,257 hands, detailed the extent of the distress in the textile industry. Of the total, only 64,393 operatives were fully employed; 15,572 were being laid off for one day each week, 55,397 for two and 28,832 for three. For more than 8,000 workers there was no work at all. This was grim news and it revived the demand in *Reynolds's Newspaper* for the breaking of the blockade, even if that meant war with the Union. Others, less closely identified with the interests of the working class, shrank from that step. Lancashire should remember that the South was as culpable as the North, since there was an embargo as well as a blockade, the *Economist* commented; moreover, 1861 would have been a year of privation without the Civil War. The enormous production and excessive exports of earlier years had resulted in several of the most important markets being glutted. And while these problems had been intensified by the war, the undoubted immediate mischief of the blockade would be outweighed by the future benefit. Enterprising merchants would open up the interior of India and the stimulus of high prices would encourage cotton production all over the world, thus assuring ample supplies at moderate prices and releasing Britain from her "painful dependence" on the Southern states. This release was "worth much temporary distress."[2]

Although the voice of caution continued to be the most influential in Britain, Charles Francis Adams saw the necessity of his country "acting with great prudence in keeping out of the hands of mischief-makers any instruments of harm on this side." No encouragement should be given to those who "steadily and systematically kept up the possibility of misunderstandings and difficulties on the other."[3] But this was exactly what Seward did. With his circular letter he deliberately reawakened suspicions of him that had been fitfully slumbering in Britain. Then came the Lyons-Seward correspondence, although public indignation was muted by displeasure with the manner in which the British case had been presented. Seward had been presented with an opportunity "to display a remarkable superiority in rhetoric and even in grammar."[4] The undeniable fact that the American had got the better of them was unlikely to lessen English irritation, and Adams viewed the affair apprehensively. The effect would be "to widen more and more the breach that is making between the two countries," he concluded gloomily. "In feeling there is now decided hostility in the popular sentiment."[5] How long would the leading men be able to control it, he asked himself.

It was in this questioning mood that Adams accepted an invitation to attend the lord mayor's banquet on November 9. At such an uneasy time he was anxious to avoid appearing "to decline civility." But one anxiety led to another, and he began to worry that he would be called upon to speak. He spent the morning thinking about what he would say, and it was as well that he did. Although it was customarily the duty of the senior diplomat (which Adams was not) to give an address, the American minister was on this occasion begged to undertake it and he grasped the opportunity to do what he could to check the popular impression that the United States was "animated by malignant hostility" to Britain.[6] He "managed to say nothing, but said it remarkably well."[7] Studiously ignoring his nation's domestic troubles he spoke for fifteen minutes, making friendly comments about England and expressing the friendly sentiments of the American people and their government. He "praised the Queen for her private virtues," one listener remarked unkindly.[8] However, the public reaction was more favourable. The speech was so complimentary, the *Times* commented, "that we could wish

America would speak more frequently to us by the mouth of her Minister, and never at all in the tone common to her press and her Secretary of State."[9] This minor personal triumph did much to revive Adams's confidence that there would be no change in British policy.

By November, Lord Russell was looking to the Port Royal expedition to clarify the American crisis. He believed that if Southerners carried their cotton to the ports controlled by the North then the game would nearly be over for the Confederacy, but that if they did not and Northerners succeeded only in holding the ground they occupied, all hope of reunion would be gone. However, even if the South was brought back he feared that its return would be accompanied "with ample guarantees for the maintenance and limited extension of slavery. Thus strengthened the cause of slavery would prevail all over the New World."[10] For this reason he wished for separation, as had some American abolitionists before the war, and he was mystified by the determination of Sumner, Harriet Beecher Stowe, and other foes of slavery to see the Union restored. But this personal opinion did not alter government policy, nor was he distracted by Seward's provocative behaviour. He fancied that the circular letter "merely meant to say 'now we have got our money from the Bankers, and we may as well brag a little!' " He did not attach much significance either to the publication of the correspondence with Lyons. "It is the business of Seward to feed the mob with sacrifices every day," he calmly observed to Palmerston, "and we happen to be the most grateful food he can offer."[11] Britain's conduct "must be strictly neutral, and will be," he informed Lyons.[12] In this spirit he fully embraced John Harding's scrupulous policy toward the blockade. Any withdrawal of recognition had to be based on the "good and valid ground" that it was "manifestly inadequate."[13] If Britain set up pretences which the law officers deemed insufficient even for remonstrance her position would be that of a bully.

Palmerston was also still set against intervention, and he used his own speech at the lord mayor's banquet to announce that there would be no interference for the sake of cotton. But he responded less phlegmatically than Russell to Seward's conduct. He took his chance to remount a hobby horse. "Every report, public, official and private that comes to us from the Northern States of America tends to shew that our relations with the

Washington government are on the most precarious footing and that Seward and Lincoln may at any time and on any pretence come to a rupture with us," he confided to Newcastle.[14] What was likely to tempt them into such an adventure, and what inspired them to pursue a policy of heaping "indignities" on Britain, was the defenceless condition of British North America. He reminded the colonial secretary that he had wanted to send reinforcements earlier, and repeated his refusal to have any truck with theoretical gentlemen who thought the chief duty of the government was to try to give away the colonies. Finally, he called on the Colonial Office to urge the Canadians to prepare during the winter the accommodation that would be required by troops sent out in the spring. Newcastle quickly rallied to his own defence and that of his department. No Little Englanders in the Colonial Office had made themselves known to him, he replied, and he reminded the prime minister that he had always advocated sending more troops to Canada in the spring. He did have to admit, however, that the weapons Palmerston assumed had been forwarded to Canada were still in England, and he ungallantly sought to charge the War Office with the responsibility. That department quickly informed Palmerston that Newcastle's request for arms had not been received until mid-October, leaving the angry prime minister to conclude that the culprit was the procrastinating colonial secretary. And Palmerston's suspicions that the Americans intended to take advantage of the defenceless condition of Canada to heap further indignities on Britain deepened with the appearance of the *James Adger* and the arrival of a report from Lyons that Bunch's exequatur had been revoked.

The Federal warship, after a fruitless search for the *Nashville*, had eventually put in to Southampton. From there her commander, Marchand, travelled up to London to see Adams on November 7. The minister urged him to use his discretion and waylay outside British waters a vessel being loaded in the Port of London with supplies for the Confederacy, but Marchand shirked further responsibility. Instead, he announced his determination to return home once necessary repairs had been made to his ship. However, by this time the American's presence had alarmed Palmerston. Prompted by Edmund Hammond, the prime minister feared that the *James Adger* was waiting to intercept and remove Mason and Slidell from the British mail steamer believed to be carrying them from the West Indies. He immediately turned to the law officers for an opinion and they informed him that the American cruiser was entitled to stop, board and search the British packet, put a prize crew aboard, and carry her off for adjudication. "But she would have no right to remove Messrs. Mason and Slidell and carry them off as Prisoners leaving the ship to pursue her voyage."[15] Initially, Palmerston seems to have misunderstood this last point, for that same day, November 11, he informed the friendly editor of the *Times* that the *James Adger* might stop the packet and either take her in as prize or take Mason and Slidell out as prisoners. Two days later, when he reported to the Queen, he did so correctly.

Whatever the legal niceties of the case, Palmerston did not relish the prospect of an affront to the dignity of the mistress of the seas. Nor did Russell, who although at home unwell was kept informed of developments. Indeed, he wanted the navy to shadow the Federal warship through the Channel and off the coast of Ireland in the hope that this would discourage any interference with British vessels. But this proposal was rejected because the sense of national frustration and irritation would be all the greater if a British warship was forced to "stand by and see the Packet searched and possibly captured at sea."[16] However, a frigate was ordered to cover the *James Adger* in British waters, to ensure that she did not commit the supreme indignity of stopping, let alone capturing the packet there.

Clearly, the only hope of avoiding an incident most Englishmen would regard as a humiliation was diplomacy not force, so Palmerston asked Adams to call upon him on November 12. At their meeting, the prime minister affected ignorance of the legality of any seizure, thus at least creating the impression that it might not be legal. He then went on to argue that even if it possessed the right the United States should not exercise it. To have an American warship put in to a British port for coal and supplies, and to permit her captain to get drunk on British brandy, and then to have the vessel rush out and commit violence on the British flag was certain to have "a very bad effect" on public opinion. Anyway the gain would not be commensurate with the risk, he continued. The arrival of two more Southerners was not going to alter the mind or policy of Her Majesty's government. Adams quickly convinced him that "it was all a false alarm" and did not disguise his wonder at such "susceptibility and exaggerated notions."[17] The *James Adger* had been sent out after the *Nashville* when it was thought that Mason and Slidell were travelling on the Confederate vessel, he explained, and was now on her way home.

Pleased with the "very satisfactory explanation" of the presence of the *James Adger*, the prime minister had turned to the question of revocation of Bunch's exequatur. Again he stressed the inexpediency of such a decision. Practically useless, because Bunch was not within Federal authority and could perform his functions without a Federal exequatur, it would further alienate British opinion. The "unfavourable feelings" aroused by the "arbitrary proceedings" of the Lincoln administration, the stoppage of cotton by the blockade, and the "diminution" of British exports by the Morrill Tariff would be intensified, Palmerston warned. Adams was surprised, for he had received no instructions to announce the revocation of the exequatur and set out to convince the British that this was another false alarm. And when he met with a recuperated Russell at the Foreign Office the following day he carried the latest despatch from Seward concerning Bunch. Conciliatory in tone and indicating no great displeasure with the consul's conduct, it would help, Adams was sure, to reduce the "very strong prejudice" against Seward in England. He read it and was well satisfied with the result. At the interview's end the foreign secretary seemed to be "somewhat mollified" and even his inscrutable features could not disguise the "gleam of satisfaction in his eye." Only after he returned to the legation did Adams discover that one of Seward's despatches was missing, but uneasiness could not dim satisfaction. It was plain to him that he was making his way "into the confidence of the Ministry by simple, straightforward dealing."[18] Given time and patience he could remove the "prejudices" against his country, but time was not to be given to him.

First, even as the members of the legation were congratulating themselves on the restoration of good feelings, the missing despatch arrived on November 19. It announced the revocation of the exequatur in language "tart in the extreme." Instead of following the normal course and simply forwarding Seward's note, Adams rephrased it "so that whilst losing none of its force, it might be stripped of its acrid character."[19] His efforts made it no more acceptable to the British, just less offensive. Russell was not pleased with Bunch—the consul had not satisfied him with his explanation for the failure to follow Lyons's instructions—but the full extent of his indiscretion was hidden by the minister who valued the presence of an experienced observer in the South. Also Bunch was protected by the determination of Palmerston and Russell to guard their "Right" to employ anyone they liked to communicate with whomsoever they had reason to address. Following Palmerston's lead, the foreign secretary rejected Seward's argument that the consul had acted improperly because he had engaged in diplomatic activity. This was the response of "profligate South American Republics" when required by a consul to afford redress for injury to British subjects, the prime minister commented to Russell. It was the duty of consuls to look after British interests and it was in the performance of this recognized duty that Bunch had negotiated with the South. And when Adams doggedly continued to argue this point Russell grew impatient. By December 9 he was describing the consul's behaviour as "not only legitimate but praiseworthy," and announcing that he did not "perceive that any advantage would be obtained by the continuance of this correspondence."[20] By that time also the Bunch affair had been virtually drowned in the storm raging around the *Trent*.

The first reports of the stopping of the mail steamer and the removal of the Confederate commissioners reached London on November 27, and no one doubted for a moment the gravity of the crisis. Russell wanted a cabinet meeting called for the very next day but Palmerston put it off until November 29, so that members out of London could attend and the opinion of the law officers be obtained. Before the meeting Russell called Adams to the Foreign Office, but the minister could add nothing to what was already known, though at the foreign secretary's request he did repeat his earlier and now embarrassing assurances about the *James Adger*. In a sombre mood the British ministers gathered in the early afternoon. The law officers confirmed the earlier opinion, that such a seizure "was illegal and unjustifiable by international law." Clearly, the British government had to demand reparation and redress. In general terms it was agreed that the United States be informed that the incident was a violation of international law and of the rights of Great Britain, and that the British government expected the act to be disavowed and the prisoners restored to British protection. If these demands were refused Lyons was to "retire" from the United States. The task of drafting precise instructions was left to Russell, but the cabinet agreed to reassemble the following afternoon to discuss them.

When they met again on November 30 they endorsed two instructions. The first repeated the "facts," stated that Britain supposed that the United States would desire to make reparation of its own accord but that in any case the Confederates had to be returned along with an apology or an expression of regret. The work of fourteen men sitting around a table, each urging his own amendment to Russell's original draft, it was a "bald" document, the foreign secretary complained. The Queen and the Prince Consort also considered the wording "meagre" and they increased the number of words, softened the tone, but left unchanged the demands. The second instruction gave the United States seven days, after the presentation of the British demands, in which to reply. If at the end of that time either no answer or an unsatisfactory one had been given Lyons was to return immediately to London. Gladstone did not like this provision and urged his colleagues at least to hear what the Americans had to say before withdrawing the minister. But they refused, no doubt satisfied that British "resistance" could not "take any milder or more procrastinating expression."[21]

As well as the instructions approved by the cabinet, Russell provided Lyons with detailed suggestions for dealing with Seward. He listed the legal points the minister should make in any discussion of the merits of the case, all of which were intended to prove the impropriety of the American act. Not the least of these was the conclusion that the British could find nothing in the case of the *Trent* to justify any complaint against her in a court of justice, therefore the "outrage" was "of the most wanton nature." Russell then added some carefully weighed advice on how to perform the "disagreeable task" of presenting the British demands to Seward. At their first meeting the minister was to prepare the American for the British despatch and ask him to settle with Lincoln what they intended to do. In this way the seven-day period would be effectively extended. Then at their second meeting Lyons was to read the despatch fully, and if Seward asked what the consequences would be of a refusal to comply with the demands the minister was to reply that he wished to leave the United States free to take its own course and to abstain from anything like menace.

Russell left little to Lyons's discretion. The minister was authorized to remain at his post if he considered the demands substantially met, but he was practically freed from the responsibility of making that decision. The cabinet was willing to accept the release of the Confederates and "to be rather easy about the apology," Russell wrote. By that he meant that if Mason and Slidell were restored to British protection "an apology or explanation" sent through Adams "might be taken as substantial compliance."[22] If they were not freed no apology would suffice. Finally, he informed the minister that the French had promised to give the British case "moral support." Consequently, Lyons should delay the formal presentation of the British demands for a few days, provided that he immediately asked for the first interview with Seward. For it would be as well if the Americans considered them in the knowledge that France supported Britain. That news would be "a heavy blow and great discouragement" to Seward, whose wish to play the European powers off against one another was well known.[23] And in this instance the British reassured themselves that they could rely on Napoleon to adhere to this "very satisfactory" line because it was "in keeping with the interests of France and the feelings of the Emperor against the Northerners."[24] Nor was he likely to deviate from it if, as Palmerston and several of his colleagues feared, Britain had to fight to obtain what she sought. An Anglo-American war would see the blockade of the South raised, enabling the French to get the cotton they so desperately needed. The worry about the European consequences of their involvement in the American war seems to have been temporarily banished from British minds by the nature of the crisis. They had no choice; they had to seek satisfaction for this insult.

Even as it couched its demands in language intended to ease an American concession, and Russell plotted the tactics of presentation with the same purpose in mind, the British government began to prepare for the worst. First Russell and then Palmerston called for a ban on the export of saltpetre and all arms, ammunition, and military stores. These measures would serve as "a good political warning" to the United States, Palmerston argued in cabinet, and would decrease the danger of war by restricting the Union's military resources. They would also limit, in the event of hostilities, the number of Englishmen shot with English ammunition fired from English rifles. "Then again is it not in our interest supposing no rupture take place between us and the Northerners," he commented in a cabinet memorandum, "that the civil war should end as soon as possible and one way to hasten its end is to withhold Fuel from the Fire?"[25] Only an end to the war would stop the merchants and manufacturers roaring for cotton and cursing the loss of exports.

The cabinet's initial response was half-hearted. They approved a ban on the export of saltpetre but resisted that on arms. There was concern that it could not be effective and that Belgian munitions manufacturers would capture traditional British markets, of which the United States was now proving one of the most lucrative. Unwilling to concede defeat, Palmerston restated his opinion with characteristic forcefulness on December 2. The present policy was "one-sided and entirely favourable to the North," he charged.[26] Federal control of the seas and espionage in Britain ensured that they received not only the arms they purchased but many of those bought by the Confederacy. However curious this concept of neutrality was, it won the support of the lord chancellor. But if their policy was unfair and therefore unneutral, the British were also guilty of an act of "egregious folly" in continuing to supply arms to a probable enemy. Others would have to defend this course in Parliament because he could not, Palmerston warned. Finally, he dismissed as "cobwebs" the argument that a ban would throw the "Gun Trade" into the hands of foreigners. Two days later the cabinet agreed to an immediate prohibition of the export of arms, ammunition, military stores, and lead. The news from the United States had convinced them that Palmerston and Russell were right.

From the outset of the crisis some cabinet members had believed war to be inevitable. They admitted that Lincoln and Seward might not have authorized the *Trent* incident but reasoned that the "mob" would not permit them to disavow it. By December their pessimism had acquired the aura of prophecy. Although the news from the United States indicated that Wilkes had acted without orders, the accounts of his reception and the tone of the press suggested that the "mob" would have virtually settled the question before the British demands were received. Now the "only chance" of avoiding a collision was for reports of British war preparations to reach Washington before Russell's despatch could be rejected. The time had come for the traditional Palmerstonian gambit of moving fleets. At Russell's direction, the Admiralty had already instructed Milne to draw his forces together, so that no vessel would be left isolated and vulnerable in the event of a sudden declaration of war by the United States. By December 6 three battleships, two frigates, and a corvette had been ordered to join Milne at Bermuda, nine ships in the first division of the Steam Reserve had been readied for commissions, and another six added to the division. These reinforcements brought the total of British tonnage on the North American Station to 12,254, with an aggregate of 1,140 guns. Somerset was well satisfied with these preparations. Without commissioning more ships Britain would soon have sufficient vessels there to blockade the coast of the United States, he informed Palmerston. "I wish the Canadian affairs were as satisfactory as our prospects at sea," he added.[27] That same day, December 6, the first military reinforcements sailed for North America.

The need to bolster the defences of Canada was obvious and imperative. Earlier schemes of fortification had not been carried out, the British had no naval force on the Great Lakes, the militia was miserably inadequate and there were no more than 5,000 regulars in the province. Nothing could be done to establish control of the lakes before spring, but more regulars could be sent out and more Canadians were expected to enrol in the militia. Cornewall Lewis and his advisers decided that 30,000 stand of arms, some officers to assist in organizing the militia, and a battery of artillery should go out immediately and that at least four regiments with artillery should be sent in all. On December 4 the cabinet approved his proposals and the first supplies and troops sailed on the *Melbourne* on December 6. But these "energetic and well conceived" plans did not relieve the anxiety about Canada. There were calls for more arms to equip more volunteers, more regulars to provide more heart to the resistance to the Americans, and for the replacement of Fenwick Williams. He did not inspire confidence in the colony, his critics claimed. What was clearly needed was a small war committee to coordinate proposals and preparations and to share the burden of responsibility carried by Lewis. Composed of Palmerston, Russell, Lewis, Somerset, Newcastle, and Granville, and with the advice of the commander-in-chief, the Duke of Cambridge, it met on December 9 and agreed to send 10,500 men as reinforcements to North America. At last Palmerston had approval for the military establishment in Canada he had long wanted.

For the prime minister the *Trent* affair was a vindication of his earlier demands. He rued the day that he had submitted to his colleagues, with their talk of insufficient barracks and their fears of dampening the spirit of colonial self-defence. Irritated by the memory of this defeat, he found in Newcastle the focus of his spleen. To both Russell and Lewis he complained privately of the colonial secretary's failure to take steps to see that the militia was properly organized, drilled, and armed. To Newcastle himself he said nothing. This was no time for public recriminations, or as he put it, to hurt the feelings of a man "totally unconscious of having omitted anything which might or ought to have been done."[28] Anyway, on balance he was well satisfied with Britain's position. "If the Federal Government comply with the demands it will be honourable to England and humiliating to the United States," he informed the Queen. "If the Federal Government refuse compliance, Great Britain is in a better state than at any former time to inflict a severe blow upon, and to read a lesson to the United States which will not soon be forgotten."[29]

Whatever the colonial secretary's past mistakes, he quickly buckled down to the task of preparing Canada for the war that he now feared was all "too likely." Monck was instructed to "take up all the vacant buildings fit for barracks" and to provide the materials for "good and warm huts."[30] He was to see that no arms or munitions crossed the border into the United States, to keep all means of transportation and all provisions out of the line of any American advance, and to make the most of the "difficulties of winter." And Newcastle expressed the hope that 100,000 volunteers would be ready to take the field by spring. All of this meant the abandonment of Monck's quiet policy. The more ostensible the Canadian preparations, at least within reasonable limits, "the more likelihood will there be that peace may yet be preserved," Newcastle believed.[31]

Newcastle was also engaged in trying to persuade Gladstone to give the Canadians a fillip by announcing imperial support for an intercolonial railway. As early as November 11 he had assured Palmerston that if only Gladstone would give him "no very large" guarantee for the railroad the colonies would "fight to the death for the Mother Country."[32] That same day two of the three Canadians sent to seek support landed in England. The third did not arrive until November 26, having had the misfortune to be shipwrecked. His two colleagues had called on Newcastle on November 14, who arranged for them to see Palmerston and he in turn passed them on to Gladstone. As everyone expected and feared, the chancellor complained of "helps to other people who might help themselves."[33] Then came the *Trent* affair. The immediate need to reinforce Canada illustrated in the most dramatic way the strategic disadvantage of not having a railroad connection between Quebec and the Maritimes. Even the road lay dangerously near the frontier with Maine. The colonists exploited their opportunity. At Newcastle's suggestion they drew up a memorandum and submitted it to the Colonial Office on December 2. Before presenting it to the cabinet Newcastle asked for the opinion of the Treasury, and before doing that officially he sent it to Gladstone privately. He urged the chancellor to adopt the colonial proposal. Proclaiming his own aversion for subsidies, he insisted that this case was exceptional. To support a railroad now would be an act of far-sighted economy. By strengthening the defences of Canada it would prevent future wars and thus save Britain untold millions. To refuse the request would be a terrible blow to the "noble colonies." For them an intercolonial railway meant independence from the United States and freedom from reliance on the Grand Trunk's connection with Portland in Maine. If they saw that this plan was hopeless they would enter the war with a faint heart, convinced "that their exertions and sacrifices" would be in vain and that in future they would be at "the mercy of — no longer a neighbour of doubtful friendship but — an enemy."[34]

Unmoved by Newcastle's emotional appeal and unimpressed by his concept of economy, Gladstone was not encouraging in his reply. From the colonial secretary he sought a statement of the annual revenue of the Canadas for the past fifteen years, the expenditures, the debt, and an estimate of the current population. He was obviously planning a careful investigation of the provinces' ability to finance the scheme themselves, and his general dislike of subsidies was in this case undoubtedly strengthened by knowledge of the expensive measures already taken to defend Canada. At the War Office Lewis had abandoned all thought of economy, compelled as he was to resume recruiting, charter transports, purchase warm clothing, and make additional provisions for arms and munitions. The final cost would be far in excess of the estimates for the year, he warned the chancellor. Meanwhile, presumably in a desperate attempt to circumvent Gladstone's predictable opposition, the Canadian emissaries had taken to the road. Seeking to make the railway a public question, they addressed meetings at Liverpool, Manchester, Oldham, Ashton, and Bristol. Yet even at this moment of intense crisis they could not win overwhelming support. Their meetings went well enough, no doubt because they were rarely more than inflammatory discussions of the *Trent*, and their cause was taken up by Palmerston's *Morning Post*. However, the influential *Times* was not won over. A railroad would have insufficient use in peacetime to be profitable, while the threat of war was too dubious a contingency to justify such a costly enterprise. Anyway, the principal burden of colonial defence should be borne by the colonists. England's duty was to "support and to second them," and this she was already performing.[35]

There was general applause in the press for the government's response to the *Trent* incident. Few questioned that a "grievous outrage" had been committed against the British flag and most agreed that there was only one honourable course. Mason and Slidell had to be restored with an ample apology. On November 30 the *Morning Post* and the *Times* revealed that these were the government's demands and that if they were not met Lord Lyons would break off diplomatic relations and return home. But the chance of the United States being reasonable seemed remote. The *Spectator*'s faith in the good sense of the silent majority, to check the "bragging wretches who guide politics in the States, and whose speeches fill the best friends of the North with a feeling of angry disgust," was soon undermined by the news of the American public's reception of Wilkes.[36] The one faint hope of peace was that "imminent danger" would frighten Seward and the New York bankers "into a state of semi-sobriety."

The prospect of war caused stock values on the London market to decline and insurance rates to rise, for Americans were certain to strike at British commerce and repudiate millions of dollars of debts. Most of Britain's exports went to the North, and war would cost her that market. Nevertheless, the situation was not as black as it might have been, the *Economist* pointed out. Exports to the North had already declined in the wake of the Morrill Tariff and the war; Northerners were now wretched customers instead of good ones. They had injured Britain by cutting her off from her main supplies of cotton, and war would see the blockade raised. It was for this very reason that *Reynolds's Newspaper* welcomed the *Trent* affair. Then, through the use of her naval superiority, Britain could effectively drive United States shipping from the seas and a powerful commercial rival would be crippled. Thus war would do Britain the minimum of economic harm and confer some measure of compensation. But dissonant voices could be heard in the tumult of patriotic feeling. The Radical *Morning Star* was calling for no threats or thoughts of force until every honourable expedient of conciliation had been exhausted. John Bright and Richard Cobden publicly made the same plea.

The two Radicals had been active in London during the two crucial meetings of the cabinet at the end of November. They drew upon their earlier associations with Milner Gibson and Villiers, the respective presidents of the Board of Trade and the Poor Law Board, to advocate moderation and restraint. Then on December 4 they took their cause to the sympathetic public of Rochdale, Bright's home and Cobden's constituency. Bright had accepted an invitation to speak there some weeks earlier and had always planned to say something on the American question. He was anxious to "break out" against those public men who had shown "how little they know, and how much less they feel, as Englishmen ought to feel, in respect to the disasters of the States."[37] He did so with a characteristic oration which overshadowed the letter from Cobden that was read to the meeting. The "Transatlantic English nation" had been rent by the insurrection of slave states whose object was "to escape from the majority who wish to limit the area of slavery," Bright declaimed.[38] In spite of this Northerners had not seen that "friendly and cordial" British neutrality they must surely have expected. Not surprisingly they had revealed their irritation, yet even this was a "measure of the high opinion" they placed on English attitudes. Turning to the *Trent*, Bright made as much as he could of the imprecise nature of the international law which was founded on precedents "not always like each other." It was almost certain that the United States government had not authorized the act, he declared, and that it would make "fitting reparation" if its legal advisers were of the opinion that the seizure was illegal. Therefore, it was essential that Britain remain calm, that the public remember how they had been dragged into the Crimean War which had cost not only enormous sums but also forty thousand lives and had seriously disturbed trade. Clearly, morality and materialism were once again in harmony.

Privately, Bright and Cobden were striving to convince Charles Sumner of the seriousness of the crisis. They imagined that he had "a kind of veto on the acts of Seward" and were sure that he was a "very peaceable and safe man." Through him the Americans had to be made to understand that "the greatest care must be taken on their part, and that they must not ignore their own altered position."[39] Bright threw himself into this task. "Be courteous and conceding to the last possible degree, now in your time of trial," he advised Sumner, "and may God help you in your struggle for freedom and humanity."[40] An offer of arbitration would save the honour of the United States and put Britain in the wrong if she refused. But come what may the United States must not let the affair grow into a war, even if it was in the right and Britain in the wrong. War with the British would deal a fatal blow to the hopes of restoring the Union. Cobden was no less insistent, though he looked beyond the immediate crisis. He repeatedly warned the American "that the cotton tie which used to keep the peace" was now pulling the other way.[41] How long would the European powers tolerate the blockade if nothing decisive happened, he asked. Not more than a year and perhaps less than six months, was his own estimate. It was time to reform the maritime code and prohibit blockades. The Union should agree to the abolition of all blockades before Europe intervened to raise that of the South. All the North needed was time, time to ensure its triumph and the death of slavery. "And the only way in which you can have time," he warned, "is by abolishing the blockade."[42]

The anxiety that fired Cobden and Bright burned even more fiercely among Northerners in Britain. The atmosphere at the American legation "would have gorged a glutton of gloom."[43] Anxious American visitors came in from London streets where miniature Confederate flags were being hawked, to ask if war would result. Their question was unanswerable and they left unreassured. Charles Francis Adams sank into despondency. All his efforts to preserve amiable relations with Britain had been jeopardized, and for such a paltry gain. The breach in Anglo-American relations that he had been struggling to prevent appeared to be opening beneath his feet. The British newspapers were so violent that he refused to read them; Forster came to dinner and "spoke without courage." Adams was embarrassed and angered by his ignorance, for he received despatches from Seward that contained not a line on the *Trent*. Convinced that his residence in London was about to be abruptly terminated he pondered whether he should go straight home or retire to the continent for the remainder of the winter and cross the stormy Atlantic during the spring. Mrs. Adams favoured braving the winter seas.

Yet there was a way out of the crisis, Adams believed, as long as the government had not compromised itself by endorsing Wilkes's act. The United States should remain true to its "honorable record" of defending neutral rights at sea, and thereby transform the surrender of the Confederates into a "great concession of principle from Great Britain."[44] Adams suggested that Seward revive the American proposal for greater protection of neutral vessels, first unsuccessfully urged on the British by James Madison early in the century. Nothing would be lost by such a move, and it would serve "to break the force of public opinion of Europe" which would certainly be against the United States if it placed itself in the position that had earned Britain the enmity of all maritime nations.

The same thought had occurred to John Bigelow in Paris. He drafted a public letter which was signed by General Winfield Scott, the former commander of the Union armies who had just arrived in the French capital. The old soldier lent the authority of his name to an expression of confidence that "the President and people of the United States would be but too happy to let these men go free, unnatural and unpardonable as their offences have been, if by it they could emancipate the commerce of the world."[45] Bigelow was excited by the response of the Paris dailies, several of which expressed the opinion that it would be fortunate if out of the crisis new regulations governing the rights of neutrals were achieved. This was the way to put England on the defensive, he wrote to Seward, echoing Adams. The United States would "lose no standing" by making concessions if it insisted that Britain surrender forever the right of visit and search of neutral vessels.

Meanwhile, Seward's unofficial ambassadors in Britain were urging him to release Mason and Slidell. Thurlow Weed had landed at Le Havre late in November, had visited Paris where Bigelow pressed him into service to persuade Scott to sign his letter, and then crossed the Channel. McIlvaine reached London soon after him. The "refined" bishop's influential friends and the tone of the press convinced him that the commissioners had to be released if war was to be averted. The doors of society also opened for the tall, slender, grey-haired figure of Weed. His reputation as "a great friend and adviser of Mr. Seward had preceded him."[46] As he listened to the talk Weed was appalled by the dislike and distrust of the secretary and alarmed by the danger of war. All of London society seemed to have heard or was retelling and embellishing the story that during the Prince of Wales's tour of North America Seward had told Newcastle that if he became secretary it would be his duty to insult Britain. The insult had been directed at Britain's flag and if necessary she was prepared to go to war to avenge it, he warned Seward. Little could be expected of the brave opposition of "Bright and his set," for they were labouring "against wind and tide." To Seward, to Lincoln, and to Simon Cameron, the secretary of war, he wrote urging "forbearance." Turn, "if needs be, even the other cheek rather than smite back at present," he implored. Only the Confederates would benefit from a war with Britain; "Slidell and Mason would be a million times less mischievous here than at Fort Warren." But like the British government and like Adams, Weed feared "the temper of Congress and our People."[47]

American preparedness for a violent British reaction to the incident had been halted by news from England. The republication on December 9 of an article from the Edinburgh *Scotsman*, reporting the law officers' opinion on the rights of the *James Adger*, relieved the *New York Herald* and the *Times* of all anxiety on the *Trent*. "This should settle the matter," the *Times* remarked. And from being valueless in its eyes Mason and Slidell became prisoners who could never be surrendered. The almost simultaneous publication of Seward's diplomatic correspondence for the year apparently did little to raise the spirit of concession. Britain had been unmasked as an enemy of American nationality. "If there be any who have thus far clung to the belief that the Great Powers of Western Europe do not really desire the triumph of the Confederate States," Horace Greeley's *Tribune* declared, "we think these facts will undeceive them."[48] Nevertheless, the chances of a peaceful settlement of the *Trent* affair were improved by these diplomatic revelations. Few who read and interpreted them in this way could doubt that Britain would seize the opportunity to divide the Union, if there was an attempt to face her down. Also, they strengthened Seward's conciliatory hand.

For all his efforts to regain public confidence in October the secretary had not stifled a vicious campaign of political and personal abuse. "Few men are now more violently attacked on all sides," Charles Francis Adams Jr. reported to his mother at the end of November.[49] He was denounced as a fanatical abolitionist or as a compromiser with slavery, as an invader of civil liberties and a warmonger, even as an alcoholic. But he controlled his fury and made no public comment on the charges. The popular applause he thirsted for came with the publication of his despatches. They excited the "greatest admiration" and went far "to reinstate Seward in the estimation of cultivated minds."[50]

By December 16, Americans had learnt from the London *Times* that Lyons had been instructed to secure the release of Mason and Slidell and an apology, and to ask for his passports if these were refused. Significantly, with one or two trifling exceptions, members of Congress refrained from inflammatory rhetoric. They were agreed that it was their duty, at a moment when the nation stood at the brink of a foreign war, to be grave, deliberate, and calm. On this question Seward had Congress under control, the younger Charles Francis Adams concluded. Another hopeful sign for those resolved to avoid a wider conflict, was the shaky condition of federal finances. A military reverse at Ball's Bluff and then the *Trent* affair had undermined the confidence of the bankers in the government and its notes. By the beginning of December they were rumoured to be considering the suspension of specie payments. For safekeeping, gold mined in California was diverted to England, while that earned by the sale of American foodstuffs was left there. Then came the reports of Britain's demands and war preparations. Share values fell sharply on the New York stock exchange and suspension seemed imminent. Worried, self-appointed spokesmen for the financial and commercial interests of New York and Boston appealed to cabinet members to avoid war unless it could be shown to be an unavoidable necessity. A war with England would "make sad work" with all interests and give "joy and gladness" to the secessionists. The market was weak and would remain so until the crisis with England was resolved, Salmon Chase's broker informed him. And he refused to sell some of the secretary's holdings of railroad stock because they were worth at least 25 cents a share but would bring no more and probably less than 17 cents each. The business community "trust you will have allayed this excitement with England," he wrote on December 20, "one war at a time is enough."[51]

Seward agreed. The daydream of a reunifying foreign war had long since faded from his mind and it was already too late to attempt to frighten Britain with words. This was "no time to be diverted from the cares of the Union into controversies with other powers, even if just causes for them could be found."[52] Concession without disgrace was possible because he had prevented the government from endorsing Wilkes, and when he met Rudolph Schleiden on December 14 he assured him that there would be a peaceful settlement. Once again he emphasized that Wilkes had acted without orders and when Schleiden referred to Welles's belated and embarrassing approval of his officer, Seward replied, "I don't care a bit what Mr. Welles said."[53] The following day he received word of the British demands, at least as they had been published in the English press. Would concessions now be prevented by a British determination to humiliate the United States? Was the tone peremptory, would there be an ultimatum, would the nation swallow its pride, what would happen to his newly-won popularity if he agreed to a humiliation? These and other questions must have been running through Seward's fertile mind when he attended a ball at the Portuguese legation on December 16. By that time the alleged British demands had been republished in the Northern newspapers, yet Seward seemed affable enough. He showed none of the irritation with Britain he had displayed in May and June. However, he did declare that if she forced war on the United States "we will wrap the whole world in flames. No power is so remote that she will not feel the fire of our battle and be burned by our conflagration."[54] He was clearly speaking for effect. It was too late to influence the British government but not Lyons. There was time to impress the minister with the need to be flexible, to exercise to the full whatever discretion had been given to him.

It was the afternoon of December 19 before Lyons met with Seward. Following Russell's instructions to the letter he went to the State Department to acquaint the American in general terms with the tenor of the despatch, and a serious secretary heard him out with dignity. It was vital for Seward that he discover the exact nature of the task that confronted him. Had a time been fixed within which the United States must reply, he asked. Lyons revealed that it was seven days. Valuable time would be saved, Seward responded, if he could have "unofficially and informally" a copy of the despatch.[55] After some hesitation and on condition that only Seward and Lincoln should see it, Lyons agreed to furnish a copy. He recognized the value of time. He was waiting for Thouvenel's expected despatch and was anxious to permit Seward to work with the president before the issue came before the entire cabinet. Returning to the legation the minister sent the despatch to Seward and "almost immediately afterwards" the American called there. He told Lyons he was pleased with his cooperative spirit, the "courteous and friendly" tone of Russell's note, in which there was no mention of the seven-day period. Seward then pressed on with the main reason for the visit. He wanted to know the consequences of refusal or procrastination. Avoiding menace, but determined to leave Seward in no doubt of Britain's resolution, the minister replied that on this point he had been left no discretion. If the answer was not satisfactory, which meant anything short of the immediate release of Mason and Slidell, he could not accept it.

Lyons returned to the State Department on Saturday, December 21, to present the British despatch officially, but Seward asked him to delay until Monday. The minister readily agreed. The earliest packet by which he could forward the American reply did not sail from New York until January 1, so a postponement of a day or two was immaterial. Also, sure that both government and people were "very much frightened," he welcomed the opportunity to play upon their fears. He was hoping for fresh news from Britain of warlike preparations and was still awaiting the arrival of the French despatch, which would convince Northerners that there was no hope of "any diversion in their favour by France" or of Britain accepting French mediation. Mercier, with whom Lyons was working very closely, did his best to impress this upon Seward. He went of his own accord to see the secretary on December 21. Compliance with the demands or war were the choices open to the United States, he insisted. There was no hope of assistance from France and Americans should not be led away by "the vulgar notion that the Emperor would gladly see England embroiled with the United States in order to pursue his own plans in Europe without opposition."[56] Seward listened patiently, then asked the Frenchman whether he had received special instructions and when he divulged that he had not, calmly commented, "Let us wait and see what your instructions really turn out to be." Although they had still not arrived on Monday, the European packet having been delayed, Lyons decided to go ahead with the official presentation of Britain's demands. To delay longer might be interpreted as vacillation, he feared, and that would be fatal. It was time to give the Americans a good lesson, and anything less than a choice between surrender or war would make them "more self-confident than ever, and lead them on to their ruin."[57] Thus at 10 a.m. on December 23, he informed Seward that he had to have a reply by noon of December 30. He had every reason to expect an answer before then and as he wrote in a note to Admiral Milne, so cautious as to be highly characteristic of Lyons, "It is not *quite* certain that it will be a refusal."[58]

Reluctantly, Lincoln's cabinet acknowledged that they must give up the Confederates. The president himself, having shared the false optimism produced by the reports of the law officers' opinion was ill-prepared for the British demands confidentially disclosed by Lyons on December 19. And before the shock had worn off a nervous Charles Sumner appeared at the White House with the alarming letters of Bright and Cobden. There was no longer any room for doubt that the United States was heading for a collision with Britain. The consequences of conflict were frightening. The Union's blockade of the South would be replaced by a British one of the North, Federal vessels would be swept from the seas, and Northern trade ruined. France would join Britain in recognizing Confederate independence and then press on with the establishment of an empire in Mexico. Finally, with Anglo-French assistance, the Confederacy would successfully establish itself. Obviously, it was vital that a rupture be avoided if the Union was to be restored. The problem, and it was now an urgent one, was how to do this without humiliation and dishonour. Arbitration was widely touted as a face-saving device and Lincoln dabbled with it as well as with an idea for making this case the recognized precedent for "all future analogous cases" between the two nations. But in both instances further discussions with the British were necessary and Seward knew that nothing short of an immediate agreement to release Mason and Slidell would satisfy Lyons.

The cabinet assembled at the White House on a bright and mild Christmas morning and for four hours discussed the crisis. Russell's despatch was read. Sumner was there and read the latest letters from Cobden and Bright. Thouvenel's instructions to Mercier had just arrived, were sent in by the French minister, and Seward read them. Other diplomatic correspondence and private letters, including at least one from Weed, were read. Their import was universally grim. The British were "thoroughly aroused" by the affront to their dignity and the honour of their flag. They were supported by the French, who would be strongly tempted to join the British in any war that would end the blockade. No one believed that the Union could afford such a war. Yet the problem remained, how to escape with as little damage as possible to national pride? Face-saving procrastination was ruled out by the terms of the British demands; anyway it was deplored by Chase as secretary of the treasury. Financially, the government could not afford delays. As he explained to his colleagues, "While the matter hangs in uncertainty, the public mind will remain disquieted, our commerce will suffer serious harm, our action against rebels will be greatly hindered, and the restoration of our prosperity, largely identified with that of all nations, must be delayed." Far better to make the sacrifice of feeling involved in releasing the Confederates immediately "than even to avoid it by the delays which explanations must occasion."[59] Fortunately, dignity could be preserved, as Adams and Bigelow had pointed out, by making concession a matter of international principle. Perhaps prompted by Adams, Seward quoted James Madison to demonstrate that in yielding the United States was remaining true to its traditional policy. The following day the cabinet reassembled and after "some verbal and formal" changes "unanimously" concurred in Seward's answer to Lyons announcing the release of Mason and Slidell. The fear of war had conquered the lingering fear that there would be a public outcry against "truckling to the power of England."[60]

The administration was saved from domestic reproach by Seward. His despatch was a masterpiece of its kind. Wilkes had acted on his own authority but not improperly. His one error had been his failure to take the vessel in as a prize. The officer's reasons were given and his oversight described as an act of "prudence and generosity." There was no cause here for Wilkes's many admirers to take offence. But in acknowledging this error the United States "was really defending and maintaining, not an exclusively British interest, but an old, honored and cherished American cause."[61] The Americans had been asked "to do to the British nation" just what they had always insisted all nations ought to do to them. Thus did Seward truly make a virtue of necessity. Yet he could not close without a few flourishes. If the safety of the Union had required the continued detention of Mason and Slidell they would have been held, but they were unimportant and the cause they represented was daily waning in influence and power. Finally, he reminded his readers that Great Britain had refused similar claims by the United States in the past. Now, Britain had adopted the American ground. It was a "smart" argument though "a little too long, and not in genuine diplomatic style."[62] Or as Seward himself explained to Lyons, his answer was intended as a compliance with the British demands but presented "in the form which would be most acceptable to the American people."[63]

The immediate publication of Seward's reply won for him private commendation and public acclaim. He had "the honours" of the affair. He had proved that the Union had not been "humiliated and disgraced," that it had not been "bullied into compliance with an unjust demand."[64] Instead, national honour remained unsullied. The surrender of the Confederates was a victory not a defeat. If there was little of this forced self-congratulation in Congress, there was also little criticism. By inviting Sumner to participate in the decision the administration had purchased for itself some protection from Congressional attacks. It quickly paid dividends. When John Hale of New Hampshire stood up in the Senate on December 26 to declare that he "would not submit to the arbitrary, the absolute demand of Great Britain to surrender these men and humble our flag even to escape war with Great Britain," Sumner quickly silenced him.[65] Seward's despatch was greeted realistically by practically all congressmen. There were more urgent duties than war with Britain. Their departure unmourned, Mason and Slidell were put aboard a British warship at a remote fishing town on the tip of Cape Cod at the beginning of the New Year.

While Northerners manfully swallowed their pride with some pretence of enjoyment, they had the satisfaction of witnessing the "frenzies and exhibitions of wild passion" in the South at the news of the commissioners' release.[66] For Confederates the settlement of the *Trent* affair was another cruelly bitter disappointment. They had hoped for so much and by mid-December had reason to believe that here was a case of wish-fulfilment. The British reaction to the incident had been all that they had dared to expect, and it seemed impossible that the North could return the two men and apologize. Had not Welles and Congress irrevocably committed the Union? There could be no backing out "without unutterable disgrace." Therefore, British intervention in the war was imminent. Soon, Southern ports would be open and Northern closed; Confederate independence would be recognized; a plentiful supply of cotton would be exported to Europe in return for all the things Southerners needed; Northern cities would be decaying and Southern growing and prospering; and there would be peace. A speedy peace was the quintessence of all these Southern hopes. From military camps soldiers wrote home elated by the promise of recognition and a short war. Speculators who had been buying up cotton at eight cents a pound, gambling that the blockade would be raised in a few months and their fortunes made, suddenly discovered that the foreign news had "put up" the planters' ideas about the value of their crops. For these soldiers and planters, for their families, friends, and fellow citizens, the release of Mason and Slidell turned hope into bitterness.

The Southern press let out a howl of impotent fury at Lincoln's "cowardice" and Seward's "duplicity" in refusing to fight the British. "A more sickening, contemptible and disgusting exhibition of diplomacy" had never been seen in European or American history.[67] And for all the wily Seward's efforts "to smother his shame in a torrent of disputation," the eyes of Europe were upon him and "neither his rounded sentences nor his elaborate quibbling would conceal the depth of his degradation."[68] The world would at last be convinced that the South was the repository of American honour and manliness. However, apart from this ephemeral consolation the only comfort the press could offer Southerners was the stale doctrine of King Cotton.

No amount of Northern "shuffling and equivocation" could offset the British need for cotton. There were four million bags of cotton in Southern warehouses waiting to be exported and there was less than two months supply of the staple left in England. The conclusion was obvious. The British would take better care of themselves than suffer an economic and social calamity when it could be averted by sending for the cotton that awaited them. They could not hope to obtain the staple from the ports controlled by the North, for at Port Royal, South Carolina, all the cotton had been burnt before it could be seized. Yet this litany was recited with less conviction than before and doubt found expression in calls for self-reliance. Only an unaided victory would be sweet, creditable, and permanent. "By relying upon the breaking of the blockade, and upon foreign interposition" Southerners had neglected to resort to "obvious and indispensable means" for their safety.[69] They had failed to establish industries and to take advantage of the weaknesses in the blockade. "If we rest idly on our oars, in the vain expectation that foreign governments or foreign merchants will come to our aid," the *Richmond Whig* warned, "we may at the end of another four months find ourselves in a far worse condition than we are at present."[70]

Jefferson Davis and his cabinet shared this concern for the future. December was a dismal month for the Confederate government. The president was under attack for his conduct of the war. Pierre Beauregard, the hero of Bull Run, encouraged the rumours that Davis had prevented him from following up that success and taking Washington. The war was going badly in Missouri and Davis was embarrassed by the charges of the secessionist governor that the situation was attributable to neglect by Richmond. Governors of several states, particularly those of Georgia and South Carolina, were "giving trouble" about providing troops and were "not acting in harmony with the Administration." On top of these military cares came financial worries. Memminger reported to the cabinet on December 6 that "means were provided until April next, but it was time to be looking ahead." The prospects were bleak. Unless the blockade was raised there was scant hope of finding fresh revenues, and there was none of reducing expenses. "God help us! I fear the worst has not come," was the silent invocation of one listener.[71] For those who had put their trust in Britain it came with the release of Mason and Slidell. Memminger was reduced to hoping against hope "for some further complication,"[72] which Davis in desperation now attempted to provoke.

On January 6 the president revived a proposal he had first made soon after Memminger's gloomy report. As the Confederacy was obtaining little revenue from the tariff he suggested that they offer free trade to all nations as "an inducement to them to raise or break the blockade."[73] But the harassed secretary of the treasury did not see how the Confederacy could get along without these duties. Judah Benjamin thought the small but highly profitable trade in and out of the South could easily support a 15 per cent duty and Hunter spoke for the rest of those present when he asserted that sufficient money could not be raised by direct taxation to pay the interest on the large and growing war debt. Thus the president's proposal was defeated in cabinet, but the very raising of it betrayed misgivings about the power of cotton to secure foreign recognition. Indeed, the financial straits of the Confederacy were already forcing the government to disregard the embargo which had been intended to exert irresistible pressure on Britain. As its supply of specie began to run short the administration was obliged to export the staple to pay for munitions. An absolute King Cotton was as impracticable as free trade.

What foreign policy was left to the Confederacy? Davis gave his answer on February 22. The occasion was his inaugural, the electorate having confirmed the provisional selection made by the Montgomery Convention just a year earlier. Although Washington's birthday had been chosen for the ceremony, it proved an inauspicious moment. Affairs were "in a blue way." Union armies and fleets seemed to be "swarming and threatening everywhere." In the west the South had just suffered its first serious military setback. The fall of Forts Henry and Donelson gave the Union forces control of the strategically vital Tennessee and Cumberland rivers. The blockade was causing hardship. Scarcity brought high prices which in turn forced "acts of self-denial and sacrifices." Abroad, "England's eye is scornful and scoffing as she turns it on our miseries," wrote Mary Chesnut. "Bad news is killing me."[74] If ever there was a time for inspirational oratory it was now. Davis did his best. Echoing the appeals of the press, he exhorted a people who had been encouraged to secede with the promise of foreign intervention to fight on unaided. But he was also addressing Britain and France. They as much as the North had to be convinced of the South's resolution. Hunter had already instructed Mason and Slidell to "take care" to emphasize in London and Paris the Confederacy's certainty of its ability to achieve its own independence and free its soil "from the invader's tread." Of course, that might require "time and sacrifices." It was important that the European powers understand this, for their interests were involved in the struggle. Continued European acquiescence in "a pretended blockade" would not only deprive them of their traditional commerce but also hurry the South down the road to self-sufficiency. Davis repeated the warning he had given a few weeks earlier. Prolonged self-reliance meant the diversion of Southern industry "from the production of articles for export" to the supply of commodities for domestic use. On the other hand, if quickly recognized and permitted to follow their interests and inclinations to cultivate foreign trade, the Southern states would "offer to manufacturing nations the most favorable markets which ever invited their commerce."[75]

Davis was not brandishing cotton, rather he was engaged in a reckoning of the gains and losses of Confederate independence. These were political as well as commercial. A Confederacy composed of all the slave states, which meant the incorporation of Maryland, Kentucky, and Missouri, would be strong enough both to protect itself from aggression and to counterbalance its northern neighbour. Its political interests like its commercial would be "auxiliary" not "adversary" to those of Britain. The promise Hunter held out to Britain privately and Davis publicly was of a truly complementary Atlantic economy, in which Southern producers of raw materials imported British manufactures "at as low a rate of duty as would be consistent with their revenue wants."[76] This was the bait, and the prospect of industrial disaster was the goad, which it was still hoped would induce Britain to intervene and supervise a favourable settlement. Thus almost against their will Confederates continued to wait anxiously and fretfully for news from across the Atlantic.

In the past Southerners had freely acknowledged that British intervention was unlikely until the Canadas were adequately protected, and whatever else it had failed to achieve the *Trent* affair had liberated Britain from this constraint. Not only had she a substantial force of regulars there but the province appeared to be improving and strengthening the militia. However, the truth of the matter was that the colonial zeal for self-defence ebbed and flowed with the danger of war. Certainly it had waned by the beginning of December as fear of an imminent war declined, but the British reaction to the seizure of the commissioners roused the torpid ministry. "There now scarcely remains a gleam of hope that peace will be preserved between England and what remains of the United States," the *Toronto Leader* judged.[77] Monck, who only a few days earlier had been fretting over the government's military inactivity, now found that he had been given carte blanche. Money was suddenly available for fortifications on the Welland Canal and Macdonald quickly produced a plan for calling out a select group of the Sedentary Militia. He promised 46,000 men shortly and 100,000 eventually.

All of this was undertaken with a show of national "unanimity pleasing to all." There were exceptions, of course. The French-Canadian response to the call for volunteers was disappointing. A meeting called to organize a company of militia in the lower part of Quebec City ended in chaos. The speaker was hissed, the lights in the hall extinguished, and the meeting broken up by a group of Irishmen who then marched through the neighbourhood cheering for the United States. Even when militia companies were formed few of the members turned out for drill. Nevertheless, it was significant that in Canada West the *Toronto Globe* joined the call for a well-drilled militia. "They may not be needed to fight, we confidently hope and believe that they will not, but preparation will do no harm to anyone," it declared. "While Britain is doing so much, Canadians should not be idle."[78] Then again, if the *Trent* incident was settled peacefully Canadians should be prepared for a period of Anglo-American irritation. "It is desirable not to over-estimate the importance of the Mason and Slidell affair as an occasion for putting the Province into an efficient state of defence," the *Leader* cautioned on December 26. The release of the commissioners was followed by an attempt on the part of the Liberal-Conservative press to convince Canadians that the crisis had taught the province a lesson. "Our militia must never again be allowed to be so utterly unfit for work of defence."[79]

The belief that continued peace with the United States was uncertain and Canadian preparedness therefore essential was shared by Lyons and Newcastle. For the colonial secretary this was "a golden opportunity" to impress upon Canadians the need to defend themselves.[80] The campaign in the ministerial press suggested that the Cartier-Macdonald coalition took the same view, which was advanced by the appointment of Macdonald as minister of militia affairs. The government recognized that the existing law had failed to maintain an efficient force, and it agreed to present a new bill to the next session of the Provincial Parliament. To prepare this measure a commission was appointed, and its members included Macdonald, Cartier, Galt, and a War Office expert, Colonel Lysons, who had been sent out to help to organize the volunteers. Monck had high hopes that the result would be a Canadian system comparable to that in England. But he soon discovered that as the threat of war receded the passion for economy grew stronger. "The financial affairs of the colony, though improving, are not yet in a flourishing condition," he admitted to Lyons.[81] Together with the evidence provided by the *Trent* affair that Britain would rush aid to the colony, and cheering reports from Washington of a "civil and conciliatory" temper,[82] this consideration served to inhibit the costly defensive zeal of the government. Work on the Welland Canal fortifications was suspended until a commission could report on the defence of the entire province. By mid-February, with the meeting of the Provincial Parliament only a month away, Monck was reporting to Newcastle that while the Militia Commission was working very well there was a difficulty over the "money question." His ministers conceded "the justice of the doctrine that in ordinary times the Province should pay for its own defences," certainly they understood that the time was coming when the British taxpayer would refuse to pay, but "practically they have hopes that they may be helped from home at this time." Some assurance that they would be given help "in the way of arms and equipment or clothing" might make "the difference between a successful and an abortive attempt" to place the Canadian force on "a satisfactory footing."[83] A year after the dissolution of the American Union the Canadian government was still looking to London.

TEN

A few months longer

THROUGHOUT DECEMBER, the British pressed on with their preparations for war. By Christmas eve more than 11,000 officers and men had either sailed or were about to leave for Canada, and instructions had been sent to Admiral Milne. The duties of his squadron would be to raise the Union blockade of the South and without cooperating directly with the Confederates "enable them to act and receive supplies," then to seal the Federal ports. Yet it was too much to hope that all Union vessels could be bottled up and privateering thereby stifled. There were rumours that the United States government, anticipating war, had sent a number of blank letters of marque to Europe, and that some American vessels in British ports were being armed and prepared to prey on British commerce. The Home Office hurriedly ordered the mayors of the principal ports to keep a sharp watch, and the Admiralty gave similar instructions to the captains in those districts. The Foreign Office decided to invite the Americans, on the outbreak of war, to abide by the provision of the Declaration of Paris banning this "objectionable system of warfare." Although it was "highly improbable" that they would agree, their refusal would free Britain from any obligation to abide by the Declaration. Steps were taken to defend the western lines of communication with the Pacific, across the isthmus of Panama and round Cape Horn. Milne was ordered to extend whatever protection he could to the British West Indies. The War Office recommended that the owners of mail steamers fit rifled 20-pounders to their vessels, and thought was given to the defence of the British coasts and the protection of Queen Victoria on the Isle of Wight from some latter-day John Paul Jones.

Enough was known of these preparations to convince observers that Britain was "in downright earnestness." This knowledge took some of the sting out of the rebuff the Confederate commissioners received when they attempted to capitalize upon the crisis. On November 27 they wrote to Russell protesting the seizure of Mason and Slidell. Instinctively, they took the same tack as Davis. They claimed "for their imprisoned countrymen the full benefit of that protection to which every private person who seeks shelter under the British flag and demeans himself according to British law has heretofore ever been held to be entitled."[1] However, when they received the instructions drafted weeks earlier for Mason and Slidell, the three Confederates attempted to initiate a discussion of the blockade. Diplomatic consistency, "real neutrality," and commercial interest all required, they argued in a second letter to Russell, that Britain enforce the international law that "blockades to be binding must be effective." On November 30 they provided him with a list of more than 400 vessels that had arrived in the South and "departed unmolested" since the Proclamation of Blockade. The foreign secretary's reply was a terse refusal "to enter into any official communication with them." The impulsive Yancey resented the "term and spirit" of this response and thought that it called for a reply from the commission. His colleagues disagreed. Convinced that the Union would soon force Britain to make common cause with the Confederacy, they were loath to erect any barrier of irritation.

If the British government ignored the Confederate diplomats, it was more difficult to disregard the activities of Unionists and Englishmen agitating for a peaceful solution to the affair. They were seeking to organize support both within influential circles and among the people for arbitration. Thurlow Weed was indefatigable. He schemed "to reach the People through the Press."[2] He breakfasted, lunched, and dined "with important personages."[3] Meanwhile, the religious community made plain its "great aversion to making war upon a form."[4] The subject was alluded to in many churches on December 8, "in a very becoming way,"[5] and on December 12 more than four thousand people attended a meeting at Exeter Hall to pray for peace.

Bright was convinced that the British government really intended war. Cobden was less gloomy. "I do not believe in war or that the old dodger wants it," he wrote on December 11. Palmerston "wishes to mount the British Lion and furnish an excuse for the present establishment and perhaps to justify further expenditures."[6] Nevertheless he was disgusted by the "cowardice" of those of his countrymen who were eager to fight the

Americans now that they were crippled by a civil war. Such belligerence compared ill with the great forbearance the English had displayed "when Washington was the capital of a United people," and together with Bright he urged Milner Gibson and Charles Villiers to disassociate themselves from any hostile measures. He even overcame his reserve and approached Gladstone, who agreed with Cobden "that we must not finally conclude in this matter until we shall have heard what America herself may have to say."[7]

Important as they considered these private appeals, the two Radicals also pressed ahead with their efforts to organize public opinion. Long committed to the compulsory arbitration of all disputes, Cobden was anxious to get up as many demonstrations as possible in favour of an arbitrated settlement of the *Trent* affair. This form of agitation was far more likely to attract widespread support than a cry for peace "which might mean submission."[8] Bright readily agreed, for he was sure that there was no town in England where a public meeting would not vote for arbitration. In fact there was at least one. A town meeting in Bright's own constituency of Birmingham declined to recommend the arbitration of the American dispute. Instead, it reaffirmed its confidence in Palmerston and Russell. Other meetings proved more cooperative. W. E. Forster spoke at Bradford, and that meeting, one at Halifax, and another at Brighton endorsed arbitration, as did much of the provincial daily press. Elated by the support of newspapers in Birmingham, Leeds, Liverpool, Glasgow, and Manchester, Cobden excitedly concluded that "if the Americans offer to submit this matter to arbitration it will be unanimously accepted in England."[9]

However exaggerated his notion of the strength and influence of this agitation, Cobden, together with Bright and others, had succeeded in making more difficult the government's task of maintaining public support for its decisive response to the *Trent* incident. But it was not bereft of allies. *Punch*'s resolute Britannia appeared beside a cannon, lanyard in hand, "Waiting For An Answer." The *Times* opposed arbitration, reminding the "pacific monitors" of the long series of earlier disputes that had ended in British concessions. And it was the *Times* and the *Morning Post*, the two organs most closely identified with Palmerston, which quickly checked the hopes of peace raised by a meeting of Russell and Adams on December 19.

The third week of December had begun in a sombre way for

the British government. Shocked and saddened by the death of the Prince Consort, it was also confronted with grim news from the United States. Lincoln's prudence in not mentioning the *Trent* in his first annual message seemed less significant than the passage of the Congressional vote of thanks to Wilkes. Here was proof that Congress would prevent any rational solution. For his part Adams was still infected with gloom. Ignorant of his own government's intentions, he met with Russell to discover those of Britain, and to try to disabuse the British of the idea that the United States in general and Seward in particular were set on a hostile course. So he took with him and read Seward's despatch of November 30, announcing that the arrest of the Confederates had been unauthorized and that the United States would not commit itself before it heard from Britain. Russell responded with an outline of his instructions and private letters to Lyons. The American felt calmer after this talk, though he was still worried by the tone of Palmerston's press allies.

The rumour that Adams had conveyed a peaceful despatch to Russell raced through the City on December 20, and stock values quickly responded. But neither Adams's conciliatory language nor the evidence of Seward's desire to avoid war guaranteed peace. What passed in London provided but a slight indication of what was happening in Washington, Russell thought. If, as the action of Congress suggested, the mob was already in power there the British demand would be rejected, and Britain had "to deal with ultimate decisions, not half-formed intentions."[10] Clearly the "mercantile sense of national honour," for which Bright was being savagely mocked by *Punch*, had to be restrained before it got out of hand, and that temptress Peace seduced the public. On December 21 the authoritative *Morning Post* denied that Adams had read a note which dealt with the *Trent* affair, while the *Times* again reviewed the history of Anglo-American relations during the past fifty years, reviving bitter memories and sharpening the sense of national indignation. "We are convinced at last that there is little dignity or wisdom in submitting any longer to treatment which, on the part of the United States, has become habitual and traditional," the *Times* concluded, "Peace can never be preserved in this way."

Yet, as Russell appreciated, the country would not approve an immediate declaration of war if the American reply was not a blunt refusal. If it was "a reasoning" the government "should send once more across the Atlantic to ask compliance," he thought.[11] He intimated as much to Adams on December 19. But there were other reasons for this reluctance to rush into a war. Lyons gave "a sad account of Canada," and then there was France. Napoleon's declared support for the British had been doubly welcome, for it had promised both to exert some influence upon the Americans and to relieve the anxiety of those Englishmen who were "persuaded that France only dreams by night and fumes by day upon vengeance for Waterloo."[12] However, by the end of December Russell and Palmerston had had ample time to reflect upon the European consequences of an American war. Hamstrung by the need to deal with the United States and protect Canada, Britain would be unable to check France. With Germany and Italy both feeling themselves in the grasp of the French emperor, it seemed that only a depleted treasury could prevent him from being in the thick of a European war by the spring.

The news that the United States had decided to release Mason and Slidell reached London on January 8, 1862. "It was announced at most of the London theatres between acts, and the audiences arose like one and cheered tremendously."[13] *The Morning Star and Dial* bravely hailed this "great victory" for the Republic. But this sympathetic and generous voice was lost in a wilderness of self-congratulation. The peaceful result was "entirely due to the mingled firmness and courtesy" with which the British government acted, the *Morning Post* declared. The Americans had been taught the much-needed lesson that it was "unsafe to presume upon British patience too far." They had been cowed by the British preparations for war. "There is no doubt about it," one Tory commented, "we put them in a precious funk."[14] Lord Derby privately rejoiced that Britain had taken a belligerent tone, for "if we are to have flung on the surface such scum as Seward and Co it is just as well that they should understand that blustering is not always safe and (as such are the motives by which they are governed) it will not in the end improve their 'personal position'."[15]

Palmerston and Russell were also pleased by the outcome of the affair. John Bright's "favourite North American Republic" had been humiliated.[16] The prisoners had been released and while there had been no formal apology there had been an unequivocal declaration that Wilkes had acted without orders.

However, some of the principles of international law laid down by Seward were far from acceptable. As the Duke of Argyll explained in a hurried private note to Sumner, if the argument that Wilkes's only error had been his failure to take the *Trent* before a prize court was not refuted England and the United States would be on the point of a collision every week. "No week may pass during which some 'Confederates' may not take passage in some neutral Packet," he warned, "and all the Captains of your navy are gravely told that they will do quite right if they take such Packets into Port before a Prize Court." Indeed, it was possible to infer from Seward's despatch "that almost every Packet passing between Dover and Calais might be liable to be taken and carried into New York on the pretext that it carried some emissary of the secessionists."[17] Ludicrous as this notion was, the British government was uneasy. Rival squadrons of Confederate privateers and Federal cruisers were reportedly on their way to British waters to prey upon or to protect American commerce. Already a Federal warship was sitting in Southampton watching the *Nashville*.

For Palmerston the situation was intolerable. A way had to be found "to avoid the scandal and inconvenience of having Federal and Confederate Squadrons watching and fighting each other in the seas around our shores." Even more important, the Americans had to understand that if they wished to remain on friendly terms with Britain they "must not be overhauling our vessels in the Channel or on the high sea, without rhyme or reason, and send them to New York for trial." He expected "some American Heroes to take great liberties" with British merchantmen "in consequence of Mr. Seward's note and in order to have a set off" against the release of Mason and Slidell, and suggested that they be dealt with in "a very summary manner."[18] The commander of any British warship falling in with a prize of British registry should be instructed to demand from the American captain the grounds which had led him to suspect the merchantman of violating the law of nations. If in his opinion the American failed to make out a *prima facie* case he was to "insist upon the release of the British ship." But that was to do exactly what they had just objected to the Americans doing, Russell pointed out, "substituting a Captain on his quarter deck for a Judge in his court." Instead of inviting international embarrassment, the foreign secretary was "disposed to be vigilant, but cautious," particularly as he was unconvinced that Americans would disrupt "bona fide commerce."[19] It was vessels carrying munitions to the South that were in danger, he replied, and they were fair game. While he asked the Admiralty to establish a system of regular cruising in British waters to ensure the protection of British vessels from "undue molestation," officers were given "stringent orders" not to do anything "which the Law Officers would deem illegal."[20] Meanwhile a British warship had been sent to Southampton to prevent a fight between the Federal cruiser and the *Nashville* within British waters.

Russell realized that in the wake of the *Trent* Britain was obliged to show a "decent deference" for the established principles of international law as she strove to discourage interference with her commerce and unwelcome naval activity around her shores. He promptly disputed the dangerous implications of Seward's despatch, but rested Britain's rejoinder on "the broad principle taken up in the French Despatch that a Packet running *bona fide* from one Neutral Port to another Neutral Port *cannot* contain contraband of war."[21] Britain would not acquiesce in the capture of British vessels under circumstances similar to those of the *Trent* even if they were taken before a prize court, Russell wrote in reply to Seward, for while that would alter the character it would not diminish the gravity of the offence against the law of nations. Next, following the French and Spanish examples, he sought to deny American vessels the bases and supplies they needed if they were to patrol European waters. On January 10 Palmerston had suggested that the *Nashville* and the Federal warship be prevented from leaving Southampton within 24 hours of each other, and an order to this effect was given to the commander of the British vessel watching them. By January 14 Russell wanted to "go to the full length of M. Thouvenel,"[22] extending the 24-hours restriction to all belligerents not requiring urgent repairs, and by January 31 a proclamation had been framed. After February 6 no warship of one belligerent would be permitted to leave port until 24 hours after the departure of a vessel of the other. Any belligerent who entered a British port would have to leave within 24 hours, and exceptions would only be made in cases of severe weather, urgent repairs, or necessary supplies. By necessary supplies the British meant coal and provisions sufficient to take a belligerent to the nearest home port.

Concern for the welfare of their commerce reinforced British fulminations against the Union's decision to sink stone-laden vessels at the entrance to Charleston harbour. Victorian indignation at this crossing of the boundaries of civilized warfare, by an act of vengeance which "could only be adopted in utter despair of the restoration of the Union, the professed object of the war,"[23] was inspired by something more than rampant morality. The sinkings were seen as "a plot against the commerce of nations and the free intercourse of the Southern States of America with the civilized world," and an "extraordinary substitution" for an effective blockade.[24] The millions of Europe "are more interested even than their princes in preserving the future commerce with the vast region of the Confederate States," Cobden warned Sumner.[25] Had the moment come for the British government to give the blockade its "earnest attention?"

From Charleston Robert Bunch was striving to bring the British government to the point. He scoffed at the success of the Port Royal expedition. Militarily insignificant, it had failed to rally any Southern Unionists and it would not release cotton for export. Planters would continue to destroy their crops first. Not five thousand bales would reach England during 1862 unless the blockade was raised, Consul Molyneux confirmed from Savannah. Nor could Britain afford to wait much longer before acting, Bunch warned. Some planters had already turned from cotton to corn and potatoes, and many others would follow them unless they saw some immediate prospect of selling their traditional crops. Even the recently picked cotton was not safe. A shortage of bagging had forced planters to store it in pens and huts, where it was certain to deteriorate. "In plain language," Bunch reported on January 8, "the fate of the Cotton Crop of 1862 hangs upon the proceedings of the next three or four months."[26]

From the government's vantage point, however, the economic consequences of the war seemed less clearcut and certainly not grave enough to justify embroilment. While there had been a substantial fall in the value of British exports to the United States, from more than £20 millions in 1860 to just over £9 millions in 1861, these losses had been cushioned, as Gladstone pointed out during a speech at Leith, by a substantial increase in trade with France. In the textile areas the woollen and worsted trades were being kept "tolerably busy." Orders from America for blankets had so exceeded the supply of wool that old refuse stuffing from French and Turkish beds had been sent to England, sold at a profit of 200 per cent, and then spun into blankets. Of course, there was no denying the depression in Lancashire. By the beginning of January, 27,000 textile operatives were reported to be without work and another 161,000 on short time. On January 3 the town of Wigan had taken the lead in forming a committee to raise funds for distressed operatives, and it was soon followed by Blackburn and Preston. Yet it was difficult to ascribe the suffering just to a shortage of cotton. The stocks at Liverpool in December 1861 were claimed to be 581,460 bales, which was more than 40,000 bales greater than the number there a year earlier. Milner Gibson at the Board of Trade was convinced that there was much more cotton in private stocks than usual; certainly Manchester had enough on hand to export some to the United States. The slump was more a matter of markets being depressed, the president of the Poor Law Board, Charles Villiers, concluded. In fact for the large cotton spinners, all of whom held heavy stocks manufactured out of the "very high priced cotton" of earlier years, the blockade was a boon, and would remain so until they had "cleared out" this expensive stock at rates that would cover the cost of production. On the other hand a war would merely depress further the existing markets.

Under the circumstances the government was unlikely to act hastily, and it was being urged to tread warily by the law officers. They had been asked to comment on yet another report from one of Milne's officers "that the blockade, either intentionally, or through want of ordinary vigilance, is most ineffective." As long as there were sufficient ships at a port to prevent access, or to pose an evident danger to vessels seeking to enter and leave, and as long as they did not voluntarily permit ingress and egress, then the fact that some vessels had successfully escaped did not " '*per se*' prevent it from being an effective blockade by international law," they replied.[27] Anyway, the inadequacy of any force was likely to be a matter of contention; therefore a neutral "ought to exercise the greatest caution" in disregarding a blockade. Indeed, that step should only be taken when those "neutrals generally having an interest in the matter" were satisfied that the power of the blockade was being abused by a state unable to institute it or unwilling to maintain it. Plainly, the law officers did not think that the blockade should be challenged and were not prepared to provide the strong legal grounds on which it might be attacked.

That the British government would continue to procrastinate was not apparent to some observers. Richard Cobden continued to urge his friend Sumner to take up the "all important topic of the blockade." He was convinced that when Parliament met there would be great pressure on the government. "All who hate democratic government will be pretending to be influenced in their opposition to the North by pity for the poor workpeople," he predicted.[28] Others would abhor the continuing and useless effusion of American blood. At heart, fully four-fifths of the members would be against the North. The only escape for the Union was to lift the blockade voluntarily, at least from all articles except contraband. Bright disagreed. "I do not see the possibility of your plan of raising the blockade being adopted," he wrote, "and the more I think of it the less reasonable does it seem." He did not share Cobden's opinion that there was "unbearable pressure from want of cotton."[29] The working people were suffering, he conceded, but many spinners and merchants had stocks and they were not anxious for any interference with the blockade. Admittedly the future looked bleak, but for the North the answer was not to lift the blockade but to use its naval power to occupy New Orleans and Mobile and then open these cotton ports to European traders.

The disagreement of the two men on the blockade was a symptom of their continuing differences on the war itself. After an initial period of doubt, which a conversation with John Lothrop Motley ended, Bright had not wavered in his belief that the Union would be restored and that the "inevitable negro" would be the great gainer. Cobden always placed peace before reunion, and the course of the war had not caused him to alter his priorities. "Is not the war hopeless?" he asked Bright early in the new year. "How can they ever lie again in the same bed?" "You might build a wall for a boundary line easier than you could extirpate the passions of hate and contempt which the South have for the North," he declared.[30] But this was the closest the kindly Cobden came to joining those friends and enemies who found Bright's conduct "irreconcilable with every principle of political right and expediency" that he had ever upheld, "and altogether at variance with the dictates of political wisdom as well as political morality."[31]

Cobden was "sorry" that Bright did not agree with him, but neither his friend's objections nor the warnings of others that by his opposition to the blockade he was placing himself on the side of those who meant "mischief" and were "quite indifferent to principles" persuaded him to cease his agitation. He continued to write to Sumner and he pressed his views on Americans in London. They did not need to be reminded of the danger. Charles Francis Adams and Thurlow Weed, Consuls Lord at Manchester and Morse at London, had feared that the settlement of the *Trent* affair would be followed by trouble over the blockade. Napoleon III was reported to be urging Britain to take action and the English newspapers had taken up the question as soon as the *Trent* crisis eased. They seized upon the "Charleston Harbor matter" as an excuse for a discussion of "the intervention of other nations to put an end to a War against the Policy and Interests of the Commercial World."[32] Operatives attending a mass meeting in Salford, which stands cheek by jowl with Manchester, made plain their feelings. There were loud shouts of "No, No" when one speaker asked them if the "paper" blockade should be respected. "These cheers at Salford, which is as Democratic a borough as any in England, and where the philo-American party of other days mustered strong, tell pretty clearly what is going on among our masses," the *Times* commented. "We can hear the whistling of the rising wind. If this war is to last we shall soon have an agitation, both out of doors and in the House of Commons, and pressure put upon the Government, for a direct interference to break the blockade."[33]

Yet the *Times* and other establishment organs continued to show little enthusiasm for embroilment in the American war. The swingeing attacks on the Union in several of the reviews were accompanied by assurances that Britain could afford to wait a while longer for the war to grind to a halt. The suspension of specie payments in the United States at the end of December and the announcement of plans to issue an inconvertible paper currency were seen as a "financial catastrophe" that marked the beginning of the war's end. "Six months more of the present rate of expenditure, and the present military establishments of both parties, must go far to exhaust themselves or their opponents," the *Edinburgh Review* concluded.[34] Interference was unnecessary, the *Economist* chimed in. It also questioned "whether the great body of the British people are yet prepared for any interposition which would even have the semblance of siding with, or aiding the establishment of a Slave Republic."[35] Meanwhile

the *Times* was minimizing the suffering and economic dislocation in Lancashire. It made the point that the distress was not
uniform, that the woollen and worsted trades were prospering.
"Nor at present can we see in the stoppage of a few mills, and
the suffering of some twenty or thirty thousand operatives," it
went on, "any call for rushing into the American squabble
before we are forced into it."[36] In Lancashire itself most of the
newspapers favoured cooperation with the South but not war
with the North, and war had always threatened to follow any
move against the blockade. This was a time for patience, the
Times announced.

Apparently Napoleon III had also decided to wait. Reports
that he would attack the blockade in his speech opening the
French Legislature on January 27 proved unfounded. Unionists
then waited nervously for the opening of Parliament on February
6. All London knew that a few members planned to bring forward the questions of Confederate recognition and the blockade,
and that they claimed the backing of almost the entire Tory
party. The discerning Adams was sure that the government was
disinclined to sustain objections to the blockade "just now," and
thought it likely that nothing would come of the agitation, but
he could not be sure. The Palmerston ministry's position in the
House provided no assurance that it would hold firm in the face
of a strong movement there for intervention.

For the Confederate representatives in London this was a
moment both of hope and frustration. They had quickly recovered from the disappointments of the Mason and Slidell affair.
They consoled themselves with the knowledge that the peaceful
settlement of the crisis was a "disgraceful humiliation" for the
North, while a "cruel" attack on the liberated commissioners in
the *Times* had been "succeeded day after day by piercingly
excruciating onslaughts upon the Lincoln concern." By mid-
January they were excitedly looking toward the meeting of
Parliament, confident that the Confederacy had seen "the last of
the darkest days."[37] Yet as one "influential active personage"
after another called on them, requesting information "with
which to swell the public pressure being made upon the Government,"[38] they were reminded of their helplessness. Instead of
the returns of customs houses, what they received from Richmond were notices of minor military successes. To all inquiries
they were obliged to reply that they expected to have conclusive

evidence of the blockade's ineffectiveness before Parliament met on February 6. Turning all of this over in his mind, as he impatiently waited for Mason to replace him, Yancey struck out at the State Department. "Considering that there is but one mission for the Department to attend to," he complained to Davis, "I must think, in the interests of our endangered country, that there has been negligence and indifference displayed by it in keeping this Commission informed upon the main point upon which it requested information."[39] Two days later, January 29, Mason reached London. He immediately let it be known that he would be happy to see anyone who wished to discuss the blockade, for he at least had the returns from some Southern ports up to the end of October, and the day after his arrival he was full of optimism. "I shall be disappointed if the Parliament does not insist on definite action by the Ministry," he wrote to Hunter, "inuring to the relief of their people as well as ours."[40]

Unionists were also striving to "fortify" their friends. McIlvaine and Weed assiduously presented their views on the war to gentlemen "prominent in English politics and society."[41] George Peabody, an American philanthropist living in London, who had set aside $500,000 for charitable works there, took Weed's advice and donated it at once. Adams sought from Seward intelligence on the filling of harbours with stones and on the efficiency of the blockade. Both he and Weed stressed to the secretary the need to encourage "moral" support for the Union. Those Englishmen who identified slavery as the fundamental issue of the war had to be "aided." However, Adams did not disguise "the fact that the policy of effecting a permanent division of the United States, by all means, fair or foul," was being "steadily pursued by a strong and influential party" in England.[42] And while he hoped that the Austrians and Italians would "fall to belabouring each other a bit,"[43] and so distract public attention from the American continent, he and the other Unionists in England were convinced that only a decisive military success would hold the British in check. Writing to Seward on January 24, Adams warned that "the course of events in America during the next six weeks must in great measure determine the future of the Government of the United States."[44]

Although Seward continued to emphasize to Adams and Weed that the United States would resist intervention with "spirit and resolution," it was no longer his policy to flaunt this determination. The *Trent* affair had dashed any lingering hopes of cowing the British, for they now had a substantial military force in Canada and a greatly strengthened fleet off the American coast. As for the task of persuading them neither to recognize the South nor raise the blockade, Seward considered that quite beyond his powers. Like Adams he concluded that the only convincing argument against foreign intervention was domestic success. It was up to the army to provide the evidence that the rebellion was being "circumscribed" and to substantiate the government's claim that the blockade would not be needed for much longer.

While he waited for the Union armies to win victories Seward skirted as many foreign issues as he could. But he did not remain inert. He approached the French with a suggestion that was designed both to purchase time and to separate them from the British. Through Dayton, he proposed that France and the United States, as the traditional defenders of neutral rights, seize the opportunity of the *Trent* settlement to fix upon Britain "in a definite form" the principles for which both nations had long contended. Nor would blockades be excluded from consideration, the Americans added temptingly. The United States was willing "either to abolish them by the general assent of all nations, or modify them in such a way as to make them, in the least possible degree, detrimental to the great interests of commerce."[45] As for the existing blockade of the Southern ports, that was "a thing more and more falling within our power to modify, if not to remove altogether," Dayton informed Thouvenel. He had taken an outline map of the United States to the Foreign Office with him and this he spread out before the foreign minister, explaining troop dispositions and what he *"supposed* to be the purpose or plan of campaign." The Union was ready to move, he emphasized, and all it wanted was *"a little time."* It was this meeting with Thouvenel, Dayton believed, which persuaded the emperor not to attack the blockade in his speech opening the Legislature.

Meanwhile, Seward was doing what he could to help to fortify the friends of the Union in England. To Adams's request for information on the blockade he replied with a report which indicated that the number of vessels running it were small, mainly British, and that its effects were really being felt in the South. "It is now as nearly absolutely effective as any blockade ever was," he boasted. Turning to the use of stone-laden vessels at Charleston, he insisted that although this was none of the business of other nations he was "desirous that the exaggerations on that subject" be corrected.[46] Two channels to the harbour had not been obstructed, he pointed out, and passage through them was prevented only by the blockading force. He also answered the criticism that the Union was not making war on slavery, and sought to sustain its "moral" supporters in England. The war was leading to a measure of emancipation, he claimed. The advance into Virginia had resulted in the freeing of 5,000 slaves there and another 9,000 had been liberated by the landing on the coast of South Carolina. With the army acting "immediately as an emancipating crusade" it was unnecessary to proclaim it and thereby alienate those Unionists who were not opposed to slavery. Slaves who fled to Union lines were being held and protected against disloyal claimants, while the government favoured compensated emancipation in the District of Columbia. It also favoured the recognition of the black states of Haiti and Liberia. Nor did Seward fail to point to the Lincoln administration's cooperation with Britain against the African slave trade.

The contentious issue of the trade carried on under the protection of the American flag had first been revived by a report from Robert Bunch in July 1861. He had warned Russell that Southerners, convinced that the United States African Squadron would be withdrawn for home service and that British vessels would not meddle with those flying United States colours, were planning to send out slavers to run between Africa and Cuba. The foreign secretary promptly ordered Lyons to inform Seward of this scheme and to ask him whether the entire squadron was going to be recalled, and if so what measures he intended to adopt to prevent slavers sheltering beneath the American flag. The American's response was unexpected. He informed the minister that a large part of the force had returned to American waters, expressed the hope that he would soon be able to send some ships back, and then disclosed that the "present administration had none of the squeamishness about allowing American vessels to be boarded and searched which had characterized their predecessors."[47] Surprised, Lyons wanted to make sure that he had understood and Seward repeated that neither he nor the cabinet would complain of searches off the coast of Africa if they were made on reasonable suspicion and in a proper manner.

This informal concession encouraged but did not satisfy the British. They knew how sensitive the American public was about visit and search, and they placed little store by the administration's resistance to popular opinion. "It is needless to say how little the present secretary of state would deem himself bound to expose himself to public obloquy by a scrupulous adherence to vague verbal assurances," Lyons added.[48] Obviously some more formal arrangement was necessary. Palmerston encouraged Russell to seek it, seeing in the claim by some Unionists in England that the war turned on slavery an effective diplomatic lever. Why should Northerners "not prove their abhorrence of slavery, by joining us and helping us ... in our operations against the Slave Trade," the prime minister suggested, "by giving us facilities for putting it down when carried under the United States Flag." Both these old men could scent at last the triumph of their long campaign to end the trade. "It would be a great glory to your administration of our Foreign affairs if you could exterminate that Hydra," Palmerston wrote without a trace of envy.[49]

On October 19 Russell wrote to Lyons instructing him to approach Seward, and on November 12 they signed an "Informal Memorandum" at the State Department. Based on Russell's despatch, it conceded what the British had long sought. Their vessels were authorized to search and detain American ships within 30 leagues of the African coast on the understanding that it was done "in a respectful manner, upon reasonable suspicion" that they were engaged in the slave trade and that "the search and detention be drawn into a precedent nowhere else, and in no other cases."[50] Although he had "hardly expected to obtain so much,"[51] Lyons doubted that the memorandum was enough to overcome distrust of Seward and he had only signed because it could be simply cancelled by one side giving notice to the other.

As the minister feared, Russell considered the agreement "worth little or nothing."[52] What he wanted was a convention, even though this meant ratification by the Senate and thus the likelihood of delay and the risk of rejection. However, further negotiations were held in abeyance during the *Trent* affair and it was February 10, 1862, before Lyons reopened this subject with Seward. The secretary said that he saw no need to go beyond the informal memorandum. The British had no reason to fear a hostile public response to the arrival at a Northern port of a British cruiser escorting an American slaver, he declared reassuringly. There had been a great change in public opinion on the slave trade, and he pointed to the case of Nathaniel Gordon as proof. Four times convicted of being a slaver, he had escaped punishment just as frequently, but this time he had been sentenced to death and Seward assured Lyons that the execution would take place. Eleven days later Gordon went to the gallows. None of this satisfied Russell. He was careful to give "full credit to Mr. Seward for his sincerity," but he protested that too much ill-feeling had been aroused in the past over the rights of visit and search for the British to act upon an informal agreement. He still wanted a convention and he was not above prodding Seward into action. The Webster-Ashburton Treaty of 1842 obliged the United States to maintain a squadron of 80 guns off Africa but now it had only one vessel bearing 22. The others had been withdrawn to aid in a blockade which inflicted "gross and serious injury on British Commerce and Manufactures."[53] Under these circumstances the very least the United States could do, Russell thought, was to consent to an efficient slave trade treaty which would enable British ships to fill the gap caused by the return of American vessels to home waters.

Lyons visited the State Department on March 15 to present Seward with Russell's draft of a treaty, but the wary secretary was still reluctant to enter into a formal agreement. For him and the administration, the signing away of the traditional American opposition to visit and search involved risk. Risk that their political opponents would exploit any "surrender" to the British. Yet, as Seward soon realized, this was a peculiarly opportune moment to act. His colleagues in the cabinet "responded warmly" to the suggestion of a treaty, as did the influential senators he sounded out. Antislavery sentiment was strong in Congress. The month of March saw debate on bills "to confiscate the property and free the slaves of rebels," to prohibit all Union officers "from employing any of the forces under their respective commands for the purpose of returning fugitives from service or labor," and to release "certain persons held in service or labor in the District of Columbia." Also, Lincoln had urged both Houses to adopt a joint resolution supporting Federal cooperation "with any State which may adopt gradual abolishment of slavery, giving to such State pecuniary aid, to be used in its discretion, to compensate for the inconveniences, public and private, produced by such change of system."[54]

Although he copied almost verbatim a draft treaty proposed by the British, Seward insisted that the United States be permitted to pose as the initiator of the settlement. He also insisted on the insertion of a clause limiting the right of search and detention to a period of ten years. In this way he effectively spiked the guns of the opposition. When the treaty was presented to the Senate there were no accusations of a "surrender," indeed not a single vote was cast against it. "Good God!" Seward exclaimed when he heard the news, "the Democrats have disappeared."[55] He was pleased with himself and he received a generous tribute from Russell, but Seward knew that sentiment alone would never prevent British intervention in the war. Military success remained the best deterrent and this the Union had finally achieved.

"At last the blows begin to tell on the side of the Union," Seward wrote to Weed in February.[56] By the end of the month he was informing Adams of the victories in the West and of plans to advance into Virginia and to seize more Southern ports. Satisfied that the Union had made a safe if narrow escape from foreign intervention, he was quick to take the diplomatic initiative. The strife in the United States had been prolonged, and Anglo-American problems created, he argued throughout February, by European sympathy and aid for the South. Specifically he complained of the "premature recognition of the insurrection as entitled to belligerent rights."[57] What was needed to extinguish a rapidly declining revolution was the revocation of belligerent recognition. The bait he dangled before the British was the willingness of the Union to go "much further and faster" in the direction of ameliorating the effects of the blockade if it had reason to expect that such concessions would be met by a withdrawal "of the belligerent privileges heretofore so unnecessarily conceded" to the insurgents.

In England, Parliament had reassembled on February 6 with the question of the American blockade still very much on everyone's mind. Were the Conservatives going to "take up the cry of justice to Lancashire?" An attack on the "sham blockade" in the *Morning Herald* on the eve of the new session added fuel to the fear that the Tories were about to assault the blockade, but it was quickly extinguished once Parliament met. Derby and Disraeli promptly declared their support for the government's policy of neutrality. However, a discussion of the blockade could not be avoided, for Mason had impressed some of their followers with his evidence that 600 vessels had run it. The two leaders responded by calling on the government to provide the country with the "real facts," the information it had received from Milne and from the consuls at American ports. The request was not made "in any spirit of cavil at the policy which Her Majesty's Government has pursued," Malmesbury, Russell's Conservative predecessor at the Foreign Office, emphasized. "I wish to repeat that no persons on this side of the House are pressing the Government to pursue any other lines of conduct than that which they seem now to be pursuing."[58]

Confident that their American policy was not going to be seriously questioned, Palmerston and Russell pressed on with it. The prime minister informed the Commons that the incidental suffering of British commercial and manufacturing interests was not "sufficient reason" to interfere in the struggle. In the Lords, the foreign secretary disclosed that the papers on the state of the blockade were already being compiled and would soon be ready. He prepared Parliament for evidence of evasions and reaffirmed the government's determination not to be too legalistic about the doctrine of effectiveness. Indeed, the opinion delivered by the law officers three weeks earlier against interference with the blockade was written up as a despatch and sent to Lyons on February 15. As for the government's motives in holding fast to nonintervention, Russell made no secret of some of them. The United States "should be persuaded of the inutility" of its efforts at reunion and should not emerge from the war convinced that it had been defeated by foreign intervention. Such a conviction would leave "a rankling feeling against that country that first interfered, an enmity and bitterness we might have to deplore for several generations."[59] Subscribing to the popular belief that the war could not go on for more than a few months, the Palmerston ministry saw no reason to interfere. As the lord chancellor commented to the prime minister, "Let them tear one another to pieces—Their own mad and evil passions and folly will reduce them in a few weeks to a state in which blockade must be abandoned."[60] Patience was the "wiser and more expedient policy," Lyons confirmed. "If the North have not made real progress towards subduing the South before the sickly season sets in (which is early in June), it must itself admit that the game is up."[61] Russell was of a like mind.

Watching the developments in Parliament, Adams's apprehension quickly dissolved. On February 6 he had confessed to the Speaker his fear that there would be a violent debate on American affairs, followed by a division. By the month's end he was satisfied that the parliamentary papers on the blockade would result in little more than some "interrogation" of ministers. The grief-stricken royal widow's rumoured desire that all exciting political questions "be evaded as much as possible in Parliament," the ministry's uncertain hold on a majority there and the Conservatives' unwillingness to topple the government and seek the approval of the electorate were all contributing to a quiescent session. Even the *Trent* settlement had helped, Adams thought, for "It has soothed the pride of this country and has dispelled the popular notion that we are intending to pick a quarrel." Then again, the distress in Lancashire was not yet "of such a kind as to give rise to much uneasiness," while Continental politics again wore "a very unsettled aspect."[62] But of all the reasons Adams identified for English civility to the United States, military success was the most important. "I am confirmed in the opinion I have heretofore expressed that nothing else is necessary here to maintain intact the friendly relations between the two countries," Adams reported to Seward on February 28. Naturally, the news from Tennessee gladdened the hearts of all Unionists in England. Adams found cause to hope that the rebellion would be crushed by midsummer, and he was sure that the danger of foreign intervention had become distant.

What cheered Northerners necessarily depressed Southerners, and James M. Mason found little to sustain his initial optimism either in the news from home or in the course of events in London. On February 10 he had an unofficial interview with Russell, from which he emerged convinced that the British government did not intend to shift its position. It was up to the Americans themselves, not any foreign nation, to determine "whether they would reconstruct the Union or live as separate and independent States," the foreign secretary had told him.[63] Lacking the Englishman's faith in the North's imminent acceptance of the futility of the struggle, Mason took little pleasure from this meeting and even less from the parliamentary papers on the blockade. Among them he found Russell's "remarkable letter" to Lyons of February 15. "I yet hope an issue will be made in Parliament on the doctrines of Earl Russell's letter," he reported to Hunter, "but at present it is a hope only."[64]

The Commons was nearly full on March 7 when William Gregory rose to speak, and the Americans were out in force. Mason and Mann were on the floor of the House, as were Thurlow Weed and Henry Adams, while Benjamin Moran and a colleague from the American legation watched intently from the diplomatic gallery. The member for Galway made a skilful speech, emphasizing his concern for the welfare of the workingman and for national honour. He reminded his listeners that Britain had already been accused by "a very eminent French jurist" (Hautefeuille) of conniving at an illegal blockade for the purpose of establishing a useful precedent. The answer to such charges, the answer to the plight of the working people, the answer to the damage to British commerce was for Britain to adhere strictly to international law. This was the essence of Gregory's speech, and that of several Tories who followed him. "If any interest of England could be served, if any honest construction of international law could be shown in support of doing what was so contrary to our interests, he would not object," Lord Robert Cecil announced, "but it seemed to him a fatal and suicidal policy to relax those laws which bind the comity of nations, and to unite ourselves to those who were our bitterest enemies when the consequence was the starving of our population and the destruction of our trade."[65]

The Union's "staunch friend and best parliamentary tactician,"[66] W. E. Forster, led the opposition to Gregory's call. Primed by the American legation, where Seward's letter to Adams on the blockade had arrived "seasonally," he seized upon a reference by Gregory to Mason's list of violations to destroy the credibility of the Confederate's information. Monckton Milnes looked at the blockade from the other standpoint suggested by Seward in his despatches to Adams—its actual consequences for Southerners. The difficulty they had "in procuring, not only the heavier articles of commerce, but medicines and the lighter and more luxurious articles," he remarked, indicated that its effectiveness was "quite sufficient for the purpose for which it was instituted." Finally the solicitor general wound up the debate for the government, making what Weed considered "a beautiful and irresistible speech."[67] Responding to the efforts of Gregory and his supporters to revive old animosities toward the United States and exploit new ones, he reminded the House of the Americans' difficulties and called for tolerance. He then went on to concede the eminence of the French jurist, to dispute his objectivity, and to agree with him "that England has as strong an interest as any Power in the world in understanding well what she is about, when she is invited to take a step that may hereafter be quoted against herself, and may make it impossible for her, with honour or consistency, to avail herself of her superiority at sea."[68] But this was no more an admission of a British preoccupation with precedents than was a leading article on the same subject in the *Times* a few days earlier. Like the newspaper, the solicitor general was simply providing members with yet another reason to approach the blockade with caution and to resist any temptation to interfere in the war. To challenge the blockade was to challenge the United States, Russell warned the Lords three days later. All Britain had to do was wait. "I trust that within three months—perhaps even sooner—we may see the close of this unfortunate civil war in America."[69]

For a bitterly disappointed James M. Mason the blockade debate, which was not carried to a division, had re-emphasized the unfriendliness of the British government. Yet that unfriendliness was still impartial, as Adams realized. If the House contained groups of Union and Confederate sympathizers, the debate had again revealed that the government and a large majority of members were not partial to one but disliked both sides to the conflict. There was a widespread animus against the United States, he reported to Seward, and a "desire that their political power should be diminished by a permanent separation."[70] The opposing interests of the two American nations could then "be turned to account either in trade or in policy." This was the "English idea" and it was "alone predominant," he thought.[71]

Neither Lincoln's proposal for compensated emancipation nor the North's military success worked any significant change in British sentiment or policy. The first was dismissed as impracticable, for where would the money come from to pay for the liberation of four million slaves, while the second was greeted as a harbinger of peace. Be wise, the British press advised Northerners, accept that the Union has been irrevocably divided. The war could now be ended "without any loss of honour" and with every prospect of securing a favourable division of territory. But the American people were not wise and their "impulsive and imaginative temperament" would overpower the government's sagacity, the *Economist* cautioned. Victory might well make them less not more willing to negotiate. "Three months may not, as we and Lord Russell lately hoped, terminate this disastrous war," it concluded, "and this country should not be unprepared for a long period of pressure and disturbance."[72]

Privately, Russell also guessed that military success would discourage quick acceptance in Washington of Southern independence. However, it did not alter his opinion that the struggle was certain to end in disunion, perhaps after a debilitating summer campaign. The Southern climate and spirit would never be conquered by the North. Had not Lincoln admitted that the Union's cause was lost in his message on compensated emancipation, Russell asked himself. Was he not saying to the South, "You would cost us too much to buy you out—so you may remain independent." Therefore Britain could and should continue to wait. Her relations with the United States were in a "smooth groove" and she had good reason to keep them there.

"I fear Europe is going to supplant the affairs of America as an exciting topic," Russell informed Lyons early in March.[73] Trouble was brewing in Poland, Prussia and Denmark were still at odds over Schleswig-Holstein and there was disquieting news from Italy. There, Baron Ricasoli had been forced to resign as prime minister after making a speech "which was supposed to countenance the warlike action of the Garibaldians against the Pope." His successor promised to be nothing more than a "mere tool" of Napoleon III, who continued to excite profound distrust. "The Emperor of the French appears to be following a system of undermining all governments which are in trouble," Russell reported to the Queen. "His agents inflame discontent, produce agitation, and this discontent and agitation are afterwards used as pretexts for interference."[74] Clearly, this was no time to risk unnecessary involvement in the American war. Britain had best continue to rest on her oars in America, always taking care that the French were not permitted to pull or to drift away. The "strict concert" was carefully maintained. Russell and Thouvenel consulted one another before they had their respective unofficial meetings with the new Confederate commissioners to England and France. A spokesman for the French government made a declaration on the blockade which was strikingly similar to Russell's despatch of February 15. To Mason it was evident "that the doctrines of Earl Russell's letter had been previously agreed on between the two Governments," which was only to be expected given "the entire accord as to American affairs existing between them."[75] And when the foreign secretary received from Lyons a warning that Seward intended to press for a withdrawal of British recognition of Confederate belligerency, he quickly established a common front with the French.

Adams had not wanted to ask the British to revoke their Proclamation of Neutrality. "The final disruption of the United States and the ultimate recognition of the seceding States" were the goals of Palmerston and Russell, he explained to Seward, and the government's popularity rested upon its foreign policy. "To ask it now to retract it is like asking it to stultify itself before the country and the world. To such a mortification it will never willingly subject itself."[76] Convinced of the futility of the exercise, Adams declined to follow Seward's repeated instructions until mid-April. He only acted then because Dayton had taken up the question in Paris. At his meeting with Russell on April 15 the minister saw it as his purpose to fasten upon the British "mistake" of the year before the responsibility for all the efforts of the rebels and their sympathizers to protract the war. He claimed that "never in history" had there been "so precipitate a recognition of belligerency." Initially heartened, the Confederates had subsequently been sustained by supplies from Britain. A withdrawal of the one and a stopping of the other, Adams argued, would put an end to the Southern delusion of British support, would do much to establish the perfect confidence of the Union in the disposition of Britain, and would hasten the revival of customary intercourse and trade.

The American minister's pessimism was well placed, for there was no chance of Britain doing what Seward asked. Palmerston and Russell regarded the request as manifestly absurd, as did Thouvenel in Paris. At a time when the North was blockading the Southern ports it was "silly" to propose that other nations withdraw their recognition of belligerency. "We might as well be asked to say that the sun does not shine at midday," Palmerston commented.[77] Russell, pointing to the raising of 400,000 troops by the United States and their inability to subdue the South after a year of war, informed Adams that the hostilities could not be treated as a "local riot." He denied that the insurrection had gained its strength and vitality from abroad; he denied that the British proclamation had been precipitate, and he claimed that the conduct of Britain had been founded on the law of nations and was no different from that of the United States when the Spanish colonies in America rebelled earlier in the century. As for the shipments of arms from Britain the prohibition of which had been revoked soon after the settlement of the *Trent* crisis, it was up to the Union blockade to prevent these reaching the South. When Britain blockaded French ports during times of war, Russell added, she did not ask the United States to prohibit American vessels from entering those ports but relied upon her own forces. In short, the foreign secretary made it clear that the British government saw no reason to change its policy and he took this opportunity to voice British resentment "that great and violent reproaches were directed against Great Britain for conduct which on the part of other nations attracted no notice and roused no resentment."[78] The first year of the war ended with Anglo-American relations pitched on the same sour note.

ELEVEN

A war of attrition

BRITISH HOPES THAT THE UNION would soon concede the futility of its struggle to recover the South grew fainter as the spring of 1862 wore on. The Northern appetite for war continued to be whetted by success. In the West the capture of Forts Henry and Donelson had been followed by the seizure of Island no. 10, which had long impeded the movement of Federal gunboats down the Mississippi. And although the battle of Shiloh was a bloody stalemate the end of April brought the capture of New Orleans. Meanwhile, in the Eastern theatre, Fort Pulaski, guarding the port of Savannah, fell to Federal forces and General McClellan launched his peninsula campaign, threatening the Confederate capital of Richmond from the rear. Clearly, this was not a time when the Northern people would contemplate giving up the fight. Indeed, Lyons saw little prospect of the North ever offering separation to the South. Independence would have to be won by Southern resolution. "The North may perhaps be sooner weary of contending for dominion than the South of struggling for independence," he thought.[1] Already the minister foresaw a war of attrition, attrition of the Northern will.

From the Confederacy Bunch reported that the military reverses were "heavily felt" but he had "no idea that any disposition exists to falter."[2] That opinion was soon endorsed by Henri Mercier, who journeyed to Richmond in April. He intended to tell the Confederate leaders, in a friendly way, that their cause was desperate, their armies beaten on every side, and that it was useless to expect any support from Europe. If they were discouraged by the recent setbacks, he thought that such language would be the final blow, inducing them to come to terms with the North and thus put an end to "a state of things which caused so grievous an interruption of trade" between Europe and America.[3] Naturally, he had discussed the proposed visit with Seward and the American had approved of the language he intended to use.

Lyons strongly disapproved of the Mercier expedition, but could do little to stop it. The fact that the Frenchman had discussed it in some detail with Seward before mentioning it to him put the British minister in a difficult position. If he made plain his opposition he might endanger his very friendly relations with Mercier and nourish in Seward's mind the idea that they were no longer acting together on the American question. There was every likelihood that it had been planted there by Mercier's proposal to travel South alone—American suspicion of Britain precluded any thought of the Englishman joining him. However, in an effort to calm Lyons's undisguised fears Mercier promised to reimpress upon Seward the closeness of his cooperation with the British minister, and he quickly withdrew his suggestion of inviting de Stoeckl, the Russian minister, to accompany him. As Lyons pointed out, the dream of Britain's enemies in Europe and the United States was an alliance of France and Russia. The visit of the two ministers to Richmond while he apparently stood aloof might create a "very disadvantageous impression" on both continents.

Mercier returned to Washington on April 24 convinced that the confidence and resolution of the Confederates had increased not diminished, that the hostility to the North was universal, that secession was a national movement, and that there was no disposition to listen to any terms other than complete independence. In short, he was sure that the restoration of the Union was impossible, and that if the European powers did not intervene the war would drag on for years. And while Lyons did not agree with all that Mercier had to say on the unanimity of Southern feelings, he, like the Frenchman, had recognized the signs of a lengthening conflict.

The longer the American struggle went on the more severe the strain on Britain's neutrality. The heart of her problem remained the blockade, which was run by many a British vessel carrying supplies and munitions to the Confederacy. What was more, London and Liverpool underwriters willingly insured the blockade runners. If the government of the United States found this irritating, even more provoking was the fitting out in British yards of vessels of war for the Confederate navy. Not surprisingly, this conduct did not measure up to the Union's standard of neutrality. Charles Francis Adams, for one, was satisfied that the South was obtaining from Britain nearly all the aid she needed to protract the war. So he repeatedly protested these activities, not because he expected to bring them to a halt but "to perpetuate the testimony for future use." He and Seward were agreed that it would be as well to have on record "the unfriendly demonstrations and proceedings of the British government and people towards the United States during the present social disturbance."[4]

Russell, without fully understanding what Adams was doing, sharply rejected his complaints. He reminded the American that Britain had not taken advantage of the blockade's imperfections to declare it ineffective. Instead, she had made allowance for the suddenness of the crisis, the Union's inadequate naval equipment, and the length of the Southern coast. However, beyond such forbearance and liberal interpretation of the law of nations, she had no intention of going. Should ships attempt to violate the blockade, capture and condemnation was the proper penalty. Britain declined to impose "unheard of restraints" upon her merchants. "The United States cannot expect that Great Britain should frame new Statutes to aid the Federal blockade and carry into effect the restrictions on commerce which the United States, for their own purposes, have thought fit to institute, and the application of which it is their duty to confine within the legitimate limits of International Law." As for the charge that Britain was providing the Confederacy with the means to continue fighting, that also was denied. Russell made the point that the bulk of the war materials shipped from England went to the Union, and he repeated his familiar explanation that vessels suspected of being equipped for the Confederacy could not be stopped without adequate proof. "It is not the custom of this country," he remarked pointedly, "to deprive any person of liberty or property without evidence of some offence."[5] But to these mutual irritants and sources of future controversy another was being added. Increasingly, the British government was pressing claims for compensation by British merchants and shippers for damages and losses resulting from the improper enforcement of the blockade.

Yet cotton continued to overshadow all other difficulties and dangers inherent in the blockade. In England and in France the condition of the textile industry and its operatives was steadily deteriorating. But the plight of France, without any Indian sources to develop, seemed particularly grave and the Confederates and their sympathizers moved to exploit the crisis. On April 8 William Lindsay, a member of the Confederate lobby in Parliament and an intimate of James M. Mason, arrived in Paris. Three days later he had an audience with the emperor, and they discussed the American war. Napoleon stressed his willingness both to follow any British lead to recognize the Confederacy and to cooperate with them to reopen the Southern ports. On April 15 the two met again when, according to Lindsay, the emperor suggested that it might soon be necessary for him to act independently of Britain, much as he desired to avoid weakening the "strict concert." All of this Lindsay reported to the British minister in Paris before hurrying to London to call on Russell. He received a cool reception.

The British government was still setting its face against intervention. As always the moment seemed inopportune. The news from across the Atlantic, of Northern success and a tightening blockade, suggested that the Union's hostility to any European interference would be stronger than ever. In Europe the Schleswig-Holstein question posed a threat to peace. No wonder Lindsay was soon followed to Paris by Austen Layard, the undersecretary of state for foreign affairs. He obtained what he sought, a reiteration of the French assurances that they would "take no step into the American business" with Britain.[6] They agreed that nothing should be done for the time being. But could even the British procrastinate for much longer?

By the beginning of May the best estimates put the number of unemployed operatives in Lancashire at 58,000, while a much larger number were working short time. Charles Villiers, the president of the Poor Law Board, was visited by "a strong muster" of Lancashire members, who enquired anxiously whether the means of the Poor Law guardians were sufficient to meet the emergency. He feared that their anxiety would soon bring them back to demand a public grant to alleviate the distress. That of course was impossible; those who were suffering must look to private sources for charity. The "great object" was to open the voluntary pockets of the country and to get rich committees to pay larger sums towards relief. In the meantime, a special commissioner was dispatched to Lancashire to investigate conditions there and report on the operation of the Poor Laws. And when the "Distress in the Manufacturing Districts" was debated in the Commons on May 9, and in the Lords three days later, the government's response to the crisis won general approval. Also, there was much praise for the "great patience and exemplary fortitude" with which the people of Lancashire were bearing their troubles. But in some mill towns patience was already wearing thin. On April 30 the first mass gathering of operatives, numbering six thousand, met at Ashton under Lyne and passed "by a very large vote" a resolution praying the government to recognize the Confederacy.

Adams watched the course of events in England "with growing distrust." He warned Seward that the "rapid increase of the distress in Lancashire is developing a state of feeling towards the United States which seeks but an opportunity to find public expression." If the government failed to bring forward positive measures of relief, and if this failure excited an outburst of popular indignation he would not be surprised to see "a very sudden change of tone, and an eagerness to precipitate an issue with the United States on the blockade."[7]

Whatever the doubts about her future conduct, the fact that Britain was still a neutral observer of the American war was a measure of the failure of Confederate diplomacy. Cotton remained an uncrowned monarch. The fear of being denied access to their principal supplier of the fibre had not proved strong enough to induce the British to prevent the outbreak of civil war. Nor had the voluntary embargo organized by Southern planters and cotton factors compelled them to impose peace on the contending parties, forcing the Union to recognize Confederate independence. Instead, the South was slowly relaxing the embargo, selling cotton for the cash with which to purchase essential supplies. She had played her trump card and lost the hand, but not the rubber. By fighting on she would demonstrate that she could not be subdued, and all the while the Union blockade would be increasing the economic pressure on Britain.

The diplomatic achievements of the Union were only slightly less meagre. British recognition of Confederate belligerency had been an early setback, while the subsequent inaction of Britain was not simply explained. Seward's bellicosity was but one of several restraining factors. The public support in Britain for a foreign policy of nonintervention, the unstable political condition of Europe, and a deep suspicion of the French emperor had all weighed heavily in the Palmerston cabinet's calculations. Of course, Seward's language and policy had further exacerbated the unfriendly Anglo-American relationship. Indeed, little had been done to temper the hostility of the British and less to win their sympathy. There had been no dramatic stroke against slavery. The Slave Trade Treaty was a poor substitute for emancipation. Finally, the Union had failed to persuade Britain to withdraw the Proclamation of Neutrality and to prevent armed vessels and supplies leaving her ports for the Confederacy. The determined effort to fix upon them the responsibility for the prolongation of the war did little to improve the disposition of the British government.

But what of Canada? Britain's concern for the province's security, intensified by the *Trent* crisis, had resulted in a sharp increase in the number of regulars garrisoned there. Nevertheless, the colony's defences were far from satisfactory and proposals for their improvement raised searching questions about the imperial relationship. Canada enjoyed the privilege of self-government, therefore she should accept the responsibility of self-defence. So at least argued many Englishmen, particularly those who resented the colony's imposition of a tariff on imported British goods, and a resolution to this effect was passed by the House of Commons in March 1862.

These arguments and many more were recited by Gladstone in opposition to the Canadian request for aid to construct the Halifax-Quebec railway. In a cabinet memorandum, he disputed the railroad's value, including its strategic significance, and asked "whether the British North American Provinces are to contribute towards the ordinary charge of their land defences." Out of a total expenditure of $9 millions in 1860 the Canadian government had spent no more than $107,000 on defence, he revealed. This was less than Britain exacted from the Ionian Islands, which had only "a twelfth part of the population of Canada." The time had come for British North America "at least to make a beginning of appreciable magnitude in the business of self-defence," the chancellor concluded, and he thought that the railway might well be the place to start.[8] However, the British government did not refuse all assistance. On April 10 the cabinet agreed to offer an imperial guarantee of interest which would lend to the colonies involved the credit of Britain and thus enable them to borrow the money with which to complete the railroad at 2½ per cent. Yet there was never any doubt that this response would prove a great disappointment to the Canadians.

The British determination that Canada shoulder the burdens of colonial defence was even more marked in their calls for an effective militia system. When the supplementary army estimates were debated in February, and the cost of the *Trent* crisis was known, several members of Parliament took the opportunity to criticize the provincial force. In reply Sir George Cornewall Lewis admitted the militia's inadequacies but voiced the belief that improvements would soon be made. Meanwhile, the colonial secretary, Newcastle, was inquiring anxiously of Monck the fate of the province's promised reforms.

On March 28, a week after he opened the new session of the Provincial Parliament, Monck forwarded to London a copy of the Militia Commission's report. It suggested sweeping and expensive changes which would have given Canada an active force of 50,000 trained men and a reserve of the same number. The governor general was well pleased and he confidently predicted the passage of a Militia Bill incorporating these proposals. Yet the opposition was soon criticizing the cost of implementing them and there were ominous signs of restiveness on the government benches. Indeed, on May 20, fifteen French-Canadian supporters of the ministry voted against second reading, the bill was defeated, and the government resigned the next day.

The collapse of the Cartier-Macdonald coalition was not the result merely of French-Canadian hostility to military preparations in time of peace. Dislike of the Militia Bill was general, particularly after Macdonald admitted that it might lead to conscription and direct taxation. The ministry's cause was not helped by Macdonald's absence from the House for a week before the vote. (He was drunk.) Even more important, perhaps, was the evidence of the coalition's dissolution on the demand for representation by population. Although this proposal had been defeated in Parliament once again, on April 1, only sixteen western votes had been cast for the government. No doubt resentment of the western defections on this crucial issue played its part in prompting a number of *Bleus* to desert the ministry on May 20.

Monck was "deeply mortified" by the defeat of the bill and he feared that it would create an impression "hostile to Canadian interests" both in Britain and the United States.[9] His fears on the first score at least were well founded. "I assure you the impression in this Country will be very bad and very prejudicial to the People whose loyalty will necessarily be doubted, at any rate for

267

a time, after such a vote of their Legislature," an angry Newcastle commented. Indeed, he warned that "if the Colony is left another winter without a Militia everybody here will consider it an announcement that Canada does not really mean to secure its independence and everybody in the States will look upon it as little less than an invitation to come and annex it."[10]

Still exposed in Canada, still worried by the unsettled problems of Europe, still distrustful of the French emperor, the British government had little cause to be pleased by the state of affairs in America. The division and emasculation of the overbearing Union had yet to be completed, whereas the difficulties of neutrality were daily increasing. In May of 1861 few observers had foreseen a long war. A year later there was every indication that it would drag on for months, perhaps years. Would neutrality, even as defined by Britain, be possible in a war of attrition?

NOTES

ONE The King was in his counting house

1. *Congressional Globe*, 36th Congress 2nd session, part 1, 73. (Turn to the Bibliographical Essay for a discussion of the other materials upon which this and the following chapters rest.)
2. Ibid., 102.
3. *New Orleans Daily Picayune*, December 23, 1860.
4. *Cong. Globe*, 36 Cong. 2nd sess., 1, 139.
5. *Charleston Daily Courier*, December 10, 1860. See also *Richmond Enquirer*, December 25, 1860.
6. Trescot to Howell Cobb, January 14, 1861, Cobb Papers, University of Georgia Library.
7. *Richmond Dispatch*, February 7, 1861.
8. Mure to Russell, December 13, 1860, Foreign Office (FO), ser. 5, vol. 744.
9. *Journal of the Congress of the Confederate States of America, 1861-1865*, 1, 27.
10. Ibid., 35.
11. Keitt to James H. Hammond, February 13, 1861, "Laurence M. Keitt's Letters from the Provisional Congress of the Confederacy," *South Carolina Historical Magazine*, LXI (January 1960), 20.
12. Cobb to Marion Cobb, February 12, 1861, "Correspondence of T.R.R. Cobb," *Publications of the Southern History Association*, XI, 174.
13. Keitt to Hammond, February 15, 1861, *S.C. Hist. Mag.*, LXI, 21.
14. Cobb to M. Cobb, February 15, 1861, *Southern History Assoc.*, XI, 178.
15. *Confederate Journal*, I, 46.
16. Ibid., 49.
17. Ibid.
18. Dunbar Rowland, *Jefferson Davis Constitutionalist*, 10 vols. (Jackson, Miss., 1923), IV, 542.
19. Bunch to Russell, February 28, 1861, FO 5/780.
20. William Howard Russell, *My Diary North and South* (New York, 1863), pp. 181-82.
21. Toombs to Stephens, June 21, 1855; Ulrich Bonnell Phillips, ed., "Correspondence of Robert Toombs, Alexander Stephens and Howell Cobb," *Annual Report of the American Historical Association for 1911*, II, 353.
22. *The Press*, June 27, 1881; clipping among Toombs Papers, Duke University Library.
23. E. Merton Coulter, *William M. Browne* (Athens, Ga., 1967), p. 64.
24. Ibid., p. 82.
25. Trescot to Miles, March 3, 1861, William Porcher Miles Papers, Southern Historical Collection, University of North Carolina.
26. *New Orleans Daily Picayune*, February 12, 1861.
27. A. R. Childs, ed., *The Private Journal of Henry William Ravenel 1859-1887* (Columbia, S.C., 1947), pp. 52-54.
28. *New Orleans Daily Picayune*, March 1, 1861.
29. Slidell to Cobb, February 13, 1861, Cobb Papers.
30. Mure to Russell, March 18, 1861, FO 5/788.

31. Diary of James H. North, August 19, 1861, Southern Hist. Coll.

32. Slidell to Cobb, February 25, 1861, Cobb Papers.

33. Frank L. Owsley, "Ambrose Dudley Mann," *Dictionary of American Biography* (New York, 1933), XII, 239-40.

34. Varina Howell Davis, *Jefferson Davis Ex-President of the Confederate States of America: A Memoir by his Wife*, 2 vols. (New York, 1890), I, 557.

35. *New York Tribune*, January 1, 1861.

36. Mary Boykin Chesnut, *A Diary from Dixie* (paperback ed., Boston, 1961), ed. Ben Ames Williams, p. 126.

37. *Gate City Guardian* (Atlanta), February 14, 1861.

38. Mary C. Simms Oliphant, Alfred Taylor Odell and T. C. Duncan Eaves, eds., *Letters of William Gilmore Simms*, 5 vols. (Columbia, S.C., 1955), IV, 333.

39. Cobb to M. Cobb, February 21, 1861, *Southern History Assoc.*, XI, 238

40. Ibid., 184.

41. *Confederate Journal*, I, 113.

42. Cobb to M. Cobb, March 7, 1861, *Southern History Assoc.*, XI, 257.

43. *Southern Confederacy* (Atlanta), March 8, 1861.

44. Ibid., April 13.

45. Toombs to Yancey, Rost and Mann, March 16, 1861; James D. Richardson, *A Compilation of the Messages and Papers of the Confederacy*, 2 vols. (Nashville, Tenn., 1905), II, 3-8.

46. *Charleston Mercury*, March 28, 1861.

47. Childs, *Ravenel Journal*, p. 59.

48. Rowland, *Jefferson Davis*, V, 62-63.

49. *Southern Confederacy*, March 15, 1861.

TWO   To preserve the Union

1. *Baltimore American and Commercial Advertiser*, November 14, 1860. (See the Bibliographical Essay for a discussion of this and other material on which the text is founded.)

2. Ibid., November 20.

3. Ibid., December 6.

4. *New York Tribune*, November 12, 1860. See also ibid., November 26.

5. *Cong. Globe*, 36th Cong. 2nd sess., appendix, p. 53.

6. *New York Herald*, October 14, 1860.

7. *New York Times*, December 24, 1860.

8. Ibid., December 26.

9. *New York Herald*, January 24, 1861. See also ibid., January 25, 26, 27, February 2, 4, 6, 7, 17, March 3.

10. John Bassett Moore, ed., *The Works of James Buchanan*, 12 vols. (reprint ed., New York, 1960), XI, 26-27.

11. Ibid., 148-49.

12. Ibid., 66.

13. *Papers Relating to Foreign Affairs*, 1861 (reprint ed., New York, 1965), pp. 31-32.

14. John D. Hayes, ed., *Samuel Francis Du Pont: A Selection from his Civil War Letters*, 3 vols. (Ithaca, 1969), I, 94.

15. Ralph Haswell Lutz, "Rudolph

Schleiden and the visit to Richmond, April 25, 1861," *Annual Report of the American Historical Association for 1915*, p. 210.

16. Frederick W. Seward, *Reminiscences of a War-Time Statesman and Diplomat 1830-1915* (New York, 1916), p. 147.

17. Roy P. Basler, ed., *The Collected Works of Abraham Lincoln*, 9 vols. (New Brunswick, N.J., 1953-55), IV, 148-49.

18. Seward to Lincoln, December 13, 1860, Lincoln Papers, reel 12.

19. Howard K. Beale, ed., *Diary of Edward Bates 1859-1866* (Washington, 1933), pp. 171-72. See also Swett to Lincoln, November 30, 1960, Lincoln Papers, reel 11.

20. Frederic Bancroft, *The Life of William H. Seward*, 2 vols. (New York, 1900), II, 151.

21. Ibid. 62-63. See also Ernest N. Paolino, *The Foundations of American Empire: William Henry Seward and U.S. Foreign Policy* (1973), p. 2.

22. *Annual Report of A. H. A. 1915*, p. 210.

23. Basler, *Works of Lincoln*, IV, 281-82.

24. Seward to Lincoln, March 11, 1861, Lincoln Papers, reel 18.

25. Cameron to Lincoln, January 2, 1861, ibid., reel 13. See also Hamlin to Lincoln, December 10, 1860, ibid., reel 11.

26. Basler, *Works of Lincoln*, IV, 161. See also Fogg to Lincoln, January 1, 1861, Lincoln Papers, reel 13.

27. David Donald, *Charles Sumner and the Coming of the Civil War* (New York, 1961), p. 384.

28. *Boston Evening Transcript*, March 19, 1861.

29. W. C. Ford, ed., *A Cycle of Adams Letters*, 2 vols. (Boston, 1920), I, 67-68.

30. Carl Schurz, *The Reminiscences of Carl Schurz*, 3 vols. (New York, 1907), II, 245.

31. Ibid., 246-47.

32. Balch to Trumbull, March 6, 1861, William H. Seward Papers, University of Rochester Library.

33. Moore, *Works of Buchanan*, XI, 174-75.

34. *New York Times*, April 1, 1861.

35. Patrick Sowle, "A Reappraisal of Seward's Memorandum of April 1, 1861, to Lincoln," *Journal of Southern History*, XXXIII (May, 1967), 234-38.

36. Basler, *Works of Lincoln*, IV, 316-18.

37. Grinnell to Seward, April 3, 1861, Seward Papers.

38. Ibid., April 6.

39. Albert A. Woldman, *Lincoln and the Russians* (paperback ed., New York, 1961), pp. 52-54.

40. Russell, *My Diary*, pp. 70-71.

41. Seward to Adams, April 10, 1861, Department of State, General Records, *Diplomatic Instructions: Great Britain*, National Archives Microfilm Publications, vol. 77, reel 76 (NA/M77/76).

42. Russell, *My Diary*, pp. 70-71.

43. Seward to Adams, July 9, 1861, Norman B. Ferris, "Tempestuous Mission, 1861-1862: The Early Diplomatic Career of Charles Francis Adams," Ph.D. thesis, Emory University, p. 274n.

44. Frederick W. Seward, *Seward at Washington as Senator and Secretary of State 1846-1861*, 3 vols. (New York, 1891), II, 556.

45. Seward to Adams, April 10, 1861, NA/M77/76.

46. Seward, *Seward at Washington*, III, 96.

47. Seward to Adams, April 10, 1861, NA/M77/76.
48. Lyons to Russell, April 23, 1861, FO 5/763. See also ibid., April 27, Russell Papers, PRO 30/22/35.
49. Seward, *Seward at Washington*, II, 366.
50. Beale, *Diary of Edward Bates*, p. 182.
51. Lyons to Head, April 19, 1861, FO 5/762.
52. Lyons to Russell, April 22, ibid.
53. Head to Newcastle, May 4, 1861, Colonial Office, series 42, vol. 627 (CO 42/627).
54. Head to Lyons, May 11, 1861, Lyons Papers, Arundel Castle, Sussex, England.
55. Beale, *Diary of Edward Bates*, pp. 183-84.
56. Adam Gurowski, *Diary*, 3 vols. (Boston, 1862), I, 29.
57. Lyons to Russell, May 10, 1861, FO 84/1137. See also ibid., May 11.
58. Ibid., May 12, FO 5/763.
59. Dallas to Seward, April 9, 1861, *Diplomatic Despatches: Great Britain*, vol. 30, reel 72 (NA/M30/72).
60. Seward to Adams, April 27, 1861, *Papers Relating to Foreign Affairs*, 1861, pp. 82-83.
61. Andrew to Head, ibid., FO 5/763.
62. Head to Andrew, ibid.
63. Cited in Beckles Willson, *Friendly Relations: A Narrative of Britain's Ministers and Ambassadors to America 1791-1930* (reprint ed., New York, 1969), pp. 202-3.
64. Cobden to Bright, November 1, 1861, British Museum Add. Ms., 43651.
65. Russell to Delane, December 20, 1861, John T. Delane Papers, Printing House Square, London.
66. T. W. L. Newton, *Lord Lyons: A Record of British Diplomacy*, 2 vols. (London, 1913), I, 17-18.
67. Lyons to Hammond, January 23, 1860, FO 5/734.
68. Lyons to Russell, May 12, 1861, FO 5/763.
69. Seward to Lyons, May 1, 1861, *Notes to Foreign Legations: Great Britain*, vol. 99, reel 37 (NA/M99/37).
70. Lyons to Russell, May 2, 1861, FO 5/763.
71. Gurowski to Sumner, Charles Sumner Papers, Houghton Library, Harvard.
72. *New York Times*, May 6, 1861. See also *New York Herald*, May 7, 1861; *Harper's Weekly*, May 18, 1861.

THREE   Looking to London

1. E. H. Cawley, ed., *The American Diaries of Richard Cobden* (Princeton, 1952), pp. 149-50.
2. Arthur R. M. Lower, *Canadians in the Making: A Social History of Canada* (Toronto, 1958), p. 185.
3. *Toronto Leader*, November 15, 1860.
4. Ibid., December 25.
5. Ibid., January 28, 1861.
6. *Quebec Morning Chronicle*, January 16, 1861. See also ibid., January 29, April 6, 8, 11, 17.
7. Ibid., April 6.
8. Willson to Seward, April 29, 1861, Seward Papers.
9. *Toronto Leader*, January 17, 1861.
10. Ibid., February 4.

11. *Quebec Morning Chronicle,* April 17, 1861.
12. *Toronto Leader,* December 25, 1860.
13. *Toronto Globe,* December 22, 1860.
14. Ibid., January 7, 1861. See also ibid., January 17, 25.
15. Ibid., February 21.
16. Ibid., January 29. See also ibid., February 5.
17. *Sarnia Observer,* February 1, 1861.
18. *Quebec Morning Chronicle,* March 13, 1861.
19. Ibid., January 29.
20. *Ottawa Citizen,* January 15, 1861.
21. S. F. Wise and Robert Craig Brown, *Canada Views the United States: Nineteenth Century Political Attitudes* (Toronto, 1967), p. 26.
22. J. M. S. Careless, *Brown of the Globe,* 2 vols. (Toronto, 1959), I, 305.
23. Ibid., 326.
24. Donald Creighton, *John A. Macdonald,* 2 vols. (Toronto, 1952-55), I, 68.
25. J. K. Johnston, ed., *The Papers of the Prime Ministers,* vol. I, *The Letters of Sir John A. Macdonald 1836-1857* (Ottawa, 1968), 13.
26. Creighton, *Macdonald,* I, 320.
27. Lyons to Russell, November 5, 1860, Governor-General's Office, RG 7/G6/9, Public Archives of Canada (PAC).
28. Head to Lyons, March 5, 1861, Lyons Papers. See also ibid., March 6, FO 5/761.
29. *Toronto Globe,* March 6, 1861.
30. Joseph Tassé, *Discours de Sir Georges Cartier* (Montreal, 1893), p. 275.
31. J. K. Johnston and Carole B. Stelmack, *The Papers of the Prime Ministers,* vol. II, *The Letters of Sir John A. Macdonald 1858-1861* (Ottawa, 1969), pp. 314-15.
32. *Toronto Globe,* April 25, 1861.
33. Ibid., April 26.
34. Ibid., May 30. See also *Address of the Hon. John A. Macdonald to the Electors of the City of Kingston with Extracts from Mr. Macdonald's Speeches,* pp. 100-7.
35. Ibid.
36. *St. Catharines Journal,* April 18, 1861.
37. *Toronto Globe,* April 20, 1861.
38. *Quebec Morning Chronicle,* May 2, 1861.
39. *Montreal Gazette,* April 22, 1861.
40. *Toronto Leader,* April 23, 1861. See also ibid., April 25.
41. Head to Newcastle, February 18, 1861, Newcastle Papers, A/308, microfilm, PAC.
42. Head to Lewis, February 24, 1861, Harpton Court Collection, National Library of Wales, Aberystwyth.
43. Head to Newcastle, March, 1861, Newcastle Papers, A/308. See also ibid., March 8.
44. Ibid., April 26.
45. Ibid., May 9. See also J. Rose to Ellice, May 3, 1861, Ellice Papers, microfilm, PAC.
46. *Toronto Globe,* May 13, 1861.
47. Head to Lyons, May 26, 1861, Lyons Papers.
48. *Toronto Leader,* April 30, 1861.
49. Head to Newcastle, May 25, 1861, Newcastle Papers A/308.
50. Ibid.
51. Ibid., April 26.
52. Head to Lyons, May 26, 1861, Lyons Papers. See also Head to Newcastle, June 25, 1861, Newcastle Papers A/308.

FOUR The Proclamation of Neutrality

1. Sir Leslie Stephen, *The "Times" on the American War: an historical study* (London, 1865), p. 8. See also *The History of the Times*, vol. II, *The Tradition Established 1841-1884* (London, 1939), p. 359.

2. Cawley, *American Diaries of Cobden*, p. 25.

3. Ibid., pp. 28-31.

4. Geoffrey Best, *Mid-Victorian Britain 1851-1875* (London, 1971), p. 229.

5. Cited in Herman Ausubel, *John Bright: Victorian Reformer* (New York, 1966), p. 23.

6. David Paul Crook, *American Democracy in English Politics 1815-1850* (Oxford, 1965), p. 204.

7. Frank Thistlethwaite, *The Anglo-American Connection in the Early Nineteenth Century* (Philadelphia, 1959), p. 8.

8. Christopher Lloyd, *The Navy and the Slave Trade* (London, 1949), p. 163.

9. Ibid., p. 171.

10. Cited in Willson, *Friendly Relations*, p. 203.

11. S. M. Ellis, ed., *A Mid-Victorian Pepys: The Letters and Memoirs of Sir William Hardman* (New York, 1913), p. 8.

12. Adams to Everett, January 24, 1862, Adams Papers, Massachusetts Historical Society, microfilm, reel 167.

13. London *Times*, January 3, 1861.

14. *Baltimore American*, February 8, 1861.

15. London *Times*, January 26, 1861.

16. *Economist*, January 19, 1861. See also *Morning Post*, January 21, 1861; ibid., January 30.

17. London *Times*, January 7, 1861.

18. London *Times*, February 2, 1861.

19. *Morning Herald*, January 25, 1861.

20. G. D. Lillibridge, *Beacon of Freedom: The Impact of American Democracy upon Great Britain 1830-1870* (Lancaster, Pa., 1955), p. 80.

21. *Economist*, January 26, 1861.

22. *Punch*, February 9, 1861.

23. *Spectator*, March 16, 1861.

24. *Morning Star and Dial*, April 1, 1861.

25. London *Times*, March 20, 1861. See also *Economist*, March 16, 1861.

26. *Morning Post*, May 4, 1861.

27. *Cornhill Magazine*, IV (August 1861), 153.

28. London *Times*, April 30, 1861. See also ibid., May 9.

29. *Morning Herald*, April 29, 1861.

30. London *Times*, May 10, 1861.

31. *Morning Post*, April 30, 1861.

32. G. W. Curtis, ed., *The Correspondence of John Lothrop Motley*, 2 vols. (New York, 1889), I, 247.

33. Kenneth Bourne, *The Foreign Policy of Victorian England 1830-1902* (London, 1970), pp. 84-85.

34. D. C. M. Platt, *Finance, Trade and Politics in British Foreign Policy 1815-1914* (Oxford, 1968), p. xiv.

35. C. P. Villiers to Bright, January 25, 1862, BM Add. Ms. 43386.

36. Ibid.

37. Bourne, *Foreign Policy*, p. 64.

38. Palmerston to Russell, April 25, 1862, PRO 30/22/21.

39. Palmerston to Clarendon, July

4, 1857; Richard W. Van Alstyne, "Anglo-American Relations, 1953-1857," *American Historical Review*, XLII (April 1937), 499. See also ibid., June 6 and December 31, 500.

40. Cawley, *American Diaries of Cobden*, pp. 177-78.

41. Algernon Cecil, *Queen Victoria and her Prime Ministers* (London, 1953), p. 124.

42. Sir Herbert Maxwell, *The Life and Letters of George William Frederick Fourth Earl of Clarendon*, 2 vols. (London, 1913), II, 206.

43. Diary of Charles Francis Adams, May 3, 1862, Massachusetts Historical Society, microfilm.

44. Derek Beales, *England and Italy 1859-1860* (New York, 1961), p. 98.

45. Bright to Cobden, February 6, 1861, BM Add. Ms. 43651.

46. Bright to Gladstone, January 1, 1861, BM Add. Ms. 44112. See also ibid., January 9.

47. Hargreaves to Cobden, December 27, 1860, Cobden Papers/6, West Sussex Record Office, Chichester.

48. Cobden to Slagg, February 4, 1861, BM Add. Ms. 43676.

49. Robert Blake, *The Conservative Party from Peel to Churchill* (London, 1970), pp. 84-93.

50. Wilbur Devereux Jones, *Lord Derby and Victorian Conservatism* (Oxford, 1956), p. 253.

51. J. Parkes to Ellice, January 3, 1861, Ellice Papers, PAC.

52. Lyons to Russell, May 8, 1860, Russell Papers, PRO 30/22/34.

53. Ibid., November 25. See also ibid., November 12.

54. Ibid., December 4, FO 5/740.

55. Ibid., December 18.

56. Palmerston memorandum, December 12, 1860, PRO 30/22/21.

57. Romaine to Milne, December 22, 1860, Milne Papers, MLN/105/1, National Maritime Museum, Greenwich.

58. *Morning Star and Dial*, January 9, 1861.

59. Clarendon to Hammond, January 13, 1861, Hammond Papers, FO 391/3, PRO.

60. Palmerston memorandum, January 6, 1861, FO 5/795.

61. Board of Trade to Foreign Office, February 2, 1861, Board of Trade Papers, 3/59/92, PRO.

62. Palmerston to Somerset, December 29, 1860, Palmerston Letterbooks, BM Add. Ms. 48582. See also John Morley, *The Life of William E. Gladstone*, 3 vols. (London, 1903), II, 82.

63. Argyll to Gladstone, December 25, 1860, BM Add. Ms. 44098.

64. Palmerston to Russell, April 14, 1861, PRO 30/22/21.

65. Bunch to Russell, March 21, 1861, FO 5/780.

66. Lyons to Russell, March 26, 1861, PRO 30/22/35. See also ibid., April 9, FO 5/762.

67. Ibid., February 4, PRO 30/22/35. See also ibid., FO 5/760.

68. Ibid., February 12.

69. Russell to Lyons, February 16, 1861, Lyons Papers. See also ibid., March 9.

70. Lyons to Russell, April 15, 1861, PRO 30/22/35.

71. Ibid., March 18.

72. Ibid., March 26.

73. Ibid., April 27.

74. *Economist*, April 27, 1861.

75. Palmerston to Russell, April 27, 1861, PRO 30/22/21.

76. *Parl. Debates*, 3rd ser., CLXII, 1378-79.

77. Hon. Mrs. Hardcastle, ed., *Life of John, Lord Campbell: Lord High Chancellor of England*, 2

vols. (London, 1881), II, Journal for May 5, 1861.

78. Law Officers Memorandum, undated, PRO 30/22/25.

79. Russell to Lyons, May 4, 1861, Lyons Papers.

80. Ibid.

81. *Parl. Debates*, 3rd ser., CLXII, 1564-66.

82. Ibid., 1763.

83. Ibid., 1833.

84. Russell to Lyons, May 15, 1861, FO 5/755.

85. *Parl. Debates*, 3rd ser., CLXII, 2078-88.

86. Lyons to Russell, May 21, 1861, FO 5/763.

87. James P. Baxter 3rd, "Papers Relating to Belligerent and Neutral Rights," *American Historical Review*, XXXIV (October 1928), 77-78. See also ibid., "The British Government and Neutral Rights," 12.

88. Roundell Palmer, *Memorials Part 1, Family and Personal 1766-1865* (London, 1896), p. 377.

89. Harding to Russell, June 6, 1861, FO 83/2211.

90. Ibid., June 24.

91. Lyons to Russell, May 6, 1861, FO 5/763. See also ibid., PRO 30/22/35.

92. Argyll to Sumner, June 4, 1861, Sumner Papers.

93. Lyons to Russell, April 15, 1861, PRO 30/22/35.

94. Ibid., May 2. See also ibid., May 6.

95. Ibid., FO 5/763.

96. Newcastle to Head, June 5, 1861, Newcastle Papers, 10885 B no. 2, University of Nottingham Library.

97. Willoughby Verner, *The Military Life of H.R.H. George, Duke of Cambridge*, 2 vols. (London, 1905), I, 311.

98. G. F. Lewis, *Letters of Sir George Cornewall Lewis* (London, 1870), pp. 397-98.

99. Russell to Lyons, May 25, 1861, Lyons Papers.

100. Russell memorandum, May 21, 1861, PRO 30/22/35.

101. Committee on Colonial Military Expenditures, *Sessional Papers*, 1861, XIII, 185.

102. Ibid., 259.

103. Palmerston to Somerset, May 26, 1861, BM Add. Ms. 48582.

104. Palmerston memorandum, May 23, 1861, PRO 30/22/35.

105. Newcastle to Head, June 5, 1861, Newcastle Papers, 10885 B no. 2.

106. Adams to Seward, May 17, 1861, NA/M30/73.

107. Adams, Diary, ibid.

108. Sarah Agnes Wallace and Frances Elma Gillespie, eds., *The Journals of Benjamin Moran 1857-1865*, 2 vols. (Chicago, 1948), II, 816 (hereafter cited as *Moran Journal*).

109. Adams to Seward, May 21, 1861, NA/M30/73.

110. Ibid., May 31.

111. *Moran Journal*, II, 875.

FIVE   A strict concert with France

1. *New York Herald*, June 3, 1861.

2. Seward, *Seward at Washington*, II, 584.

3. Ibid., 576.

4. Cited in David Donald, *Charles Sumner and the Rights of Man* (New York, 1970), p. 21.

5. Seward to Sanford, May 20, 1861, Seward Papers.

6. Seward to Adams, May 21, 1861, NA/M77/76.
7. Ibid.
8. Donald, *Sumner and Rights of Man*, pp. 20-22.
9. Sumner to Seward, June 12, 1861, Seward Papers.
10. Lyons to Russell, May 23, 1861, FO 5/764.
11. Schleiden to Sumner, June 5, 1861, Sumner Papers.
12. Schurz, *Reminiscences*, II, 242-43.
13. Curtis, *Motley Correspondence*, I, 395.
14. Seward, *Seward at Washington*, II, 590.
15. *Papers Relating to Foreign Affairs*, 1861, pp. 97-98.
16. Seward, *Seward at Washington*, II, 590.
17. Lyons to Russell, June 6, 1861, FO 5/765.
18. Lyons to Milne, May 12, 1861, MLN/107. See also ibid., May 25, Admiralty Papers (Adm), series 128, vol. 56.
19. Ibid., June 10, MLN/107.
20. *Montreal Gazette*, May 28, 1861.
21. *Toronto Globe*, May 22, 1861.
22. Ibid., May 27.
23. *Toronto Leader*, May 28, 1861.
24. *Quebec Morning Chronicle*, May 28, 1861.
25. Johnston and Stelmack, *Papers of the Prime Ministers*, II, 344-51.
26. *Quebec Morning Chronicle*, June 4, 1861.
27. *Richmond Whig*, May 18, 1861.
28. Keitt to Hammond, May 15, 1861, *S.C. Hist. Mag.*, LXI, 23.
29. *Confederate Journal*, I, 214.
30. Yancey, Rost, and Mann, to Toombs, June 1, 1861, *Official Records of the Union and Confederate Navies*, National Archives Microfilm Publications (NA/M275), reel 30.
31. Argyll to Sumner, June 4, 1861, Sumner Papers.
32. Lyons to Russell, February 12, 1861, PRO 30/22/35. See also ibid., April 15, May 6, 20.
33. Cited in Lynn M. Case and Warren F. Spencer, *The United States and France: Civil War Diplomacy* (Philadelphia, 1970), p. 51.
34. Cowley to Russell, July 2, 1861, PRO 30/22/57.
35. Lyons to Russell, April 27, 1861, PRO 30/22/35.
36. Russell to Lyons, May 18, 1861, FO 5/755.
37. Ibid., May 25, Lyons Papers.
38. Cowley to Russell, May 16, 1861, Cowley Papers, FO 519/11, PRO.
39. Lyons to Russell, June 10, 1861, PRO 30/22/35. See also ibid., June 4; ibid., June 8, FO 5/765.
40. Ibid., June 14, PRO 30/22/35.
41. Ibid., June 17, FO 5/766.
42. Ibid., June 18, PRO 30/22/35.
43. W. C. Ford, ed., *The Letters of Henry Adams 1858-1891* (London, 1930), pp. 90-94. See also Adams, Diary, June 10, 1861.
44. Adams to Seward, June 14, 1861, NA/M30/73. See also Adams, Diary, June 12, 1861.
45. *Moran Journal*, II, 828.
46. G. P. Gooch, ed., *The Later Correspondence of Lord John Russell 1840-1878*, 2 vols. (London, 1925), II, 320.
47. Adams to Seward, June 21, 1861, Adams Letterbooks.
48. Adams to R. H. Dana Jr., June 14, ibid.
49. Seward to Adams, June 21, 1861, NA/M77/76.
50. Adams to Everett, July 12, 1861, Adams Letterbooks.
51. Adams, Diary, July 25, 1861.
52. *Morning Star and Dial*, July 25, 1861.

53. Adams, Diary, July 11, 1861. See also ibid., July 13.
54. Cowley to Russell, July 16, 1861, PRO 30/22/57.
55. Palmerston's comments on Russell to Adams (draft), July 18, 1861, FO 5/755.
56. Law Officers to Russell, June 25, 1861, FO 83/2211.
57. Russell to Lyons, June 29, 1861, FO 5/756.
58. Cowley to Russell, June 28, 1861, PRO 30/22/57. See also ibid., July 2.
59. Russell to Lyons, July 6, 1861, FO 5/756.
60. Russell to Lyons (draft), July 10, ibid.
61. Palmerston memorandum, PRO 30/22/27.
62. Cowley to Russell, July 12, 1861, FO 519/11.
63. Russell to Lyons, July 20, 1861, FO 5/756.
64. Ibid., July 24, Lyons Papers.

65. Ibid., July 19, FO 5/756.
66. Russell to Lyons (draft), July 26, 1861, FO 5/755.
67. Russell circular, July 28, 1861, PRO 30/22/31. See also Cabinet opinions, July 1861, PRO 30/22/27; Russell memorandum, July 30, ibid.
68. Russell to Lyons, August 8, 1861, FO 5/756.
69. Somerset to Milne, July 29, 1861, MLN/107.
70. Russell to Adams, July 31, 1861, NA/M30/73.
71. *Moran Journal*, II, 856.
72. Cowley to Russell, August 20, 1861, FO 519/11.
73. Russell to Lyons, August 17, 1861, Lyons Papers.
74. Adams, Diary, August 23, 1861.
75. Adams to Russell, August 23, 1861, NA/M30/73.
76. Cowley to Russell, August 13, 1861, PRO 30/22/57.

SIX   The blockade begins

1. *New York Times*, June 30, 1861.
2. Trescot to Corwine, October 26, 1860, Department of State, *Domestic Letters* (NA/M40/51).
3. Seward to Adams, June 19, 1861, *Papers Relating to Foreign Affairs*, 1861, pp. 106-9.
4. Basler, *Works of Lincoln*, IV, 431.
5. Ibid., 429.
6. *Cong. Globe*, 37th Cong. 1st sess., p. 55.
7. Lyons to Russell, July 20, 1861, FO 5/768.
8. Ibid., PRO 30/22/35. See also ibid., FO 5/768.
9. Seward to Adams, July 21, 1861, *Papers Relating to Foreign Affairs*, 1861, pp. 117-21.

10. T. C. Pease and J. G. Randall, eds., *Diary of Orville Hickman Browning*, 2 vols. (Springfield, Ill., 1925), I, 488-89.
11. *Papers Relating to Foreign Affairs*, 1861, p. 118.
12. Seward, *Reminiscences*, pp. 178-79.
13. Ibid., p. 181.
14. Seward to Adams, August 17, 1861, NA/M77/77.
15. Lyons to Russell, September 2, 1861, FO 5/770.
16. Ibid., June 24, FO 5/766.
17. Lyons to H.M.'s Consuls, June 20, ibid.
18. Lyons to Bunch, July 5, 1861, FO 5/767.

19. Edward A. Trescot, "The Confederacy and the Declaration of Paris," *American Historical Review*, XXIII (July 1918), 826-35.
20. Diary and Reminiscences of Stephen Mallory, I, 10-11, Southern Historical Collection.
21. Trescot, *American Historical Review*, XXIII, 834-35.
22. Rembert W. Patrick, *Jefferson Davis and his Cabinet* (Baton Rouge, 1944), p. 97.
23. D. G. Wright, *A Southern Girl in '61: The War-Time Memories of a Confederate Senator's Daughter* (New York, 1905), p. 30.
24. Toombs to Stephens, July 5, 1861, Toombs Papers.
25. Hunter to Yancey, Rost and Mann, July 29, 1861, NA/M275/30.
26. Mallory, Diary, I, 9.
27. Trescot, *American Historical Review*, XXIII, 831-33. See also Trescot to Hunter, August 3, 1861, NA/M275/30.
28. Chesnut, *Diary from Dixie*, p. 91.
29. *Wilmington Daily Journal*, August 20, 1861.
30. *Charleston Mercury*, July 8, 1861. See also ibid., July 2, 4, 15, 16.
31. Laura A. White, *Robert Barnwell Rhett* (New York, 1931), pp. 209-10.
32. Trescot to Hunter, August 3, 1861, NA/M275/30.
33. Hunter to Yancey, Rost and Mann, August 24, ibid.
34. Toombs to Stephens, July 5, 1861, Toombs Papers.
35. *Charleston Mercury*, June 29, 1861.
36. *Confederate Journal*, I, 300.
37. Yancey to S. Reid, July 3, 1861, Yancey Papers. See also Yancey to R. Chapman, ibid.; Yancey to B. C. Yancey, ibid., B. C. Yancey Papers, Southern Historical Collection.
38. Yancey and Mann to Toombs, July 15, 1861, NA/M275/30.
39. Yancey, Rost, and Mann to Toombs, August 7, ibid.
40. Mann to Gregory, August 7, 1861, Gregory Papers.
41. Yancey and Mann to Toombs, August 1, ibid.
42. Yancey, Rost, and Mann to Toombs, August 7, ibid.
43. Ibid.
44. Yancey to B. C. Yancey, August 15, 1861, B. C. Yancey Papers.
45. Adams to Seward, July 12, 1861, NA/M30/73.
46. Palmerston to Milner Gibson, July 7, 1861, BM Add. Ms. 48582.
47. Milner Gibson to Palmerston, July 9, 1861, Broadlands Mss., Historical Manuscripts Commission, London.
48. *Morning Post*, October 8, 1861.
49. Bunch to Russell, June 12, 1861, FO 5/780.
50. Harding to Russell, July 27, 1861, FO 83/2211.
51. Russell to Lyons, August 9, 1861, FO 5/756.

SEVEN   Britain rests on her oars

1. London *Times*, August 26, 1861.
2. *Speeches of John Bright on the American Question* (reprint ed., New York, 1970), pp. 3-7.
3. Adams to J. Forbes, August 30, 1861, Adams Letterbooks.
4. James D. Bulloch, *The Secret Service of the Confederate States*

in Europe (reprint ed., New York, 1959), pp. 53-54.

5. Ibid., p. 67.

6. Adams to Russell, August 15, 1861, NA/M30/73.

7. Russell to Adams, August 22, ibid.

8. Adams to Seward, October 5, 1861, ibid.

9. *Moran Journal*, II, 877-78.

10. Palmerston to Russell, August 25, 1861, PRO 30/22/21.

11. Ibid.

12. Somerset to Palmerston, August 19, 1861, Broadlands Mss.

13. Palmer, *Memorials*, pp. 461-62.

14. Palmerston to Lewis, August 26, 1861, Broadlands Mss.

15. Lewis to Palmerston, August 27, ibid.

16. Somerset to Palmerston, August 30, ibid.

17. Newcastle to Head, August 27, 1861, Newcastle Papers, 10882 B no. 2.

18. G. F. Lewis, *Letters of Lewis*, p. 401.

19. Monck to Delane, August 31, 1861, Delane Papers.

20. Newcastle to Palmerston, August 30, 1861, Broadlands Mss.

21. *Parl. Debates*, 3rd ser., CLXIII, 1517-27.

22. Head to Newcastle, June 29, 1861, CO 42/627. See also ibid., August 27, September 9.

23. London *Times*, September 2, 1861.

24. Palmerston to Russell, September 9, 1861, PRO 30/22/21.

25. Palmerston to Newcastle, September 1, 1861, BM Add. Ms. 48582.

26. Ibid.

27. Newcastle to Palmerston, September 3, 1861, Broadlands Mss.

28. Palmerston to Russell, September 9, 1861, PRO 30/22/21.

29. Russell to Palmerston, September 6, 1861, Broadlands Mss.

30. Palmerston to Russell, September 9, 1861, PRO 30/22/21.

31. Ibid., September 17.

32. Gladstone to Lewis, September 21, 1861, BM Add. Ms. 44236.

33. Henry Lord to Seward, September 13, 1861, Department of State, *Consular Despatches: Manchester* (NA/T219/1).

34. Bright to Cobden, August 31, 1861, BM Add. Ms. 43384.

35. *Bright on the American Question*, pp. 3-4.

36. Sir William Gregory, *An Autobiography* (London, 1894), p. 214.

37. London *Times*, October 3, 1861.

38. Cobden to Bright, September 7, 1861, BM Add. Ms. 43651. See also ibid., September 3; ibid., September 4.

39. Bright to Cobden, September 6, 1861, BM Add. Ms. 43384.

40. Forster to Cobden, September 8, 1861, Cobden Papers/6.

41. Bright to Cobden, September 6, 1867, BM Add. Ms. 43384.

42. Cobden to Bright, October 14, 1861, BM Add. Ms. 43651.

43. Lord to Seward, October 15, 1861, NA/T219/1.

44. Bright to Cobden, October 3, 1861, BM Add. Ms. 43384.

45. Layard memorandum, September, 1861, Layard Papers, BM Add. Ms. 38987.

46. Palmerston to Russell, October 6, 1861, PRO 30/22/21.

47. Layard memorandum, September, 1861, BM Add. Ms. 38987.

48. Lyons to Russell, October 4, 1861, PRO 30/22/35.

49. Russell to Palmerston, October 17, 1861, Broadlands Mss.

50. London *Times*, October 16, 1861.

51. *Morning Star and Dial*, October

15, 1861. See also ibid., October 17.

52. Russell to Palmerston, October 17, 1861, Broadlands Mss.
53. Palmerston to Russell, October 18, 1861, PRO 30/22/14B.
54. Ibid.
55. Ibid., November 7, Broadlands Mss.
56. Ibid., October 18, PRO 30/22/14B.
57. Harding to Russell, October 30, 1861, FO 83/2212.
58. *Morning Star and Dial*, October 30, 1861.
59. Adams to Seward, October 18, 1861, NA/M30/73.
60. Adams to Palfrey, October 18, 1861, Adams Letterbooks.
61. Cited in Harold Temperley and Lillian M. Penson, *Foundations of British Foreign Policy from*

Pitt to Salisbury (Cambridge, 1938), p. 295.
62. *Toronto Leader*, July 29, 1861.
63. Ibid., August 1.
64. Ibid., August 5.
65. *Quebec Morning Chronicle*, August 9, 1861. See also *Montreal Gazette*, ibid.; *Toronto Leader*, August 26, 1861; *Quebec Morning Chronicle*, September 24, 1861.
66. *Toronto Globe*, July 23, 1861.
67. Ibid., July 27.
68. Ibid., August 16.
69. Ibid., September 12.
70. Ibid., September 16. See also ibid., September 23.
71. Head to Newcastle, September 23, 1861, marginalia, CO 42/627.
72. Elliot to War Office, October 14, 1861, CO 43/127.

EIGHT Mason and Slidell

1. Morris to Russell, September 9, 1861, Mowbrey Morris Papers, 11/229, Printing House Square, London.
2. Russell to Dasent, September 15, 1861, Delane Papers.
3. Lyons to Russell, August 23, 1861, PRO 30/22/35.
4. Hayes, *Du Pont Letters*, I, 155.
5. Beale, *Diary of Bates*, p. 195.
6. Lyons to Russell, October 8, 1861, FO 5/771. See also ibid., October 14, PRO 30/22/35.
7. *Letters of John Hay and Extracts from his Diary*, 3 vols. (reprint ed., New York, 1969), I, 33.
8. Lyons to Russell, August 23, 1861, PRO 30/22/35. See also ibid., August 27, September 2, 6, 13, 24, 27.
9. Ibid., October 14.
10. Ibid.
11. Clarendon to Brougham, Sep-

tember 29, 1861, Brougham Papers, University College, London.
12. Palmerston to Russell, September 26, 1861, PRO 30/22/21.
13. Russell to Lyons, September 28, 1861, FO 5/756.
14. Seward to Lyons, October 14, 1861, FO 5/772.
15. *Boston Evening Transcript*, October 19, 1861.
16. Lyons to Russell, October 28, 1861, PRO 30/22/35.
17. Bigelow to Seward, September 23, 1861, Seward Papers.
18. Seward, *Seward at Washington*, II, 627.
19. Ibid., 635.
20. Lyons to Russell, October 28, 1861, FO 5/773.
21. Lyons to Milne, October 28, 1861, MLN/107.

22. *Harper's Weekly*, November 2, 1861.

23. Seward, *Seward at Washington*, II, 627.

24. Seward to Dayton, November 7, 1861, Seward Papers.

25. Lyons to Russell, November 8, 1861, FO 5/773.

26. *Richmond Dispatch*, August 31, 1861. See also ibid., August 26, 23.

27. Catharine Hopley, *Life in the South*, 2 vols. (London, 1863), II, 69.

28. *DeBow's Review*, VI, September, 1861.

29. *Richmond Dispatch*, August 24, 1861. See also ibid., August 27.

30. Mallory, Diary, I, 16.

31. *Charleston Daily Courier*, September 25, 1861.

32. *Richmond Dispatch*, October 11, 1861.

33. *Richmond Whig*, October 16, 1861.

34. *Wilmington Daily Journal*, October 28, 1861. See also *Richmond Dispatch*, October 24, 1861; *Charleston Daily Courier*, October 28, 1861.

35. Russell, *My Diary*, p. 237.

36. Chesnut, *Diary from Dixie*, pp. 123-24.

37. *Richmond Whig*, September 14, 1861.

38. *Charleston Mercury*, October 29, 1861.

39. Hunter to Mason, September 23, 1861, NA/M275/30.

40. Browne to Mason, October 29, ibid.

41. Mallory, Diary, I, 15.

42. Mason to Hunter, October 5, 1861, NA/M275/30.

43. Virginia Mason, ed., *The Public Life and Diplomatic Correspondence of James M. Mason* (Roanoke, Va., 1903), pp. 199-213.

44. *New Orleans Daily Picayune*, October 5, 1861. See also ibid., October 31.

45. Diary of Charles Wilkes, November 16, 1861, Wilkes Papers, Library of Congress.

46. Ibid., November 8.

47. Wilkes to Welles, November 15, 1861, NA/M275/1.

48. P. T. Barnum to Wilkes, December 11, 1861, Wilkes Papers.

49. C. F. Adams Jr., "The Trent Affair," *Proceedings of the Massachusetts Historical Society*, XLVI (November 1911), 49.

50. George Templeton Strong, *Diary of the Civil War 1860-1865*, ed. Allan Nevins (New York, 1962), pp. 192-93.

51. *New York Herald*, November 22, 1861.

52. Diary of Thomas Bragg, November 26, 1861, Southern Historical Collection. See also ibid., November 27.

53. Richardson, *Messages and Papers of the Confederacy*, I, 141-43.

54. *Toronto Leader*, October 8, 1861. See also ibid., October 11, 15.

55. *Montreal Gazette*, October 26, 1861.

56. *Toronto Globe*, November 18, 1861.

57. Monck to Newcastle, November 1, 1861, Newcastle Papers, A/308.

58. Ibid., November 22.

59. Ibid.

60. Ibid., November 30.

61. Monck to Lyons, December 5, 1861, Lyons Papers.

62. Lyons to Russell, November 22, 1861, PRO 30/22/35.

63. Seward to Adams, November 27, 1861, NA/M77/77.

64. *New York Times*, November 30, 1861. See also ibid., December 3.

NINE One war at a time

1. Adams to Seward, November 1, 1861, NA/M30/74.
2. *Economist*, November 16, 1861.
3. Adams to Seward, November 1, 1861, NA/M30/74.
4. London *Times*, November 5, 1861.
5. Adams, Diary, November 4, 1861.
6. Adams to Seward, November 15, 1861, NA/M30/74.
7. *Moran Journal*, II, 903-4.
8. Nancy Mitford, ed., *The Stanleys of Alderley* (London, 1939), p. 267.
9. London *Times*, November 11, 1861.
10. Russell to Lyons, November 2, 1861, Lyons Papers.
11. Russell to Palmerston, November 12, 1861, Broadlands Mss.
12. Russell to Lyons, November 8, 1861, FO 5/757.
13. Russell to Layard and Hammond, November 16, 1861, BM Add Ms. 38987.
14. Palmerston to Newcastle, November 7, 1861, BM Add. Ms. 48582.
15. Law Officers to Russell, November 12, 1861, FO 83/2212.
16. Hammond memorandum, November 11, 1861, FO 391/7.
17. Adams, Diary, November 12, 1861. See also Russell to Lyons, November 16, 1861, Lyons Papers.
18. Adams, Diary, November 13, 1861.
19. Ibid., November 21.
20. Russell to Adams, December 9, 1861, FO 5/791.
21. *George Douglas, Eighth Earl of Argyll, Autobiography and Letters*, 2 vols. (London, 1906), II, 179-80.
22. Russell to Lyons, December 1,

1861, Lyons Papers. See also ibid., December 6, FO 5/758.
23. Clarendon to Russell, December 4, 1861, PRO 30/22/29.
24. Palmerston to Russell, December 6, 1861, PRO 30/22/21.
25. Palmerston memorandum, November 30, 1861, Cab/A/141, Broadlands Mss.
26. Ibid., December 2, Cab/A/147.
27. Somerset to Palmerston, December 6, 1861, Broadlands Mss.
28. Palmerston to Lewis, December 5, ibid. See also Palmerston to Russell, December 6, 1861, PRO 30/22/21.
29. Brian Connell, *Regina v Palmerston: The Correspondence between Queen Victoria and Her Foreign Prime Minister 1837-1865* (London, 1962), p. 311.
30. Newcastle to Monck, December 5, 1861, Newcastle Papers, 10885 B no. 2.
31. Ibid., December 7, 10886 B no. 3.
32. Newcastle to Palmerston, November 11, 1861, Broadlands Mss.
33. E. W. Watkin, *Canada and the States: Recollections 1851-1886* (London, 1887), p. 84.
34. Newcastle to Gladstone, December 5, 1861, Newcastle Papers, 10890 C no. 2.
35. London *Times*, December 9, 1861.
36. *Spectator*, November 30, 1861.
37. Bright to Cobden, November 4, 1861, BM Add. Ms. 43384. See also ibid., November 16.
38. *Bright on the American Question*, pp. 11-67.
39. Cobden to Bright, December 6, 1861, BM Add. Ms. 43651.
40. "Bright-Sumner Letters," *Proceedings of the Massachusetts*

Historical Society, XLVI (November 1911), 150-52.

41. Cobden to Sumner, November 27, 1861, BM Add. Ms. 43676. See also ibid., November 29; ibid., December 5.

42. Ibid., December 6.

43. Henry Adams, *The Education of Henry Adams* (reprint ed., Boston, 1960), p. 119.

44. Adams to Seward, December 3, 1861, NA/M30/74.

45. John Bigelow, *Retrospections of an Active Life*, 5 vols. (New York, 1903-13), I, 385-89.

46. Connell, *Regina v Palmerston*, p. 311.

47. Weed to Seward, December 4, 1861, Lincoln Papers, reel 29. See also ibid., December 6, Seward Papers; ibid., December 7, 10; Weed to Lincoln, December 7, 1861, Lincoln Papers, reel 30; Weed to Cameron, December 3, 1861, Simon Cameron Papers, Library of Congress; ibid., December 7.

48. *New York Tribune*, December 10, 1861.

49. Ford, *Cycle of Adams Letters*, I, 73-74.

50. Ibid., 89-90.

51. Hanna to Chase, December 20, 1861, Salmon P. Chase Papers, Library of Congress.

52. Seward to Adams, December 27, 1861, NA/M77/77.

53. *Annual Report of American Historical Association for 1915*, p. 214.

54. Russell, *My Diary*, pp. 587-88.

55. Lyons to Russell, December 19, 1861, FO 5/777. See also ibid., PRO 30/22/35.

56. Ibid., December 23, FO 5/777.

57. Ibid., PRO 30/22/14C.

58. Lyons to Milne, December 23, 1861, MLN/107.

59. David Donald, ed., *Inside Lincoln's Cabinet: The Civil War Diaries of Salmon P. Chase* (New York, 1954), pp. 53-55.

60. Pease and Randall, *Browning Diary*, I, 518-19.

61. Seward to Lyons, December 26, 1861, NA/M99/38.

62. Gurowski, *Diary*, I, 135.

63. Lyons to Russell, December 27, 1861, FO 5/777.

64. Gurowski, *Diary*, I, 135. See also Minturn to Seward, December 28, 1861, Seward Papers; Everett to Seward, December 30, ibid.; Shipman to Welles, January 1, 1862, Welles Papers; *Boston Evening Transcript*, December 30, 1861; *New York Times*, December 29, 1861; *New York Tribune*, December 30, 1861; *Baltimore American* December 31, 1861.

65. *Cong. Globe*, 37th Cong. 2nd sess., part 1, 176-77. See also ibid., 207-13; ibid., 241-45.

66. *Baltimore American*, January 2, 1862. See also *New York Herald*, January 4, 1862.

67. *New Orleans Daily Picayune*, January 1, 1862. See also ibid., January 3.

68. *Charleston Daily Courier*, January 6, 1862.

69. *Charleston Mercury*, January 17, 1862.

70. *Richmond Whig*, January 16, 1862.

71. Bragg, Diary, December 6, 1861.

72. Memminger to Cobb, January 1, 1862, *Annual Report of American Historical Association for 1911*, II, 587.

73. Bragg, Diary, January 6, 1862.

74. Chesnut, *Diary from Dixie*, p. 187.

75. Rowland, *Jefferson Davis*, V, 201-2.

76. Richardson, *Messages and Papers of Confederacy*, II, 172.
77. *Toronto Leader*, December 17, 1861. See also ibid., December 19.
78. *Toronto Globe*, December 17, 1861. See also ibid., December 18.
79. *Montreal Gazette*, December 31, 1861.
80. Newcastle to Monck, January 4,

1862, Newcastle Papers, A/309.
81. Monck to Lyons, January 13, 1862, Lyons Papers.
82. Ashmun to Galt, January 8, 1862, Alexander T. Galt Papers, M.G. 27/1/DA/2, PAC. See also Rose to Ellice, February 2, 1862, Ellice Papers.
83. Monck to Newcastle, February 14, 1862, Newcastle Papers, A/308.

TEN   A few months longer

1. Richardson, *Messages and Papers of the Confederacy*, II, 126-27.
2. Weed to Seward, December 18, 1861, Seward Papers.
3. Ford, *Cycle of Adams Letters*, I, 84.
4. *Moran Journal*, II, 925.
5. Adams, Diary, December 8, 1861.
6. Cobden to Bright, December 11, 1861, BM Add. Ms. 43651.
7. Gladstone to Cobden, December 13, 1861, BM Add. Ms. 44136.
8. Cobden to Bright, December 17, 1861, BM Add. Ms. 43651.
9. Cobden to Chevalier, December 14, 1861, Cobden Papers/47. See also ibid., December 29.
10. Russell to Palmerston, December 20, 1861, Broadlands Mss.
11. Ibid., December 16.
12. Gladstone to Brougham, December 27, 1861, Brougham Papers.
13. *Moran Journal*, II, 940.
14. Ellis, *Mid-Victorian Pepys*, p. 83.
15. Derby to Granville, January 23, 1862, Granville Papers, PRO 30/29/18.
16. Jasper Ridley, *Lord Palmerston* (London, 1970), p. 555.
17. Argyll to Sumner, January 10, 1862, Sumner Papers.
18. Palmerston to Russell, January 15, 1862, PRO 30/22/21. See also

ibid., January 10; Palmerston to Hammond, January 13, 1862, FO 391/7.
19. Russell to Palmerston, January 15, 1862, Broadlands Mss.
20. FO to Admiralty, January 13, 1862, FO 5/853.
21. Argyll to Sumner, January 10, 1862, Sumner Papers.
22. Russell to Hammond, January 14, 1862, FO 391/7.
23. Russell to Lyons, December 20, 1861, FO 5/758.
24. Liverpool Ship Owners Association to Russell, January 13, 1862, FO 5/853.
25. Cobden to Sumner, December 19, 1861, BM Add. Ms. 43676.
26. Bunch to Russell, January 8, 1862, FO 5/843.
27. Law Officers to Russell, January 25, 1862, FO 83/2213.
28. Cobden to Sumner, January 23, 1862, BM Add. Ms. 43676.
29. Bright to Cobden, January 9, 1862, BM Add. Ms. 43384. See also ibid., January 10.
30. Cobden to Bright, January 7, 1862, BM Add. Ms. 43652.
31. Paulton to Cobden, December 26, 1861, Cobden Papers/99.
32. Weed to Seward, January 6, 1862, Seward Papers.

33. London *Times*, January 23, 1862.
34. *Edinburgh Review*, CXV, January 1862.
35. *Economist*, January 25, 1862.
36. London *Times*, January 25, 1862.
37. Richardson, *Messages and Papers of Confederacy*, II, 153-54.
38. Ibid., 155.
39. Ibid., 158.
40. Ibid., 160.
41. Thurlow Weed Barnes, *The Life of Thurlow Weed*, 2 vols. (Boston, 1884), II, 362. See also Weed to Blatchford, January 12, 1862, Seward Papers.
42. Adams to Seward, January 31, 1862, Adams Papers, reel 167.
43. Ford, *Cycle of Adams Letters*, I, 106.
44. Adams to Seward, January 24, 1862, NA/M30/74.
45. *Papers Relating to Foreign Affairs*, 1862, pp. 310-13.
46. Seward to Adams, February 17, 1862 (no. 186), NA/M77/77.
47. Lyons to Russell, September 10, 1861, Slave Trade Papers, FO 84/1137.
48. Ibid., November 8.
49. Palmerston to Russell, September 24, 1861, PRO 30/22/21.
50. Informal memorandum, November 13, 1861, FO 84/1137.
51. Lyons to Russell, November 15, 1861, PRO 30/22/35.
52. Russell to Lyons, October 19, 1861, FO 84/1137.
53. Russell to Lyons, February 28, 1862, FO 84/1170.
54. *Cong. Globe*, 37th Cong. 2nd sess., part II, 1102.
55. A. T. Milne, "The Lyons-Seward Treaty of 1862," *American Historical Review*, XXXVIII (April 1933), 513-14.

56. Seward, *Seward at Washington*, III, 63.
57. Seward to Adams, February 4, 1862, NA/M77/77. See also ibid., February 5, 13, 28.
58. *Parl. Debates*, 3rd ser., CLXV, 113-14.
59. Ibid., 116-18.
60. Westbury to Palmerston, February 9, 1862, Broadlands Mss.
61. Lyons to Russell, February 7, 1862, PRO 30/22/36. See also ibid., February 11.
62. Adams to Seward, February 28, 1862, NA/M30/75. See also ibid., February 13, NA/M30/74; Adams to Everett, February 21, 1862, Adams Papers, reel 167.
63. Russell to Lyons, February 11, 1862, FO 5/817.
64. Mason, *James M. Mason*, p. 264.
65. *Parl. Debates*, 3rd ser., CLXV, 1229.
66. *Moran Journal*, 11, 961.
67. *Parl. Debates*, 3rd ser., CLXV, 1202.
68. Ibid., 1212.
69. Ibid., 1243.
70. Adams to Seward, March 13, 1862, NA/M30/75.
71. Adams, Diary, March 29, 1862. See also ibid., April 7.
72. *Economist*, March 29, 1862.
73. Russell to Lyons, March 1, 1862, Lyons Papers. See also ibid., March 15; ibid., March 22.
74. G. E. Buckle, ed., *Letters of Queen Victoria*, 2nd ser., 3 vols. (London, 1926), I, 22-23.
75. Mason, *James M. Mason*, p. 264.
76. Adams to Seward, March 27, 1862, NA/M30/75.
77. Palmerston memorandum, April 25, 1862, FO 391/17.
78. Russell to Lyons, April 17, 1862, FO 5/818.

ELEVEN   A war of attrition

1. Lyons to Russell, April 11, 1862, FO 5/827.
2. Bunch to Russell, February 25, 1862, FO 5/843.
3. Lyons to Russell, April 14, 1862, FO 5/828.
4. Seward to Adams, April 1, 1862, NA/M77/77.
5. Russell to Adams, March 27, 1862, NA/M30/75. See also ibid., May 6, 1862.
6. Layard to Hammond, April 25, 1862, BM Add. Ms. 38959.
7. Adams to Seward, May 8, 1862, NA/M30/75.
8. Gladstone memorandum, December 14, 1861, BM Add. Ms. 44593.
9. Monck to Newcastle, May 23, 1862, Newcastle Papers, A/308.
10. Newcastle to Monck, June 14, 1862, ibid., A/309.

BIBLIOGRAPHICAL ESSAY

Confederacy

WILLIAM HOWARD RUSSELL's *My Diary North and South* (1863) is the most frequently cited British commentary on the attitudes of Southerners in the spring of 1861, for he was an excellent reporter. An edited version, more suitable for general readers, was published in 1954 under the title *My Civil War Diary*. Also useful and interesting, though somewhat dramatized, is Catharine Hopley's *Life in the South* (2 vols., 1863). An indispensable Southern source is Mary Boykin Chesnut's *A Diary from Dixie*, edited by Ben Ames Williams and reissued in a paperback edition (1961). Another intelligent observer, though not as well placed as Mrs. Chesnut, was the planter-botanist Henry Ravenel. See *The Private Journal of Henry William Ravenel 1859-1887*, edited by A. R. Childs (1947). Interesting comment is also to be found among the letters published in the fourth volume of the *Letters of William Gilmore Simms*, edited by Mary Simms Oliphant, Alfred Taylor Odell and T. C. Duncan Eaves (5 vols., 1955). Many of the other published journals and memoirs are disappointingly trivial, at least for the period covered in this volume, as for example the reflections of Senator Louis Wigfall's daughter—D. Girand Wright, *A Southern Girl in '61: The War-Time Memories of a Confederate Senator's Daughter* (1905). For the work of the Montgomery Convention see the very full correspondence between T. R. R. Cobb and his wife published in the eleventh volume of the *Publications of the Southern History Association*. A few of the letters of Laurence M. Keitt, a member of the South Carolina delegation, have been published in the *South Carolina Historical Magazine*, LXI (1960). Robert Barnwell Rhett Jr. took an understandably sympathetic view of his father's proposed policy in "The Confederate Government at Montgmery," *Battles and Leaders of the Civil War*, I (1887). Laura A. White's *Robert Barnwell Rhett: Father of Secession* (1931) is an adequate biography but Rhett's newspaper, the *Charleston Mercury*, should be consulted. Important manuscript collections for this period are the Howell Cobb Papers, held by the Library of the University of Georgia, and the William Porcher Miles Papers, part of the excellent Southern Historical Collection at the Library of the University of North Carolina, Chapel Hill. The Collection includes the diary and reminiscences of Stephen Mallory (all too brief for the Civil War period); the diary of Thomas Bragg, who was appointed attorney-general in November 1861; the papers of Benjamin C. Yancey, the brother of William Lowndes and a former diplomat; the diary of Edward Clifford Anderson, a purchasing agent in Britain, and the fragmentary diary of James Heyward North, who accompanied him. Only a few miles from Chapel Hill is Duke University and that Library holds a broad collection of manuscripts, but many are fragmentary. Two examples are the Robert Toombs and the Jefferson Davis Papers.

The Confederate President has attracted a number of biographers. He was excoriated by a contemporary, Edward Pollard, whose *Life of Jefferson Davis* has been reprinted (1969), and many of his former colleagues were extremely critical of him and his policies in their memoirs. However, Davis has won the sympathy of some historians. Allen Tate's brief, undocumented but sympathetic biography, *Jefferson Davis: His Rise and Fall*, first published some forty years ago has also been reprinted (1969). The best modern study is Hudson Strode's three-volume work: *American Patriot* (1955), *Confederate President* (1959), and *Tragic Hero* (1964). Davis settled some personal scores in his *Rise and Fall of the Confederate Government* (1881), which is available in an abridged paperback edition (1961). For the most part, however, it is a laboured apologia. Many of Davis's letters, as well as his speeches and papers, were collected by Dunbar Rowland in the ten volumes of *Jefferson Davis: Constitutionalist* (1923). This should be supplemented with *Jefferson Davis: Private Letters 1823-1889* (1966), edited by Hudson Strode, although there is little correspondence from the war years. Also, the first volume of a massive edition of *The Papers of Jefferson Davis*, edited by Haskell M. Monroe, Jr. and James T. McIntosh has now been published (1971). Helpful and

at times revealing is Varina Howell Davis's *Jefferson Davis Ex-President of the Confederate States of America: A Memoir by his Wife* (2 vols., 1890). Of the two studies that deal with Davis and his cabinet colleagues the better is Rembert Patrick's *Jefferson Davis and his Cabinet* (1944). The title of Burton J. Hendrick's *Statesmen of a Lost Cause: Jefferson Davis and his Cabinet* (1939) is somewhat misleading because he discusses Confederate diplomacy at some length. But the standard against which all examinations of Confederate foreign relations are measured is Frank Lawrence Owsley's *King Cotton Diplomacy*. First published in 1931 it is now in a second edition, revised by Harriet Chappell Owsley (1959); it replaced James M. Callahan's *Diplomatic History of the Southern Confederacy* (1901). A savage contemporary assault upon Confederate diplomacy is that by Paul Pecquet DuBellet, *The Diplomacy of the Confederate Cabinet at Richmond and Its Agents Abroad*, edited by William Stanley Poole and published in the Confederate Centennial Studies, no. 23 (1963). See also the article by Henry Blumenthal, "Confederate Diplomacy: Popular Notions and International Realities," *Journal of Southern History*, XXXII (1966). Of the biographies of Davis's first secretary of state the latest is by **William Y.** Thompson, *Robert Toombs of Georgia* (1966). The published "Correspondence of Robert Toombs, Alexander Stephens and Howell Cobb," edited by Ulrich B. Phillips and to be found in the *Annual Report of the American Historical As-*

sociation of 1911, II, is not helpful for the period of Toombs's cabinet service. However, some of the letters to Cobb do suggest the fervour with which free trade was advocated as a foreign policy by certain influential Southerners. For a biography of Toombs's successor see H. H. Simms, *Life of Robert M. T. Hunter* (1935). "The Correspondence of Robert T. M. Hunter," edited by Charles H. Ambler and published in the second volume of the *Annual Report of the American Historical Association for 1916* is of no use for the Civil War years. A mildly revisionist article is that by William S. Hitchcock, "Southern Moderates and Secession: Senator Robert M. T. Hunter's Call for Union," *Journal of American History*, LXI (1973). E. Merton Coulter has rescued the assistant secretary of state from obscurity in *William M. Browne* (1967). As for the original Confederate commissioners to Europe, there is an old biography of Yancey by John Witherspoon Du-Bose, *The Life and Times of William Lowndes Yancey, A History of Political Parties in the United States, From 1834 to 1864, Especially as to the Origins of the Confederate States* (1892), which has been reprinted in two volumes (1942). Clement Eaton devoted one chapter of the revised edition of *The Mind of the Old South* (1967) to Yancey. The Yancey Papers held by the Alabama Department of Archives and History, Montgomery, are useful but fragmentary for this period. Frank Owsley wrote the brief note on Ambrose Dudley Mann in the *Dictionary of American Biography*, XII (1933), and a little more has been written of him in the introduction to *"My Ever Dearest Friend," the letters of Ambrose Dudley Mann to Jefferson Davis 1869-1889* (1960). This is another volume in the Confederate Centennial Studies and is edited by John Preston Moore. Neither Mason nor Slidell has been dealt with adequately by biographers. Mason's daughter, Virginia Mason, wrote and edited *The Public Life and Diplomatic Correspondence of James M. Mason* (1903), which as the title suggests does contain lengthy quotations from his correspondence, private as well as official. The Mason Papers are held by the Library of Congress. There is no similar deposit for Mason's fellow diplomat and the absence is obvious in Louis Martin Sears's *John Slidell* (1925). However, Slidell correspondence is to be found in other collections, such as the Howell Cobb Papers. For the observations of John Bigelow, who was sent to France by Seward to help frustrate the efforts of the Southern commissioners, see "The Confederate Diplomats," *Century Magazine*, XLII (1891). Most of the diplomatic correspondence of the Confederacy, the Pickett Papers, has been published. The great bulk is to be found in vol. 30 of the *Official Records of the Union and Confederate Navies in the War of the Rebellion* (31 vols., 1894-1927). These have also been microfilmed by the National Archives (NA/M275). There is also a good selection of despatches in the second volume of James D. Richardson's *A Compilation of the Messages and Papers of the Confederacy* (2 vols., 1905). For aspects of Confederate activities in Britain see J. Franklin Jameson, "The London Expenditures of the Confederate Secret Service," *American Historical Review*, XXXV (1930); James D. Bulloch, *The Secret Service of the Confederate States in Europe or How the Confederate Cruisers Were Equipped* (2 vols., 1883), was reprinted as one (1959). For an extensive modern discussion of the building of the Confederate Navy in Britain see Frank J. Merli, *Great Britain and the Confederate Navy 1861-1865* (1970). Charles P. Cullop's *Confederate Propaganda in Europe, 1861-1865* (1969) centres upon Henry Hotze and the *Index*. Those activities will be considered in the concluding volume of this study.

Union

THE UNHAPPY AND UNFORTUNATE Buchanan has found an understanding biographer in Philip Shriver Klein, *President James Buchanan* (1962). John Bassett Moore edited the twelve volumes of *The Works of James Buchanan* (1908-11). The material on Buchanan's successor dwarfs that on all other presidents. The standard biography is by J. G. Randall, *Lincoln the President* (4 vols., 1945-55). The final volume was completed by Richard N. Current. There are at least two good shorter studies, Lord Charnwood's *Abraham Lincoln* (1920), and Benjamin P. Thomas's *Abraham Lincoln* (1952). Both have been reprinted, the first as a paperback and the second in a clothbound edition (1968). There are two large and accessible collections of Lincoln's works and correspondence. Roy P. Basler edited *The Works of Abraham Lincoln* (9 vols., 1953-55), and the Abraham Lincoln Papers in the Library of Congress have been microfilmed as part of the Presidential Papers series. For Lincoln's relations with his cabinet see Burton J. Hendrick, *Lincoln's War Cabinet* (1946), which has been re-printed in paperback (1961). Several of Lincoln's colleagues kept diaries. Of these the sketchiest is that by the first secretary of treasury, see David Donald, ed., *Inside Lincoln's Cabinet: The Civil War Diaries of Salmon P. Chase* (1954). A much fuller record, except for the early period of the war, and one that is now available in an edition that shows how it was amended over the years, is *The Diary of Gideon Welles* (3 vols., 1960), edited by Howard K. Beale. Beale also edited *The Diary of Edward Bates 1859-1866* (1933). Some of the papers of Chase, Welles, and Simon Cameron, the first secretary for war, are held by the Library of Congress. The appointment of Seward as secretary of state, and his subsequent manoeuvring, are discussed in William Baringer's *A House Dividing: Lincoln as President-Elect* (1945); Glyndon G. Van Deusen, *William Henry Seward* (1967), is a solid biography founded upon massive research; H. Draper Hunt, *Hannibal Hamlin of Maine* (1969), deals with Lincoln's use of Hamlin in the tricky negotiations with Seward. Reference to them is also to be found in the John Bigelow Papers held by the New York Public Library. See also Glyndon G. Van Deusen's article, "Seward and the Secession Winter of 1860-1," *Canadian Historical Association Papers*, 1966. A jaundiced contemporary observer was Gideon Welles whose *Lincoln and Seward* has been reprinted (1969). For Seward's career see also *The Works of William H. Seward*, edited by George E. Baker (5 vols., 1853-84); Frederic Bancroft, *The Life of William H. Seward* (2 vols., 1900); the three volumes of Frederick Seward's biography of his father, *Seward at Washington as Senator and Secretary of State 1846-1861* (1891), are very important because they contain much correspondence to be found nowhere else, but as Van Deusen warns it must be used with caution. Frederick served as his father's assistant and his *Reminiscences of a War-Time Statesman and Diplomat 1830-1915* (1916) should be consulted. Finally, there is the very large collection of Seward Papers at the Library of the University of Rochester. Located there also are the papers of Thurlow Weed, Seward's political crony. A new study of Seward's foreign policy, emphasizing his concern for commercial rather than territorial expansion, is Ernest N. Paolino's *The Foundations of American Empire* (1973).

Much of the diplomatic correspondence of the United States was published in the *Papers Relating to Foreign Affairs*, which Seward was the first secretary to submit to Congress annually, beginning in 1861. However, the use of these volumes is not sufficient for any study of American diplomacy. They contain selected correspondence only and passages were omitted from some of the letters included. The essential source remains the records of the Department of State in the National Archives, Washington, many of which are available on microfilm. For Britain, there are the diplomatic instructions to the minister in London and the diplomatic despatches from him, the notes to and from the British legation in Washington, and correspondence with American consuls. That with the consul-general to Canada, and the consuls at Liverpool and Manchester proved useful for this study. Thomas Dudley, who was appointed consul at Liverpool by Lincoln, has contributed an article on his activities, "Three Critical Periods in our Diplomatic Relations with England," *Pennsylvania Magazine of History and Biography*, XVII (1893). See also Brainerd Dyer, "Thomas H. Dudley," *Civil War History*, I (1955). However, Dudley's activities properly belong to the second volume of this study. Lincoln's contributions to foreign policy have received exaggerated treatment, both in importance and style, from Jay Monaghan, *Diplomat in Carpet Slippers: Abraham Lincoln Deals with Foreign Affairs* (1945), reprinted in paperback (1962). Another dramatic account is that by Philip Van Doren Stern, *When the Guns Roared: World Aspects of the Civil War* (1965). *Heard Round the World: The Impact Abroad of the Civil War* (1969), edited by Harold Hyman, contains some useful essays. Among them are those on Britain, by H. C.

Allen, and France, by David H. Pinckney. Seward's role in the deliberations and negotiations concerning Fort Sumter is discussed by Richard N. Current, *Lincoln and the First Shot* (1963). A lengthy article on the attempt of the South to secure a peaceful withdrawal of the Federal troops is that by Ludwell H. Johnson, "Fort Sumter and Confederate Diplomacy," *Journal of Southern History*, XXVI (1960). Patrick Sowle, "A Reappraisal of Seward's Memorandum of April 1, 1861, to Lincoln," *Journal of Southern History*, XXXIII (1967), reasons that Seward intended to announce his direction of Union policy in the *New York Times*. The Ashmun mission to Canada is discussed by F. Lauriston Bullard in "Abraham Lincoln and George Ashmun," *New England Quarterly*, XIX (1946). Yet another mistake of the secretary's was to employ the choleric Adam Gurowski. There is a biography, Leroy H. Fischer, *Lincoln's Gadfly: Adam Gurowski* (1964), but Gurowski's *Diary* (3 vols., 1862-66) is much livelier reading. He was also one of Charles Sumner's correspondents. See the Charles Sumner Papers at the Houghton Library, Harvard. It is surprising that Lord Lyons has not attracted the attention of more historians. The only biography remains that by T. W. L. Newton, *Lord Lyons: A Record of British Diplomacy* (2 vols., 1913). The Lyons Papers are indispensable but access to them at Arundel Castle, Sussex, has necessarily been restricted because they are being catalogued. However, they were made available to this author at the West Sussex

Record Office, Chichester. Lyons's equally capable American counterpart, Charles Francis Adams, has been well served by his most recent biographer. Martin Duberman's *Charles Francis Adams 1807-1886* (1961), reprinted in paperback (1968), has replaced the short study by Charles Francis Adams Jr. (1900). Henry Adams, who accompanied his father to England to serve as his secretary, touches upon the falling out with Sumner in his brilliant autobiography *The Education of Henry Adams*, also reprinted in paperback (1960). On this topic see David Donald, *Charles Sumner and the Coming of the Civil War* (1961). There is a good selection of Adams correspondence in Worthington Chauncey Ford, ed., *A Cycle of Adams Letters* (2 vols., 1920). In addition, see the *Letters of Henry Adams 1858-1890* (1930), also edited by Ford. However, the essential sources are the diary and letterbooks of Charles Francis Adams, held by the Massachusetts Historical Society. They are available on microfilm and the Adams Papers are slowly being published. The Adams Papers should be supplemented with the second volume of *The Journal of Benjamin Moran* (2 vols., 1949) edited by Sarah Agnes Wallace and Frances Elma Gillespie. There is an unpublished doctoral dissertation on the first year of the Adams mission in Britain by Norman B. Ferris, "Tempestuous Mission, 1861-1862: the early career of Charles Francis Adams" (Emory University, 1962). For an aspect of Union activity in Britain of which Adams strongly disapproved see Harriet Chappell

Owsley, "Henry Shelton Sanford and Federal Surveillance Abroad 1861-1865," *Mississippi Valley Historical Review*, XLVIII (1961).

The literature of Franco-American relations during the war years, a relationship that the British, profoundly distrustful of Napoleon III, watched carefully, has been growing in recent years. Thus to Henry Blumenthal's survey, *A Reappraisal of Franco-American Relations 1830-1871* (1959), has been added Daniel Carroll's competent study of the French minister to the United States, *Henri Mercier and the American Civil War* (1971), and Lynn Case has brought his well-established interest in the subject to a massive conclusion in Lynn M. Case and Warren F. Spencer, *The United States and France: Civil War Diplomacy* (1970). Unfortunately, this book's size and topical organization, which leads to considerable overlapping of material, is likely to discourage many readers. A brief overview of the response of the French government to the American war has been provided by Jean-Guy Larrégola in his two-part article, "Le Gouvernement Français Face à La Guerre de Secession," *Revue d'Histoire Diplomatique*, LXXXIII (1969). A recent study of *Napoleon III and Mexico* (1971) is by Alfred Jackson Hanna and Kathryn Abbey Hanna. For the extent to which Napoleon's ill-fated Mexican adventure was bound up with his European diplomacy see Nancy Nichols Barker, *Distaff Diplomacy: The Empress Eugénie and the Foreign Policy of the Second Empire* (1967); "France, Austria, and the Mexican Adventure, 1861-1864,"

French Historical Studies, III (1963), also by Miss Barker; *and* Noel Blayau, *Billaut: Ministre de Napoléon III d'après ses papiers personnels 1805-1863* (1969). Another useful study of the relations of the United States with a European power is that by Albert A. Woldman, *Lincoln and the Russians*, which was first published in 1952 but reissued as a paperback (1961).

The difficulties of the Navy Department, as it sought to make the blockade effective, can be explored in the *Official Records of the Union and Confederate Navies*. In addition, see Richard S. West, *Gideon Welles: Lincoln's Navy Department* (1943); Robert M. Thompson and Richard Wainwright, eds., *Confidential Correspondence of Gustavus Vasa Fox, Assistant Secretary of the Navy 1861-1865* (2 vols., 1918-1919); John D. Hayes, ed., *Samuel Francis Du Pont: A Selection from his Civil War Letters* (2 vols., 1969). Charles Wilkes proved to be another of Welles's difficulties. His biographer, Daniel MacIntyre Henderson, touches upon Wilkes's wilfulness, harshness, and insubordination in *The Hidden Coasts: A Biography of Admiral Charles Wilkes* (1953). There is also an article, W. W. Jeffries, "The Civil War Career of Charles Wilkes," *Journal of Southern History*, XI (1945). The Wilkes Papers, which include a diary, are held by the Library of Congress. His most famous Civil War exploit and its international repercussions have been discussed fully by historians. T. L. Harris, *The Trent Affair* (1896), and Evan John, *Atlantic Impact* (1952) cover much of the ground but are by no means definitive. Dean E. Brundage, "The Trent Affair and the British Press," an unpublished master's thesis (Georgetown University, 1948), is workmanlike without being important. A great number of articles have been written on the subject, several of them by Charles Francis Adams Jr. Arnold Whitridge contributed a lively piece, "The Trent Affair, 1861: An Anglo-American Crisis that almost led to War," to *History Today*, IV (1954). Others have sought to identify the persons or factors that preserved peace. The Prince Consort's contribution was known to many people at the time and Theodore Martin duly paid tribute to it in his biography of Victoria's husband (1874-80). Sir John W.

Wheeler-Bennett included an essay on "The Trent Affair: How the Prince Consort saved the United States," in his *A Wreath for Clio: Studies in British, American and German Affairs* (1967). Norman B. Ferris had broadened the discussion to include the London *Times* in his article, which is to be found in *Civil War History*, VI (1960). Victor H. Cohen has written on "Charles Sumner and the *Trent* Affair," *Journal of Southern History*, XXII (1956), while Lynn M. Case claims a vital role for the French in "La France et l'affaire du *Trent*," *Revue Historique*, CDLIX (1961). A straightforward summary of this affair is to be found in James A. Rawley's *Turning Points of the Civil War* (1966).

Canada

THE INTERPLAY OF CANADA, the United States, and Great Britain was the subtitle chosen by John Bartlet Brebner for his grand survey of the *North Atlantic Triangle*, several chapters of which discuss aspects of the period studied here. First published in 1945 it is now available in a paperback reprint (1966). From the same series is Lester B. Shippee's *Canadian-American Relations 1849-1874* (1939). Still useful is James M. Callahan's *American Foreign Policy in Canadian Relations* (1937). An aspect of Canadian-American relations is dealt with by D. F. Warner, *The Idea of Continental Union: Agitation for the Annexation of Canada to the United States, 1849-1893* (1960). C. P. Stacey has destroyed "The Myth of the Un-

guarded Frontier, 1815-1871," *American Historical Review*, LVI (1950). The two essays by S. F. Wise in the little book that he co-authored with Robert Craig Brown, *Canada Views the United States: Nineteenth Century Political Attitudes* (1967) are excellent. A helpful book is Arthur R. M. Lower's *Canadians in the Making: A Social History of Canada* (1958). On immigration see Norman Macdonald, *Canada: Immigration and Colonization, 1841-1903* (1966), and a brief statement of her findings by Helen I. Cowan, *British Immigration Before Confederation* (1968), the second of the Canadian Historical Association's Historical Booklets. *The Reciprocity Treaty of 1854* has been analysed by Donald C. Masters (1937) and reprinted in paperback

(1963). Alvin Charles Glueck has investigated *Minnesota and the Manifest Destiny of the Canadian Northwest* (1965).

The Canadian response to the disruption of the Union has received considerable attention: Fred Landon, "Canadian Opinion of Southern Secession 1860-1861," *Canadian Historical Review*, I (1920); James J. Talman, ed., "A Canadian View of Parties and Issues on the Eve of the Civil War," *Journal of Southern History*, V (1939); W. L. Morton, "British North America and a Continent in Dissolution, 1861-1871," *History*, XLVII (1962); ibid., *The Critical Years: The Union of British North America 1857-1873* (1964); Helen G. Macdonald, *Canadian Public Opinion on the American Civil War* (1926); however, the most detailed study, though lacking in colour, is that by Robin W. Winks, *Canada and the United States: The Civil War Years* (1960). There is an important and very helpful article by Hubert Néant, "Le Canada et la Guerre de Secession," *Revue D'Histoire Diplomatique*, LXXVII (1963), for he quotes extensively from reports of the French consul there. On Canadian hopes for increased commerce along the St. Lawrence see Samuel McKee Jr., "Canada's Bid for the Traffic of the Middle West: A Quarter Century of the St. Lawrence Waterway, 1849-1874," *Canadian Historical Association Papers* (1940). The report of the chief emigration agent is to be found in Colonial Office 42, vol. 626. The extent of newspaper patronage is discussed by Robert A. Hill, "A Note on Newspaper Patronage in Canada during the later 1850's and early 1860's," *Canadian Historical Review*, XLIX (1968). The opening chapter of P. B. Waite's *The Life and Times of Confederation 1864-1867: Politics, Newspapers, and the Union of British North America* (1967) should also be consulted. On black settlements in Canada West, and the opposition to them, William H. Pease and Jane H. Pease have written "Opposition to the Founding of the Elgin Settlement," *Canadian Historical Review*, XXXVIII (1957), and *Black Utopia: Negro Communal Experiments in America* (1963). Robin W. Winks has added a more general work, *The Blacks in Canada* (1971).

The decade of sectional antagonism in Canada, or aspects of it, are discussed by J. M. S. Careless, *The Union of the Canadas: The Growth of Canadian Institutions, 1841-1857* (1967); Morton, *The Critical Years*; J. M. S. Careless, *Brown of the Globe* (2 vols., 1959, 1963); ibid., "The Toronto Globe and Agrarian Radicalism, 1850-1867," *Canadian Historical Review*, XXIX (1949), ibid., "Mid-Victorian Liberalism in Central Canadian Newspapers, 1850-1867," XXXI (1950); Paul Grant Cornell, "The Alignment of Political Groups in the United Province of Canada, 1854-1864," ibid., XXX (1949); George W. Brown, "The Grit Party and the Great Reform Convention of 1859," ibid., XVI (1935); Frank H. Underhill, "The Development of National Political Parties in Canada," ibid.; O. D. Skelton, *The Life and Times of Sir Alexander Tilloch Galt* (1920). The only biography of Sir George Etienne Cartier is that by John Boyd (1914). However, there is an unpublished doctoral dissertation by Henry Bruce MacLeod Best, "George-Etienne Cartier" (Laval University, 1969). In addition, Joseph Tassé, *Discours de Sir Georges Cartier* (1893) should be consulted as should an article by John Irwin Cooper, "The Political Ideas of George Etienne Cartier," *Canadian Historical Review*, XXII (1942). The material on Cartier's political partner, Macdonald, is voluminous. He has been fortunate in his biographer, Donald Creighton, *John A. Macdonald* (2 vols., 1952, 1955). Creighton has also written a perceptive article, "Sir John A. Macdonald and Kingston," *Report of the Canadian Historical Association*, 1950. T. W. L. MacDermot sought to analyse "The Political Ideas of John A. Macdonald," *Canadian Historical Review*, XIV (1933). The Public Archives of Canada holds a very large collection of Macdonald Papers, and is publishing much of it together with Macdonald correspondence held elsewhere. The first two volumes of *The Papers of the Prime Ministers* are *The Letters of Sir John A. Macdonald 1836-1857* (1968) and *1858-1861* (1969). There is a competent study of *Sir Edmund Head: A Scholarly Governor* (1954) by D. G. G. Kerr. Head was a friend of Sir George Cornewall Lewis, a member of the Palmerston cabinet, and some of his correspondence is to be found in the Lewis Papers, called the Harpton Court Collection, in the National Library of Wales, Aberystwyth. Naturally, Head also wrote privately to the colonial secretary, Newcastle, and the Public Archives of Canada holds microfilm copies of those Newcastle Papers

catalogued under North America. But additional items of correspondence, pertinent to the colony and the American Civil War, are to be found in other sections. The manuscripts are located at the Library of the University of Nottingham. The official correspondence between the governor-general and the Colonial Office is to be found in the CO 42 series, but the Records of the Governor-General's Office in the Public Archives of Canada should also be consulted. Both Head and his successor, Monck, established close and cordial relations with Lyons in Washington, and correspondence from them both is to be found in the Lyons Papers. W. L. Morton has written an affectionate description of Monck and his family entourage in the introduction to *Monck Letters and Journals 1863-1868 Canada from Government House at Confederation* (1970). See also the essay Morton contributed to John S. Moir, ed., *Character and circumstance: essays in honour of Donald Grant Creighton* (1970). No discussion of one of Monck's immediate problems, improving the militia, or the condition of the British regular esablishment in the colony, would be complete without reference to C. P. Stacey's *Canada and the British Army 1846-1871* (rev. ed., 1963). See also George F. G. Stanley, *Canada's Soldiers: The Military History of an Unmilitary People* (rev. ed., 1960), and the introductory chapters in Richard A. Preston's *Canada and "Imperial Defense"* (1967), and Donald C. Gordon's *The Dominion Partnership in Imperial Defense, 1870-1914* (1965).

Britain

THE WRITINGS OF mid-century British travellers to the United States have been analysed by Max Berger, *The British Traveller in America 1836-1860* (1943). An older and briefer account is that by E. D. Adams, "The Point of View of The British Traveller in America," *Political Science Quarterly*, XXIX (1914). Allan Nevins has edited a broad selection of British accounts in *America Through British Eyes* (rev. ed., 1948). There is an excellent modern edition of Alexis de Tocqueville's *Democracy in America*, edited by J. P. Mayer and Max Lerner (1966).

Cobden and Bright continue to fascinate historians. To such traditional studies as John Morley's *Life of Richard Cobden* (2 vols., 1881); J. A. Hobson's *Richard Cobden: The International Man* (1918); W. H. Dawson's *Richard Cobden and Foreign Policy* (1926); and G. M. Trevelyan's *John Bright* (1913) have been added Herman Ausubel's brief biography, *John Bright: Victorian Reformer* (1966), and Donald Reads's thoughtful comparative study *Cobden and Bright: A Victorian Political Partnership* (1967). There is also an excellent essay on "John Bright and the Creed of Reform" in Asa Briggs's *Victorian People: A Reassessment of Persons and Themes 1851-1887*, first published in 1954 but reprinted in paperback, with minor revisions (1965). John H. Derry includes a lengthy chapter on Cobden and Bright in his book *The Radical Tradition: Tom Paine to Lloyd George* (1967). An important source is *The American Diaries of Richard Cobden* (1952), edited by E. H. Cawley. *The Diaries of John Bright* (1930), edited by R. A. J. Walling, are more helpful with respect to America for the period beginning February 1862. G. D. Lillibridge, *Beacon of Freedom: The Impact of American Democracy upon Great Britain 1830-1870* (1955) overstates the case. More judicious is David Paul Crook, *American Democracy in English Politics 1815-1850* (1965). Two brief but very good introductions to the Anglo-American relationship in the mid-Nineteenth Century are Frank Thistlethwaite, *The Anglo-American Connection in the Early Nineteenth Century* (1959), and H. C. Allen, *Conflict and Concord: The Anglo-American Relationship since 1783* (1959). The development of the American economy has been briefly analysed and described, in a manner easily understood by non-economists, by Douglas C. North, *The Economic Growth of the United States 1790-1860* (1961). See also George Rogers Taylor, *The Transportation Revolution 1815-1860* (1951) and Marvin Fisher, *Workshops in the Wilderness: The European Response to American Industrialization* (1967). Some of the pertinent economic statistics are to be found in *The Statistical History of the United States from Colonial Times to the Present* (1965). For the specific American challenge in shipping see J. H. Clapham, *An Economic History of Modern Britain: Free Trade and Steel 1850-1886* (1932); and John G. B. Hutchins, *The American Mari-*

time *Industries and Public Policy 1789-1914* (1941). British efforts to break their total dependence upon American cotton are discussed by Arthur W. Silver, *Manchester Men and Indian Cotton 1847-1872* (1966); Frenise Logan, "India—Britain's substitute for American Cotton, 1861-1865," *Journal of Southern History*, XXIV (1958); and E. M. Earle, "Egyptian Cotton and the American Civil War," *Political Science Quarterly*, XLI (1926). For the slackening of the Anglo-American humanitarian ties see, in addition to Thistlethwaite, Merle Curti, *The American Peace Crusade 1815-1860* (reprint ed., 1965); Christine Bolt, *The Anti-Slavery Movement and Reconstruction: A study in Anglo-American Cooperation 1833-1877* (1969); and *Victorian Attitudes to Race* (1971), by the same author.

British motives in abolishing slavery and attempting to suppress the slave trade are the subject of a continuing historical debate. The traditional emphasis, by Coupland and Mathieson, was upon humanitarianism, but this interpretation was vigorously challenged by Eric Williams, *Capitalism and Slavery* (1944), subsequently reprinted several times. That brought a rejoinder from the followers of the humanitarian school led by G. R. Mellor, *British Imperial Trusteeship 1783-1850* (1951). More direct is Roger T. Anstey, "*Capitalism and Slavery*: a critique," *Economic History Review*, XXI (1968). For example, Anstey exposes Williams's "strange" approach to Palmerston's long campaign against the slave trade. A recent account of the anti-slavery movement in Britain is

that by Howard Temperley, *British anti-slavery 1833-1870* (1972). Johnson U. J. Asiegbu has subjected the British to fresh criticism in his *Slavery and the Politics of Liberation 1787-1861: A Study of Liberated African Emigration and British Anti-Slavery Policy* (1969). Discussing the treatment of blacks freed by the British antislaving patrols, he argues that the "voluntary" emigration of these liberated Africans to the British West Indian colonies took on all the trappings of a thinly disguised slave trade. Also, that the British Navy could have stifled the trade by pressing ahead with inshore cruising in the 1840s but that they were more interested in obtaining cheap labour for the West Indies from foreign slavers. The role of the British Navy has been described by Christopher Lloyd, *The Navy and the Slave Trade* (1949); and W. E. F. Ward, *The Royal Navy and the Slavers: The Suppression of the Atlantic Slave Trade* (1969). A useful quantitative study of the trade is Philip D. Curtin's *The Atlantic Slave Trade* (1969). As for suppression of the trade and Anglo-American relations see W. E. B. DuBois, *The Suppression of the African Slave Trade to the United States of America 1638-1870* (reprint ed., 1965); Richard W. Van Alstyne, "The British Right of Search and the African Slave Trade," *Journal of Modern History*, II (1930); Hugh G. Soulsby, *The Right of Search and the Slave Trade in Anglo-American Relations 1814-1862* (1933); H. E. Landry, "Slavery and the Slave Trade in Atlantic Diplomacy 1850-1861," *Journal of Southern History*,

XXVII (1961); Warren S. Howard, *American Slavers and the Federal Law* (1963). On the other aspects of the diplomatic relationship see the fine study by Kenneth Bourne, *Britain and the Balance of Power in North America 1815-1908* (1967); Frederick Merk, *The Oregon Question: Essays in Anglo-American Diplomacy and Politics* (1967); Richard Van Alstyne, "Anglo-American Relations, 1853-1857," *American Historical Review*, XLII (1937); Kenneth Bourne, "The Clayton-Bulwer Treaty and the Decline of British Opposition to the Territorial Expansion of the United States, 1857-1860," *Journal of Modern History*, XXXIII (1961).

The full range of Britain's foreign relations is discussed in the second volume of *The Cambridge History of British Foreign Policy 1783-1919* (Cambridge, 1923) by Sir A. W. Ward and G. P. Gooch. A briefer and more limited account is that by R. W. Seton-Watson, *Britain and Europe 1789-1914: A Survey of Foreign Policy* (1937). An important book is D. C. M. Platt's *Finance, Trade and Politics in British Foreign Policy 1815-1915* (1968). Kenneth Bourne and D. C. Watt have edited a collection of essays, *Studies in International History* (1967). There is a good selection of documents in Harold Temperley and Lillian M. Penson, *Foundations of British Foreign Policy from Pitt to Salisbury* (1938), but *The Foreign Policy of Victorian England 1830-1902* (1972), by Kenneth Bourne, is much more valuable, not least because of his fine introduction to the selected documents. Aspects of the

uneasy Anglo-French relationship are also discussed by Derek Beales in his analytical study, *England and Italy 1859-1860* (1961); James Phinney Baxter 3rd, *The Introduction of the Ironclad Warship* (reprint, 1968); and Philip Appleman, William A. Madden and Michael Wolff, eds., *1859: Entering an Age of Crisis* (1959).

There are numerous biographies of Palmerston. Of these the standard remains that by H. F. C. Bell, *Lord Palmerston* (2 vols., 1936), but Douglas Southgate, *"The Most English Minister . . .": The Policies and Politics of Palmerston* (1970) should be consulted as should Jasper Ridley, *Lord Palmerston* (1970). A useful selection is that edited by Brian Connell, *Regina v Palmerston: The Correspondence between Queen Victoria and Her Foreign and Prime Minister 1837-1865* (1962). However, Palmerston's private letterbooks in the British Museum and the Broadlands Mss. held by the Historical Manuscripts Commission, London, are indispensable. The Broadlands Mss. also include the papers of Palmerston's son-in-law, the Earl of Shaftesbury, and among them are items that relate to the American Civil War. Lord John Russell has attracted less attention than Palmerston, but there are three biographies: Spencer Walpole, *Life of Lord John Russell* (2 vols., 1889); A. Wyatt Tilby, *Lord John Russell: A Study in Civil and Religious Liberty* (1930); and John Prest, *Lord John Russell* (1972). Selections from Russell's correspondence have been published, four volumes in all, but as with Palmerston there is a wealth of manuscript material open to scholars. The Russell Papers can be consulted at the Public Record Office, London.

A good introduction to Victorian Britain is Asa Briggs's *The Age of Improvement 1783-1867* (1959). Also valuable is his *Victorian People* (1954), and *The Age of Reform 1815-1870* (2nd ed., 1962), by Sir Llewellyn Woodward. For two other useful surveys see W. L. Burn, *Age of Equipoise: A Study of the Mid-Victorian Generation* (1964), and Geoffrey Best, *Mid-Victorian Britain 1851-1875* (1971). On politics, consult *The Conservative Party from Peel to Churchill* (1970) by Robert Blake; John Vincent's *The Formation of the Liberal Party 1857-1868* (1966); W. E. Williams's *The Rise of Gladstone to the Leadership of the Liberal Party 1859-1868* (1934) and Donald Southgate, *The Passing of the Whigs, 1832-1886* (1962). For Bright's reaction to the American crisis see the essay by J. G. Randall which was included in his *Lincoln: The Liberal Statesman* (1947), and R. J. Zorn's article, "John Bright and the British Attitude to the American Civil War," *Mid-America*, XXXVIII (1956). Many of Bright's letters to Charles Sumner have been published in the *Proceedings of the Massachusetts Historical Society*, XLV (1911-12) and XLVI (1912-13) but much valuable material remains in the Bright Mss. The bulk are held by the British Museum but there is a small collection in the Library of University College, London. However, much of this is family correspondence and there is little mention of the American war, at least for the period studied in this volume. There are a few pertinent items in the Joseph Parkes and the Brougham Papers held by University College Library. There is a large collection of Cobden Papers in the British Museum but the substantial holdings of the West Sussex Record Office should not be overlooked. The response of the Conservative party to secession and then civil war in America has been discussed briefly by Wilbur Devereux Jones, "The British Conservatives and the American Civil War," *American Historical Review*, LVIII (1953). Jones has also written a biography of the Conservative leader, *Lord Derby and Victorian Conservatism* (1956). Robert Blake, *Disraeli* (1967), makes only passing reference to the American Civil War and the Disraeli Papers, at Hughenden, are disappointing on this topic for the period studied. Another brief account is that by Arnold Whitridge, "British Liberals and the American Civil War," *History Today*, XII (1962).

The British government's policy and the factors that shaped it have prompted many articles and books. E. D. Adams, *Great Britain and the American Civil War*, first published in two volumes almost fifty years ago, but later reprinted in one (1958), is a work of superior scholarship. B. Villiers and W. H. Chesson, *Anglo-American Relations 1861-1865* (1919), is of little value. Much more useful is D. Jordan and E. J. Pratt, *Europe and the American Civil War* (1936), as is *Europe Looks at the Civil War*, edited by Belle Becker Sideman and Lillian Friedman and available in paperback (1962). A more recent study is that by Joseph M. Hernon, Jr., *Celts, Catholics and Copperheads: Ireland Views the American Civil War* (1968). Max Beloff contributed a perceptive note, "Historical Revision No. CXVIII: Great Britain and the American Civil War," *History*, XXXVII (1952). See also E. Ginzberg, "The Economics of British Neutrality During the American Civil War," *Agricultural History*, X (1936); Amos Khasigian, "Economic Factors and British Neutrality, 1861-1865," *Historian*, XXV (1963); Martin Paul Claussen, "The United States and Great Britain, 1861-1865: Peace Factors in International Relations," a doctoral dissertation (University of Illinois, 1938), but the findings were published as an article in the *Mississippi Valley Historical Review*, XXVI (1940). An undistinguished master's thesis is Benjamin Sacks' "Lord Palmerston's Diplomatic Partisanship in Favour of the Confederate States During the American Civil War, April, 1861–October, 1862" (McGill University, 1927). Of far higher quality are the articles by Joseph M. Hernon, Jr., "British Sympathies in the American Civil War: A Reconsideration," *Journal of Southern History*, XXXIII (1967), D. G. Wright, "Bradford and the American Civil War," *The Journal of British Studies*, VIII (1969), and D. P. Crook, "Portents of War: English Opinion of Secession," *Journal of American Studies*. IV (1970). Robert Huhn Jones has provided a very helpful guide to "The American Civil War in British Sessional Papers," *Proceedings of the American Philosophical Society*, CVII

(1963), but his article "Anglo-American Relations 1861-1865, Reconsidered," *Mid-America*, XLV (1963) rests entirely upon the correspondence published in the British "Blue Books." More revealing are the unpublished volumes of Foreign Office correspondence with the minister in Washington and the consuls at the major American ports. Of the consuls in the South, Robert Bunch at Charleston soon emerged as the principal commentator on Confederate affairs. For a study of these men see Milledge L. Bonhan, *The British Consuls in the Confederacy* (1911). Other pertinent Foreign Office records are the reports of the law officers and the Slave Trade Papers. In addition, the Colonial Office (Canada), Admiralty, War Office, and Board of Trade Papers contain important material. Then there are the papers of the British ministers and officials concerned with what was happening in America. Selections from some of these have been published, as for example G. F. Lewis, ed., *Letters of Sir George Cornewall Lewis* (1870); Nancy Mitford, ed., *The Stanleys of Alderley: Their Letters Between 1851-1865* (1939); Roundell Palmer, *Memorials Part 1, Family and Personal 1766-1865* (1896); C. Collyer, "Gladstone and the American Civil War," *Proceedings of the Leeds Philosophical Society*, VI (1951). But important manuscript collections, in addition to those already mentioned, are the Gladstone (BM); Edmund Hammond (PRO), the permanent undersecretary at the Foreign Office; Admiral Milne (National Maritime Museum, Greenwich); A. H. Layard

(BM), who in the summer of 1861, following Russell's departure from the Commons for the Lords, was appointed under-secretary of state for foreign affairs; and Ripon (BM), at this time still Earl de Grey, under-secretary of state for war.

The myth of British labour's total support for the Union, despite the suffering the Civil War caused them, and opposition to slavery, has now been dispelled. The traditional view and the extent to which it has been challenged can be quickly traced through a number of articles—J. H. Park, "The English Workingman and the American Civil War," *Political Science Quarterly*, XXXVII (1924); R. Greenleaf, "British Labour against American Slavery," *Science and Society*, XVII (1953); Royden Harrison, "British Labour and the Confederacy", *International Journal of Social History*, II (1957); J. R. Pole, *Abraham Lincoln and the Working Classes of Britain* (1959); and the chapter on "British Labour and American Slavery" in Royden Harrison's *Before the Socialist: Studies in Labour and Politics 1861-1865* (1965). Much more substantial is the doctoral dissertation on Lancashire and the American Civil War by Mary Ellison which is about to be published under the title *Support for Secession: Lancashire and the American Civil War* (1973). On the Lancashire cotton famine, which will be discussed in the second volume of this study, the standard work is that by W. O. Henderson, *The Lancashire Cotton Famine 1861-1865*, first published in 1934 but now revised with an updated and extremely helpful bibliography (1969). A useful contemporary work is R. Arthur Arnold's *The History of the Cotton Famine* (1864), and a rare record of a victim of the famine is "The Diary of John Ward of Clitheroe, Weaver, 1860-1864," edited by R. Sharpe Spence, *Transactions of the Historic Society of Lancashire and Cheshire*, CV (1953). E. A. Brady, "A Reconsideration of the Lancashire Cotton Famine," *Agricultural History*, XXXVII (1963), argues that the famine was the result more of over-production of cotton yarn and textiles in earlier years than the loss of Southern cotton. Of course, this was argued by the *Economist* and even the London *Times* at the time, but most people continued to hold the American war responsible.

Newspapers and Periodicals

THE DANGERS OF USING NEWSPAPERS, particularly of equating their columns with public opinion, are well known. Some acute suggestions on how to use American newspapers in the late nineteenth century are to be found in Ernest R. May's *American Imperialism: A Speculative Essay* (1968). However, the extent to which newspapers truly reflect public opinion may in this instance be less important than the fact that they saw themselves as public spokesmen, were used by politicians to influence and shape opinion, and in some cases were quoted by foreign newspapers as representative of public sentiment in their nation. Thus

Lincoln, as president-elect, was sufficiently concerned about the influence of the *New York Tribune* to ask some of his supporters to try and silence Greeley on the subject of peaceful secession. The *New York Herald*'s fulminations made good copy in both Canada and Britain and the *New York Times* was closely identified with Seward. In Canada the principal organs were clearly political instruments. The Reform leader, George Brown, owned and helped to edit the *Toronto Globe* while the Cartier-Macdonald Coalition used the *Quebec Morning Chronicle* and the *Toronto Leader*. Finally, several of the British papers were selected because of their avowed political persuasion. *The Morning Herald* was the acknowledged Conservative organ, the *Morning Star and Dial* spoke for the Cobdenite Radicals, and *Reynolds's Newspaper* claimed to speak for the working people. The *Morning Post* was widely regarded, in Britain and abroad, as Palmerston's mouthpiece, and by 1861 the influential London *Times* also fell into that category. Palmerston had established a flatteringly close and confidential relationship with John Delane, the editor. These newspapers were quoted in the United States not only because they, like the others, were believed to represent the opinions of important segments of the British public but also because they apparently offered clues to what the prime minister was thinking and planning.

INDEX